Public Anthropology in a Borderless World

Studies in Public and Applied Anthropology

General Editors: Sarah Pink, *RMIT University, Melbourne, Australia,* and Simone Abram, *Durham University and Leeds Beckett University*

The value of anthropology to public policy, business and third sector initiatives is increasingly recognized, not least due to significant innovations in the discipline. The books published in this series offer important insight into these developments by examining the expanding role of anthropologists practicing their discipline outside academia as well as exploring the ethnographic, methodological and theoretical contribution of anthropology, within and outside academia, to issues of public concern.

Public Anthropology in a Borderless World

Edited by

Sam Beck and Carl A. Maida

berghahn
NEW YORK · OXFORD
www.berghahnbooks.com

First published in 2015 by

Berghahn Books

www.berghahnbooks.com

Library of Congress Cataloging-in-Publication Data

Public anthropology in a borderless world / edited by Sam Beck and Carl A. Maida.
    pages cm. -- (Studies in public and applied anthropology ; volume 8)
  Includes bibliographical references and index.
    ISBN 978-1-78238-730-5 (hardback)— ISBN 978-1-78533-515-0 paperback —
ISBN 978-1-78238-731-2 (ebook)
 1. Public anthropology. I. Beck, Sam. II. Maida, Carl A.
  GN398.5.P83 2015
  301.01--dc23

                                                                 2015002050

British Library Cataloguing in Publication Data

A catalogue record for this book is available from the British Library

ISBN 978-1-78238-730-5 hardback
ISBN 978-1-78533-515-0 paperback
ISBN 978-1-78238-731-2 ebook

To the legacy of Eric R. Wolf

CONTENTS

ILLUSTRATIONS

ACKNOWLEDGMENTS

———— ∞∞∞ ————

Sam Beck would like to acknowledge Dean Alan Mathios and Former Associate Dean Carole Bisogni of the College of Human Ecology, Cornell University, who have supported his anthropological work and without whom this volume would not have been possible. Carl Maida would like to acknowledge the support of his colleagues at UCLA Institute of the Environment and Sustainability and the UCLA Clinical and Translational Science Institute. We are both grateful to Marion and Vivian Berghahn for their continuing support and encouragement.

INTRODUCTION

—⊗⊗⊗—

Carl A. Maida and Sam Beck

But what must anthropology look like if it is to be the study of human freedom and liberation, of human possibility and necessity? It must have a sense
of shared humanity.
—Eric R. Wolf, Foreword to Stanley Diamond's *In Search of the Primitive*

The Prospect of Transformational Research for Public Anthropology

For more than a century, anthropologists have been called upon to act as
experts and educators on the nature and lifeways of people worldwide,
and to understand the human condition in broader comparative perspectives. As a discipline, anthropology has been public arbiter, advocate,
and even defender of the cultural integrity, authenticity, and autonomy
of indigenous people across the globe. Public anthropology today fulfills
the discipline's original purpose through ongoing praxis, the dialectical
and polemical relationship of theory and practice, grounding theories in
lived experience and placing empirical knowledge in deeper historical
and comparative frameworks. As such, public anthropology questions its
own culturally based epistemology and is now answering calls to engage
with and give voice to issues of concern to a global public facing natural,
social, economic, and cultural crises. At the same time, public anthropologists can, and arguably should, act as experts and advocates, critiquing
the oversimplified assertions of politicians, government officials, and the
media, and attempting to redress human problems associated with inequities and injustices. Public anthropology, then, is anthropology of a critical nature.

Anthropologists wishing to pursue this approach to improving the
human condition can do so by producing texts, films, and exhibits for

public consumption, and by actively engaging *with* people on the ground to make change through research, education, and political action based on dialogue. Public engagement necessitates choices about how to carry out fieldwork—namely, how we consciously choose those we do research with, together determine our conceptual frames, decide on collaborative research methods, and construct ways of communicating about our work to the appropriate audiences. It also requires careful and critical elucidation of issues needing attention and the people who raise them.

This particular sense of engagement with people in the field (Beck and Maida 2013; Low and Merry 2010) points to Paulo Freire's (1970) important contribution to this vision of public anthropology. We embrace the centrality of what Freire called critical consciousness (*conscientizacao*), which implies raising the consciousness of the educator—the anthropologist, in this case—*and* the public, as their relationship must engage each in dialogue, co-participation, and co-construction. Brian McKenna (2013: 448–449) suggests that Freire's work also overlaps with anthropological engagement practices: "Freire was, in fact, an anthropological educator. He founded an educational movement based, in part, on conducting an ethnographic evaluation of a community to identify the generative themes (or 'dangerous words') which matter profoundly to people and which, for just this reason, contain their own catalytic power." This style of reflexive, engaged practice within anthropology also entails tracing a particular form of history making and understanding both the relationship between anthropology and history on the one hand (Cole and Wolf 1974; Roseberry 1989; Wolf 1982)—notably the global history of capitalism, political expansion, and state power—and the significance of frontiers on the other. Such an approach can be a powerful tool to make the invisible visible, surface assumptions, identify contradictions, and improve possibilities for critical practice.

In this book we advocate a transformational approach to public anthropology. Transformational research shifts consciousness toward recognizing that anthropology provides grounded perspectives on the structural factors and power relationships underlying social and economic disparities in marginalized populations (S. Schensul et al. 2014). This approach, based on principles of personal and group transformation, holds researchers responsible for collaborating with communities and groups to *co-construct* research, thereby enhancing the constituents' ability to carry out subsequent transformational change studies rooted in and shaped by the local community. Defining and securing a satisfactory quality of life for the world's most vulnerable and exposing the market-based commodification of the global natural and cultural commons (Harvey 2011; Nonini 2007) are key priorities of transformational research. Local communities' responses to macro forces "range from adaptation, social networking, organizing, and coalition building, to various types of resistance" (Hyland and Bennett 2005). Social suffering—that is, the assemblage of human problems caused by inequitable distribution of political, economic, and social power—and the various human responses to the social problems that are subject to these forms of power are central to transformational work (Kleinman, Das, and Lock 1997). A transformational research approach addresses multiple and diverse publics, whether students, academicians, policy makers, the general public, or people and groups encountered in the field, and always accounts for the structures of power and differentiation that facilitate or constrain desired social change.

Public anthropology, then, is fertile ground for anthropological exploration of opportunities for engagement inside and outside both the discipline and the objects of research, with specific reference to transformative change at the individual, group, and societal levels. This volume offers a roadmap for those seeking praxis, a bigger role for anthropological knowledge, and societal action.

The Continuing Debate over Public Anthropology

Calls to connect anthropology to real-world contexts, conditions, and processes have episodically elicited movement in the discipline's history. A history of public anthropology as we frame it is yet to be written. We are more concerned with illuminating the very nature of what is now pressing anthropology to address a wider range of public concerns and nontraditional audiences. Beyond its disciplinary history, anthropology gives ethnographic practice a deep historical dimension that is critical to contextualizing the material world and lived experience as foundational and authentic, and transformative when anthropological knowledge is made public. At the same time, we seek to highlight multiple and different points of view in this project. Whereas Robert Borofsky (2007) defined public anthropology as a field that "engages issues and audiences beyond today's self-imposed disciplinary boundaries," our more specific conception of the term reaches beyond public anthropology as audience for academic knowledge to anthropology as a means to support and bring about positive change. Borofsky focused "on conversations with broad audiences about broad concerns," but public anthropology necessarily includes much more than just conversations and narrowly confined intellectual exchanges: it embraces the co-construction of knowledge, the communication of that knowledge to diverse publics, and as appropriate, various forms of intervention, including political action.

In 2000, Merrill Singer's widely circulated article in *Anthropology News*, titled "Why I Am Not a Public Anthropologist," essentially rearticulated a major disciplinary divide between those who practice applied anthropology and those who do not. We could pose a dichotomy between anthropologists who work in the academy and those who do not, but this would fail to acknowledge that anthropology departments teach applied anthropology and academically employed anthropologists practice application; further, anthropologists employed outside the university may also teach in academic departments. Also misguided, Singer observed, is the notion that "the life of the mind" (scholarly work) and the life of practice (application) are separate, distinct activities. Indeed, some (e.g., S. Schensul 1985) argue that scholarly work is best understood as social "experimentation" (practices) because regardless of whether it is conducted inside or outside of academia, it requires conceptualization, methodology, and results. Anthropology cannot afford a division between research and practice.

Moreover, anthropological knowledge claims and expertise can and do play a significant role in today's civil society and should be acknowledged accordingly. More than 70 percent of the field is employed outside the university, contributing to theory and practices from the vantage points of multiple settings, disciplines, and institutions (Wasson et al. 2012). Anthropologists work in the private, nonprofit, and government sectors. They partake in media discussions, news and editorial writing, filmmaking, performance, criticism, and evaluation. They also engage in policy arenas at local, state, national, and global levels, and many are active players in public policy development. Their perspectives cannot and should not be ignored.

Nevertheless, some sectors of the anthropological academy continue to stigmatize any anthropological work that goes beyond writing published in journal articles and books, or involves policy research, interventions, or other activities besides teaching, publishing, and academic service. However, we tend to concur with Paul Rabinow (2011: 115), who stated "that the social sciences have been linked—and will continue to be linked—in multiple ways with policy and politics for as long as they have been (or are) in existence." In the same vein, Martha Balshem (1993: 134) described false dividing lines within anthropology, such as "theory versus practice, pure science versus human needs, concern versus competencies and intellectual ferment versus practical affairs." These reifications persist, even as universities entreat researchers to produce scholarship that is "engaged with the community," providing expertise for local and broader problem solving and learning at the same time.

Judith Goode (1981: 320) discovered early on that social science was being used "to explain failure" rather than attempting "to contribute to achieving goals" through a research style bridging academic and problem-solving models, an approach Goode and her students used in their work on the neighborhood movement in Philadelphia. Encouraging students to do socially meaningful work as part of their academic anthropological training can further destigmatize the image of alternative styles of research. The work of the Hispanic Health Council in Hartford, Connecticut, also represents this methodological alternative: community residents collaborate on research and program development, produce common products, and advocate for change, radically blurring the distinction between "researcher" and "client" by design (S. Schensul and Borrero 1982; Singer 2003). The Institute for Community Research, founded in Hartford in 1987 to build model programs in partnership with communities and organizations that promote justice and equity, uses participatory action research to address disparities in health, education, and culture (J. Schensul 2005).

Public anthropology plays a crucial role in responding to pressing issues; however, it need not, as Singer implied, serve merely as an academic vehicle that dismisses or supplants applied anthropology. Across the discipline, anthropologists will have to engage in an anthropological praxis that makes their own position in society a part of professional practice, not just a function of self-reflection or reflexivity. This position is especially controversial for academic anthropology, as it questions the very basis of what the academy understands as professional social science research (McKenna 2010). However, to agree that anthropology is neither objective nor value-free is to acknowledge that fieldwork can be an act of intervention as well as interpretation and thus warrants use of a conceptual framework that understands the nature of such interventions and interpretations, and is sensitive to their broader impacts. By its very name, public anthropology recognizes something about the anthropologist's social position, the nature of the work, and the forces, ideas, and processes that inform this disciplinary construct. If anthropology is a form of knowledge production, the question remains: "Knowledge for whom and for what purpose?" In response, the discipline can participate in uncovering conditions that generate socioeconomic and other disparities and injustices in vulnerable and marginalized social groups.

George Marcus (2008: 48) pointed out that the edges of ethnography's contemporary application are where anthropologists are redefining practical boundaries of their projects in multiple theaters of reception, asking basic questions of scale, function, purpose, and ethics as ethnography shifts away from the study of culture and toward the process of knowledge production. Similarly, Aihwa Ong (2010: 101) envisions a new analytical approach whereby contemporary anthropologists are "shaping truth claims about the human in different domains of human action," arguing that "anthropology is really the study of how cultures and knowledges define what it means to be human in a particular context." Hence, knowledge changes constantly as humans adapt by constructing new approaches to solve the problems of survival and everyday life, and contemporary anthropological practice must come to terms with the evolving struggles between humans and their environments. Active participation in knowledge production will allow a more accurate representation of the challenges facing the groups and communities we study. This shift toward active creation of knowledge holds the promise of ethnography as a multi-sited field where groups are not just the objects of research but become partners in the ethnographic project (Smith 1999). In some ways this has always been the case, since informants were needed to produce ethnographic constructs. In the past, informants were part of story development or rated mention in acknowledgments; now, they bring themselves in as collaborators, co-constructing research and weighing in on how research findings are communicated.

Following the lead of Michael Burawoy, who took public sociology in an inclusive direction, we advocate for a public anthropology among other anthropologies. Burawoy maintained that "public sociology is part of a broader division of labor that also includes policy sociology, professional sociology, and critical sociology" (2005: 9), and that sociology's public face cannot be separated from its professional, policy, and critical dimensions. To be sure, anthropology—particularly academic (or "professional," in Burawoy's terms) anthropology—has never been independent of publics; indeed, "most anthropology has been 'engaged' and 'public' in intention" (Field and Fox 2007: 4). Similarly, Basil Sansom (1985: 6) recognized that "in the main the discipline has also been self-sustaining, producing its own consumers though also relying on some generalized public support."

The same can be said of universities, which were never independent of publics. This especially concerns what are tellingly called public universities, but private educational institutions sustained by donations also have their relevant publics. However, it is questions of engagement—with which publics, how, and with what intensity—that define a public anthropology and differentiate it from other anthropological practices. As a form of community-engaged scholarship, this style of practice can create environments for transformation challenging disparities and inequalities. And the transformative process is bi-directional, because co-produced research, as an educational and empowering set of experiences, returns to the university through dialogue and can inform scholarly questions like those asked by Ester Barinaga and Patricia S. Parker (2013: 9): "How can we learn from organized civic forces without silencing the voices of those we work with? How can we be part of a political dialogue without reproducing the symbolic and economic distance between the academy and civil society?" Eventually, the discipline can promote public anthropology, as we have defined it, as central to professional practice and begin to respond to these questions.

Many anthropologists have mentioned the centrality of advocacy in their work (S. Schensul and J. Schensul 1978), inasmuch as engaged anthropology does not itself *speak for* (advocate), but *speaks with* by helping to amplify the voices of the vulnerable, marginalized, and silenced through the co-construction of knowledge about problems affecting the study community. Others in the discipline often see their job as mediating to improve mutual understanding between cultures by either writing about them or acting as translational agents. Although writing and being read is a more passive approach to helping others grasp and adjust to cultural diversity, it is also an act of advocacy, since "the revelations of advocacy are usually those of making the socially invisible, observable; that is, by re-framing the relation of the audience to their social surroundings," as Peter Harries-Jones (1985: 227) observed. By contrast, Charles R. Hale (2007: 105) defines activist anthropology as a practice that "involves a basic decision to align oneself with an organized group in a struggle for rights, redress, and empowerment and a commitment to produce knowledge in collaboration and dialogue with the members of that group."

Anthropologists' negotiation or mediation with informants, clients, and research subjects can arrive at either an advocacy or an activist position. An example of advocacy is the Vicos Project carried out by Alan Homberg and other Cornell University anthropologists (Isbell 2013; Ross 2010), in which the project became a landowner and a peasantry eventually took control of the land. Sol Tax (1988), on the other hand, derived his concept of "action anthropology" from his work on the Fox Project among the Meskwaki Indians, where he realized that the anthropologist's influence needed to be better understood and used to benefit the group under study. Tax's method more closely resembles activist anthropology, given that "the anthropologist must operate within the framework of goals and activities initiated by groups seeking to direct the course of their own development" (Chambers 1989: 22). In line with Tax and his work are David and Pia Maybury-Lewis, who founded Cultural Survival in 1972 to advocate for the rights of the world's indigenous peoples (Lamphere 2009), and Sheldon Davis, who started the Anthropology Resource Center in 1975 to promote the human rights of indigenous people in the Americas (Wali 2012). And Alaka Wali founded the Center for Cultural Understanding and Change at the Field Museum to integrate the museum's arts and sciences programs through participatory action research with Chicago-area community organizations, promoting widespread participation in the arts and civic activism in environmental conservation, restoration, and education projects (Wali 2006; Wali et al. 2003).

In a similar vein, Peggy Sanday (1976; 1998) coined the term "public interest anthropology," a perspective with its own theory and method. Its purpose is twofold: to offer theory and analysis in the service of problem solving to make change, and to make anthropology available to the general public. Dedication to social justice, human rights in the broadest sense of the term, and democratic principles is central to public interest anthropology. While writing, as an anthropological public practice, is Sanday's chief expression of public interest anthropology, it is not the only possible practice. Her suggestion to blur the distinction between action and theory leaves the door open for research-based action as another form of public anthropology. Still, this ethically grounded style of practice remains rooted in anthropological holism and relies on ethnographic data and conceptual categories to guide engaged research and analysis of civil society and the public sphere of debate and action (Sanday 2004).

Public Anthropology and the Public Sphere

The idea of the public sphere emerged with the development of the nation-state, industrialization, and urbanization. "The public" came into being with mass literacy, government-printed pronouncements, the spread of popular literature and theatrical culture, and the intellectual and political culture that grew with the popularity of salons, coffeehouses, and taverns (Woloch and Brown 2012). It also took the form of politically engaged constituents asserting their power to determine their own fate, that is, a civil society actively engaged in the politics of the day. The public struggled against royalism and adapted to and challenged prevailing aristocratic elites, each case requiring its political will to enter the fray, improve its condition, and be heard (Thompson 1963; 1971). The advance of liberal market capitalism was key to the public sphere's development as an institutional space between private life and the state (Habermas 1991). Markets expanded as goods were traded over ever wider geographic areas, and with this surge in production and commerce came the requirement for more knowledge. A commercial class—the bourgeoisie—emerged and multiplied, and its urban domicile became the model for status and the aesthetics of urban consumption. This increasingly literate class promoted literary culture and a turn toward the politics of civic issues, becoming part of an "Enlightened" public sphere of middle-class and aristocratic elements that appeared first in eighteenth-century Britain, France, and Germany (Melton 2001).

In the colonial era and then the new republic of the United States, civic culture was maintained by a few educated, powerful individuals who shared a sensibility and adhered to common rules of discourse. The broader educated classes cultivated a civic role through self-improvement and the nurturance of an urban cultural legacy, chiefly through libraries, philosophical and historical societies, mechanical and agricultural associations, and informal discussion groups (Bender 1993a). After the Civil War, America's civic culture was eroded by an urban order increasingly oriented to cultural diversity and egalitarianism, and by social and cultural segregation in spatial and institutional configurations, although these trends were clearly present in earlier periods too. By the late nineteenth century, two major hubs of public engagement had emerged: the urban labor and agrarian populist movements; and the universities, where civic activity promoted professional knowledge and practical interests (Bender 1993b). The federal Morrill Act of 1862 established land-grant colleges in the United States to further these goals.

Anthropological engagement, as an aspect of the nineteenth-century development of science for public use, was typically based in museums such as the American Museum of Natural History in New York and the Pitt Rivers Museum in Oxford. At this time British imperialism reigned, and the agrarian political economy was giving way to industrialization and urbanization. It was also a period of American expansionism and territorial annexation. This was the setting of the founding of the Royal Anthropological Institute in London in 1871, and the Bureau of Ethnology in 1879 (which became the Bureau of American Ethnology in 1897). The academic world was still far from its twentieth-century self-segmentation, in which specializations of various sorts split off to create self-referential languages and discourses. Academicians and public scholars outside the academy engaged in discourses that cut across disciplines and reached a lay audience through public print media, presentations, and debates. Erve Chambers (1989) noted that as early as 1838, professional anthropologists were involved in the Aboriginal Protection Society in London, and Michele Hanks (2004) documented the history of the Women's Anthropological Society, established in 1885, which supported housing improvements for the poor in the nation's capital. Because these activities and institutions lay outside the world of the academy, they lost ground as the academy took over the social science disciplines.

In the 1920s and 1930s, a "culture war" was fought on two fronts (Hegeman 1999; Manganaro 2002): "against ethnocentric supremacism," and "against biological determinism" (Eriksen 2006: 5). Margaret Mead, Ruth Benedict, and Franz Boas, of course, were notables in these culture wars, as were Zora Neale Hurston (1935) and Ashley Montagu (1951). In the 1930s and 1940s, Alan Lomax (1993) collected thousands of field recordings of rural Southern folk songs and interviews with legendary folk, blues, and jazz musicians for the Library of Congress's Archive of Folk Song. During World War II and the early Cold War years, Mead and Benedict sought to make the cultures of allies and enemies alike available to both the U.S. government (Price 2002a) and the general public by founding a research project entitled Columbia University Research in Contemporary Cultures (Beeman 2000). At this time, the sociologist C. Wright Mills's work at Columbia University's Bureau for Applied Social Research included, among other projects, a study of Puerto Rican immigrants in New York City (Sterne 2005), and St. Clair Drake and Horace Cayton (1945) published a classic study of the Great Migration and African American life on Chicago's South Side based upon research conducted by Works Progress Administration fieldworkers.

The concerns of the early twentieth-century culture wars and the wartime uses of anthropology remain central to Western discourses tied to postcolonial and neoliberal interests. Faye Harrison (1991: 5) has suggested that collaborative relationships in the field, together with dissemination to wider audiences, could establish a cultural critique of hegemonic ideologies and discourses: "A decolonizing and decolonized anthropology can indeed benefit from an 'experimental moment,' but one directed toward the empowerment of its studied populations." The culture wars are certainly not over, and anthropology's position within the postcolonial situation is still being debated inside and outside the university.

Eriksen (2006) has described anthropology's withdrawal from the public soon after World War II, as social and cultural anthropology became institutionalized, dominant forces in academic debate, and at times public discourse, on world cultures. However, there were exceptions; many in the field had an impact outside of postwar anthropological circles, including Laura Bohannan (1954), Claude Lévi-Strauss (1955), Dorothy Lee (1959), Oscar Lewis (1961), Colin Turnbull (1961), Jules Henry (1963), Charles Keil (1966), Edward T. Hall (1966), Napoleon A. Chagnon (1968), Jane Goodall (1971), Marshall Sahlins (1974), Edmund Carpenter (1974), Marvin Harris (1977), John Gwaltney (1980), Marjorie Shostak (1981), Melvin Konner (1982), Eric Wolf (1982), and Sidney Mintz (1985). Today, according to Roberto J. Gonzalez (2004a: 2), "few anthropologists could be considered celebrities in the United States, but that does not mean that none speak to the public." Contemporary American anthropologists whose works reach a wider public include Nancy Scheper-Hughes (1992), Ruth Behar (1993), Meredith F. Small (1998), Paul Farmer (2003), Nina Jablonski (2006), Philippe Bourgois and Jeffrey Shonberg (2009), David Graeber (2011), and Agustín Fuentes (2012). The contemporary Mexican anthropologists Gonzalo Aguirre Beltrán, Salomón Nahmad Sitton, and Arturo Warman also have broad readerships (Gonzalez 2004b).

American anthropologists have a rich history of positioning themselves in the struggle for social justice and democratization (Rylko-Bauer et al. 2006). This history is the foundation of public anthropology. A public anthropologist brings *praxis* to bear in understanding the deep historical dimensions of the culture and society under study. Professional scholarship within anthropology, or scholarship for scholarship's sake, cannot by itself attain this. However, the discipline was slow to recognize anthropologically trained individuals doing public anthropology outside academic frameworks or anthropology departments. Only lately has public scholarship surfaced as a legitimate approach demonstrating scholarly acumen; therefore it has not been a basis for tenure and promotion decisions in this discipline or in others, especially regarding social scientists holding progressive perspectives. Working in a discipline with a critical tradition of values that give rise to progressive thinking, anthropologists are predisposed to express unpopular views, thereby making any public anthropology a threat to the mainstream. In this light, anthropologists, as public scholars, have often been cautious in the public sphere—especially in the 1960s—lest they be seen as antiestablishment social critics or countercultural leaders, or even labeled subversive.

Even as anthropology risked ostracism by mainstream academics outside the discipline, it also had to contend with attempts to keep the discipline marginalized so as to reduce its impact in the social arena itself, as when City University of New York administrators proposed to significantly reduce or eliminate funding for anthropology, along with philosophy, across the system during the mid-1970s New York City fiscal crisis. At some institutions, funding became a tool for manipulating departmental policies within the social sciences to align scholarship with hegemonic, rather than public, purpose. In the United States today, public intellectuals do not have unrestricted access to mainstream market media—indeed, even engaged journalists complain about self-censorship and the restricted flow of authentic information. It is ironic that journalists themselves are ostracized and marginalized in the media market of mainstream U.S. journalism. In certain European and Latin American countries, by contrast, public intellectuals participate considerably more in public discourse, and even radical ideas still crop up in normalized media.

Given the challenges humanity faces today, the idea of the public sphere and its usefulness for anthropological practice need critical examination. Habermas's idealized construct of the liberal public sphere follows from his model of communicative action, in which a lifeworld based on ideal speech situations is set off from an economic realm grounded in instrumental rationality (Kloppenberg 1994). Feminist historians like Nancy Fraser (1990: 59) pointed out that the liberal public sphere "rested on, indeed was importantly constituted by, a number of significant exclusions," notably bourgeois gender norms that assigned feminine domesticity to a separate private sphere. Moreover, the "separate spheres" notion that emerged in society and politics at the dawn of liberal modernity, which restricted the bourgeois public sphere to male domains of action, has become hegemonic, extending throughout society. Feminist critiques aim to broaden the idea of a public sphere to include, following Fraser (1990: 77), a "multiplicity of publics … both in stratified and egalitarian societies." This broader conception of multiple publics has the liberatory potential to expose more and more sectors of society to a wider range of issues. This clearly has an impact on anthropological practice, especially with respect to indigenous peoples and marginalized groups typically excluded from public debates over the global commons, sustainability, and the quality of life. Meanwhile, negotiations of major international agreements about these global issues are tending toward decreased transparency. These exclusionary practices exemplify, according to Richard Westra (personal communication), how an impetus that has, since the dawn of the liberal era, progressively opened a public sphere in society can be reversed by increased restriction today. We can construe this trajectory as a reversal of the liberatory dynamic of democratic modernity as well.

Coming to terms with this potential reversal of democratic modernity requires anthropological elucidation of the ways diverse societies reproduce their material existence, notably around the social demand for basic goods, the allocation of resources, and fair compensation for productive work (Westra 2006). Through critical study of changing institutional arrangements in the global economy, including acts of domination, and the various styles of resistance to these forms of power, anthropological inquiry and praxis can inform a modern idea of citizenship and social inclusion and help ensure continuation of public spheres in diverse societies.

A Critical Turn in Anthropological Knowledge

After World War II and the subsequent reorganization of U.S. higher education, prompted mainly by the Cold War, academicians often hid their political views by asserting a value-free, objective professional practice (Price 2004; 2008). In anthropology, this effectively silenced all but mainstream voices until *The New York Review of Books* printed Joseph Jorgensen and Eric Wolf's (1970) revelations about anthropologists' participation in the American war in Southeast Asia, specifically their role in U.S. counterinsurgency efforts in Thailand (Price 1998; Wakin 1992; Wax 2008). This kind of silencing is complex. It entails avoiding political confrontation— what Laura Nader (1996) refers to as "coercive harmony." More recently, recruiting anthropologists to participate in the Human Terrain System program in the Iraq and Afghanistan wars (Glenn 2007; Gonzalez 2004a) provoked an outcry. "Embedded" in military units, anthropologists help shape military operations by providing information about the social and cultural context that is assumed to be advantageous in counterinsurgency. Neither the American Anthropological Association nor the Society for Applied Anthropology (American Anthropological Association 2009; Forte 2011) supports this role. Ironically, even anthropologists in the Human Terrain System program were apt to shift their sympathies to the people, redirecting their loyalties or, at the very least, taking an ethical stance based on the principle of non-maleficence ("do no harm"). The social scientists on the ground believed they would help prevent unnecessary deaths by collaborating with the U.S. military to communicate with "locals."

Anthropologists' efforts for the Allies in World War II, a "declared" war, differ from their involvement in "undeclared" wars or extended military engagements like Vietnam, Iraq, and Afghanistan, according to Thomas H. Eriksen (personal communication), in that the latter wars were invasions. When World War II revealed Americans' relative ignorance of the cultures and societies of enemies and allies alike, anthropologists were recruited to support the war effort. George Murdock's *Cross-Cultural Survey* at Yale University's Institute of Human Relations, funded by the Carnegie and Rockefeller Foundations, hired anthropologists to assist the U.S. military's wartime operations in the Pacific, then to help govern Pacific nations liberated from the Japanese. With continued funding from the armed forces and the Central Intelligence Agency after the war, the Institute's Human Relations Area Files provided information to government agencies seeking anthropological knowledge (Price 2008; Rohde 2013). During the Cold War, programs funded federally and by foundations recruited students and academics to pursue language and cultural studies of specific interest to the national security state. Much of the netted information could be used in ways not intended by the researchers. These anthropologists' activities contributed to Cold War strategies not only because the fieldwork generated information about little studied cultures and societies, but because anthropologists, like Peace Corps volunteers and Fulbright Program scholars, were also there to struggle for "the hearts and minds" of the people.

At this time anthropologists also turned toward the study of revolutions, notably the revolutionary movements affecting peasantries in different parts of the world along with the expansion and penetration of commercial agriculture (Wolf 1969). In predominantly peasant countries, disruptive exposure to the market forces of a capitalist world economy was sparking agrarian conflicts. Writing in *The New York Review of Books*, Stanley Diamond (1970) described how the Igbo in Biafra, who were predominantly farmers, were resisting a Nigerian state backed by global financial and oil interests. At the time, anthropology was starting to critique modernization and development theory by studying the dependency of countries at the periphery of the world system. Anthropologists and other social scientists studied dynamics of political patronage (Scott and Kerkvliet 1977), focusing on groups that mediate between peasants and the larger society and "connect the village to the wider ranging elites in markets or political networks" (Wolf 1969: xii). Writings on Third World peasant-based revolutions in the Vietnam War era reflected the sense of urgency felt by those conducting postwar anthropological fieldwork in peasant societies and thrust anthropology into public discourses on colonialism and neocolonialism. At the University of Michigan in 1965, Eric Wolf and Marshall Sahlins helped organize the anti-war movement's first "teach-in," which according to David Price (2002b: 5) is "a still vibrant model of public education that bypasses the filters and constraints of traditional media outlets." In Washington, DC, that same year, Wolf and Sahlins, together with Morton Fried, also helped organize the first national teach-in to advance public discussion of U.S. policies in Southeast Asia, an event that the national media covered widely (Price 2004).

Although anthropology has had a public face since its inception (Eriksen 2006; Lamphere 2004; Sanday 1976; Scheper-Hughes 1995; Vermeulen 2008), the notion of a public anthropology gained ground in the 1960s because domestic liberation movements in North American and European societies and national liberation movements in the colonized world opened the way to discovering "the other," and anthropology's core values enabled interpretation, translation, and amplification of the other's voice. Under postcolonial conditions today, the battle is as viable as ever. Stanley Diamond's (1974: 1) critique of the situation begins: "Civilization originates in conquest abroad and repression at home. Each is an aspect of the other." Diamond understood that "the search for the primitive" cannot be separated from civilization's longing for an idealized mode of existence that it projects onto "primitive societies." His critique extended to anthropologists who, through the colonial encounter, came to view the cultural "other" as "primitive" compared to imperial "civilizations" that produced anthropologists to provide "expert discourse" used to understand "primitive" lifeways in the interests of maintaining their hegemony. Diamond (1974: 94) then offered a corrective: "Unless the anthropologist confronts his own alienation, which is only a special instance of a general condition, seeks to understand its roots and subsequently matures as a relentless critic of his own civilization, the very civilization which converts man into an object, he cannot understand or even recognize himself in the man of another culture or that other man in himself."

Commenting on Diamond's critique, Eric Wolf (1974: xi) locates dual epistemological crises in our civilization and our definition of human nature: "The crisis in the Western world and its imperial hinterland, which is also the crisis of humanity, cannot be confined to social, economic or technological 'problems': it inheres in our definition, our very understanding of man." Using abstract models to study humanity as a "problem" propagates an "official definition of reality" and thereby denies the "integral relation of theory and praxis," Wolf argues, calling for an anthropology that "can also posit new possibilities for ourselves" and "political action consistent with our insights" (1974: xii, xiii). Public anthropology, which likewise bridges theory and praxis, can help overcome these epistemological crises through its conscious methodological trajectory from dialogue and the co-construction of knowledge in the field situation to political action.

Yet anthropologists cannot be complacent about their capacity to produce this kind of knowledge. Knowledge made public can always be inverted—a "latent oppression" that is unseen but always present. Instead of advancing the cause of liberation and creating a context conducive to greater understanding and tolerance, anthropologists' knowledge production may cause cruelty and injury to a population because of how research is carried out and how, and by whom, research results are reported and used (Singer 2008). Here critical public anthropology is needed to elucidate power structures and their effects on global inequalities and disparities (Maida 2008; Nader 1969). A critique of traditional anthropology that emerged in the late 1960s and early 1970s (Asad 1973; Deloria 1969; Gough 1968, Huizer and Mannheim 1979; Hymes 1969; Said 1978) centered on anthropological fieldwork, which is unavoidably based on asymmetries of privilege and power, and the textual basis of professional practice in anthropology. Even public anthropology is normatively understood as textual (Eriksen 2006). Text-based work is an important product of public anthropology since its purpose is to educate and increase public consciousness, something we do not wish to minimize or reduce. However, in the context of late capitalist political economy and a critical anthropology (Arrighi 1994; Hedges 2009; Klein 2008; Maskovsky and Susser 2009; Wallerstein 1976), texts alone are insufficient.

The epistemological move toward public anthropology poses a challenge to the "normal scientific" anthropological paradigm, as Kuhn (1962) put it, amid internal calls for greater engagement and reflexivity, significant market pressure on the discipline, and higher learning institutions' demands concerning curriculum, service, and development (Giroux 2007; Strathern 2001). Beyond their long-standing community-partnered activities, universities are strengthening ties with private corporations as a form of "engagement." Moreover, market pressures are affecting academic disciplines as well, especially their curricula. Government, corporate, and foundation funding is setting the parameters of academic research, and the marketplace even appears to influence teaching, as the Internet is used to educate tens of thousands at a time. In an academic arena where disciplines compete for funding and students, anthropology is seeking greater public recognition in response to complaints in the profession that anthropological knowledge is seldom found in public venues and is invisible in public spheres. The American Anthropological Association (AAA) has encouraged its members to become significantly more public-oriented, stressing op-ed articles and investigative journalism as vehicles (Bird 2009; 2010; Boyer 2010; Checker, Vine, and Wali 2010; Dyck and Waldram 1993; Fikry 1980; Geilhufe 1979; Peterson 2010; Shore and Wright 1997; Vesperi 2010; Wedel et al. 2005), although this move has also provoked critique (McKenna 2009). One effort by the AAA produced the traveling award-winning exhibit *Race: Are We So Different?* which directly engages the public to rethink conventional but unscientifically supported ideas about race; other AAA efforts in the works will focus on migration (Mullings 2013: 3).

Anthropologists have long been involved in addressing the public. We argue that a public anthropology was foundational to the discipline, at least in U.S. anthropology, Franz Boas's anti-racist and anti-xenophobic work being an early example. However, it took generations of anthropologists to establish this critical stance, often in the face of considerable pressure to silence questioning voices within and outside the discipline. In the 1970s and 1980s, tenure track appointments were few, relative to the number of doctorates conferred. Then as now, the most forward-thinking mentors advised graduate students to at least think about alternatives to academic careers and encouraged them to write for a general public. These decades witnessed the early development of anthropologies of Europe and North America, in part a response to limited funding for field research in more faraway environments. This prompted anthropology to expand into the world of complex societies because students were told that primitives and peasants were disappearing.

At this time, historically informed political economic anthropologists produced work exploring the nature of capitalism at the global and local levels, and the relations between capitalism and other modes of production. A critical anthropology of development also reached beyond traditional anthropological and policy audiences to address new publics. Similarly, critical medical anthropology emerged to assert the fundamental importance of political economy in health (Biehl and Petryna 2013; Singer et al. 1992). With this changing disciplinary matrix came an academic public anthropology that not only addressed societal transformation but also supported desired change. This form of engagement is increasingly recognized and accepted as a necessary aspect of anthropological practice. This is not to deny that anthropologists were involved in making change in the past by applying anthropology in government or the private sector, or working to identify and resolve problems for private nonprofit organizations. Only now is an anthropology that addresses a wider public beginning to gain legitimacy in the academy. Within and beyond anthropology, efforts are on the rise to translate scientific knowledge for use in public discourse that can speed the address of problems experienced in the everyday lived world.

Over the last two decades, anthropologists began to self-consciously identify themselves as "public anthropologists." Within the discipline, *an anthropology for the public* gained prominence due to a unique set of circumstances. A "crisis of representation" (Denzin 1996: 135) and the reflexive turn in the human sciences pushed anthropologists toward a deeper understanding of ways people construct knowledge and of the relationship between a particular group's knowledge production and its behavior and lived experience. The anthropology of lived experience (Clifford and Marcus 1986; Geertz 2000; Marcus and Fisher 1986; Turner 1986) emerged in response to this crisis, raising issues of gender, class, and race. However, a fully reflexive interpretive anthropology clearly needs to study these issues in broader historical and political economic frames, and to critically evaluate the anthropologist's stance in the field encounter.

In this direction, Robert Desjarlais and C. Jason Throop call for phenomenological approaches and ethnographic field methods to "attend at once to the tangible realities of people's lives and to the often interrelated social, biological, corporeal, sensorial, discursive, cultural, political, economic, psychological, and environmental dimensions of those realities" (2011: 97). For example, anthropological studies of craft apprenticeships combine phenomenological, educational, historical, and economic approaches to understand the varieties of skilled practice (Marchand 2008), reflecting a move toward such methodological synergies. These concerns are, in part, a consequence of global economic penetration and political domination of the communities under study—and of academic knowledge itself, by neocolonial and neoliberal design. In critical anthropological circles, how anthropology constructs its knowledge in response to these forms of control and domination was a signal concern (Hymes 1969) well before this epistemological crisis of the mid 1980s.

What counts as knowledge is socially constructed (Berger and Luckmann 1967); each discipline defines its varied approaches to knowledge production and what its particular sense of knowledge is. Acknowledging academic knowledge production as the object of research, Michael Gibbons et al. (1994) identified the emergence, during the post–World War II era, of a new form of knowledge production that is context-driven, problem-focused, and interdisciplinary. Gibbons and his colleagues contrasted this newer form to an earlier mode of knowledge production that is academic, investigator-initiated, and discipline-based. Chris Argyris and Donald Schon discuss the specificities of the newer knowledge production in such terms as "theorizing-in-action" (1974) and "reflective practice" (Schon 1984) to define the situation. Many who do fieldwork find themselves changing the subject of research as new realities they confront in the field—that is, *in context* and *in process*—compel them to integrate theory with practice. Hence, context-driven research implies studies undertaken in the process of action that tries to solve lived problems encountered while conducting fieldwork. This transitional process, which actually occurs during graduate training in anthropology, is clearly what initial and subsequent fieldwork experiences are about; however, many academicians devote limited attention to this dialectical process.

Participatory action research (Greenwood and Levin 2006) and community-based participatory research (Israel et al. 1998) are kindred methods that acknowledge this dialectical process and integrate the scholar/researcher's expertise of with local-level (or indigenous) expertise to effect sociocultural change. The approach, which dates to the 1920s in Germany, was brought to the United States by the psychologist Kurt Lewin and spread to several disciplines, including sociology, anthropology, and most recently community development (Pottier 1997; Sillitoe 2002) and public health (Minkler and Wallerstein 2011). Lewin advanced understanding of the reality of social phenomena; the constancy of relations; and the relations among structural properties of a dynamic whole, the subparts within a social field, and the subjective and objective elements within that field. He proposed an analysis of group life that moves from perception to action, and from subjective to objective phenomena, concluding that "circular causal processes" regulate action in individuals and groups. This clearly points to the reflexivity at the core of transformational research. In Lewin's (1951: 199) field-theoretical psychology, individual perception or "fact-finding" is linked to both individual and group action through circular causality, as the content of the perception "depends upon the way in which the situation is changed by action. The result of the fact-finding in turn influences or steers action." Lewin (1935: 41) thus views human behavior as a dynamic interplay of forces *"derived from the relation of the concrete individual to the concrete situation*, and, so far as internal forces are concerned, from the mutual relations of the various functional systems that make up the individual." His emphasis on dynamical systems nudged the social sciences toward the view that "a wider and wider realm of determinants must be treated as part of a single, interdependent field" (Cartwright 1951: xii).

Further, Lewin saw the need to move beyond disciplinary boundaries in order to study social phenomena through a coherent system of constructs. This "deterritorializing" of knowledge is evident in anthropological studies of biomedicine, sociolinguistics, and cross-cultural psychology, where an interdisciplinary framework combining neurobiology, culture, cognition, and narrative is key to understanding the range of social phenomena. Scientists in the emerging field of social neuroscience view encounters, such as participatory forms of research, as ways to enhance the social interaction essential to the reflective learning derived from, in this case, fieldwork based on grounded theory (Glaser and Strauss 1967). Interpersonal encounters that come about through participant-observation may, in turn, be supported by neural circuits linking perception and action for "close coupling and attunement between self and other," and for synaptic plasticity (Meltzoff et al. 2009: 285).

Participatory research methods seem straightforward enough at first blush, but their implementation generates numerous contradictions that must be resolved in context and in process, as research and action are carried out (Hampshire, Hills, and Iqbal 2005). Mixing expertise creates a relationship—variously called cooperative, partnered, collaborative, contractual, and consultative—whose very nature frequently leads to methodological concerns concerning power. Michael Burawoy (1998: 15) argued that action research cannot succeed without addressing the "multiple dimensions of power" and their hierarchies. He upheld the extended case method of the Manchester School (Evens and Handelman 2006) as a model for action research, one that informs his idea of a reflexive science that "elevates dialogue as its defining principle and intersubjectivity between participant and observer as a premise" (Burawoy 2009: 39). As a move toward this reflexive methodological innovation, the extended case method provides four extensions to legitimate the many alternative ethnographies that have "moved beyond thick description to incorporate historical and political sensibilities" but stop short of the model of science he proposes: "The extended case method undertakes four extensions, corresponding to intersubjectivity, process, structuration, and theory reconstruction. The first extension makes the observer a participant, experiencing the world of the Other; the second extends observations over time and space, allowing us to interpret those experiences as process; the third extends from the local to the extralocal, historicizing our interpretation of process as shaped by forces; and the fourth extends theory, making the previous three extensions possible and connecting us to communities of theorists" (Burawoy 1998: 15). As participatory research methods continue to develop, additional conceptual and methodological knowledge frames like those Burawoy proposed, together with revised ethical guidelines (Finnis 2004), will further refine the practice within anthropology.

Toward a Redefined Public Anthropology

Since the mid twentieth century at least, significant shifts have affected both everyday consciousness and public thinking about the nature of work and community life. These changes clearly impact anthropological practice. It is safe to say that consciousness is based on what we do and where we are situated in society, the economy, and the work we do inside and out of academia. The organization of our daily lives is reflected in the way we think about things, our perception of our existence, the kind of world we create for ourselves, and our chances to improve ourselves and the world we live in. Throughout the postwar decades, a mix of corporate and state power increasingly reshaped the contours of everyday life in communities and workplaces, including the university. According to Louise Lamphere, Helena Rangoné, and Patricia Zavella (1997: 1), "cultural conceptions are being transformed by those who control hegemonic institutions *and* by workers, clients, patients, family members, and citizens affected by these institutions." Corporate power has increasingly insinuated itself into the decision-making processes of the state. This is no novelty: economic elites have always exerted influence on the politics of the state and the dominant values of society at large, clearly influencing what is considered "common sense." This "power elite," as Mills (1956) understood it, presents its own interests and projects as the indisputable common interest of all members of society. Antonio Gramsci (1971) termed the elite's influence over how society at large thinks and represents reality "ideological hegemony."

In this market-driven ideology, namely neoliberalism, anthropology must compete for funding and students. The business strategies universities have adopted to accommodate the neoliberal shift are changing the power structure and functions of higher education (Menand 2010). Public and private nonprofit universities alike have had to learn how to compete with ascendant for-profit institutions to benefit from government, foundation, and corporate largesse. This is not just a matter of how higher education organizes itself to produce knowledge, but also how its delivery of educational services accommodates the marketplace where students seek employment. That is, "colleges and universities must accelerate the pace of curricula restructuring to expand the flexible interactive modes of teaching and learning that are sought by the workforce and made possible by the technology revolution" (Broad 1998: vi). The labor market seeks workers with particular skills and knowledge and pressures post-secondary institutions to deliver such individuals. The resultant restructuring of higher education has shifted beliefs about the value of college, and these changed views are now part of both the students' and their parents' social reality as consumers. As with any innovative product or service, a consumer may be unaware of the change in the original commodity and may not recall the move away from its original purpose, in this case from liberal education to workforce preparation. Like other products or services that change rapidly in late capitalism's current neoliberal mode, higher education has incorporated innovations that render it a revalued commodity, widely disseminated and socialized throughout the culture. A generation of parents now believes that institutions of higher education are training grounds for their children to acquire secure, well-paid jobs that will justify the high cost of education.

To be clear, neoliberalism is based on neoclassical theories of economics that posit private enterprise, made possible by liberal trade policies and open markets, as the most efficient economic form. According to neoliberalism, the private sector should determine state policies whenever it believes that government will be able to operate more efficiently and improve the economy. Privatization, a core ideological value of the neoliberal regime, has simultaneously pushed its way into a social sphere that values individual autonomy and choice, and shifted financial risk from government and corporations onto individual taxpayers. Under neoliberalism, the concept of class is abandoned for a neoliberal subjectivity characterized by personal consumption and sets of interpersonal transactions—an identity that is decontextualized and autonomous, most notably from labor processes. In Jean and John Comaroff's (2000: 306) view, class inequality under neoliberal conditions, or "millennial capitalism," is no longer rooted in work and production structures but in "mechanical solidarities of 'identity' in constructing selfhood and social being," and hence in "personal trait or lifestyle choice." A cogent example is the economic collapse during the first and second decades of this century, a transformation that has fragmented class consciousness and modernist forms of life, especially middle-class lifeways. In this crisis of neoliberalization and "millennial manifestation of market rule" (Peck, Theodore, and Brenner 2012: 268), financial institutions were rescued, whereas individual taxpayers were left to fend for themselves.

A recent shift in academic research as well causes the research university to function as an arm of the national and global economy, and as a source of the civilian knowledge workforce and military research. With these functions comes a two-pronged managerial regime. First, based upon Frederick Winslow Taylor's scientific management, it uses task analysis to control academic workplaces, including both administrative and curricular directions. Second, it carries out social management, transferring corporate-sector organizational and leadership styles, including entrepreneurship and monetization principles, to university governance oriented to the profit motive. Observing this shift, Pierre Bourdieu (2004: vii) warned: "Many research scientists or research teams are falling under the control of large industrial companies seeking to secure a monopoly on commercially very profitable products, through patents; and the boundary, which has long been blurred, between fundamental research, in university laboratories, and applied research, is tending to disappear completely." The monetizing of university-based knowledge production means that comparatively open-ended approaches, like those of anthropological research focused on interpretive analytics, are being eased out.

As an intervention, Paul Rabinow (2011: 114) suggests "rethinking" the styles of inquiry, accepted practices, and scholarly products of the interpretive sciences, beginning with "experimentation," or "simply trying out different configurations of inquiry or critique," notably through collaborative practices or "assemblages" of people and projects within common, or shared, venues for such experimentation. As in modernist experiments to create "spaces of critical practice," for Rabinow (2011: 117) the first step is "to invent practices of knowledge production, dissemination and critique that resolutely refuse the (liberal and symbolic capital-laden) individualism" of the human sciences as they are currently practiced. Abandoning methodological individualism for a more collaborative style would essentially "redesign" anthropology to more appropriately address the contemporary situation, so as to "remediate the practices, forms, and determinations of inquiry and pedagogy—and thereby make new capacities possible" (2011: 143). Following Bourdieu's notion of blurred boundaries in the research enterprise, Rabinow regards such collaborative research activities as "hybrid assemblages" within and at the edge of universities.

Along with these shifting knowledge structures, the roles of intellectuals—both private and public, within and outside of the corporate economy—have changed in the borderless world of the post–Cold War globalizing political order. Despite the politically stratified "three worlds" of the previous Cold War era, as characterized by Peter Worsley (1984), population flows across these geographical borders dramatically influenced intellectual life both in and outside the academy at the time. According to Richard A. Posner (2001: 5), many "of the most distinguished academic public intellectuals" in the second half of the twentieth century were foreigners, refugees, and immigrants. In U.S. anthropology, a tradition of foreign-born academic public intellectuals began with Franz Boas, was carried on by Eric Wolf and Talal Asad in the postwar years, and continues today in the public voices of Saba Mahmood, Didier Fassin, Aihwa Ong, Alaka Wali, and João Biehl, all strongly interested in human rights and social justice.

In a borderless world, many public intellectuals, native-born and émigré alike, find that the sum of their experiences at the margins of multiple social worlds is a cosmopolitan identity. Tony Judt (2010) referred to marginalized intellectuals like himself as "edge people" who, "born at intersecting margins," maintain tangential relationships to nation and community of origin and hence embrace cosmopolitanism as "the normal condition of life." Advantageously perched at the margins, public intellectuals can influence the public sphere; Judt even went on to cite a particular "obstinacy of character" that impels them to provide counterarguments, alternative views, and critiques of what human life can be, and moreover to encourage the public—that is, ordinary people—to take charge of public and common spaces and help manage the democratization of everyday life. In *Public Power in the Age of Empire,* Arundhati Roy (2004: 39) wrote: "If we want to reclaim the space for civil disobedience, we will have to liberate ourselves from the tyranny of crisis reportage and its fear of the mundane. We have to use our experience, our imagination, and our art to interrogate those instruments of the state that ensure that 'normality' remains what it is: cruel, unjust, unacceptable." Following Roy, anthropologists, as public intellectuals, will need to engage their various publics, or audiences, to understand the dynamics of war and peace in our time, namely that peace should not merely mean the absence of war (Rylko-Bauer and Singer 2011). Likewise, in the economic sphere the public must be convinced that normality should not reflect extreme disparities between a few wealthy individuals who control the vast bulk of wealth and a general population that must struggle to survive.

This book reflects its authors' experiences exploring an anthropologically informed approach of engagement that acknowledges that this discipline is at once value-based, historical, and scientific. Critical and political, it embraces advocacy and at times activism, not just as a strategy for generating data but as a commitment to support and effect change for society's most vulnerable members and for those living in oppressive conditions.

The first set of essays focuses on participatory action research. Jean Schensul focuses on the "co-construction" of public knowledge through participatory action research, whereby politically oriented activist researchers and politically motivated community actors create new knowledge together. She emphasizes the process by which individuals of different backgrounds, knowledge bases, and experiences integrate and synthesize multiple sources of information into a consensus perspective leading to action. Alaka Wali and Madeleine Tudor set out to rethink and experiment with participatory action research strategies based in a museum. Their applied research and public action work investigates how the process through which residents care for place and contest it relates to consequences for both the people and the built and natural environments. Multimedia strategies, when integrated into participatory action research methods, help forge pathways for community empowerment. Carl Maida explores how practitioners of professional and lay knowledge collaborated to improve urban quality of life in a working-class Latino community. Focusing on the building of a community of practice to address environmental justice concerns, the chapter demonstrates how professionals and residents moved toward common ground. Participatory action research turned community and academic stakeholders into partners designing and carrying out a research project to understand and reduce toxic risks.

The next set of essays attempts to come to terms with critical issues facing public anthropological engagement. Josiah Heyman accepts partisan engagement in public issues as a given and looks instead at what actually happens in such practices. He critically analyzes how engagement actually occurs and what this says about how the social process of political engagement affects value choices and tactical decisions in such politics. After reflecting on the distinction between radical and reformist approaches, he leaves this initial dichotomy behind to examine the social and political process of engagement. Merrill Singer explores how the anthropologist can at once serve as scientist and public social critic, and posits that social criticism can inform public anthropology. He examines anthropological involvement in knowledge-based assaults on the causes of social suffering and structural violence, attacks that respond to a core epistemological dilemma within the discipline—"Knowledge for what?"—with the applied reply "the practical transformation of the real world." Louise Lamphere's autobiographical take on public anthropology concerns the study of critical social issues, continued collaboration with communities, and public policy making. She elaborates on how her generation's participation in social movements initially catalyzed a change in anthropological research and teaching, opening up research on a host of critical social issues of concern to the populations studied.

Judith Goode discusses how, in anthropology's epistemological transition, research subjects changed from populations of "others" to "ourselves," and anthropologists' possible audiences for anthropological knowledge production and related action roles broadened. With this transition came new ways of framing research in terms of critical theories of power-knowledge, which created complex, often critical views of professional "expertise" that complicated communication with publics. Asking "Anthropology for Whom?" Angela Stuesse reflects on the promises and pitfalls of activist research. The "Austin School" of activist anthropology promotes sustained collaboration with an organized collective and presupposes a concrete, bounded, organized group of individuals or organizations with whom one works throughout the various stages of research. Through fieldwork, however, Stuesse found that the "communities in struggle" with whom anthropologists align themselves are often much more amorphous and transitional, at times even metaphorical or imagined. Raúl Acosta also begins with a question: "Just how public is public anthropology supposed to be?" He then reflects on studies that highlight the dialogical character of anthropological research. In the new spaces— from grassroots dialogues to those fostered by emerging media—being carved out for anthropology's public engagement, activists' calls for "dialogue" and "democracy" are often appropriated by powerful governmental interests. Acosta offers an analytical framework for effective public use of anthropology to understand processes of grassroots resistance and hegemonic appropriation.

Authors of the final set of essays seek to understand public anthropology in diverse arenas, including radio and television, visual culture, and urban design. Thomas Hylland Eriksen recognizes how a public anthropology can contribute to a shift from a fragmented, reductionist view of humanity to an image of the world as a whole. Pointing to the need to reflect seriously on *what* we say, to *whom,* and *how,* he sees academic anthropologists as too often concentrating on problems that are internal to the discipline, that is, academically defined. While anthropologists have been busy doing other things, he claims, neoliberal, xenophobic, and reductionist perspectives on humanity have gained currency as "real science." Udi Mandel Butler asks: *Who* are the publics in a public anthropology? Should *the public* be regarded as the population sector interested in newspapers, books, and other media outlets where anthropologists can have a voice? Or should the public, in a public anthropology, be understood in a broader sense of promoting the use of anthropological knowledge outside the academy in domains that affect people's day-to-day lives? He frames his answers through the lens of a public anthropology of visual culture that emphasizes how subjects experience images that affect their emotions, identities, and imaginations.

Sam Beck shows how urban graffiti, an aesthetic created *in* and *of* low-income communities of color, became a commodity for mass consumption, often without attribution. This brought graffiti artists into conflict with state authority as they fought to sustain graffiti as a lifestyle rather than a commodified art form. Today, gentrification and displacement have limited the movement, either eliminating it as a force and presence on the landscape or civilizing it for art gallery patrons. Graffiti survives as an urban aesthetic and a social movement of resistance, albeit tamed by the elite imaginary of urban planners, corporate real estate developers, and marketers of urban living. Finally, Tony Asare, Erika Mamley Osae, and Deborah Pellow show what it means to take anthropology out of the academy and use it to confront critical public concerns by collaborating with communities and thereby influencing social policies. They see slums as an outcome of urban poverty as well as failed policies, poor governance, inappropriate legal and regulatory frameworks, dysfunctional land markets, unresponsive financial systems, and not least a lack of political will. By documenting a project that helped solve a housing shortage through appropriate design and accessible financing, they illustrate how poor community residents became participants in a project that radically changed their living circumstances.

Together, the contributors to this volume reposition public anthropology as an anthropology of and in communities that meaningfully and productively engages in a world of intensifying disparities to fulfill a real-world purpose.

Acknowledgments

We would like to thank Ian Coulter, Thomas Hylland Eriksen, George Marcus, Brian McKenna, Dick Roberts, Jean Schensul, Sydel Silverman, Merrill Singer, Alaka Wali, Richard Westra, and Bruce Woych for their close readings of earlier versions of the manuscript and their suggested revisions, and to Jaime Taber for expert copy-editing of the final manuscript.

Carl A. Maida is a professor at the UCLA Institute of the Environment and Sustainability in the College of Letters and Science, where he teaches courses on action research methods and conducts community-based research on urban sustainability. His anthropological research in Los Angeles focuses on how various urban social formations—social networks, mutual aid groups, and associations based on ethnic, community, and voluntary ties—serve as arenas for making sense of atypical events and move into the vacuum to act as pathways through crisis, and will often form the basis of social movements on behalf of health and environmental quality of life. He also directs the UCLA Pre-College Science Education

Program, and conducts studies of project-based and inquiry-based learning in schools and action research in community-based organizations funded by the National Science Foundation, National Institutes of Health, US Environmental Protection Agency, Robert Wood Johnson Foundation, Ford Foundation, Howard Hughes Medical Institute, and The California Endowment. He is a Fellow of the American Association for the Advancement of Science, the American Anthropological Association, and the Society for Applied Anthropology.

Sam Beck is Senior Lecturer and Director of the Urban Semester Program at Cornell University. His interests have focused primarily on intergroup relationships expressed as ethnicity, race, and class under a variety of conditions, processes, landscapes, and modes of production. He teaches a fifteen-credit academic program in which students learn ethnographic methods as tools for learning from experience. He guides students' experiences in their internships and community service/participation in critical reflection seminars. He is actively engaged in the North Brooklyn community, receiving from Churches United for Fair Housing (CUFFH) the Daisy Lopez Outstanding Leader of the Year Award. Cornell University recognized him with two Merrill Presidential Scholar Outstanding Educator Awards (2011, 2012) and the Kendall S. Carpenter Memorial Advising Award.

References

American Anthropological Association. 2009. "AAA Commission on the Engagement of Anthropology with the US Security and Intelligence Communities." Final Report on Army Human Terrain System Proof of Concept Program. http://www.aaanet.org/issues/policy-advocacy/CEAUSSIC-Releases-Final-Report-on-Army-HTS-Program.cfm.

Argyris, Chris, and Donald A. Schon. 1974. *Theory in Practice: Increasing Professional Effectiveness*. San Francisco: Jossey-Bass.

Arrighi, Giovanni. 1994. *The Long Twentieth Century*. London: Verso.

Asad, Talal, ed. 1973. *Anthropology and the Colonial Encounter*. New York: Humanities Press.

Balshem, Martha. 1993. *Cancer in the Community: Class and Medical Authority*. Washington, DC: Smithsonian Institution Press.

Barinaga, Ester, and Patricia S. Parker. 2013. "Community-Engaged Scholarship: Creating Participative Spaces for Transformative Politics." *Tamara: Journal for Critical Organization Inquiry* 11, no. 4: 5–11.

Beck, Sam, and Carl A. Maida. 2013. *Toward Engaged Anthropology*. New York: Berghahn Books.

Beeman, William O. 2000. "Introduction: Margaret Mead, Cultural Studies, and International Understanding." In *The Study of Culture at a Distance*, ed. Margaret Mead and Rhoda Métraux. New York: Berghahn Books.

Behar, Ruth. 1993. *Translated Woman: Crossing the Border with Esperanza's Story.* Boston: Beacon Press.

Bender, Thomas. 1993a. "The Cultures of Intellectual Life: The City and the Professions." In *Intellect and Public Life: Essays on the Social History of Academic Intellectuals in the United States.* Baltimore: Johns Hopkins University Press.

———. 1993b. "The Erosion of Public Culture: Cities, Discourses, and Professional Disciplines." In *Intellect and Public Life: Essays on the Social History of Academic Intellectuals in the United States.* Baltimore: Johns Hopkins University Press.

Berger, Peter L., and Thomas Luckmann. 1967. *The Social Construction of Reality: A Treatise on the Sociology of Knowledge.* New York: Anchor Books.

Biehl, João, and Adriana Petryna. 2013. "Critical Global Health." In *When People Come First: Critical Studies in Global Health,* ed. João Biehl and Adriana Petryna. Princeton: Princeton University Press.

Bird, S. Elizabeth, ed. 2009. *The Anthropology of News and Journalism: Global Perspectives.* Bloomington: Indiana University Press.

———. 2010. "Anthropological Engagement with News Media: Why Now?" *Anthropology News* 51, no. 4: 5, 9.

Bohannan, Laura (Elenore Smith Bowen, pseud.). 1954. *Return to Laughter.* New York: Harper and Row.

Borofsky, Robert. 2007. "Defining Public Anthropology: A Personal Perspective." http://www.publicanthropology.org/public-anthropology/.

Bourdieu, Pierre. 2004. *Science of Science and Reflexivity.* Chicago: The University of Chicago Press.

Bourgois, Philippe, and Jeffrey Schonberg. 2009. *Righteous Dopefiend.* Berkeley: University of California Press.

Boyer, Dominic. 2010. "Digital Expertise in Online Journalism (and Anthropology)." *Anthropological Quarterly* 83, no. 1: 73–96.

Broad, Molly Corbett. 1998. "Foreword." In *What Business Wants from Higher Education,* ed. Diana G. Oblinger and Anne-Lee Verville. Phoenix, AZ: American Council on Education / Oryx Press.

Burawoy, Michael. 1998. "Critical Sociology: A Dialogue between Two Sciences." *Contemporary Sociology* 27, no. 1: 12–20.

———. 2005. "For Public Sociology." 2004 Presidential Address. *American Sociological Review* 70, no. 1: 4–28.

———. 2009. *The Extended Case Method: Four Countries, Four Decades, Four Great Transformations and One Theoretical Tradition.* Berkeley: University of California Press.

Carpenter, Edmund S. 1974. *Oh What a Blow That Phantom Gave Me.* New York: Holt, Rinehart and Winston.

Cartwright, Dorwin. 1951. "Introduction." In *Field Theory in Social Science Selected Theoretical Papers,* ed. Dorwin Cartwright. New York: Harper and Row.

Chagnon, Napoleon A. 1968. *Yanomamö: The Fierce People.* New York: Holt, Rinehart and Winston.

Chambers, Erve. 1989. *Applied Anthropology: A Practical Guide.* Long Grove, IL: Waveland Press.

Checker, Melissa, David Vine, and Alaka Wali. 2010. "A Sea Change in Anthropology? Public Anthropology Reviews." *American Anthropologist* 112, no. 1: 5–6.

Clifford, James, and George E. Marcus, eds. 1986. *Writing Culture.* Berkeley: University of California Press.

Cole, John W., and Eric R. Wolf. 1974. *The Hidden Frontier: Ecology and Ethnicity in an Alpine Valley.* New York: Academic Press.

Comaroff, Jean, and John L. Comaroff. 2000. "Millennial Capitalism: First Thoughts on a Second Coming." *Public Culture* 12, no. 2: 291–343.

Deloria, Vine, Jr. 1969. *Custer Died For Your Sins*. New York: Macmillan.

Denzin, Norman K. 1996. "The Epistemological Crisis in the Human Disciplines: Letting the Old Do the Work of the New." In *Ethnography and Human Development: Context and Meaning in Social Inquiry*, ed. Richard Jessor, Anne Colby, and Richard A. Shweder. Chicago: University of Chicago Press.

Desjarlais, Robert, and C. Jason Throop. 2011. Phenomenological Approaches in Anthropology. *Annual Review of Anthropology* 40: 87–102.

Diamond, Stanley. 1970. "Who Killed Biafra?" *The New York Review of Books* 14, no. 4: 17–26.

———. 1974. *In Search of the Primitive*. New Brunswick, NJ: Transaction Publishers.

Drake, St. Clair, and Horace R. Cayton. 1945. *Black Metropolis: A Study of Negro Life in a Northern City*. New York: Harcourt, Brace and Company.

Dyck, Noel, and James B. Waldram. 1993. *Anthropology, Public Policy and Native Peoples of Canada*. Montreal: McGill-Queens University Press.

Eriksen, Thomas H. 2006. *Engaging Anthropology*. New York: Bloomsbury Academic.

Evens, T.M.S., and Don Handelman. 2006. "Introduction: The Ethnographic Praxis of the Theory of Practice." In *The Manchester School: Practice and Ethnographic Praxis in Anthropology*, ed, T.M.S. Evens and Don Handelman. New York: Berghahn Books.

Farmer, Paul. 2003. *Pathologies of Power: Health, Human Rights and the New War on the Poor*. Berkeley: University of California Press.

Field, Les, and Richard G. Fox, eds. 2007. *Anthropology Put To Work*. Oxford: Berg.

Fikry, Mona. 1980. "On Anthropology and Policy Studies." *Current Anthropology* 21, no. 5: 682–684.

Finnis, Elizabeth. 2004. "Anthropology and Participatory Research: Ethical Considerations in International Development." *NEXUS* 17, no. 1: 32–62.

Forte, Maximilian C. 2011. "The Human Terrain System and Anthropology: A Review of Ongoing Public Debates." *American Anthropologist* 113, no. 1: 149–153.

Fraser, Nancy. 1990. "Rethinking the Public Sphere: A Contribution to the Critique of Actually Existing Democracy." *Social Text* 25/26: 56–80.

Freire, Paulo. 1970. *Pedagogy of the Oppressed*. New York: Continuum.

Fuentes, Agustín. 2012. *Race, Monogamy, and Other Lies They Told You: Busting Myths About Human Nature*. Berkeley: University of California Press.

Geertz, Clifford. 2000. "The State of the Art." In *Available Light: Anthropological Reflections on Philosophical Topics*. Princeton, NJ: Princeton University Press.

Geilhufe, Nancy L. 1979. "Anthropology and Policy Analysis." *Current Anthropology* 20, no. 3: 557–579.

Gibbons, Michael, Camille Limoges, Helga Nowotny, Simon Schwartzman, Peter Scott, and Martin Trow. 1994. *The New Production of Knowledge: The Dynamics of Science and Research in Contemporary Societies*. London: Sage.

Giroux, Henry A. 2007. *The University in Chains: Confronting the Military-Industrial-Academic Complex*. Boulder: Paradigm.

Glaser, Barney, and Anselm Strauss. 1967. *The Discovery of Grounded Theory: Strategies for Qualitative Research*. Chicago: Aldine.

Glenn, David. 2007. "Former Human Terrain System Participant Describes Program in Disarray." *Chronicle of Higher Education*, 5 December.

Gonzalez, Roberto J. 2004a. *Anthropologists in the Public Sphere: Speaking Out on War, Peace, and American Power*. Austin: University of Texas Press.

———. 2004b. "From Indigenismo to Zapatismo: Theory and Practice in Mexican Anthropology." *Human Organization* 63, no. 2: 142–150.

Goodall, Jane.1971. *In the Shadow of Man*. Boston: Houghton Mifflin.

Goode, Judith. 1981. Teaching Urban Anthropology within a Problem-Solving Framework. *Urban Anthropology* 10, no. 4: 319–330.

Gough, Kathleen. 1968. "Anthropology and Imperialism." *Monthly Review* 19, no. 11: 12–27.

Graeber, David. 2011. *Debt: The Frist 5,000 Years*. Brooklyn, NY: Melville House.

Gramsci, Antonio. 1971. *Selections from the Prison Notebooks*. Ed. and trans. Quinton Hoare and Geoffrey Nowell Smith. New York: International.

Greenwood, Davydd J., and Morten Levin. 2006. *Introduction to Action Research: Social Research for Social Change*. 2nd ed. Thousand Oaks, CA: Sage.

Gwaltney, John. 1980. *Drylongso: A Self-Portrait of Black America*. New York: Random House.

Habermas, Jürgen. 1991. *The Structural Transformation of the Public Sphere: An Inquiry into a Category of Bourgeois Society*. Cambridge, MA: The MIT Press.

Hale, Charles R. 2007. "In Praise of 'Reckless Minds': Making a Case for Activist Anthropology." In *Anthropology Put to Work*, ed. Les W. Field and Richard G. Fox. Oxford: Berg.

Hall, Edward T. 1966. *The Hidden Dimension*. Garden City, NY: Doubleday.

Hampshire, Kate R., Elaine Hills, and Nazalie Iqbal. 2005. "Power Relations in Participatory Research and Community Development: a Case Study from Northern England." *Human Organization* 64, no. 4: 340–349.

Hanks, Michele M. 2004. *The Women's Anthropological Society, 1885–1899: Contesting and Defining Women's Professionalism in U.S. Anthropology*. Mount Holyoke College Department of Anthropology.

Harries-Jones, Peter. 1985. "From Cultural Translator to Advocate: Changing Circles of Interpretation." In *Advocacy and Anthropology: First Encounters*, ed. Robert Paine. St John's Newfoundland: Institute of Social and Economic Research, Memorial University of Newfoundland.

Harris, Marvin. 1977. *Cannibals and Kings: The Origins of Cultures*. New York: Random House.

Harrison, Faye V. 1991. "Anthropology as an Agent of Transformation: Introductory Comments and Queries." In *Decolonizing Anthropology: Moving Further Toward an Anthropology for Liberation*, ed. Faye V. Harrison. Washington, DC: American Anthropological Association.

Harvey, David. 2011. "The Future of the Commons." *Radical History Review* 109: 101–107.

Hedges, Chris. 2009. *Empire of Illusion: The End of Literacy and the Triumph of Spectacle*. New York: Nation Books.

Hegeman, Susan. 1999. *Patterns for America: Modernism and the Concept of Culture*. Princeton, NJ: Princeton University Press.

Henry, Jules. 1963. *Culture Against Man*. New York: Random House.

Huizer, Gerrit, and Bruce Mannheim, eds. 1979. *The Politics of Anthropology: From Colonialism and Sexism Toward a View from Below*. Boston: Walter de Gruyter.

Hurston, Zora Neale. 1935. *Mules and Men*. Philadelphia: J.B. Lippincott.

Hyland, Stanley E., and Linda A. Bennett. 2005. "Community Building in the Twenty-First Century." In *Community Building in the Twenty-First Century*, ed. Stanley E. Hyland. School of American Research Advanced Seminar series. Santa Fe, NM: School of American Research.

Hymes, Dell, ed. 1969. *Reinventing Anthropology*. New York: Random House.

Isbell, Billie Jean. 2013. "Lessons from Vicos." In *Toward Engaged Anthropology*, ed. Sam Beck and Carl A. Maida. New York: Berghahn Books.

Israel, Barbara A., Amy J. Schulz, Edith A. Parker, and Adam B. Becker. 1998. "Review of Community-Based Research: Assessing Partnership Approaches to Improve Public Health." *Annual Review of Public Health* 19: 173–202.

Jablonski, Nina G. 2006. *Skin: A Natural History*. Berkeley: University of California Press.

Jorgensen, Joseph, and Eric R. Wolf. 1970. "A Special Supplement: Anthropology on the Warpath in Thailand." *The New York Review of Books* 15, no. 9: 26–35.

Judt, Tony. 2010. "Edge People." *The New York Review of Books* 57, no. 5: 11.

Keil, Charles. 1966. *Urban Blues.* Chicago: University of Chicago Press.

Klein, Naomi. 2008. *The Shock Doctrine: The Rise of Disaster Capitalism.* New York: Picador.

Kleinman, Arthur, Veena Das, and Margaret Lock, eds. 1997. *Social Suffering.* Berkeley: University of California Press.

Kloppenberg, James T. 1994. "Democracy and Disenchantment: From Weber and Dewey to Habermas and Rorty." In *Modernist Impulses in the Human Sciences, 1870–1930,* ed. Dorothy Ross. Baltimore: Johns Hopkins University Press.

Konner, Melvin. 1982. *The Tangled Wing: The Biological Constraints on the Human Spirit.* New York: Holt, Rinehart and Winston.

Kuhn, Thomas S. 1962. *The Structure of Scientific Revolutions.* Chicago: University of Chicago Press.

Lamphere, Louise. 2004. "The Convergence of Applied, Practicing, and Public Anthropology in the 21st Century." *Human Organization* 63, no. 4: 431–443.

———. 2009. "David Maybury-Lewis and Cultural Survival: Providing a Model for Public Anthropology, Advocacy, and Collaboration." *Anthropological Quarterly* 82, no. 4: 1049–1054.

Lamphere, Louise, Helena Rangoné, and Patricia Zavella. 1997. "Introduction." In *Situated Lives: Gender and Culture in Everyday Life,* ed. Louise Lamphere, Helena Rangoné, and Patricia Zavella. New York: Routledge.

Lee, Dorothy. 1959. *Freedom and Culture.* Englewood Cliffs, NJ: Prentice-Hall.

Lévi-Strauss, Claude. 1955. *Tristes Tropiques.* Paris: Librairie Plon. [1973. *Tristes Tropiques.* Trans. John and Doreen Weightman. London: Jonathan Cape.]

Lewin, Kurt. 1935. "The Conflict between Aristotelian and Galileian Modes of Thought in Contemporary Psychology." In *A Dynamic Theory of Personality.* New York: McGraw-Hill.

———. 1951. "Frontiers in Group Dynamics." In *Field Theory in Social Science: Selected Theoretical Papers,* ed. Dorwin Cartwright. New York: Harper and Row.

Lewis, Oscar. 1961. *The Children of Sanchez.* New York: Random House.

Lomax, Alan. 1993. *The Land Where the Blues Began.* New York: Pantheon.

Low, Setha, and Sally Engle Merry. 2010. "Engaged Anthropology: Diversity and Dilemmas." *Current Anthropology* 51, supplement 2: S203–S226.

Maida, Carl A. 2008. *Pathways Through Crisis: Urban Risk and Public Culture.* Lanham, MD: AltaMira Press.

Manganaro, Marc. 2002. *Culture, 1922: The Emergence of a Concept.* Princeton, NJ: Princeton University Press.

Marchand, Trevor H.J. 2008. "Muscles, Morals and Mind: Craft Apprenticeship and the Formation of the Person." *British Journal of Educational Studies* 56, no. 3: 245–271.

Marcus, George. 2008. "Collaborative Options and Pedagogical Experiment in Anthropological, Research on Experts and Policy Processes." *Anthropology in Action* 15, no. 2: 47–57.

Marcus, George, and Michael Fisher. 1986. *Anthropology as Cultural Critique.* Chicago: University of Chicago Press.

Maskovsky, Jeff, and Ida Susser. 2009. *Rethinking America: The Imperial Homeland in the 21st Century.* Boulder: Paradigm.

McKenna, Brian. 2009. "When Anthropology Disparages Journalism It Shortchanges Citizens, Damages Profession." *Society for Applied Anthropology Newsletter* 20, no. 1: 24–28.

———. 2010. "Exposing Environmental Health Deception as a Governmental Whistleblower: Turning Critical Ethnography into Public Pedagogy." *Policy Futures in Education* 8, no. 1: 22–36.

———. 2013. "Paulo Freire's Blunt Challenge to Anthropology: Create a *Pedagogy of the Oppressed* for Your Times." *Critique of Anthropology* 33, no. 4: 447–475.

Melton, James Van Horn. 2001. *The Rise of the Public in Enlightenment Europe.* Cambridge: Cambridge University Press.

Meltzoff, Andrew N., Patricia K. Kuhl, Javier Movellan, and Terrence J. Sejnowsky. 2009. "Foundations for a New Science of Learning." *Science* 325 (17 July): 284–288.

Menand, Louis. 2010. *The Marketplace of Ideas: Reform and Resistance in the American University.* New York: Norton.

Mills, C. Wright. 1956. *The Power Elite.* New York: Oxford University Press.

Minkler, Meredith, and Nina Wallerstein. 2011. *Community-Based Participatory Research for Health: From Process to Outcomes.* San Francisco: Jossey-Bass.

Mintz, Sidney W. 1985. *Sweetness and Power: The Place of Sugar in Modern History.* New York: Viking.

Montagu, Ashley. 1951. *Statement on Race.* New York: Oxford University Press.

Mullings, Leith. 2013. "Communication, Engagement and Outreach." *Anthropology News* 54, no. 9/10: 3.

Nader, Laura. 1969. "Up the Anthropologist: Perspectives Gained from Studying Up." In *Reinventing Anthropology,* ed. Dell Hymes. New York: Random House.

———. 1996. "Coercive Harmony: The Political Economy of Legal Models." *Kroeber Anthropology Society Papers* 80: 1–13.

Nonini, Donald M. 2007. "Introduction: The Global Idea of 'the Commons.'" In *The Global Idea of 'the Commons,'* ed. Donald M. Nonini. New York: Berghahn Books.

Ong, Aihwa. 2010. "In Conversation with Professor Aihwa Ong." Interview by Vineeta Sinha. *Kroeber Anthropological Society* 100, no. 1: 95–103. http://kas.berkeley.edu/documents/ Issue_99-100/8-InConversation.pdf.

Peck, Jamie, Nik Theodore, and Neil Brenner. 2012. "Neoliberalism Resurgent? Market Rule after the Great Recession." *South Atlantic Quarterly* 111, no. 2: 265–288.

Peterson, Mark Allen. 2010. "Journalism as Trope." *Anthropology News* 51, no. 4: 8–9.

Posner, Richard A. 2001. *Public Intellectuals: A Study of Decline.* Cambridge, MA: Harvard University Press.

Pottier, Johan. 1997. "Towards an Ethnography of Participatory Appraisal and Research." In *Discourses of Development: Anthropological Perspectives,* ed. Ralph D. Grillo and R. L. Stirrat. Oxford: Berg.

Price, David H. 1998. "Cold War Anthropology: Collaborators and Victims of the National Security State." *Identities: Global Studies in Culture and Power.*4, no. 3/4: 389–430.

———. 2002a. "Lessons from Second World War Anthropology." *Anthropology Today* 18, no. 3: 14–20.

———. 2002b. "Past Wars, Future Dangers, Future Anthropologies." *Anthropology Today* 18, no. 1: 3–5.

———. 2004. *Threatening Anthropology: McCarthyism and the FBI's Surveillance of Activist Anthropologists.* Durham, NC: Duke University Press.

———. 2008. *Anthropological Intelligence: The Deployment and Neglect of American Anthropology in the Second World War.* Durham, NC: Duke University Press.

Rabinow, Paul. 2011. *The Accompaniment: Assembling the Contemporary.* Chicago: University of Chicago Press.

Rohde, Joy. 2013. *Armed with Expertise: The Militarization of American Social Science Research During the Cold War.* Ithaca, NY: Cornell University Press.

Roseberry, William. 1989. *Anthropologies and Histories: Essays in Culture, History, and Political Economy.* New Brunswick, NJ: Rutgers University Press.

Ross, Eric B. 2010. "Reflections on Vicos: Anthropology, the Cold War, and the Idea of Peasant Conservatism." In *Vicos Then and Now: A Half Century of Applying Anthropology in Peru*, ed. Ralph Bolton, Tom Greaves, and Florencia Zapata. Lanham, MD: AltaMira.

Roy, Arundhati. 2004. *Public Power in the Age of Empire*. New York: Seven Stories Press.

Rylko-Bauer, Barbara, and Merrill Singer. 2011. "Political Violence, War and Medical Anthropology." In *A Companion to Medical Anthropology*, ed. Merrill Singer and Pam Erickson. San Francisco: Wiley.

Rylko-Bauer, Barbara, Merrill Singer, and John van Willigen. 2006. "Reclaiming Applied Anthropology: Its Past, Present, and Future." *American Anthropologist* 108, no. 1: 178–190.

Sahlins, Marshall. 1974. *Stone Age Economics*. Chicago: Aldine.

Said, Edward. 1978. *Orientalism*. New York: Random House.

Sanday, Peggy Reeves. 1976. *Anthropology and the Public Interest: Fieldwork and Theory*. New York: Academic Press.

———. 1998. "Opening Statement: Defining Public Interest Anthropology." 97th Annual Meeting American Anthropological Association, Philadelphia, PA. http://www.sas.upenn.edu/~psanday/pia.99.html.

———. 2004. "Public Interest Anthropology: A Model for Engaged Research." http://www.sas.upenn.edu/~psanday/PIE.05.htm.

Sansom, Basil. 1985. "Canons of Anthropology?" In *Advocacy and Anthropology: First Encounters*, ed. Robert Paine. St John's Newfoundland: Institute of Social and Economic Research, Memorial University of Newfoundland.

Schensul, Jean J. 2005. "Strengthening Communities through Research Partnerships for Social Change: Perspectives from the Institute for Community Research." In *Community Building in the Twenty-First Century*, ed. Stanley E. Hyland. School of American Research Advanced Seminar series. Santa Fe, NM: School of American Research.

Schensul, Steven L. 1985. "Science, Theory, and Application in Anthropology." *American Behavioral Scientist* 29, no. 2: 164–185.

Schensul, Steven L., and Maria Borrero. 1982. "Introduction: The Hispanic Health Council." *Urban Anthropology* 11, no. 1: 1–8.

Schensul, Steven L., and Jean Schensul. 1978. "Advocacy and Applied Anthropology." In *Social Scientists as Advocates*, ed. George H. Weber and G.J. McCall. Thousand Oaks, CA: Sage.

Schensul, Stephen L., Jean J. Schensul, Merrill Singer, Margaret Weeks, and Marie Brault. (in press). "Conceptual and Methodological Approaches to the Role of Anthropology in Community and Societal Change." In *Handbook of Methods in Cultural Anthropology*, ed. Lance Gravlee and Russell Bernard. Lanham, MD: Rowman and Littlefield.

Scheper-Hughes, Nancy. 1992. *Death Without Weeping: The Violence of Everyday Life in Brazil*. Berkeley: University of California Press.

———. 1995. "The Primacy of the Ethical: Propositions for a Militant Anthropology." *Current Anthropology* 36, no. 3: 409–440.

Schon, Donald A. 1984. *The Reflective Practitioner: How Professionals Think In Action*. New York: Basic Books.

Scott, James C., and Benedict J. Kerkvliet. 1977. "How Traditional Rural Patrons Lose Legitimacy: A Theory with Special Reference to Southeast Asia." In *Friends, Followers, and Factions: A Reader in Political Clientism*, ed. Steffen W. Schmidt, James C. Scott, Carl Landé, and Luara Guasti. Berkeley: University of California Press.

Shore, Chris, and Susan Wright. 1997. *Anthropology of Policy: Perspectives on Governance and Power*. London: Routledge.

Shostak, Marjorie. 1981. *Nisa: The Life and Words of a !Kung Woman*. Cambridge, MA: Harvard University Press.

Sillitoe, Paul. 2002. "Participant Observation to Participatory Development: Making Anthropology Work." In *Participating in Development: Approaches to Indigenous Knowledge,* ed. Paul Sillitoe, Alan Bicker, and Johan Pottier. ASA Monographs 39. London: Routledge.

Singer, Merrill. 2000. "Why I am Not a Public Anthropologist." *Anthropology Newsletter* 41, no. 6: 6–7.

———. 2003. "The Hispanic Health Council: An Experiment in Applied Anthropology." *Practicing Anthropology* 25, no. 3: 2–7.

———. 2008. "Applied Anthropology." In *A New History of Anthropology,* ed. Henrika Kulick. Malden, MA: Blackwell.

Singer, Merrill, Freddie Valentín, Hans Baer, and Zhongke Jia. 1992. "Why Does Juan García Have a Drinking Problem? The Perspective of Critical Medical Anthropology." *Medical Anthropology* 14, no. 1: 77–108.

Small, Meredith F. 1998. *Our Babies, Ourselves: How Biology and Culture Shape the Way We Parent.* New York: Anchor Press/Doubleday.

Smith, Linda Tuhiwai. 1999. *Decolonizing Methodologies: Research and Indigenous Peoples.* London: Zed Books.

Sterne, Jonathan. 2005. "C. Wright Mills, the Bureau for Applied Social Research, and the Meaning of Critical Scholarship." *Cultural Studies <=> Critical Methodologies* 5, no. 1: 65–94.

Strathern, Marilyn. 2001. "Blowing Hot and Cold." *Anthropology Today* 17, no. 1: 1–2.

Tax, Sol. 1988. "Pride and Puzzlement: Retro-introspective Record of 60 Years of Anthropology." *Annual Review of Anthropology* 17: 1–21.

Thompson, E.P. 1963. *The Making of the English Working Class.* New York: Random House.

———. 1971. "The Moral Economy of the English Crowd in the Eighteenth Century." *Past and Present* 50: 76–136.

Turnbull, Colin M. 1961. *The Forest People.* New York: Simon and Schuster.

Turner, Victor W. 1986. "Dewey, Dilthey, and Drama: An Essay in the Anthropology of Experience." In *The Anthropology of Experience,* ed. Victor W. Turner and Edward M. Bruner. Urbana: University of Illinois Press.

Vermeulen, Hans F. 2008. "Anthropology in the Netherlands: Past, Present, and Future." In *Other People's Anthropologies: Ethnographic Practice on the Margins,* ed. Aleksandar Bošković. New York: Berghahn Books.

Vesperi, Maria. 2010. "Attend to the Differences First: Conflict and Collaboration in Anthropology and Journalism." *Anthropology News* 51, no. 4: 7–9.

Wakin, Erik. 1992. *Anthropology Goes to War: Professional Ethics and Counterinsurgency in Thailand.* Madison: University of Wisconsin, Center for Southeast Asian Studies.

Wali, Alaka, ed. 2006. *Collaborative Research: A Practical Introduction to Participatory Action Research (PAR) for Communities and Scholars.* Chicago: The Field Museum Center for Cultural Understanding and Change.

———. 2012. "The Arc of Justice: Indigenous Activism and Anthropological Intersections." *Tipití: Journal of the Society for the Anthropology of Lowland South America* 9, no. 2. Article 2. http://digitalcommons.trinity.edu/tipiti/vol9/iss2/2.

Wali, Alaka, Gillian Darlow, Carol Fialkowski, Madeleine Tudor, Hilary del Campo, and Douglas Stolz. 2003. "Methodologies for Interdisciplinary Research and Action in an Urban Ecosystem in Chicago." *Conservation Ecology* 7, no. 3: 2. http://www.consecol.org/vol7/iss3/art2/.

Wallerstein, Immanuel M. 1976. *The Modern World System: Capitalist Agriculture and the Origins of the European World-Economy in the Sixteenth Century.* New York: Academic Press.

Wasson, Christina, Mary Odell Butler, and Jacqueline Copeland-Carson, eds. 2012. *Applying Anthropology in the Global Village.* Walnut Creek, CA: Left Coast Press.

Wax, Dustin M., ed. 2008. *Anthropology at the Dawn of the Cold War: The Influence of Foundations, McCarthyism, and the CIA.* London: Pluto Press.

Wedel, Janine R., Chris Shore, Gregory Feldman, and Stacy Lathrop. 2005. "Toward an Anthropology of Public Policy." *Annals of the American Academy of Political and Social Science* 600: 30–51.

Westra, Richard. 2006. "Sociomaterial Communication, Community and Ecosustainability in the Global Era." In *Sustainability and Communities of Place*, ed. Carl A. Maida. New York: Berghahn Books.

Wolf, Eric R. 1969. *Peasant Wars of the Twentieth Century.* New York: Harper and Row.

———. 1974. "Foreword." In Stanley Diamond, *In Search of the Primitive.* New Brunswick, NJ: Transaction.

———. 1982. *Europe and the People Without History.* Berkeley: University of California Press.

Woloch, Isser, and Gregory S. Brown. 2012. "Living the Enlightenment: The Public Sphere." In *Eighteenth-Century Europe: Tradition and Progress, 1715–1789*, ed. Isser Woloch and Gregory S. Brown. New York: Norton.

Worsley, Peter. 1984. *The Three Worlds: Culture and World Development.* Chicago: University of Chicago Press.

Chapter 1

COMMUNITY-BASED RESEARCH ORGANIZATIONS
Co-constructing Public Knowledge and Bridging Knowledge/Action Communities Through Participatory Action Research

———— ⬡⬡⬡ ————

Jean J. Schensul

Most of the scientific knowledge incorporated into public dialogues is generated in academic settings and delivered to public audiences by scientists. In this chapter I argue that affected communities should play a central role in constructing local knowledge and using it to address complex local and global social issues by engaging multiple publics in finding solutions. Having always loved inquiry and despised social, economic, and racialized inequities, I chose this approach because it allows me, and others, to fuse these passions into socially responsible methodologically rigorous participatory research to further social justice in this world.

Terms used to describe this approach include action research (AR), action science (AS), participatory action research (PAR), and community-based participatory research (CBPR) (S. Schensul et al. 2014). I prefer PAR because it has a long history of implementation and use in anthropology, sociology, and psychology, and because it emphasizes the social and structural factors contributing to disparities and injustices. "Affected communities" refers to communities of identity (Israel et al. 2005; Minkler and Wallerstein 2010) or construction that are affected by inequitable social, economic, and health structures and policies, and wish to remedy these injustices by bringing about significant change. Because they constitute a focus, a place, and a set of collaborators, these communities are the first "publics" for participatory action research. In this chapter, "co-

construction" refers to the processes by which politically oriented activist researchers and politically motivated community actors who are members of affected communities, create new knowledge and reinforce individual and group agency (J. Schensul 1998; 2005; 2009; 2010; J. Schensul et al. 2004; 2008; S. Schensul and J. Schensul 1978).

Despite growing emphasis on community engagement in university settings, mainstream science continues to cling to the right to produce and reproduce knowledge without obligation to share it with the people from who it is collected. Likewise, anticipation of effects on populations and communities (rather than individuals) is neither expected nor required. PAR responds to these deficits with a transformative approach to community development in which researchers and community actors, activists, and residents co-construct knowledge through transparent, readily accessible research methods and find ways of using it together for community change. But despite PAR's increasing popularity, as reflected in a growing literature, mainstream science and social science disciplines still see this approach as a dramatic shift in the way knowledge is produced, shared, and used. The PAR paradigm involves joint decisions about research design, methodology (including methods for forging equitable, action-oriented research partnerships), data analysis procedures, results interpretation and representation, obligations to act, and strategies for action. Below I review several different approaches to PAR as a means by which affected publics produce credible knowledge for public use. These include comprehensive community development and critical pedagogy, both of which are usually enacted from a university or other educational institution. I then discuss the community-based research organization (CBRO) as a unique form of social "intermediary" that facilitates co-construction of new knowledge and community control over knowledge and its uses over time in a way that promises sustainability of both process and outcome. I illustrate this concept with the example of a CBRO that I founded in Hartford, Connecticut, with the help of many others, the Institute for Community Research, which today boasts a thirty year history of collaborative participatory community-based research and knowledge development and application.

Historical Context of Knowledge Co-construction for Social Change

Over the past seven decades, researchers, research administrators, and communities have evolved many different ways of addressing the pressing ethical and practical need for a politically motivated, action-oriented approach to conducting research. In the 1930s and 1940s, social science–driven action research efforts were shaped by the work of Kurt Lewin, a radical psychologist of German Jewish origin whose work often is overlooked by anthropologists applying action research principles. Though Lewin is often cited as the founder of action research as a form of social engineering, his motivations, rooted in his belief in social justice, have been largely ignored. Lewin believed in participating in attempts to improve relations between groups with unequal power (i.e., middle- and upper-middle-class white organizations and low-income, recent African American migrants to the northeastern United States) and studying the results. Questioning the sustainability of "conversations" and joint plans, in a radical departure at the time he advocated—prioritizing stronger intragroup identity and self-esteem through the struggle for recognition of group rights. This, he argued, was both the primary way "minority" groups could claim an equal place at the decision-making table and a process that should be reinforced through study. Lewin's work as an interdisciplinary social scientist was visionary in many ways: it linked research with activism; connected Western colonial policies to inequitable policies and practices within the United States that were rooted in racial discrimination; and recognized that the self-esteem, power, and influence of marginalized and indigenous groups lay in reclaiming their histories and identities through struggle (Lewin 1946: 46).

Anthropology is a discipline that values and depends upon diversity and difference. The "work" of anthropology is to uncover and understand differences and commonalities among peoples and communities, account for those differences, and explain them to the scientific public. Typically the researcher has dominated or controlled the lens through which cultural patterns and differences have been described, defined, and explained. In anthropology, those carrying out the research and those participating in it have always worked in close proximity, and active collaboration between key informants and local experts and researchers is not uncommon. Reasons both ethical and social lie behind the emergence of various means for reducing class, national, ethnic-racialized, and other social distances between researchers and local communities and ensuring local voice is heard. These include valuing the "emic" perspective (ensuring that language-based perspectives and interpretations of the researched are taken into consideration in analysis and representation), member checking (asking respondents to verify that researcher models are correct), and collaborative writing (polyvocality) or collaborative production of audiovisual materials. These forms, ranging from generation of empirical knowledge to co-construction of partial knowledge, address one question relevant to the accumulation and dissemination of anthropological knowledge:

whether the research results are socially valid and meaningful to colonized or marginalized voices and represent them fairly and appropriately.

Van Willigen has noted that "the history of anthropology, both basic and applied, is the history of the power relationships between anthropologists and the people studied" (van Willigen 2002: 43). In the study of "anthropologically valued difference," both class and the privileging of science-based knowledge challenge the ability of studied communities to influence broader perspectives without the social scientist's "permission," endorsement, or leadership. Many other questions thus focus on the multiple dimensions of the power differential between those who are formally educated to acquire social science knowledge in the Western social sciences tradition, and those who acquire experiential knowledge through narratives, lived experience, tradition and ritual, observation, and social learning. These questions, which I have tried to address in my work, have to do with how knowledge is defined and who "owns" it; what priorities govern the organizations through which researchers work; how the research needs and interests of "affected" communities emerge and intersect with researchers' interests and needs; whether those needs and interests are being addressed; what methodologies are used to address them and whether the methods, theories, frameworks, and interpretations align with and engage the community's perspectives and cultural knowledge base; how the research results are shared and used, both within the local community and/or affected group and with other audiences; and finally, how communities can use and invent research theory and methodology to create their own knowledge. Answering these questions begins to address in a more profound way the relationship between knowledge construction, the active decolonization of anthropological knowledge, and its public uses.

Many other approaches to co-construction and public representation of local or indigenous knowledge have emerged since Lewin's time. They attempt to forge relationships that reflect upon, address, and work to minimize power differentials with the goal of reducing inequities and improving social welfare. They also aim to maximize community voice and activism through the "democratization of science" (J. Schensul 2002). Together, these objectives constitute the central components of PAR, which can be summarized under the rubrics of *community development* and *critical pedagogical* approaches.

Community development approaches focus on integrating research with holistic or systemic efforts to transform local communities through programs, service delivery, economic development, and policy transformation. Early community development approaches integrated research with action in multiple ways. Through research, for example, Tax's students discovered that it was lack of economic development, and not discriminatory interethnic relationships that resulted in the situation faced by the Mesquakie and turned to generating funds to support small-scale industry and a cultural center. Under the leadership of Stephen Schensul, research was integrated with community development in the Mexican American community in such a way that community leaders and activists worked alongside academically based researchers and students to conduct community-based research that supported the development of many institutions and organizations that reflected the needs, responded to the demands and staked out the presence of an emergent Mexican American community in a changing civil rights environment (S. Schensul 1980). As a partnership between academic researchers and various sectors of an underrepresented, marginalized community, over time this model created a seamless interface between research, training, community development, and civil rights advocacy that continues to this day.

Among the notable achievements of this ten-year development program were two significant instances in the history of community-produced knowledge for action: a "commando raid" by educational activists and researchers collaborating to document inadequate pedagogy in ESL classrooms and advocate for bilingual education (S. Schensul 1978), and a National Institute of Mental Health grant to a community-based organization to conduct research on the "*cuarentena*," a culturally specific practice of protecting women during the first month of pregnancy. The organization thus had full management and control of all aspects of the research. A team, consisting of an anthropologist (S. Schensul), a community-based psychiatrist, and several community leaders who were trained as community researchers (Gaviria et al. 1982) together defined the study, gathered data, analyzed the data, and used the results at first to build a program to revive the *cuarentena* as a cultural practice, and later, a women's health advocacy center, Mujeres Latinas en Accion. Early on the model demonstrated the benefits of community-driven, locally generated knowledge and community mobilization through a combination of lived experience and flexible social science methodology.

Cornell University has been another influential base for community-engaged research in community and institutional settings. Whereas the terms action anthropology and action research originated in community development work in Chicago, Cornell contributed the notion of participatory action research. The Cornell version of PAR, rooted in Vicos (Dobyns et al. 1971: 8; Greaves et al. 2010) and Mondragon (Whyte 1991), used vertical alliances and in the case of Vicos, "devolution" of power and ownership to the workers to engage communities and industries in all aspects of research. It crystallized the notion of full participation of non-academically trained partners in an alliance to conduct all aspects of research for community use.

The University of Memphis has mounted a similar program over the past three decades, moving toward a PAR model that draws on a long history of civil rights activism to address historical inequities facing the African American community in Memphis. Guided by scholar-activist faculty, students in the anthropology and urban affairs/public policy programs engage with facets of community development ranging from education and cultural identity to food justice and food systems. They learn the principles of PAR and attempt to operationalize them with faculty guidance, and to interrogate issues of power and power imbalances wherever they can. The University of Memphis has the added advantage of attracting young local leaders and activists into their program, thereby enabling them to use ethnographic research methods and anthropological theory in generating local knowledge in their own communities. These examples of the potential contributions enabled by university departments, administrations, and programs dedicated to engaged scholarship for comprehensive community development through participatory knowledge development and strategic actions are among many summarized in comprehensive analyses and edited volumes (see Bennett and Whiteford 2014; Ervin et al. 2005; Hyland 2005; Kadia and van Willigen 2005; Park et al. 1993; Rylko-Bauer et al. 2006; J. Schensul and LeCompte 2012; van Willigen 2002).

Critical pedagogical experiments in PAR and community development rely on faculty engagement in a form of activist-oriented critical pedagogy focused on transforming post-secondary students by involving them in co-construction of knowledge and action for community-wide change. Some anthropologists and educators use critical pedagogy to engage students (who may themselves be teachers) in reflexive analysis of their own situation and lived experience, as the basis for transformative action (Greenman and Dieckmann 2004; Phillips et al. 2010). Such analysis begets critical consciousness or understanding of social, political, economic, and other contributing factors to oppressive structures (Berg and J. Schensul 2004; Cammarota 2008; Freire 1970; 1981). Diverse methodologies exist to evolve critical consciousness through inward reflection, group discussion, and the framing of questions that students answer through research in their own communities or through "studying up," for example by analyzing the structures and policies that characterize institutions with power over their lives (Gusterson 1997). Many forms of PAR address the formation of critical consciousness, intention to act, and action. Some emphasize reflection/engagement and co-construction of new knowledge based on lived experience (Fine and Torre 2006; Maguire 2006); others are based on externally oriented activities involving reflection, as well as data collection, analysis, and the transformation of research results into interactive dissemination practices. The Latin American framing of PAR, based on the work of Paulo Freire, aims to evolve critical consciousness via dialectical exploration of contradictions between lived experience and structural realities. Though Freire was unable to continue his work in Brazil, it has influenced several generations of critical educators, public health research activists, and anthropologists. Among them is Fals Borda, whose approach integrates research and active engagement to mobilize and transform structures and processes, and promote resistance movements (Fals Borda and Rahman 1991). Our own research at the Institute for Community Research has also been heavily influenced by critical pedagogical theory and the work of Paulo Freire.

Most forms of youth-oriented PAR develop individual and collective agency by concentrating on co-construction of cognitive models for action (Aguilera 2009; Cammarota 2008) rather than the co-construction of local knowledge (culture) as the basis for action. In my own history of PAR with youth and adults, I have found that agency develops via the interaction between *belief* in the capacity to act (self- and group efficacy), *collective action*, and cultivation and use of *participatory research-based inquiry skills*. The addition of inquiry skills (research) enables learners and teachers to engage with multiple publics; communicate effectively; learn the skills of questioning, documenting, and analysis; and deal with contradictions and differences in beliefs and practices. This approach to PAR reinforces the importance of taking responsibility for *knowing*, as well as for knowledge (Berg et al. 2009).

Another element in a critical or decolonizing pedagogy is the constitution of indigenous knowledge as the basis for reframing educational and development structures (Akenya 2012; Barnhardt 2005). The importance of indigenous knowledge comes to the fore when local educational or environmental institutions are constructed to maintain colonizing structures and self-depreciating mentalities and thereby deny the legitimacy of indigenous or local knowledge and ways of knowing. Only under considerable pressure do such institutions respond to the needs and interests of indigenous populations. As Akenya notes, "The ideas and principles of indigenous-knowledge discursive frameworks are rooted and actionable in local and grassroots political organizing and a form of intellectual activism" (2012: 8)

Responses to repressive institutional regimes require new approaches based on indigenous cultural principles, pedagogy, and learning and working processes. These approaches fall along a continuum: learning *from* local peoples to create externally generated models and materials; learning *with* local people to create more effective, mutually generated models and materials; and learning *through* local people by equipping them with the supplemental skills and methods they need, along with their own intellectual and experiential capital, to create their own learning and knowledge development institutions. Critical educators and educational anthropologists have been at the forefront in creating new research methodologies, indigenous research agendas, and partnerships for exploring the evolution of these new ways of knowing (Brodkey 1987; Cintron-Moscoso 2009; Erickson 1987; Greenman and Dieckmann 2004; Kwon 2008; London and Chabran 2004; Mehan 2008).

Despite these examples of engaged scholarship in diverse institutional settings, university and schooling structures increasingly serve the overriding goal of producing knowledge and an employable labor force geared to advancing national or global science, technology, business, industry, and military interests (Dickson 1988; Frickel and Moore 2006; Langley et al. 2008; Rhoads and Torres 2006). Thus much of the dedicated and resoundingly excellent work carried out by educators within university and schooling structures is constrained by local political forces, publication and promotion requirements, privatized funding sources, and conservative trustees' vested interests. For this reason, alternative structures are required to develop new forms of knowledge and mobilize political will to use them more freely for community development and social justice. In these nontraditional institutions—which include, for instance, museums (Wali 2006; Wali et al. 2001), cultural centers, and nontraditional or after-school educational programs—communities can create and act upon local knowledge independently or jointly with community-responsive scientists (specializing mainly in public health) and social scientists unrestricted by the pedagogical constraints of bureaucratic institutions.

One such venue is the community-based research organization. CBROs are often overlooked as sources of new knowledge creation because, at least in the United States and at the time of first writing this chapter, they were not formally organized in an association (e.g., of nonprofits or international NGOs) or movement. And the knowledge they generated does not always reach the national or international scientific community. These organizations are both responsive to the growing recognition that local, tacit, and indigenous knowledges are a source of important social innovation, and able to reach multiple publics via ongoing engagement with affected communities and the Internet as well as scientific institutions. Further, CBROs experience fewer bureaucratic constraints when generating their research agendas, and enacting the results of their research, and are more able to use research to mobilize communities and the larger public for action. Searching resourcefully, one can locate many such organizations in the United States and others organized in PAR or action research networks around the globe (J. Schensul 2010). As of 2012 a new organization came into being under the umbrella of Community-Campus Partnerships for Health, called the Community Network for Research Equity and Impact (CNREI) with a membership of more than 450 organizations. The mission of CNRE is to carry out this charge and to ensure equivalence with their university partners.

Community-Based Research Organizations

My interest in and commitment to CBRO development grew from an observation based on the previously mentioned Chicago experience: without proper infrastructure, embedding research in community organizations is insufficient to guarantee continuing community control of research and its results. When the university research team that had initiated the Chicago research partnerships dispersed, the community lost its research capacity because it had not established other structures to ensure its ability to continue to mount independent socially and scientifically significant research.

Steve Schensul and I moved to Hartford in 1977. At that time, the Hartford-based research and advocacy organization La Casa de Puerto Rico was one of several such organizations nationally that had formed in response to the civil rights movements. La Casa de Puerto Rico's mission was to work through community committees to gather information about the emergent Puerto Rican community and use it to transform education, housing, health, and other infrastructure to improve the quality of life for Puerto Ricans and other Latinos. The vision of Maria Borrero a health worker at the time, and anthropologist Stephen Schensul at the University of Connecticut Health Center, was to create a stable core of community-based academic researchers and trained community researchers who together could gather health information and advocate for structural changes while also contributing to the scientific literature. The primary way of operationalizing this vision was the creation of the Hispanic Health Council (HHC), a second generation Puerto Rican CBRO working on issues of health equity. A critical element in the early growth of (HHC), was the ability of the anthropologists (Steve and I, later joined by Merrill Singer followed by David Himmelgreen, Nancy Romero-Daza, and others) to generate National Institutes of Health (NIH) funding that included indirect costs. The acquisition of funding with substantial indirect costs to cover project administration, allowed HHC to function independently in a colonialized local funding environment where funders did not understand why communities should do research rather than service, and foundation funding was based on obtaining donations for charitable work. This strategy also provided much of the financial infrastructure for the Institute for Community Research (ICR), which I founded in 1987 and directed until 2004, when I stepped aside to take the position of full-time senior scientist and to continue the pursuit of NIH funding; Margaret Weeks, an NIH-funded AIDS researcher, replaced me as executive director.

These experiences at the HHC and ICR, along with years of exploring other such organizations, led me to conceptualize the CBRO as a type of public knowledge-producing entity whose organizational structure offers a new approach to public anthropology. Other scientists have also written about CBROs. In the late 1990s, the Loka Institute built the first U.S.-based network of independent CBROs, the Community Research Network, which was intended to organize and influence science policy (Sclove et al. 1998). Mary Brydon-Miller and colleagues described some CBROs under the rubric of popular culture (Brydon-Miller et al. 2008). However, until the creation of the CNREI, I had not found other such examples, despite increasing anthropological interest in NGO formation and political economy, and considerable interest in NGOs in general, internationally.

CBROs are independent, activist-oriented research organizations that conduct research jointly with under-resourced, marginalized, under-served, underrepresented communities and groups, and then work with them to use the results to bring about change locally, nationally, and internationally. "Knowledge for CBROs is power, and CBROs focus knowledge development on increasing community voice, providing support for participatory democracy and the elimination of environmental, health, educational and cultural injustices and disparities. This strategy links local knowledge with national and international issues" (J. Schensul 2010). As alternative sources of knowledge and knowledge production, CBROs are important nodes in the international network of organizations and centers that constitute third-sector science.

The primary mission of CBROs is to combine the results of multiple, often innovative forms of knowledge generation—achieved through partnerships between CBRO researchers and local residents or community-based organizations—with critical approaches to social transformation. The principal "public" for CBRO research is the local community of affected residents; other publics include the scientific community, the general public, businesses, and policy makers. All are crucial to changing social norms and practices that promote and endorse social justice processes and outcomes. CBROs are bridge organizations whose personnel necessarily include researchers with varying degrees of formal education and research experience and commitment and people from local communities who share the same goals. This crossroads—the intersection of staff, community, and the world of science—is a fertile environment for generating new knowledge and new ways of knowing.

Clearly, some of the functions of the activist-oriented university base and the CBRO overlap, but significant structural differences provide CBROs with opportunities unavailable even to those universities with strong community-engaged research centers and programs. Typically CBROs begin in response to a significant social problem, situation, or event that provokes calls for transformative change: the anti-apartheid movement in South Africa (Brydon-Miller 2008), the health of African American girls in Cincinnati, the death of a child because of inadequate, unresponsive health care delivery (Schensul and Borrero 1982; S. Schensul and J. Schensul 1978). They see research as both a means of learning about these issues' causes and how to address them, and a way of organizing people to work toward those ends.

A social justice mission is central to the definition of a CBRO and key to its public presentation. The Highlander Research and Education Center in Kentucky, for example, states as its mission that it works with "people fighting for justice, equality and sustainability, supporting their efforts to take collective action to shape their own destiny. Through popular education, participatory research, and cultural work, we help create spaces—at Highlander and in local communities—where people gain knowledge, hope and courage, expanding their ideas of what is possible. We develop leadership and help create and support strong, democratic organizations that work for justice, equality and sustainability in their own communities and that join with others to build broad movements for social, economic and restorative environmental change" (Highlander Research and Education Center, 2014). Many well-known PAR researchers such as John Gaventa have trained at the Highlander Center.

The mission of the HHC, mentioned above, is to improve the health and well-being of Latinos and other diverse communities through research, service, and advocacy. The ICR defines its mission as "using the tools of research in collaboration with communities and their allies to promote justice and equity in a diverse world." ICR increases community and CBO capacity to conduct research through research collaborations and participatory action research with children, youth and adults in the United States, India, and China. The Society for Participatory Research in Asia (PRIA), a Delhi-based, Asia-oriented CBRO, dedicated to deepening democracy uses "knowledge is power" as its logo. PRIA's mission is: "To work towards the promotion of policies, institutions and capacities that strengthens the voices against marginalization of communities and increase the participation of the marginalized in society." (Society for Participatory Research in Asia website, 2014). PRIA's connections reach beyond

India, and it is currently working with the University of Victoria, Canada, to offer Internet-based distance-learning courses in PAR and the creation of infrastructure to support civil society.

CBROs try to reflect and be part of the communities where they are located, and for this reason they are heavily staffed by members and representatives of the communities of identity that they serve. Harmony Garden's primary research staff, for example, consisted of women from a local African American housing project who were trained by PAR researcher/directors and conducted activist PAR to improve girls' lives. Most of the personnel at the HHC, including some of its researchers, are from the Hartford area. Highlander personnel come mainly from Kentucky and Tennessee, and are recruited from local communities where the organization works.

CBROs build bonding and bridging structures (J. Schensul 2005). Bonding structures forge strong links within communities of identity to promote specific interests. Bridging structures bind communities of identity to other, disconnected or oppositional community organizations to move toward accomplishing comprehensive public goals. In both cases, CBROs recognize that partnerships are critical for identifying resources, gathering information, developing allies, and organizing to "get things done." Often it takes years to build trust *within* communities of identity struggling with extreme circumstances or high levels of historical discrimination, or groups that are under suspicion for political reasons or lack of residential documentation. Thus CBROs need a "bank" or reservoir of partnerships to call upon for different purposes. Elsewhere we have referred to this process as building "living alliances" (Radda and J. Schensul 2011).

In keeping with social justice principles, CBROs strive to reduce or eliminate both internal and partnership hierarchies of class, racial/ethnic identity, formal education, income, and knowledge orientation. Their structural and financial independence allows them to avoid the typical university hierarchies that structure salary schedules, and to evaluate and promote individuals for multiple types of performance related to complex work goals and settings. Good CBRO administrative principles ensure opportunities for everyone's voice to be heard in organizational and project decision-making (J. Schensul 2010).

CBROs endorse a holistic approach, forging joint research agendas and programs to address policies and practices affecting entire communities as best they can within funding constraints and other resource limitations. The work CBROs undertake generally proceeds within the context of community-wide transformation. Patchwork projects outside of a strategic plan for "holistic" or dynamic system change rarely evolve a future, and CBROs cannot afford to spend time on singular efforts that are not part of a larger movement or strategic plan for development. Good community research, built on local knowledge and holding potential for transformational change, requires methodological sophistication. This calls for innovative community-wide research designs, including randomized controlled trials in community settings, which, contrary to the opinions of many, residents may prefer because the results stand up to traditional scientific scrutiny. Using new and often resident-generated ways of collecting information—including mixed-method research that takes advantage of narrative, photography, cultural or ethno-epidemiology, and other culturally embedded approaches—promotes a systemic vision and transformational process.

To facilitate research programs, CBROs like the ICR prefer to form their own institutional review boards (IRBs), ethical review committees that are composed of people who understand community and research personnel as well as individual-level research risks. IRB members can train community researchers in research ethics and vice versa in the flexible CBRO environment and can also participate in university IRB deliberations to provide sound advice to researchers attempting community-based research partnership projects, which are still new to university-based research practice. The typical CBRO's less bureaucratic structure facilitates rapid decision-making, contractual agreements, and creative transfers of funds, all of which makes work in partnership with community organizations more efficient while at the same time enhancing trust.

The first audience or "public" for CBRO research results is the local community, where the issues are located and the CBROs and community researchers do their research. Disseminating research results is thus an ethical as well as a practical consideration. CBROs may disseminate research results through reports, press releases, and performance ethnography (i.e., theatrical performances, speech, videos, music, and other audiovisual media, usually with community participation and directorship). CBRO dissemination differs from sharing data through publications, because its purpose is to inspire viewers to inquire, critique, and mobilize to effect changes in policies, service delivery, or the environment. Thus it is dialogic, politically motivated and intended to be transformational. At the same time reaching the world of science and science policy is critical to the CBRO enterprise because it reinforces legitimacy with scientists, the media, and evidence-based policy makers. This requires other efforts, including publication in peer-reviewed journals and presence at conferences and other scholarly or policy-related events where research methodology and topical discussions on the subject matter of the research take place.

Finally, CBRO-based researchers join forces with others to promote and advocate for new methodologies and new approaches to science. Community-based participatory research in health is a good example (Israel et al. 2005; Minkler and Wallerstein 2010). The existing, substantial advocacy infrastructure for CBPR consists of university faculty conducting CBPR, advocacy organizations, community research networks, community partners, and broker membership agencies like Community-Campus Partnerships for Health (CCPH) that include community agencies and schools of public health and medicine. CCPH and many others have advocated for increased CBPR funding through the National Institutes of Health, as is clearly reflected in recent NIH social and behavioral science solicitations. Other research advocates working in CBROs have promoted research on important technological advances, such as the female condom (Weeks et al. 2010), or focused on expanding research methodologies for the conduct of community-based participatory interventions or systems science (Hovmand, 2014; J. Schensul and LeCompte, 2012). A critical contribution of CBROs to new forms of knowledge development is their activism to promote standard, highly innovative qualitative and mixed-methods research methods. Interactive mixed-methods research methodologies have blossomed in recent years through communities' receptivity to knowledge development via visual, art-based, and interactive research methods and tools, alongside traditional practices of knowledge transmission through story, narrative, ritual, and enactment.

Not every CBRO shares all of these principles, and their implementation varies considerably from one organization to another. Central to all of them, however, are organizational independence, local embeddedness, a multilevel or holistic approach, and use of innovative participatory research methodology and tools to address social justice issues and reduce inequities in relation to their constituencies.

Now I turn to illustrate these principles with an example—the Institute for Community Research (ICR). ICR was founded in 1987 as a CBRO with a commitment to holistic, community-based collaborative research for social justice. We formed ICR at a time when Fals Borda was beginning his work in Colombia and Nina Wallerstein was starting to write about action research and community-based participatory research for health. Clearly "something was in the air" as these disparate efforts began to appear on the Internet, in conferences, and eventually in the literature. Created as a response to local needs, we also saw ICR as a national/international model for interdisciplinary multisectoral and cross-national community-based participatory research. Founding staff and board understood that the work of the Institute needed to integrate health, community development, education, and cultural conservation/representation and to find methodologies for promoting social justice. With this vision and perspective, ICR sought and found its niche in the political economy of the Hartford area, across the state and beyond.

The Institute for Community Research

The ICR continues to embody the principles outlined above. In 1987, I, as director, along with a small staff and the board of directors envisioned an organization that would conduct participatory and collaborative research to promote social justice in the areas of health, education, and culture across the lifespan. The city of Hartford, Connecticut, influenced by the models of the Hispanic Health Council and La Casa de Puerto Rico, offered a positive environment for community-based research. At the same time, it functioned as a "feudal town" where control over decisions about the city's neighborhoods was largely concentrated at City Hall and in the hands of the large insurance companies, hospitals, and developers that dominated the economic landscape. I have referred to this type of racialized, ethnically segregated city as a form of socially constructed "urban apartheid" (J. Schensul 1997), characterized by sustained and significant economic, health, and other disparities across neighborhoods. In this context the ICR crafted its mission, calling for collaboration in the use of research theories, methods, and results to address structural inequities and their consequences and for efforts to bridge these structural divides. Many small decisions and actions have operationalized this mission daily and over time.

ICR staff has always been a true cross-section of the local community, reflecting its diversity of ethnicity, social race, age, education level, spirituality, language, and culture matching the composition of the larger, increasingly globally representative racial/ethnic and social communities in the area. ICR personnel are a mix of politically motivated researchers; local health educators; and health, education, and cultural activists. They are hired for their commitment to social justice; their experience working in impoverished, marginalized and culturally diverse communities; and their willingness to take a team approach to applying research skills or learning research methods to address the structural inequities confronting residents of Hartford and elsewhere. From the outset, ICR researchers forged relationships with community organizations, community groups, voluntary associations, and service hubs such as libraries and clinics. Our goal in establishing these relationships was twofold: to identify people of like mind, and to discuss possible research projects conducive to collaborative creation of new knowledge-based solutions to social issues that would truly represent Hartford's invisible communities. Our success in competing for NIH and other federal funding for our research program generated substantial amounts of money, which we cost-shared equitably with our partners. The ability to attract "outside money" that other organizations were not able to obtain, and to share it equally across partners meant that we did not have to compete with our local partners for scarce local resources. Instead we could help them and ourselves to grow financially and in other ways, while we accomplished our joint goals. Chief among the complex dynamics that shape the ICR/partner research agenda is its staff capacity. Negotiating PAR projects requires matching researcher skills, interests, and track record including publications in peer-reviewed journals with community need. If communities wish to conduct research on a topic in which ICR staff have no experience, skills, training, publications, or research history, the organization cannot respond immediately (or even at all) to that issue. However, ICR staff may refer community groups to others who do have the skills, build consortia that include researchers at other institutions, or try to reframe the research to meet existing skill sets.

Early on, the ICR evolved several different "lines of collaborative research work" based on its "cornerstone principles" — action research, collaboration, "interventions" (i.e., evaluable action to promote change of any kind in an ongoing social context), and culture. It operationalizes these principles in partnerships with community organizations and services, as well as with residents and voluntary groups, for basic or formative research, intervention studies, participatory action research, and cultural conservation and development. Lines of collaborative work have materialized in long-standing programs of collaborative or alliance-based research and PAR. These lines of work include HIV/AIDS and substance abuse prevention among youth and adults, health and mental health problems among older adults, and adult and youth-led PAR for transformational change addressing many different topics. The ICR Community Gallery shares research results, performance ethnography, and interactive experiences designed to reduce social distance across multiple publics. Figure 1.1 illustrates the theoretical framework guiding the organization toward overall community development based on its mission. It displays the model's primary theoretical approaches: (1) development of critical consciousness; (2) affirmation of cultural and other forms of identity; (3) expansion of economic, social, and personal resources; (4) formation of alliances across groups for work on specific issues; and (5) integration of global and local technological advances. These theoretical approaches are linked to Putnam's notions of bonding (within groups), and bridging (across groups).

The model delineates ways in which these theoretical areas are operationalized in the ICR's spheres of work. Each specific, complex sphere reflects the incorporation of multiple theoretical approaches, as designated by directional arrows. Finally, the outcomes identify how the major forms of research engagement (middle column) emerge from community engagement; move toward achieving transformative outcomes desired by

THE ICR INTERVENTION MODEL

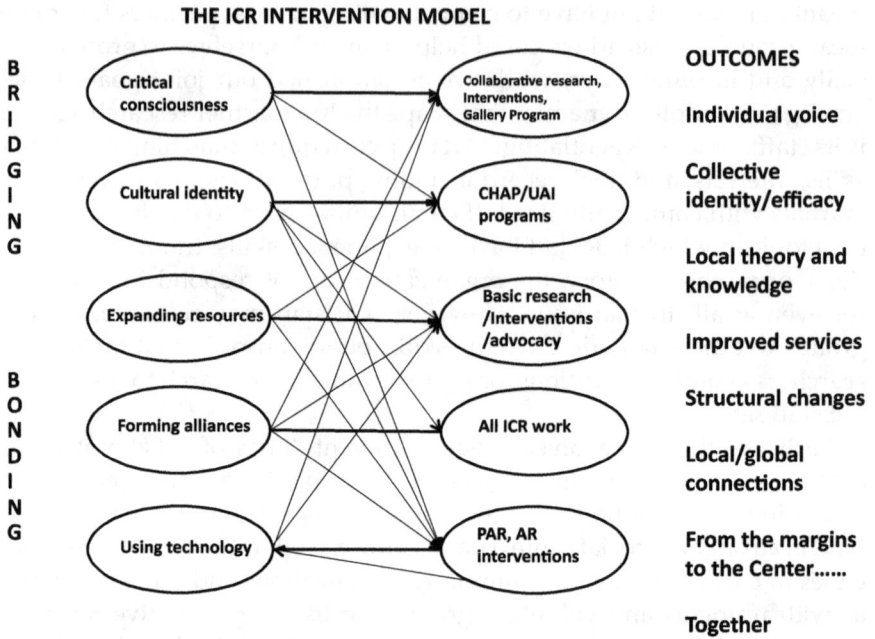

Figure 1.1. ICR intervention model

individuals, groups, and communities; and link local efforts to national and international movements.

The theoretical framework begins with the notion of critical consciousness, which Paulo Freire introduced in the 1970s. This concept calls for learning and pedagogical processes involving reflection on and engagement with the inequities that stem from differences in power, resources, and privilege, a process he called "concientizacion" (Freire 1970; 1981). Building critical consciousness is central to the decolonization of knowledge and lies at the heart of the PAR process, affecting individuals, the group, and the process of moving to transform the world. Brydon-Miller expresses this as "Embracing the notion of knowledge as socially constructed, and recognizing that all research is embedded within a system of values and promotes some model of human interaction, we commit ourselves to a form of research which challenges unjust and undemocratic economic, social and political systems and practices" (Brydon-Miller et al. 2008: 11). PAR builds critical consciousness by centering the knowledge production process through critical reflection of those directly affected by structural inequalities on their lived experience (Phillips et al. 2010).

"Knowing, to Freire, means being an active subject who questions and transforms. To learn is to recreate the way we see ourselves, our education and our society" (Shor 1993). In other words, "knowing" intersects with identity construction, a fluid construct (Berg et al. 2009; Levinson 2005). Knowledge construction, according to ICR principles, is a mixture of lived experience, culture, and history reconstructed through secondary literature and community narratives, together with the use of interactive ethnographic field research methods. These three main ways of understanding reality—lived experience, secondary sources and community narratives, and ethnography—converge in most ICR partnership projects and are triangulated to produce both processes and outcomes that all project partners agree upon.

The ICR collaborates with community partners in the co-construction and representation of knowledge in three main ways, which I describe below.

Cultural Representation

Many people from cultural, national, or ethnic communities of identity live in the Northeastern United States but are not recognized in its economic, social, and political life. The ICR works with them to represent their cultures, experiences, and art forms to the public, thus reinforcing identity and intergroup communication through two programs, the Connecticut Cultural Heritage Arts Program (CHAP) and the Urban Artists Initiative (now ended). CHAP facilitates representation and indigenous economic development of new, marginalized, or unknown groups. CHAP was first developed by me, and David Marshall, another anthropologist at the Connecticut Commission on the Arts who recognized that ICR could provide a good base for the Connecticut Folk Arts Program. We developed the founding application to the National Endowment on the Arts together. Together we hired the CHAP founding program director, Rebecca Joseph, another anthropologist. Several years later when she left to take a position with the National Park Service, archeological curator Lynne Williamson took over the directorship of the program and has nurtured it with continued NEA and other funding for more than two decades. CHAP offers collaborative exhibits, marketplaces, and various performance events through the ICR gallery and other off-site public programs, as well as a New England–wide mentorship program to foster the development of new heritage artists who create and perform music and dance, paint, carve, weave, cook, decorate, crochet, quilt, and collect, for both their own communities and broader audiences (Williamson et al. 2000). The program also maintains an archive of materials, cultural artifacts, information, and photographs for use by the public.

The Urban Artists Initiative was a twelve-year program founded and directed by David Marshall (Connecticut Commission on the Arts) and

Rebecca Joseph (ICR), and subsequently arts administrator Maryland Grier and well-known installation artist Colleen Coleman. This program identified and organized emerging artists and presenting organizations recruited from a broad diversity of communities and ethnic and national groups. More than 350 artists and arts organizations participated in training courses, numerous well-attended public exhibits, performances, conferences, mentorships, and other activities that advanced their careers while building the visibility of their work and their communities in the twelve Connecticut cities where the program was conducted. The program changed the cultural landscape of the state bringing diversity to arts funding, performance, and exhibition.

Alliances

Alliances are forged in the conduct of all research in which ICR plays a role. An alliance can be defined as agreement between two or more organizations to advance a common goal. ICR's alliances are "living alliances," a term encompassing the notion that community development work requires long-term presence and relationships across many sectors, which continue and are solidified, reinforced, renewed, and nurtured over time. As Radda and Schensul note, living alliances, once established, enable allies to organize to achieve (or participate in) specific outcomes at specific times in connection with an ongoing process of community transformation (Radda and J. Schensul 2011). Alliances that include organizations committed to transformative work may be vertical (cutting across institutions and "levels," i.e., state, city, etc.) or horizontal (among organizations at the same ecological level, e.g., clinics). They may consist of as few as two or three organizations or as many as eighty. The process of forging alliances to accomplish specific research and action goals expands social capital while creating an environment for constructing new knowledge. Alliances reach out to community residents, block clubs, tenants' associations, and so on to ensure the inclusion of resident voices as alliance members and as research partners in a community-based process.

One of the ICR's earliest alliances reflected a community-wide need to collect basic data on HIV knowledge and risk in Hartford. In 1988, the ICR formed a core horizontal community research alliance with the Urban League of Greater Hartford, the Hispanic Health Council, and the City of Hartford Health Department, all of which worked closely with the main ethnic, racial, and cultural communities affected by HIV at the time (J. Schensul et al. 1989). These organizations, concerned by the profound effects of HIV especially among substance users, found state support, which they cost-shared, to jointly conduct the first knowledge, attitudes, and behaviors studies. Over time this group expanded to include AIDs Project Hartford and Latinos contra SIDA (now renamed Latino Community Services) and share resources for developing and assessing culturally framed HIV preventive interventions. Further expansions added organizations involved in case management and HIV prevention education. Now, much later, some of the same organizations and newer ones have joined, with experience in research and development of female-focused prevention methods, as well as peer-driven harm reduction. When any organization in this loose alliance holds an HIV/AIDS related event, others support it, and all collaborate to honor World AIDS Day. New approaches addressing adherence issues and prevention through medication have been instrumental in maintaining the links among these organizations.

Similarly, a loose network of gerontologists, state public health geriatric advocates, older adult activists, and activist agencies, together with residents of senior housing, have been working for more than a decade to create resident-engaged participatory research and intervention projects in low-income senior housing. The work began with a study of exposure to HIV risk that involved an Area Agency on Aging and a total of thirteen low-income senior housing residences in Chicago and Hartford. Residents complained that some male residents were learning to inject drugs from their friends on streets outside the buildings; others were fearful of the injection drug users who sought out stairwells of buildings to shoot up in safety. Still others complained that male residents were inviting female commercial sex workers into the building, bringing drugs, HIV exposure, and the threat of robbery into the buildings. Finally, some residents whose adult children were HIV-infected were upset that other residents misunderstood HIV transmission and objected to their children's visits. With NIH funding, we collectively mounted a two-city study that explored HIV knowledge, exposure, and risk behaviors among residents. We worked with tenants' associations to engage them in the study, which involved sensitive behavior, and combined this with follow-up HIV education (J. Schensul et al. 2003).

During the course of the study, residents identified depression as a problem in their buildings. Working with residents, building managers, and a team of mental health researchers and geriatric psychiatrists, we conducted a study of depression in six buildings, following it with mental health services provided directly in the buildings. (Radda and J. Schensul 2011; Robison et al. 2009; J. Schensul et al. 2006). Our work with older adults attracted the interest of a vaccine researcher at the University of Connecticut Health Center who wanted to promote flu vaccination uptake among older adults who experienced barriers to vaccination.

Using existing state and city networks, we mobilized a vertical alliance to support a program to develop resident-driven flu and vaccination education. Residents raised their own questions about flu and vaccinations, obtained answers that satisfied them by interrogating experts, and created health education materials to support a building intervention. With additional funding, residents formed a Vaccination for Prevention Committee. Drawing on vertical alliance members for informational expertise, our research team helped the committee to plan a vaccination campaign that included resident pro-vaccination testimony, a pro-vaccination poster contest, vaccination games, and culturally embedded ways to keep healthy, and to create a flu education and vaccination film (J. Schensul et al. 2009). Now, a new vertical alliance has been formed through several grants from the National Institute of Dental and Cranial Research to address the major problem of inadequate dental care for older adults. The grants support collaborations with residents of senior housing to find ways to improve their health care and evaluate these apaches. As in the earlier project, residents work with researchers to develop campaign and other intervention materials and think through the intervention. In the process they uncover structural barriers to dental care and query disparities in oral health. Over time some have become involved in the vertical alliance as oral health activists.

PAR as Critical Pedagogy in Action

Most PAR projects involve partnerships between researchers and community residents in the co-construction of knowledge and participation in many aspects of a study. Community residents may become familiar with and involved in all aspects of the study. Further research approaches and community knowledge, and ways of knowing may also be discussed and exchanged. But the means of reconstituting and generating new knowledge through ethnographic research methods is not always available for use, even when community residents participate in the creation and refinement of research methods.

PAR as practiced at the ICR, is an approach to critical pedagogy in action that engages people of all ages in a process of resident-led research resulting in group knowledge generation and interventions geared toward transforming self, group, and society. Residents including young people and teens examine their identities and experiences, forge close group relationships, together define the topic of study, learn and adapt ethnographic methods shared by researchers who either hail from their communities or are well known there, conduct data analysis, and generate interpretations from their "emic" point of view (J. Schensul et al. 2008). Through learning/ knowing, they come to own both the results (i.e., the knowledge) and the inquiry methodologies, which they can then transfer to other situations. The academically trained researchers who work with them are members of the community or have long experience there.

About this form of PAR, Phillips and Berg state: "This method seeks to fully engage (participants) in a process of inquiry, action and reflection that facilitates their understanding of how their world is structured, their understanding of the contradictions that they may experience, and their ability to work as a group to determine what they can do to impact it" (Phillips et al. 2010: 180). The results of PAR projects are presented to the public in the form of installations, performances, videos, mixed media, and actions solicited and engaged over time. The many advantages of PAR as an approach to activist development for community change include the following:

(a) Critical self-reflection and the shift from perceiving lack of educational achievement, low income, and other inequities as matters of individual responsibility to understanding that these issues are rooted in structural and social determinants;

(b) Understanding that lived experience provides important and valued knowledge;

(c) Recognizing that knowing involves actively seeking information through self-reflection *and* from others;

(d) Learning that interviewing and other ways of engaging people in information collection are at once a way of obtaining information, a community organizing strategy, and a way to build social capital;

(e) Gaining technical skills in reading, math, computer software, and writing;

(f) Learning to use and to question sources of information;

(g) Gaining communication and negotiation skills within the PAR group and with publics that are the focus of advocacy.

Formal evaluation of this approach shows that whereas group formation and issue learning occur during the research phase, it is through engagement in political activism that youth and adults transform their identities and begin to view themselves as scholar-activists (Berg et al. 2009) Similar work with adults shows that collective critical consciousness results from the combination of research and transformative action (Weeks et al. 2009). PAR at the ICR offers communities a means for inventing research theory and methodology to create and promote their own knowledge and activism base.

Data Ownership and Sharing in Knowledge Co-construction Settings

Data ownership and sharing are critical to all participatory action research projects. In every collaborative ICR project, all parties "own" both the data and the knowledge resulting from the work. Throughout the life of a project, agreements made both in advance and as needed determine how the study results should and can be used. Because a project's main purpose is to address a community problem, it is advantageous to share research results as quickly as possible so that they can be used. Procedures are established in formal contractual agreements and internal memos that detail rules for ownership, mutual respect, and use of data. An example from an early ICR collaborative project, the Urban Women's Development Project (J. Schensul et al. 2008), illustrates how such agreements are instituted. Over the course of five years, five community organizations partnered to develop a project to engage women in the community in defining their concerns (i.e., the affected population) and then planning to collect information needed to address them. Even before they received funding, the five organizations detailed the roles, responsibilities, and budgeting that would support the collaboration. They agreed that participants would be involved in all aspects of data definition, collection, and dissemination; that each would receive copies of the participant-generated data; that no organization would use the data without consulting with the project steering committee; and that presentation of the data, regardless of who "owned" it, would be enhanced by the presence of organizational and community representatives. All parties agreed that the city of Hartford should have access to the first year's de-identified survey data, in order to better promote and advocate for urban women (J. Schensul et al. 2008). In this four-year project, other issues came to the fore (e.g. dropping out of high school, child care needs, and violence against women) and women participants took leadership in researching and advocating to bring about changes in these areas.

Data ownership and sharing becomes more complex when the producers are youth. First, data produced by high school youth do not always stand up to intellectually rigorous review, and sharing these data may unnecessarily subject teens to criticism by those who fail to see that the most important aspect of youth-led research is the process of coming to know and act, not the production of adult-quality research data and results. Given constraints imposed by time, skill sets, and available instruction, youth-led research may be marked by non-representative samples, less-than-rich qualitative data, and analytical limitations. Preferably, youth present the results of their research to their peers and the wider public;

and their voices along with the data carry weight in policy and programmatic decision-making.

Sharing Results with Different Publics

Sharing of results should begin in a project's planning stage, and planning for dissemination should continue through the end. The Rapid Sociodemographic Assessment Project (RSA), one of the ICR's earlier large-scale PAR efforts, demonstrates how initial planning creates an infrastructure for later dissemination and use. The RSA project involved thirteen neighborhoods, six municipalities, and more than eighty community organizations and neighborhood groups in a community action-oriented survey and critique of census categories. The project had multiple objectives: (1) to qualify organizations to understand survey and qualitative research by *doing* it; (2) to place written results, databases, and the capacity to use them in the hands of community organizations in marginalized communities; (3) to enable community organizations to challenge census racial and ethnic designations and try to change them; (4) to recruit people to conduct the next census, (5) to encourage competing organizations to forge alliances by helping them understand that private and governmental actions to segment the city by class and race/ethnicity underpinned and fostered the competition among them (Simmons 1998); and (6) to spin off other critical analysis activities that identified and explored the reasons for income and occupational disparities.

Many community groups participated in developing the core survey, and local groups developed neighborhood-specific surveys according to neighborhood needs. ICR policy required working with all groups and ensuring intergroup cooperation. Neighborhood meetings and the requirement to participate in survey development for neighborhood use brought most organizations to the table, despite considerable racialized and economic competition among groups. The lead organizations organizing community researchers or data collectors received neighborhood data files and neighborhood reports. Larger agencies acted as repositories for organizations that wanted planning and historical data, and as bases for results dissemination. ICR researchers provided technical assistance in using the databases until agencies learned how to query the databases themselves.

Opportunities for dissemination emerge at times, particularly at the end of a study. In the last year of a decade of National Institute on Drug Abuse research on substance youth and lifestyle among young people in Hartford, the idea emerged to create thirteen 3- by 9-foot panels depicting youth lifestyle and drug use over that period of time. The study team—

made up of young researchers from the community, older anthropologists including myself, and a community physician—decided that a "street drama" technique was the best way to reach young people with the results of their information sharing. Our idea was to create portable panels that could be placed on any street corner, or in front of a club or bar, to foster discussion. The city ultimately made it impossible to use this tactic, but we did create the panels as well as a traveling multimedia installation that created opportunities for dialogue in youth centers, City Hall, and other public venues of all sizes throughout Connecticut and at sites in Vancouver, Minnesota, Montreal, and Mexico (J. Schensul et al. 2012).

Other ways of disseminating or sharing data with public audiences include musical, dance, and spoken word performances; film; and dialogues about the implications of results and gallery installations. When these dissemination methods are interactive, they continue the process of co-construction at a community level, eliciting new, useful information from all parties to further the social change process.

Summary

The illustrations above show how CBROs position themselves in and with communities to enhance the potential for a fully shared knowledge development and utilization experience. Trusted CBROs can help to democratize science by opening doors to interrogate others' research results and making the process of theory formulation transparent. Researchers who wish to collaborate with communities to make knowledge need good skills and flexibility to invent or co-create new ways of listening, observing, capturing, speaking, telling, describing, documenting, and measuring. Most people, even those in desperate situations, desire new information and have situational and experiential knowledge to offer. Finding ways to match questions, designs, and methods to community needs; transforming community questions into researchable designs; and learning from local ways of generating, keeping, and sharing traditional or tacit knowledge and problem solving are challenges requiring highly imaginative methodological training and the highest degree of understanding of and sensitivity to local community conditions.

CBROs like the ICR are settings where creative researchers can interact daily with creative community residents and professionals to build new knowledge relevant to the transformation of inequitable community structures and processes. They can create new capacities for knowledge development and problem solving. The projects they develop in collaboration with others result in new alliances and social networks that often are maintained over time. The research skills used in co-constructing knowledge through project implementation are generalizable to other action research projects. As bridge organizations, CBROs connect community-based organizations and community residents to broader social institutions, structures, networks, and resources. They may also be able to help initiate new community organizations and link them with established networks. CBROs enhance community assets and capacities. And because of their ability to network with similar organizations and dedicated researchers and activists elsewhere, CBROs are in a position to bring national and international knowledge and resources to local communities, and vice versa. Thus they and their networks can and do participate actively in a global knowledge exchange system.

CBROs face numerous challenges and limitations, and the ICR is no exception. Major problems include staffing, constant fluctuations in funding, the need to respond to changing constituencies, and legal issues arising from work with undocumented populations or people who lack or cannot afford official documentation (drivers' licenses, DUNS numbers, business licenses, income tax returns, etc.). Access to libraries and other information sources hinges on collaboration with universities, which in turn entails trade-offs and time spent on proper negotiation. The overall political environment requires constant adaptation and adjustment to assure consistency across mission, operations, and funding.

Nevertheless, to work hand in hand with publics that confront serious challenges—stigma, survival, visibility, access to resources, rapid unsupported growth—while also contributing important knowledge and cultural resources is a continuously rewarding venture because these independent research and action organizations "share a commitment to democratic practice, a respect for people's knowledge and a conviction that together knowledge and collective action can bring about positive change" (Brydon-Miller et al. 2008).

Jean J. Schensul, PhD (Minnesota), senior scientist and founding director, Institute for Community Research, Hartford, is an interdisciplinary medical/educational anthropologist. She is the recipient of a number of collaborative community-based National Institutes of Health research grants, as well as other federal, state, and foundation grants. She has published widely on these topics, as well as community engagement, communitybased knowledge development and research methodology. Dr. Schensul is the recipient of the Solon T. Kimball Award for Public Policy Research in Anthropology, with Stephen Schensul, and the Bronislaw Malinowski Award for Lifetime Achievement in Anthropology, and author/editor *Ethnographer's Toolkit,* 1st and 2nd editions with Margaret LeCompte.

References

Aguilera, Dorothy. 2009. "Participatory Action Research as Pedagogy for Equity and Social Justice." In *Education: Intersection of Youth Voice, Reflection, Action in a Public High School: Denver, CO*. http://oln.educationnorthwest.org/webfm_send/196.

Akenya, Francis A. 2012. "Critical Analysis of the Production of Western Knowledge and Its Implications for Indigenous Knowledge and Decolonization." *Journal of Black Studies* 20, no. 10: 1–21.

Barnhardt, Ray. 2005. "Creating a Place for Indigenous Knowledge in Education: The Alaska Native Knowledge Network." In *Place-Based Education in the Global Age: Local Diversity*, ed. Gregory Smith and David Gruenewald. Hillsdale, NJ: Lawrence Erlbaum Associates.

Bennett, Linda, and Linda Whiteford, eds. 2013. "Anthropology and the Engaged University: New Vision for the Discipline within Higher Education." *Annals of Anthropological Practice*, vol. 37, no. 1: 2–18.

Berg, Marlene, and Jean Schensul. 2004. "Participatory Action Research with Youth." Special issue of *Practicing Anthropology* 26, no. 2.

Berg, Marlene, Emil Coman, and Jean Schensul. 2009. "Youth Action Research for Prevention: A Multi-level Intervention Designed to Increase Efficacy and Empowerment Among Urban Youth." *American Journal of Community Psychology* 43, nos. 3/4: 345–359.

Brodkey, Linda. 1987. "Writing Critical Ethnographic Narratives." *Anthropology & Education Quarterly* 18, no. 2: 67–76.

Brydon-Miller, Mary, Ismael Davids, Namrata Jaiti, Brinton M. Lykes, Jean Schensul, Susan Williams. 2008. "Popular Education and Action Research: Voices from the Field." In *Handbook on Educational Action Research*, ed. Susan Noffke and Bridget Somekh, 495–507. Thousand Oaks, CA: Sage.

Cammarota, Julio. 2008. "The Cultural Organizing of Youth Ethnographers: Formalizing a Praxis-Based Pedagogy." *Anthropology & Education Quarterly* 39, no. 1: 45–58.

Cintron-Moscoso, Federico. 2009. "Cultivating Youth Proenvironmental Development: A Critical Ecological Approach." *Ecopsychology* 2, no. 1: 33–40.

Dickson, David. 1988. *The New Politics of Science*. Chicago: University of Chicago Press.

Dobyns, Henry F., Paul L. Doughty, and Harold D. Lasswell. 1971. *Peasants, Power and Applied Social Change: Vicos as a Model*. Beverly Hills, CA: Sage.

Erickson, Frederick. 1987. "Transformation and School Success: The Politics and Culture of Educational Achievement." *Anthropology & Education Quarterly* 18, no. 4: 335–356.

Ervin, Alexander. 2005. *Applied Anthropology Tools and Perspectives for Contemporary Practice*. Needham Heights, MA: Allyn and Bacon.

Fals Borda, Orlando, and Mohammad Anisur Rahman. 1991. *Action and Knowledge: Breaking the Monopoly with Participatory Action Research*. New York: Apex.

Fine, Michelle, and María Elena Torre. 2006. "Intimate Details: Participatory Action Research in Prison." *Action Research* 4, no. 3: 253–269.

Freire, Paulo. 1970. *Pedagogy of the Oppressed*. New York: Herder and Herder.

———. 1981. *Education for Critical Consciousness*. New York: Continuum.

Frickel, Scott, and Kelly Moore, eds. 2006. *The New Political Sociology of Science: Institutions, Networks and Power*. Madison: University of Wisconsin Press.

Gaviria, Moises, Gwen Stern, and Stephen L. Schensul. 1982. "Sociocultural Factors and Perinatal Health in a Mexican-American Community." *Journal of the National Medical Association* 74, no. 10: 983–989.

Greaves, Thomas, Ralph Bolton, and Florencia Zapata. 2010. *Vicos and Beyond: A Half Century of Applying Anthropology in Peru*. Lanham, MD: AltaMira Press.

Greenman, Nancy, and Jack A. Dieckmann. 2004. "Considering Criticality and Culture as Pivotal in Transformative Teacher Education." *Journal of Teacher Education* 55: 240–255.

Gusterson, Hugh. 1997. "Studying Up Revisited." *PoLAR: Political and Legal Anthropology Review* 20, no. 1: 114–119.

Highlander Research and Education Center. 2014 Mission. http://highlandercenter.org/about-us/mission/.

Hovmand, Peter. 2014. *Community Based System Dynamics.* New York: Springer.

Hyland, Stanley, ed. 2005. *Community Building in the Twenty-First Century.* Santa Fe, NM: School for Advanced Research.

Israel, Barbara, Eugenia Eng, Amy Shultz, Edith Parker. 2005. *Methods in Community Based Participatory Research for Health.* San Francisco: Jossey-Bass.

Kadia, Satish, and John van Willigen. 2005. *Applied Anthropology: Domains of Application.* Westport, CT: Praeger.

Kwon, Soo Ah. 2008. "Moving from Complaints to Action: Oppositional Consciousness and Collective Action in a Political Community." *Anthropology & Education Quarterly* 39, no. 1: 59–76.

Langley, Chris, Stuart Parkinson, and Philip Webber. 2008. "Behind Closed Doors: Military Influence, Commercial Pressures and the Compromised University." Report, Science for Global Responsibility.

Levinson, Bradley. 2005. "Citizenship, Identity, Democracy: Engaging the Political in the Anthropology of Education." *Anthropology & Education Quarterly* 36, no. 4: 329–340.

Lewin, Kurt. 1946. "Action Research and Minority Problems." *Journal of Social Issues* 2, no. 4: 34–46.

London, Jonathon, and Melissa A. Chabran. 2004. "Youth-Led REP: Building Critical Consciousness for Social Change." *Practicing Anthropology* 26, no. 2: 45–50.

Maguire, Patricia. 2006. "Uneven Ground: Feminisms and Action Research." In *Handbook of Action Research,* ed. Peter Reason and Hillary Bradbury. Thousand Oaks, CA: Sage.

Mehan, Hugh. 2008. "Engaging the Sociological Imagination: My Journey into Design Research and Public Sociology." *Anthropology & Education Quarterly* 39, no. 1: 77–91.

Minkler, Meredith, and Nina Wallerstein. 2010. *Community-Based Participatory Research for Health: From Process to Outcomes.* Hoboken, NJ: John Wiley & Sons.

Park, Peter, Mary Brydon-Miller, and Bud L. Hall. 1993. *Voices of Change: Participatory Research in the US and Canada.* Westport, CT: Bergin and Garvey.

Phillips, Evelyn, Marlene Berg, Chiedza Rodriguez, Damion Morgan. 2010. "A Case Study of Participatory Action Research in a Public New England Middle School: Empowerment, Constraints and Challenges." *American Journal of Community Psychology* 46, no. 1: 179–194.

Radda, Kim E., and Jean Schensul. 2011. "Building Living Alliances: Community Engagement and Community-Based Partnerships to Address the Health of Community Elders." *Annals of Anthropological Practice* 35, no. 2: 154–173.

Rhoads, Robert A., and Carlos Alberto Torres, eds. 2006. *The University, State and Market: The Political Economy of Globalization in the Americas.* Stanford, CA: Stanford University Press.

Robison, Julie, Gretchen Diefenbach, Jean Schensul, William Disch, Emil Coman, Sonia Gaztambide, Kim Radda. 2009. Mental health in senior housing: racial/ethnic patterns and correlates of major depressive disorder. *Aging & Mental Health* 13, no. 5: 659–673.

Rylko-Bauer, Barbara, Merrill Singer, and John van Willigen. 2006. "Reclaiming Applied Anthropology: Its Past, Present, and Future." *American Anthropologist* 108, no. 1: 178–190.

Schensul, Jean J. 1997. "Urban Apartheid and the Privatization of Public Resources." Paper presented at the Session on Urban Segregation, Development and Change, Society for Applied Anthropology Annual Meeting, Seattle, WA.

———. 1998. Community-based risk prevention with urban youth. School Psychology Review.

———. 2002. Democratizing Science through Social Science Research Partnerships. *Bulletin of Science Technology & Society* 22: 190.

———. 2005. "Strengthening Communities through Research Partnerships for Social Change: Perspectives from the Institute for Community Research." In *Community Building in the Twenty-first Century,* ed. Stanley Hyland. Santa Fe, NM: School for Advanced Research.

———. 2009. Community, culture and sustainability in multilevel dynamic systems intervention science. *American Journal of Community Psychology* 43, nos. 3/4: 241–256.

———. 2010. "Engaged Universities, Community Based Research Organizations and Third Sector Science in a Global System." *Human Organization* 69, no. 4: 307–320.

Schensul, Jean J., Marlene J. Berg, and Ken M. Williamson. 2008. "Challenging Hegemonies: Advancing Collaboration in Community-Based Participatory Action Research." *Collaborative Anthropologies* 1: 102–138.

Schensul, Jean J., and Margaret D. LeCompte. 2012. *Ethnography in Practice: a Mixed Methods Approach. Volume 7 Ethnographer's Toolkit,* 2nd ed. Lanham, MD: AltaMira Press.

Schensul, Jean J., Judith A. Levy, and William.B. Disch. 2003. "Individual, Contextual, and Social Network Factors Affecting Exposure to HIV/AIDS Risk among Older Residents Living in Low-Income Senior Housing Complexes." *Journal of Acquired Immune Deficiency Syndromes* 33: S138–S152.

Schensul, Jean J., Georgina Burke, Merrill Singer, Miriam Torres. 1989. "AIDS Knowledge: Attitudes and Behaviors Survey in a Multi-Ethnic Neighborhood of Hartford." Institute for Community Research Publication, Phase II.

Schensul, Jean J., Marlene Berg, Sandra Sydlo. 2004. "Core elements of participatory action research for educational empowerment and risk prevention with urban youth." *Practicing Anthropology* 26, no. 2: 5–9.

Schensul, Jean J., Julie Robison, Carmen Reyes, Kim Radda, Sonia Gastambide, William Disch. 2006. "Building Interdisciplinary/Intersectoral Research Partnerships for Community-Based Mental Health Research With Older Minority Adults. *American Journal of Community Psychology* 38, nos. 1/2: 79–93.

Schensul, Jean J., Kim Radda, Emil Coman, Elsie Vazquez. 2009. "Multi-Level Intervention to Prevent Influenza Infections in Older Low Income and Minority Adults." *American Journal of Community Psychology* 43, no. 3: 313–329.

Schensul, Jean J., Colleen Coleman, Sarah Diamond. 2012. "'Rollin' n Dustin': Using Installation and Film for Interactive Dissemination of Drug Study Results to Youth in Participant Communities." In *Popularizing Research: Engaging New Genres, Media, and Audiences,* ed. Peter Vannini. New York: Peter Lang Publishing.

Schensul, Stephen L. 1978. "Commando Research." *Practicing Anthropology* 1, no. 1: 13–14.

———. 1980. "Anthropological Fieldwork and Sociopolitical Change." *Social Problems* 27, no. 3: 309–319.

Schensul, Stephen L., and Jean J. Schensul. 1978. "Advocacy and Applied Anthropology." In *Social Scientists and Advocates: Views from the Applied Disciplines,* ed. George Weber and George McCall. Beverly Hills, CA: Sage.

Schensul, Stephen L., and M. Borrero. 1982. "Introduction to the Hispanic Health Council." *Urban Anthropology* 11, no. 1: 1–8.

Schensul, Stephen L., Jean Schensul, M. Weeks, M. Singer, and M. Brault. 2014. *Participatory Methods and Community-Based Collaborations, Handbook of Research in Cultural Anthropology,* 2nd Edition, ed. H.R. Bernard and Clarence Gravlee, 185–214. Lanham, MD: Roman & Littlefield.

Sclove, Richard, Madeleine Scammell, and Breena Holland. 1998. *Community Based Research in the United States: An Introductory Reconnaissance, Including Twelve Organizational Case*

Studies and Comparison with the Dutch Science Shops and the Mainstream American Research System. Amherst, MA: Loka Institute.

Shor, Ira. 1993. "Education is Politics: Paulo Freire's Critical Pedagogy." In *Paulo Freire: A Critical Encounter*, ed. Peter McLaren and Peter Leonard. London: Routledge Press.

Simmons, Louise B. 1998. "A New Urban Conservatism: The Case of Hartford, Connecticut." *Journal of Urban Affairs* 20, no. 2: 175–198.

Society for Participatory Research in Asia. 2014. http://www.pria.org/about-us.

van Willigen, John. 2002. *Applied Anthropology: An Introduction*, 3rd ed. Westport, CT: Bergen and Garvey.

Wali, Alika. 2006. *Collaborative Research: A Practical Guide to Participatory Action Research for Communities and Scholars*. Chicago: Field Museum.

Wali, Alika, Elena Marcheschi, Rebecca Severson, Mario Longoni. 2001. "More than a Hobby: Adult Participation in the Informal Arts." *Journal of Arts Management, Law and Society* 31, no. 3: 212–222.

Weeks, Margaret R. Mark Convey, Julia Dickson-Gomez, Mark Convey, Julia Dickson-Gomez, Jianghong Li, Kim Radda, Maria Martinez, Eduardo Robles. 2009. "Changing Drug Users' Risk Environments: Peer Health Advocates as Multi-Level Community Change Agents." *American Journal of Community Psychology* 43, nos. 3/4: 330–344.

Weeks, Margaret R. Jianghong Li, Emil Coma, Maryann Abbot, Laurie Sylla, Michelle Corbett, Julia Dickson-Gomez. 2010. "Multilevel Social Influences on Female Condom Use and Adoption Among Women in the Urban United States." *AIDS Patient Care and STDs* 24, no. 5: 297–309.

Whyte, William F. 1991. *The Growth and Dynamics of the Worker Cooperative Complex*. Ithaca, NY: Cornell University Press.

Williamson, Lynne, Jeremy Brecher, Ruth Glasser, Jean Schensul. 2000. "Using Ethnography to Influence Public Programming, Volume 7 of Ethnographer's Toolkit." In *Using Ethnographic Data: Interventions, Public Programming and Public Policy*, ed. Jean J. Schensul and Margaret D. LeCompte, vol. 7. Lanham, MD: AltaMira Press.

Chapter 2

CROSSING THE LINE
Participatory Action Research in a Museum Setting

———— ∞∞∞ ————

Alaka Wali and Madeleine Tudor

A museum is a problematic setting for public anthropology. Natural history and anthropology museums are colonial holdovers that, having originated in "cabinets of curiosity," now display collections of objects from "others"—typically non-Western, previously colonized subjects of anthropological study—and maintain an authoritative voice in the interpretation of cultural constructs (Haas 1996; Stocking 1985). Nevertheless, museum-based communications methods afford potential benefits for building collaboration and integrating research findings into action strategies because they tend to be multimedia, non-didactic, and interactive. The challenge is to take the museum-based strategies literally out of the museum for direct engagement with community partners.

This chapter discusses our efforts, through the Center for Cultural Understanding and Change,[1] to rethink and experiment with participatory action research (PAR) strategies from a museum. Our applied research and public action work have focused on the relationship between the process of residents' caring for and contesting place, and the consequences of that process for both the people and the built and natural environments. We have used museum-inspired multimedia strategies integrated into PAR methods to create pathways to empowerment for our community partners. Below, we first outline the fundamentals of our approach to PAR and the integration of multimedia techniques. Then we discuss the outcomes of our experiments with various communication strategies, specifically mapping, the Web, and videography, and community exhibits.

———————

Notes for this chapter begin on page 85.

Museum-Based Participatory Action Research: Theory and Principles

Participatory action research is by definition a form of public anthropology. Long a marginal strategy in the social sciences, it has gained more acceptance lately as anthropologists and social scientists find themselves increasingly situated in nonacademic settings. Although there is a common understanding of what constitutes PAR (i.e., involvement of research subjects in actual investigation, with the objective of contributing to change or betterment in the subjects' social situation/context), a wide variety of approaches fall under the PAR rubric (Schensul et al. 2008; Tolman and Brydon-Miller 2001; Wali 2006). The theoretical underpinning of PAR work is the premise that research (i.e., the systematic gathering of information toward the advancement of knowledge) is most useful when it is highly transparent and directly relevant to solving the problem at hand.

PAR approaches date back to the 1950s (Tax 1958). More recent iterations have been influenced by feminist theory and new theorizing in "collaborative anthropologies" (Lassiter 2008). Feminist theory questions the quest for "objectivity" in research practice and argues that a transparent approach, which admits researcher bias but also includes multiple voices as part of the research process, can produce valid results (Morawski 2001; Schrijvers 2001: 19–30). By de-centering the researcher's authority, feminist theory provided a framework for a more inclusive approach to inquiry (Morgen 1990; Rapp and Ross 1981). Meanwhile, the necessity of research for action, and of inclusionary approaches to conducting good research, further validates PAR strategies. Despite ongoing critique of these theories, PAR's proven power to enhance insight into complex social phenomena and yield effective results has increased its stature (Freire 1989).

Notwithstanding its growing acceptance, however, PAR as a research methodology and action strategy faces challenges—not least the question of determining how to most effectively use research findings to inform action. The path from "knowing something" to "acting on it" is not linear. Hence, crossing the line from research to action requires a multifaceted approach. PAR approaches may differ in their degree of involvement of subjects in research design, actual field work, and analysis of results. The expected outcomes may also differ. In other words, *participatory* and *action* take on a wide array of characteristics. At The Field Museum, we developed specific principles to guide our PAR work. First, we aimed to start from a position of trust between our partners in the project and ourselves as the researchers. This meant that before undertaking research itself, we had to establish a relationship with clear roles and responsibilities. Second, the different types of experience the partners brought to the project were stated explicitly. We had experience and expertise in conducting qualitative research. Community partners had rich "local ecological knowledge," expertise in understanding the social context, and networks, as well as research experience. We did not, however, expect them to conduct the research.[2] A third principle was flexibility in customizing research to partner needs, though we also made sure to dialogue about unrealistic expectations early on in the collaboration, as many of our partners' research needs were outside our realm of expertise. Finally, our efforts incorporated museum-style communication methods.

Presenting Research

Scholars are most comfortable presenting research in written texts where they can tackle complex ideas and explain their research findings in detail. Indeed, written text dominated all modes of research presentation until just the last decade. Recently, however, the proliferation of visual technologies and cyber-based formats has begun to erode the written word's dominance in conveying scholarship. Audiovisual elements are becoming central modes of communication and can no longer be perceived as mere "supplements" to the text (see Wesch 2009). University-based scholars are creatively pursuing visual modes and also using the Web, videography, and photography to engage students. Visual anthropology has attained sophistication; it is not just a documentary endeavor but an integral aspect of research methodologies (Harper 2009).

The use of visual media as research method is not new to anthropology. For nearly a century, anthropologists have used photography and film as tools in their analyses, visually documenting, interpreting, and communicating social and cultural life, from daily activities to the performance of ritual to artistic representations of identity, affiliations, and power relations (J. Collier and M. Collier 1986; Mead 2003 [1975]; Pink 2003; 2007). Visual methods are attractive to anthropological inquiry because they provide a material interface between objectivity and subjectivity that acts as a window into social process and its interpretation, and as an artifact produced within its own historical and disciplinary context. Visual methods also allow anthropologists to cross the line from research to action by engaging participants in creating visual cultural material that exchanges, produces, and represents knowledge.

Whereas the value of using visual media to further anthropological inquiry beyond formal uses of documentation has been debated (mainly with respect to the degree to which visual representations present positivist or mediated realities; see Pink [2003] for historical perspective), applications of visual methods in anthropological research continue to develop in both theory and practice. The inherent visual quality of photographs and other visual media offers an avenue for mediating the relationship between outsider and insider perspectives, and contemporary digital media facilitate its centrality to a range of applied visual methods. Sarah Pink (2007: 3) asserts that the main contemporary use of visual anthropology is its application to social issues through "visual representations informed by anthropological theory, analysis of visual aspects of culture, and the use of visual ethnographic research methods."

Photovoice (Wang 1999, cited in Harper 2009), participatory videography, and sketch mapping are examples of tools we have used to engage participants in the research process, where they create and/or contribute perspectives on content and context. By revealing various meanings that emerge as people interpret their world, this approach can instill a deeper, more nuanced understanding of the research inquiry in both researchers and participants (Wolowic 2008).

The Museum Setting

As mentioned above, museums have long employed non–text-based communication strategies to communicate knowledge to public audiences in ways that are entertaining and interactive as well as educational. These communication strategies rely on 3-D (i.e., objects) and 2-D multimedia to create sensory experiences that convey knowledge more holistically than text alone can.

In the late 1980s, museums increasingly added audiovisual elements to exhibits, jettisoning the strategy of dioramas and glass cases filled with objects or authoritatively labeled specimens (see Haraway 1989 for a critique of dioramas). The Field Museum undertook this shift under the leadership of Michael Spock, whom many in the museum community consider a pioneer in applying new theories of learning (especially for children) to museum settings. Spock was tasked with transforming The Field Museum's permanent exhibits into appealing immersive experiences. His approach relied on layering information to make it accessible to children and adults with diverse learning styles and attention spans. Thus, information was embedded in objects surrounded by stage sets that evoked context. Interactive games and video displays enhanced central messages or allowed an entertaining delivery of supplementary information. Text was minimized, relegated mostly to conveying central messages at the reading level of an 8- to 12-year-old, or providing information about objects' provenance. The new approach to communication generated considerable debate within the museum. The curators (i.e., scholar-researchers) perceived this shift as a loss of the ability to communicate information. Because large spaces were needed to create immersive experiences, fewer objects or specimens were used; meanwhile, minimized label text meant curators had less space to expound didactically on objects and their meaning. Spock and the exhibits team, on the other hand, felt that accommodating visitors' own knowledge base and comfort level was a way to reach more of them (Freire 1989).

How much information to communicate and how to do so effectively remain matters of ongoing debate in the museum community. Our attempts to grapple with these questions began during the development of a new exhibit for The Field Museum between 1995 and 1997. Titled *Living Together: Common Concerns, Different Responses,* the exhibit presented anthropology's perspective on the reasons for cultural diversity. It used comparison across cultures (marking The Field Museum's first inclusion of cultural practices from the United States) to suggest that social groups' different responses to common human concerns (such as constructing a home, forging community or social bonds, and embodying personhood) are due to the interaction between their environments, their histories, and sheer human creativity. Departing from the traditional mode of exhibiting cultures through a regional lens (e.g., hall of Africa, hall of the Pacific), the exhibit juxtaposed objects from different cultures to force a comparative view of peoples' responses to common concerns by showcasing similarities and differences among cultures. It also incorporated video, interactive games, and photography to layer the central messages and communicate the ways people create culture.

The experience of working on the exhibit influenced our understanding of effective deployments of non–text-based media to communicate relatively complex ideas. Ultimately, we realized that these same techniques were suited to translating participatory research into action with our community partners. To that end, we began to experiment with taking the museum outside of its walls.

Crossing the Line from Research to Action: Experimental Outcomes

Locating Cultural Practices: Mapping Assets

The use of maps to convey more than geographical information dates to prehistoric times (Woodward and Lewis 1998). Maps are effective communicative devices, affording a way to locate processes in place and to visualize relationships through immediately understandable representations. Anthropologists have productively used maps and mapping in applied work for many years. Environmental anthropology projects, for example, have incorporated sketch maps to help people envision patterns of natural resource use, territorial boundaries, and even cosmological principles (Alcorn 2000; Chapin 2001). In urban work, maps were popularized through the influence of urban planners—especially John Kretzmann and John McKnight, who pioneered the use of "asset maps." They presented an alternative to the standard "needs assessment" approach to "fixing" community problems, instead making a case for creating social change by building on communities' existing talents and capacities. They developed social asset mapping (Kretzmann and McKnight 1993) to help urban planners and community development organizations identify the skills and organizational forms that urban poor relied on.[3] Anthropologists Stan Hyland and Linda Bennett (2005) applied asset mapping to community development work in Memphis, Tennessee. In both cases, maps were created through "participatory" processes that allowed participants to determine how they wanted to represent their "landscapes" or "asset-scapes."

We have used asset mapping in both Chicago and the Andes/Amazon region of Peru, applying our knowledge of maps' effectiveness in urban settings to our work in the Andes/Amazon and vice versa. The cross-site learning has enriched our experience. Working in a museum context—specifically, a natural history museum with its traditional focus on understanding human-environment interfaces—influenced our work with maps. However, we bypassed the more traditional human ecological theories undergirding museum research by grounding our inquiry in theoretical concepts rooted in the examination of place, space, and place attachment—a common denominator for understanding the relationship between social organization and its location in physical space. Space and place theoreticians have long provided anthropologists and other social scientists with key insights into the complex, dynamic processes by which people adapt to their environments (Pellow 1996).

Ethnographic research has yielded myriad studies of how people invest their environments with meaning that shapes and is shaped by normative patterns of gender, ethnicity, status, kinship, and cosmology (e.g., Ardener 1993; Birdwell-Pheasant and Lawrence-Zuniga 1999; Bourdieu 2003 [1971]; Conquergood 1992; Pellow 1996; Rapoport 1969; Spain 1992), which can then be compared cross-culturally (Low and Lawrence-Zuniga 2003). The ongoing development of this research has expanded its focus on the urban context, a fruitful setting for investigating processes of social change. Setha Low's (2000: 127–128) clarification of spatial categories as the "*social production of space* [which] includes all those factors—social, economical, ideological, and technological—that result … in the physical creation of the material setting" and the "*social construction of space* [which] is the actual transformation of space—through peoples' social exchanges, memories, images, and daily use of the material setting—into scenes and actions that convey meaning," were particularly helpful for understanding how tangible and intangible assets are manifest in the landscape and provided a concrete way to locate urban cultural processes within both physical and social geographies.

This focus led us to add a place-based dimension to Kretzmann and McKnight's asset mapping strategy in a participatory research project on Chicago's Southeast Side, popularly known as the Calumet Region.

The project aimed to engage communities in the restoration and stewardship of significant wilderness habitats—remnants of prairie, savannah, and woodlands.[4] We supplemented Kretzmann and McKnight's asset mapping methods with ethnography to provide a thick description of the key players, associations, and institutions, as well as the networks and relationships extending from each asset. We defined assets as follows: (1) the

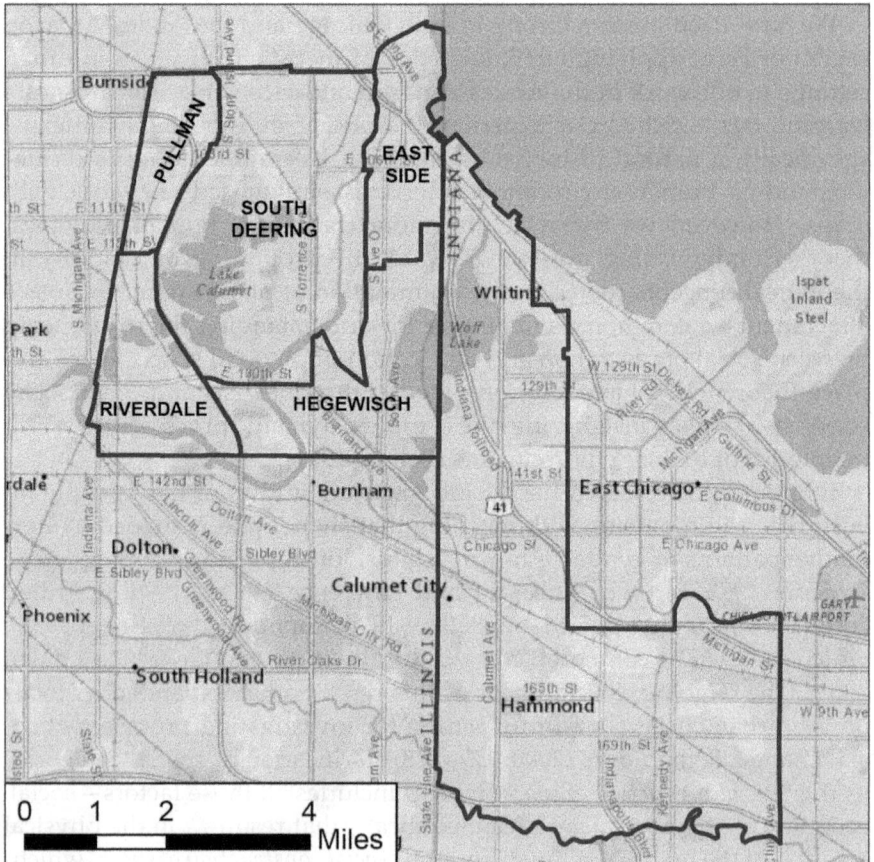

Figure 2.1. The Calumet Region spans the southeastern Chicago metropolitan area and northwestern Indiana.

visible manifestations of people's capacity to organize, such as institutions and organizations (places of faith, voluntary associations, community-based organizations, etc.); (2) other, less manifest ways people organize themselves, including family and friend networks; and (3) the attitudes and values that underlie strategies and guide action (Field Museum Website 2011). Our research revealed the diversity of social assets in their different locations. For example, we identified differences between longtime residents—former steel mill workers and newer residents of the region (including many Latinos and African Americans who moved to the region after deindustrialization). Both groups were attached to their homeplace, but their differing reasons for this attachment affected their action strategies.

As we wrote the technical report of our ethnographic findings, we knew few people would want to wade through the details. Therefore, we represented the assets of the diverse residents by locating them on base

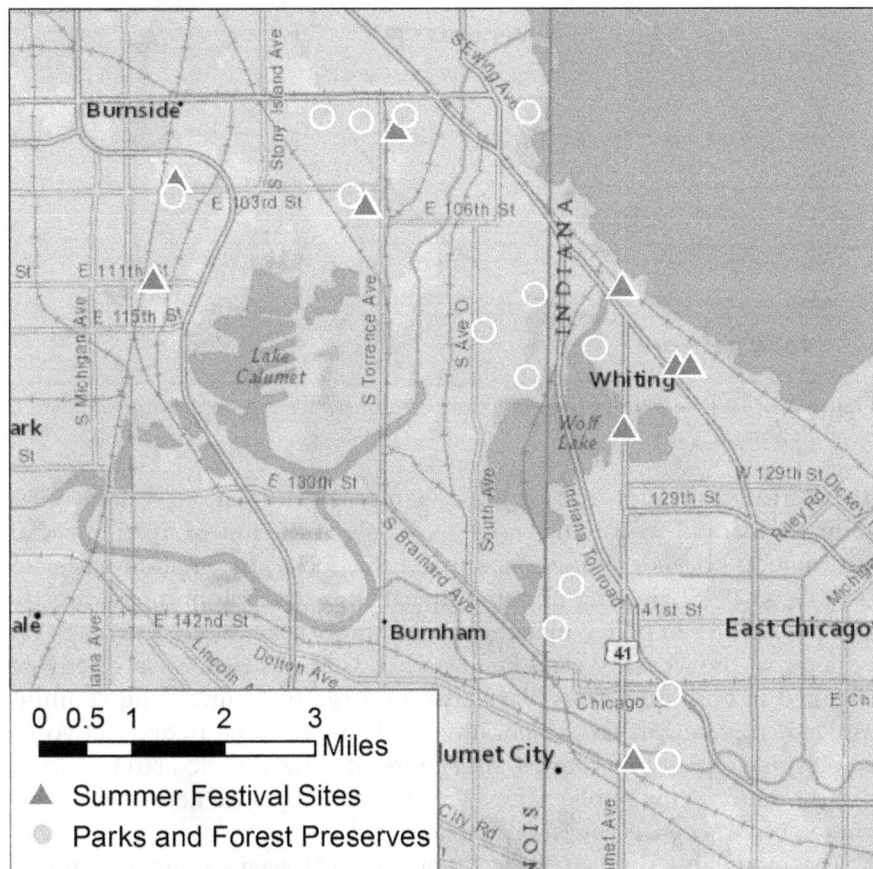

Figure 2.2. This interactive asset map shows the relationship of neighborhood festivals to green space.

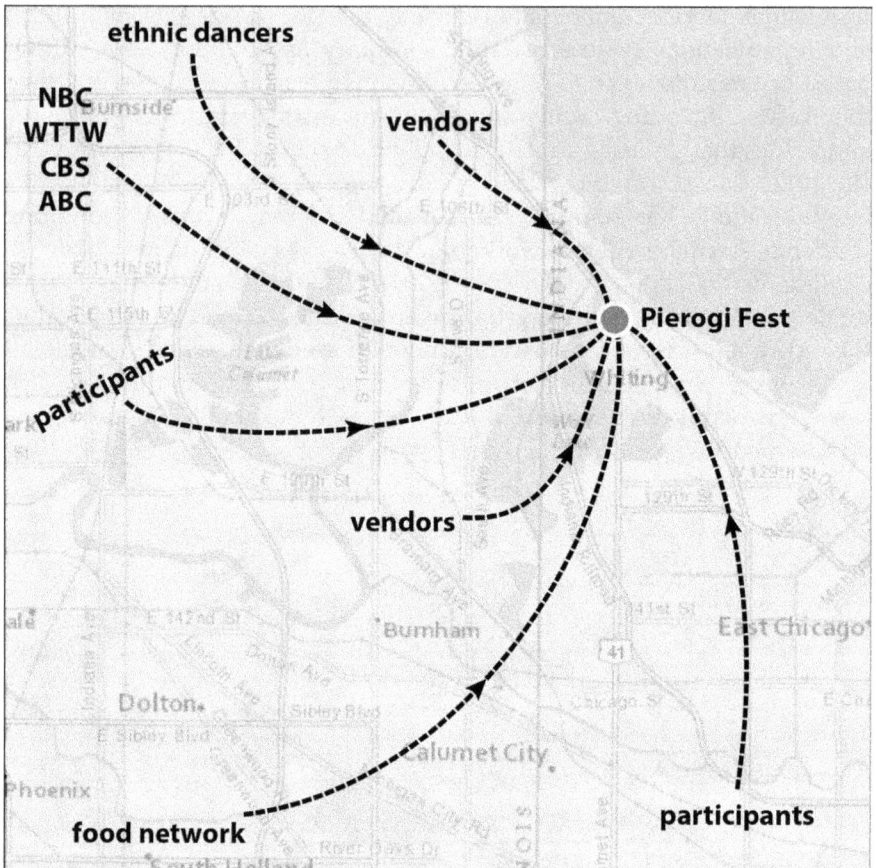

Figure 2.3. This version of the asset map demonstrates regional connections to a popular annual festival.

maps created through use of the geographic information system (GIS) software that was becoming more accessible at the time. Layering social information on geographic maps made the social information easier to read (Scott 1998), helping us communicate our research findings directly and powerfully to policy makers and community activists. The maps revealed that the working-class neighborhoods of this region were actively engaged in both quotidian place-creation (e.g., by maintaining community and private gardens, celebrating heritage, or constructing networks across geographic boundaries) and more organized civic activism (e.g., protest marches for public safety, environmental justice activism, or formation of local conservation organizations).

The maps also showed the relationships between different forms of activism and organization, pinpointing nodes or clusters in the Calumet landscape where stewardship strategies could effectively take root. In other words, the asset maps laid a foundation for an alternative approach to community engagement. Subsequently, the City of Chicago Department of Environment, particularly the Deputy Commissioner, a longtime environmental activist, became a major user of the maps, using them to advocate for more participatory land-use planning processes and execution of environmental remediation work in neighborhoods with strong activist presence.

Integrating ethnographic data into geographic representation also became a critical strategy for environmental conservation efforts in Peru and Bolivia. We understood that the strategy of using asset mapping to reverse portrayals of the urban poor could also work for marginalized forest dwellers—people long considered "backward" and in need of "development." Even environmental conservation organizations perceived forest dwellers as contributors to deforestation and environmental degradation and thus part of the "problem," even though long-term anthropological research in Amazonian societies[5] demonstrated that forest dwellers had long managed their use of natural resources without degrading these fragile habitats. Local people struggled to retain local ecological knowledge and distinct cultural practices that continued to shape livelihood strategies.

We worked with nongovernmental organizations in both countries to conduct asset mapping in communities adjacent to protected areas of high biological value.[6] We trained community-selected facilitators to collect information in their home communities about natural resource use, social organization, and cultural practices (Del Campo and Wali 2007). The information was entered into a GIS-linked database that generated the asset maps. Bolivian municipal authorities used the asset maps to petition for secure land title for the communities, and the maps also furthered land-use planning processes based on community-identified concerns. In Peru, the maps were incorporated into the Park Management Plan and also used for community land-use planning. In fact, the Peruvian NGO has done the asset mapping about every two years, each time expanding the number of communities involved (eighty-nine communities participated in the 2008 mapping, more than ninety communities participated in 2012). Information from the asset maps has also been incorporated into community "quality of life" plans designed to enable participating communities to set priorities for improving subsistence-based livelihoods.

In sum, asset maps integrating cultural information with natural resource use or environmental knowledge and perceptions, whether in urban or non-urban contexts, translate research into action in directly visible ways. The strength of the approach relies on local people's participation

76 | ALAKA WALI AND MADELEINE TUDOR

in identifying social assets and communicating results in an accessible format.

Websites and Visual Media

A second strategy we relied on to translate research into action was the use of websites and videos. Websites, videos, and other photographic media have become a ubiquitous, almost required feature of many research projects (the National Science Foundation now often requires that research grant proposals discuss how results will be disseminated to broader audiences). Unlike the asset maps, which were most directly useful to actual participants advocating for specific resources, the websites and videos were used to create general public awareness of local perspectives in a vibrant, dynamic format.

We first experimented with a website as a dissemination tool in the Calumet project, hoping to reach area residents and local and external groups interested in environmental and economic revitalization of the region. The site featured various visual and multimedia formats, such as thematically grouped photo slide shows, video segments, and the geographically based asset maps discussed above. We combined these visual methods to capture and communicate the informal and formal activism in the Calumet Region, and to show how local assets, especially intangible ones, are grounded in place and can connect with environmental and economic revitalization strategies.

To construct the website, we used exhibit development strategies of communicating scientific research to broad audiences, such as layering of information, providing multiple media formats, and ease of navigation through the findings. The Web medium was more forgiving than that of the typical 3-D exhibition, which produces content in large-scale graphics and displays objects in stationary cases. We organized the information in the website by themes, such as "place," "geographic asset maps," and "communities in motion." Each theme presented the research findings through the photos and maps. The communities in motion section contains four 3- to 4-minute videos linked to a map. Each video expounds on a specific aspect of community activism, showcasing the various ways of defining activism itself. As the website's visitors click through the different sections or watch the videos, the overriding message is that the people of the region work constantly to improve their homeplace and quality of life, and that this work is organized through the construction of informal and formal social relationships.

Since then we have created websites[7] for all participatory research projects to present the research in an appealing format with photographs

Figure 2.4. This photograph is part of a slideshow that depicts how residents transform space through public art and music. Photo copyright 2002, Hannah Anderson Graver, The Field Museum.

and minimal text. In that sense, they can be integrated into social action because they democratize learning. However, we have not managed to transform any of them into more direct action tools. We have discovered that effective use of websites requires a concerted strategy of training partners to use the information they contain. Increasingly, we have used the Web to create interactive "toolkits" that community partners can download and incorporate into community education curricula or into their action strategies (see http://archive.fieldmuseum.org/research_collections/ccuc/ccuc_sites/newallies/).

More recently, our team of anthropologists worked between 2009 and 2011 with the City of Chicago Department of Environment, conducting participatory action research in diverse neighborhoods to find out how to more effectively engage residents in reducing the carbon footprint and mitigating harmful effects of climate change (Hirsch et al. 2011). Initially, we placed research reports on websites. Then we transformed these reports into recommendations for action strategies that people can access through a Web-based "toolkit" created in partnership with community organizations that participated in the climate change research. The toolkit (http://climatechicago.fieldmuseum.org/) contains guides, videos, and other forms of interactive media showcasing local efforts to address climate change and enhance quality of life. Besides using the Web as a place to access the tools, we have set up working pages and photo sites to facilitate partners' participation in development of the tools.

Community Exhibits

Whether and how to engage communities in the creation of exhibitions that communicate the complexity of scientific content accessibly, engagingly, and effectively (Karp and Levine 1991; Weil 1999) are questions spurring ongoing debate among and between scholars and museum professionals. Much discussion about transforming museums into engaged public education institutions has concerned what happens in the physical space of the institution and the degree to which—and ways in which—exhibitions should be made more representative and inclusive of the communities whose voices and experiences they depict (Boyd 1999). Although museum exhibition strategies have changed significantly in response to critique, exhibitions remain an arguably limited form of engagement for anthropologists interested in public interest work.

Exhibitions, no matter how cutting-edge, polyvocalic, or decentered, are limited vehicles for change because of the way they "deliver" information, their location and audience's expectations, and the museum's economic and political dynamics. As multimedia experiences that must both entertain and inform, exhibitions can provoke critical thought but cannot satisfy the need to grasp the complexity of social phenomena. Furthermore, natural history museums have mainly marketed themselves as "family-friendly," child-oriented places—unlike art museums, which continue to be seen as "temples" of learning and civic appreciation of timeless masterpieces. Therefore audiences in natural history museums expect to cruise through exhibits, pausing briefly to wonder at an amazing artifact or allow children to push buttons. According to audience research, the average museum visitor spends between three and five minutes at any given exhibit. Lastly, museum administrators have responded to recent economic downturns and political controversies by forgoing more innovative or provocative exhibits in favor of safer, "blockbuster" displays they think will expand attendance.

To overcome these constraints and unleash exhibitions' potential as vehicles of communication for action, we have experimented with creating exhibitions on community issues in community spaces together with community partners. Drawing on our previous work to engage communities in the exhibit development process and expertise in exhibition development and production, we developed a community-based exhibits program as part of a larger project to build cohesion across social and economic boundaries in the new mixed-income community of Lake Park Crescent, built in Chicago's historic Bronzeville community. In the 1950s and 1960s, this neighborhood came to be known for its density of public housing. Culturally it rivaled the Harlem Renaissance, boasting a rich history of arts as community activism. Local artists, for example, started the community-based mural movement with the "Wall of Respect" mural created in 1967, featuring African-American heroes.

Lake Park Crescent (LPC) was part of a large-scale effort by the city administration to remedy the deleterious effects of massive neglect and abandonment of public housing complexes. The Chicago Housing Authority was nationally known for the scale of its problems, including the scandalous conditions of life in the complexes (Cabrini Green and Robert Taylor Homes were subjects of scathing journalistic accounts such as Alex Kotlowitz's *There Are No Children Here*). In 1999, the city initiated a Plan for Transformation to tear down massive public housing projects and replace them with mixed-income developments. Rather than acknowledge the abandonment of these complexes and their residents, the plan's creators offered their replacement as a better alternative for the urban poor, arguing that mixed-income housing would prevent their isolation and offer them a better chance at "self-improvement." The plan had the support of most major Chicago-based foundations that contributed financing for ancillary programs, including post-occupancy social programs for the new developments (Vale and Graves 2010).

Lake Park Crescent, built on the site of a torn-down public housing project, consisted of a high-rise building and six flats. The plan called for initial occupancy of rental units and eventual construction of condominiums and row houses. LPC's private developer invited us to collaborate in post-occupancy efforts. Despite misgivings about the overall plan, we offered to participate by using ethnographic research on residents' assets to guide creative programming and social services (Nichols and Wali 2009). The project was an opportunity to empower residents to form social bonds and create community despite negative stereotypes. We functioned as part of a collaboration that also included the residential property developer and partnering social service agencies. Though arts and other creative programs provided a foundation for building community,[8] we soon discovered that more was needed to make residents' assets highly visible, both within the LPC development and between LPC and the surrounding community. We developed the exhibits program as a strategy to bring residents together and expand residents' social networks into the adjacent community.

The program was twofold: the first phase made residents' assets visible to themselves and each other; the second showcased residents' perceptions and connections to the surrounding neighborhood. These efforts demonstrated the wealth of resources that LPC residents brought to the area. We based the model on previous exhibition projects with significant community engagement components, in which participants contributed to and critiqued the content themes, messages, and examples throughout the exhibit's development. More influential was a partnership with a community-based organization that wanted to develop an exhibit, based on the *Living Together* exhibit (see above), that showcased shoes as a metaphor for lived experience. The organization wanted the exhibit to bolster its presence within and beyond its service area, with the ultimate goal of increasing its resource base. Our role was to advise the organization about collecting oral histories—and shoes—from local residents and develop them into an exhibition format.

These experiences were invaluable for us and educational for the partners, who learned the ins and outs of exhibition development, including community engagement and communication strategies. However, they were not without challenges. We learned the importance of providing parameters to guide participants in contributing to the interpretive process, which involves thinking about subject matter abstractly and visually, as well as from different perspectives. The exhibits program combined participatory visual methods with exhibition techniques and presentation formats that reframe and validate less-visible subject matter, such as social assets, in ways that educate and entertain. We used the techniques of participatory photography and "photovoice" or "photo elicitation" to engage residents in creating exhibit content by examining photos relevant to particular themes guided by research findings, interpreting the photos' content and context, and choosing which ones to display. Throughout the program, the exhibit creation process served as a medium through which residents could share their perspectives and reflections on the research findings. We began the participatory exhibit program with a meeting of residents, where we presented some of the emerging research findings on LPC residents' social assets and networks. Then we introduced the idea of creating a small and simple yet impactful exhibit of photographs with interpretive text and quotes. We gave an overview of the exhibit development process and its value in framing and translating complex content. This discussion gave us an opening to introduce residents to the idea of being "curators" of their community.

With the help of the newly formed LPC Residents Arts Council, we put out an open call for photo submissions and then selected three depicting how arts programs, cooking classes, and a residents' walking club were creating common ground for building networks across social divides in this new community. We interviewed resident participants in the project

BUILDING NETWORKS
Connecting Residents at Lake Park Crescent

Making connections to this wealth of resources—
neighbor to neighbor—will make this new community blossom!

"You're meeting different people out on the walk and finding out
different things we have in common with each other."

Carolyn Mitchell

Pictured (left to right): Kathy Wilson, Johnnie Gardner,
Carolyn Mitchell, and Gregory Winbush, members of the
Lake Park Crescent Walking Club, make use of the track
at nearby Mandrake Park.

Photograph courtesy of H. Stovall Jr., 2006.

Figure 2.5. Lake Park Crescent exhibit photos represented the value that residents placed on home and community.

and worked with them to craft short label texts and cull poignant quotes that best reflected the research findings. A professional designer came on board to create poster-style panels featuring the photographs, enlarged and framed by their titles, explanatory text, and quotes. The panels were displayed in the lobby of the LPC main building. At the opening of the installation, the ward alderman commented on the photos and the positive image they created of LPC. Residents took pride in seeing their own work prominently displayed and stated that it made LPC a "nice place to live."

The second phase of the exhibit program, titled *Neighborhood Gems: People and Places of North Kenwood/Oakland,* was broader in scope geographically, involved more project participants, and displayed more photographs. The goal of this phase was to connect LPC with the surrounding North Kenwood/Oakland (designated a community area within the larger geography of Bronzeville) by showcasing the people, structures, and social interactions its residents valued. This new set of images presented LPC as part of North Kenwood/Oakland and North Kenwood/Oakland as a changing, vibrant neighborhood.

We modified the structure of this phase by holding an instructional session in basic photography and distributing disposable cameras to interested residents to increase participation in the project. We then led an event where residents critiqued the photos with the photographers. The photo panels were displayed in additional LPC buildings and sites throughout the community, including a high-profile neighborhood art center with a diverse audience, a local Citibank branch, and a neighborhood childcare center.

The exhibit, in its diverse community venues, contributed to the process of "placemaking" for LPC residents. Its physical manifestation of connections to meaningful places in the neighborhood increased residents' comfort with neighborhood institutions and organizations and simulta-

Figure 2.6. An exhibits program participant attends the exhibit's opening at a neighborhood art center. The top image on the left panel is of the recently restored mural *A Time to Unite,* which several residents photographed. Photo copyright 2009, Sarah Sommers, The Field Museum.

neously provided neighborhood residents with a pathway connecting to LPC. At the exhibit opening at the art center, a longtime community activist (who later became interim ward alderman) commented on the project's importance to integrating LPC and its residents into the neighborhood. She also suggested that the property developer or the Chicago Housing Authority hire Clinton Nichols, our ethnographer and project manager, to continue the work (unfortunately, funding never materialized).

The photo exhibits successfully raised the profile of LPC as a great place to live and lessened the stigma attached to Chicago Housing Authority residents by facilitating the process of looking beyond stereotypes. The exhibit projects resulted in positive image-building for the residents, which in turn encouraged higher-income residents to stay on there, forestalling instability on the rental market. Toward the end of the project, the Resident Art Council decided to stay together and continue programming. These same members, along with others, also began participating in community organizations such as the school council and community policing efforts. The exhibits remain as permanent installations at LPC. Clearly, community-based exhibits can usefully catalyze certain types of action for social change. The act of creating an exhibit, the physical installation, and the opportunity it affords for ongoing dialogue can empower activists to coalesce across social boundaries.

Conclusion

These experiments with PAR in the museum taught us that public visual culture is powerfully communicative and can facilitate crossing the line from research to action. By drawing on its idioms, we have deepened both the participatory processes in our research and public programs, and the empowerment needed to take action.

As shown here, different visual methods integrated into participatory action research can be equally effective. The impact of the medium does not depend on the placement of the media strategy—that is, on whether it is part of the actual research process or whether it communicates the research findings. Each medium (maps, websites, videos, exhibits) has its own advantages and shortcomings, so the choice of medium (or combination of media) should be determined by the type of action it aims to influence. Museum-based techniques make combinations of media and interplay between text and visual elements more effective in integrating research into action.

The efforts we describe here also contain useful insights for PAR work overall. The particular kind of give-and-take that PAR requires between researcher and collaborator can be mutually rewarding *and* mutually frustrating. Research findings emerging from joint efforts give both researchers and community partners a sense of deep satisfaction and ownership of the insights into everyone's lifeways. Most anthropologists treasure field experience for the personal rewards that friendships and relationships bring, and these relationships are even deeper when the research is collaborative and everyone understands its benefits. Nevertheless, the process is frustrating because there is no linear connection between research and direct action. Even when research is effectively communicated or translated, action based on its results may be limited or require a long time to bear fruit.

In the Calumet project, for example, even though both community organizations and the environment commissioner used the website, actual social change along the lines the research envisioned has been slow and uneven. Over the past decade, community organizations we identified and collaborated with in the original project have taken different paths to contest public and private efforts that they viewed as injurious to their constituents. Although the Department of Environment embraced the study's results, other city agencies did not, and certain economic development plans continued to pose challenges to local well-being.

In the Peruvian case, asset mapping and subsequent collaborative efforts ultimately increased the participating communities' resources, helping them establish the sustainability of their natural resource use and ward off pressures from extractive industries (oil companies and illegal loggers). Currently, we are continuing our collaborative, asset-based community engagement with conservation efforts in Peru.

All this raises questions about how to measure the impact of PAR, and in what time frame. We now know that project time frames (e.g., three-year funding cycles) are inadequate to the work of social change. For more than a decade we have stayed involved with partners in the Calumet Region, and we are currently collaborating with local organizations to explore a National Heritage Area designation for the area. We have also found new ways to incorporate museum-based multimedia strategies and improve collaborative processes. These efforts reflect our determination to cross the line from research to action by working side by side with partners over the long term to effect social change.

Alaka Wali is Curator of North American Anthropology at The Field Museum. She received her BA at Harvard University and her PhD at Columbia University. She has conducted research in both the neotropics (Central and South America) and in the urban United States (New York and Chicago). In the years that she has been at The Field Museum, she has expanded the efforts of the Museum to build partnerships with community-based organizations to promote greater understanding of cultural and social assets, improve quality of life, and develop more effective stewardship of natural resources. She is the author of two books and more than forty articles and monographs, and has received numerous grants for research.

Madeleine Tudor has worked at The Field Museum since 1997. Her projects have ranged from creating nontraditional educational tools that help urban communities build on cultural and ecological assets, to ethnographic research into the materiality of heritage and place-making, to engaging diverse communities around common concerns. A consistent part of her work involves translating anthropological concepts and research results into a variety of formats, including video, Web, print, and exhibitions, for a range of audiences. She has worked on a number of temporary exhibitions at The Field Museum and at local organizations, including *Urban Gardens: Growing Chicago's Communities* and *Design Innovations in Manufactured Housing*. Current projects include developing a new collection of contemporary urban material culture and building connections between people and place in the Calumet Region of Illinois and Indiana. Ms. Tudor's educational background is in history and anthropology.

Notes

1. The Center for Cultural Understanding and Change (CCUC) was founded in 1995 as part of The Field Museum's efforts to more effectively engage its audiences and constituents by taking up contemporary concerns related to cultural diversity. From 1995 to 2004, CCUC acted as an independent unit within the museum's academic division, relying almost completely on grants to conduct applied research. In 2004, during a major reorganization of the academic divisions, CCUC joined the Environmental and Conservation Programs (dedicated to promoting direct action for environmental conservation) to create the Environment, Culture and Conservation Division (ECCo). Between 2004 and 2010, the two units strived for synergy, finally deciding in 2010 to merge and continue working as a single unit. In 2013, The Field Museum created the Science Action Center for Conservation & Culture to further ECCo's work to translate scientific understandings into on-the-ground results. The Science Action Center's current staff numbers about twenty-five ecologists, anthropologists, and educators. Its work focuses on the Andes/Amazon region and the Chicago metropolitan region (www.fieldmuseum.org/conservation).
2. We did not feel able to adequately train community partners in research techniques, for if research expertise and credentialing are taken seriously, then how can they be imparted in a relatively short period of time? Rather, we used students to conduct the actual research.
3. Long before Kretzmann and McKnight, however, anthropologists such as Carol Stack (1997 [1974]), BettylouValentine (1978), and others had observed that urban poor women were resourceful in developing social strategies to counter the structures of

racism and impoverishment they faced. These anthropologists argued against punitive welfare policies that purported to change behavior (see also van Willigen 2005 for a more historical perspective).

4. Based on findings of a 1994 biological survey by the Illinois Department of Natural Resources, restoration and stewardship of the Calumet Region was identified as a high priority by the Chicago Wilderness Coalition, an organization devoted to conservation efforts concerning biologically diverse habitats throughout the Chicago metropolitan ecosystem, which extends from southern Wisconsin to northern Indiana. Ironically, the Calumet Region is the heart of Chicago's manufacturing/steel industry, and many of its wilderness sites border defunct steel plants and other industrial structures.

5. These include indigenous peoples and other subsistence-oriented groups like rubber tappers, fisher peoples, and small-scale farmers who have long lived in the Amazon's varied habitats.

6. The Field Museum began the effort to conserve large tracts of Amazonian landscapes in 1994 as an experiment by a small group of ecologists. The group—called Environmental and Conservation Programs—was affiliated with the Rapid Assessment Program of Conservation International. It conducted rapid inventories of selected areas throughout the Amazon and reported its recommendations for setting aside protected areas. In 1999, frustrated with Conservation International's methods, the group initiated the Rapid Biological Inventories program (http://fm2.fieldmuseum.org/rbi). In 2001, I was invited to join the group and develop a community-based social component for the inventories. In two instances—one in the Pando Region of Northern Bolivia and the other in the buffer zone of the Cordillera Azul National Park in Northern Peru—we undertook close collaboration with local partners to develop community-based conservation efforts (for a full account, see Wali 2006).

7. The websites are accessible via http://fieldmuseum.org/science/research/area/science-action/communities.

8. We based our use of arts programs to bring residents together across income boundaries on research conducted on the social impact of making art in informal settings (Wali et al. 2002).

References

Alcorn, Janis B. 2000. "Border Rules and Governance: Mapping to Catalyze Changes in Policy and Management." *Gatekeeper Series*, no. 91. London: International Institute for Environment and Development.

Ardener, Shirley, ed. 1993. *Women and Space: Ground Rules and Social Maps*. Oxford: Berg.

Birdwell-Pheasant, Donna, and Denise Lawrence-Zuniga. 1999. *House Life: Space, Place, and Family in Europe*. Oxford: Berg.

Bourdieu, Pierre. 2003 [1971]. "The Berber House." In *The Anthropology of Space and Place: Locating Culture*, eds. Setha M. Low and Denise Lawrence-Zuniga. Malden, MA: Blackwell Publishing.

Boyd, Willard L. 1999. "Museums as Centers of Controversy." *Daedalus: Journal of the American Academy of Arts and Sciences* 128, no. 3: 185–228.

Chapin, Mac. 2001. *Indigenous Landscapes: A Study in Ethnocartography*. Washington, DC: Center for the Support of Native Lands.

Collier, John Jr., and Malcolm Collier. 1986. *Visual Anthropology*. Albuquerque: University of New Mexico Press.

Conquergood, Dwight. 1992. "Life in Big Red: Struggles and Accommodations in a Chicago Polyethnic Tenement." In *Structuring Diversity: Ethnographic Perspectives on the New Immigration*, ed. Louise Lamphere. Chicago: University of Chicago Press.

Del Campo, Hillary, and Alaka Wali. 2007. "Applying Asset Mapping to Protected Area Planning and Management in the Cordillera Azul National Park, Peru." *Ethnobotany Research and Applications* 5, no. 1: 25–36

Field Museum Website. 2011. "Journey Through Calumet: Communities in Motion in Southeast Chicago and Northeast Indiana" (16 August). http://archive.fieldmuseum.org/calu met/.

Freire, Paulo. 1989. *Pedagogy of the Oppressed.* New York: Continuum.

Haas, Jonathon. 1996. "Power, Objects, and a Voice for Anthropology." *Current Anthropology* 37: 1–22.

Haraway, Donna. 1989. *Primate Visions: Gender, Race and Nature in the World of Modern Science.* New York: Routledge.

Harper, Krista. 2009. "Using Photovoice to Investigate Environment and Health in a Hungarian Romani (Gypsy) Community." *Practicing Anthropology* 31, no. 4: 10–14.

Hirsch, Jennifer, Sarah Van Deusen Phillips, Edward Labenski, Christine Dunford, and Troy Peters. 2011. "Linking Climate Action to Local Knowledge and Practice: A Case Study of Diverse Chicago Neighborhoods." In *Environmental Anthropology*, ed. Helen Kopina and Eleanor E. Shoreman. New York: Berghahn Books.

Hyland, Stanley E., and Linda A. Bennett. 2005. "Introduction." In *Community Building in the Twenty-First Century*, ed. Stanley E. Hyland. Santa Fe, NM: School of American Research Press.

Karp, Ivan, and Steven D. Levine. 1991. "Museums and Multiculturalism." In *Exhibiting Cultures: The Poetics and Politics of Museum Display*, ed. Ivan Karp and Steven D. Levine. Washington, DC: Smithsonian Institution Press.

Kotlowitz, Alex. 1992. *There Are No Children Here.* New York: Anchor Books.

Kretzmann, John P., and John L. McKnight. 1993. *Building Communities from the Inside Out: A Path Toward Finding and Mobilizing a Community's Assets.* Chicago: ACTA Publications.

Lassiter, Luke Eric, ed. 2008. "Introduction." *Collaborative Anthropologies* 1: vii–xii.. Lincoln: University of Nebraska Press.

Low, Setha M. 2000. *On the Plaza: The Politics of Public Space and Culture.* Austin: University of Texas Press.

Low, Setha M. and Denise Lawrence-Zuniga, eds. 2003. *The Anthropology of Space and Place: Locating Culture.* Malden, MA: Blackwell.

Mead, Margaret. 2003 [1975]. "Visual Anthropology in a Discipline of Words." In *Principles of Visual Anthropology*, ed. Paul Hockings, 3rd ed. The Hague: Mouton de Gruyter.

Morawski, Jill. 2001. "Feminist Research Methods: Bringing Culture to Science." In *From Subjects to Subjectivities: A Handbook of Interpretive and Participatory Methods*, ed. Deborah L. Tolman and Mary Brydon-Miller. New York: New York University Press.

Morgen, Sandra, ed. 1990. *Gender and Anthropology: Critical Reviews for Research and Teaching.* Washington, DC: AAA.

Nichols, Clinton, and Alaka Wali. 2009. "Building Community Cohesion at Lake Park Crescent: Mixed-Income Housing Development." Report to The John D. and Catherine T. MacArthur Foundation.

Pellow, Deborah. 1996. *Setting Boundaries: The Anthropology of Spatial and Social Organization.* Westport, CT: Bergin and Garvey.

Pink, Sarah. 2003. "Interdisciplinary Agendas in Visual Research: Re-situating Visual Anthropology." *Visual Studies* 18, no. 2: 179–192.

———, ed. 2007. *Visual Interventions: Applied Visual Anthropology.* New York: Berghahn Books.

Rapoport, Amos. 1969. *House Form and Culture*. Englewood Cliffs, NJ: Prentice-Hall.

Rapp, Rayna, and Ellen Ross. 1981. "Sex and Society: A Research Note from Anthropology and Social History." *Comparative Studies in Society and History* 23, no. 1: 51–72.

Schensul, Jean J., Marlene J. Berg, and Ken M. Williamson. 2008. "Challenging Hegemonies: Advancing Collaboration in Community-Based Participatory Action Research." In *Collaborative Anthropologies*, vol. 1, ed. Luke Eric Lassiter. Lincoln: University of Nebraska Press.

Schrijvers, Joke. 2001. "Participation and Power: A Transformative Feminist Research Perspective." In *Power and Participatory Development: Theory and Practice*, ed. Nici Nelson and Susan Wright. London: ITDG.

Scott, James. 1998. *Seeing Like a State: How Certain Schemes to Improve the Human Condition Have Failed*. Binghamton, NY: Vail-Ballou Press.

Spain, Daphne. 1992. *Gendered Spaces*. Chapel Hill: University of North Carolina Press.

Stack, Carol B. 1997 [1974]. *All Our Kin: Strategies for Survival in a Black Community*. New York: Basic Books.

Stocking, George W., ed. 1985. *Objects and Others: Essays on Museums and Material Culture*. Madison: University of Wisconsin Press.

Tax, Sol. 1958. "The Fox Project." *Human Organization* 17, no. 1: 17–19.

Tolman, Deborah L., and Mary Brydon-Miller. 2001. "Interpretive and Participatory Research Methods: Moving toward Subjectivities." In *From Subjects to Subjectivities: A Handbook of Interpretive and Participatory Methods*, ed. Deborah L. Tolman and Mary Brydon-Miller. New York: New York University Press.

Vale, Lawrence J., and Erin Graves. 2010. *The Chicago Housing Authority's Plan for Transformation: What Does the Research Show So Far?* Cambridge, MA: Massachusetts Institute of Technology, Department of Urban Studies and Planning.

Valentine, Bettylou. 1978. *Hustling and Other Hard Work: Life Styles in the Ghetto*. New York: Macmillan Free Press.

van Willigen, John. 2005. "Community Assets and the Community-Building Process: Historic Perspectives." In *Community Building in the Twenty-First Century*, ed. Stanley E. Hyland. Santa Fe, NM: School of American Research Press.

Wali, Alaka, ed. 2006. *Collaborative Research: A Practical Introduction to Participatory Action Research (PAR) for Communities and Scholars*. Booklet produced by The Field Museum Center for Cultural Understanding and Change.

Wali, Alaka, Rebecca Severson, and Mario Longoni. 2002. "Informal Arts: Finding Cohesion, Capacity, and other Cultural Benefits in Unexpected Places." Report to the Center for Art Policy at Columbia College. http://archive.fieldmuseum.org/research_collections/ccuc/ccuc_sites/Arts_Study/pdf/Informal_Arts_Full_Report.pdf.

Wang, Carolyn. 1999. "Photovoice: A Participatory Action Research Strategy Applied to Women's Health." *Journal of Women's Health* 8, no. 2: 185–192.

Weil, Stephen E. 1999. "From Being *about* Something to Being *for* Somebody: The Ongoing Transformation of the American Museum." *Daedalus: Journal of the American Academy of Arts and Sciences* 128, no. 3: 229–258.

Wesch, Michael. 2009. "Mediated Culture / Mediated Education." Keynote address at the Association for Learning Technology Conference, Manchester, England, 8 September. Transcript available online in ALT Open Access Repository, http://repository.alt.ac.uk/656/.

Wolowic, Jennifer. 2008. "See What Happens When You Give Us the Camera." Paper presented at the annual meeting of the Society for Applied Anthropology, Memphis, Tennessee, 25–29 March.

Woodward, David, and Malcom Lewis. 1998. *History of Cartography*, vol. 3. Chicago: University of Chicago Press.

Chapter 3

MONITORING THE COMMONS
Giving "Voice" to Environmental Justice in Pacoima

⸻ ◈◈◈ ⸻

Carl A. Maida

This chapter explores how practitioners of professional and lay knowledge worked together to improve urban quality of life in Pacoima, California, a working-class Latino community in Los Angeles. The focus is on building a community of practice on behalf of environmental justice concerns, and on demonstrating how professionals and residents moved toward common ground on environmental health issues, including toxic exposures. The "community of practice" is an organizational form that complements the current *knowledge economy*—namely, the "production and services based upon knowledge-intensive activities" (Powell and Snellman 2004: 199)—which since the late twentieth century has accelerated with advances in information production and dissemination. Promising to "radically galvanize knowledge sharing, learning, and change" (Wenger and Snyder 2000: 139), a community of practice provides a framework for understanding social learning in complex organizations, specifically the notion of "knowing." For novices and experts alike, knowing within a community of practice is based upon socially defined *competence*, or the ability to act and be viewed as a competent member, and ongoing *experience* within the context of the community. According to Wenger (2000), "belonging" to a particular community is based upon engagement, imagination, and alignment within a social learning system that supports and sustains members and the community itself. Communities of practice provide the framework for "social learning," because members share a sense of joint enterprise indicative of the level of learning energy within the community; interact on the

---

Notes for this chapter begin on page 114.

basis of mutuality, which points to the depth of social capital generated by mutual engagement; and share a repertoire of resources, indicating the degree of participants' self-awareness. This framework—of knowing, belonging, and social learning through more informal styles characteristic of communities of practice—provides members with the skills to meaningfully engage in knowledge production, exchange, and transformation in complex organizations.

"Citizen science" is an approach that supports the expansion of communities of practice by bridging researchers and the lay public, across diverse populations and subpopulations (Bonney et al. 2009). Regarding the production or transfer of critical knowledge, citizen science is decidedly personal and interpersonal in style, enacted from the "bottom up" and most often at the local level. As conceptualized by Irwin (2001) and Bäckstrand (2003), it involves science initiated and carried out by citizens not trained to be professional scientists. Early lay efforts to monitor common-pool resources and common property were carried out by users who depended upon a given resource for long-term sustenance. These efforts focused on meeting local and regional challenges of environmental degradation and resource depletion that threatened watersheds, fisheries, and pasturage, with a goal of building consensus among users of a particular resource "so that joint benefits will outweigh current costs" (Ostrom et al. 1999: 281). Initial interest in citizen science concerned ecological and environmental health sciences, as average citizens became more aware of the impact of science and technology on their personal lives and their community's quality of life (Brossard et al. 2005). Biomonitoring, or body-burden research, emerged in response to growing public demand for information about humans' exposure to chemicals in the environment (Morello-Frosch et al. 2005). Since then, community residents collaborating with environmental health scientists in universities and community-based organizations have monitored workplace toxins, air and water pollution, household lead, flame retardants in consumer products, and environmental chemicals in breast milk (Little 2009; Morello-Frosch et al. 2009). On-the-ground data collection techniques, such as "ground-truthing," use residents' knowledge to identify pollution sources located in their communities (Heaney et al. 2007) and verify compiled data derived from standardized risk-screening environmental indicators (Ash and Fetter, 2002; Bouwes et al. 2001).

In the more engaged communities worldwide, civic communities of practice have emerged to address quality of life issues, such as health care, housing, and the environment (Snyder and Wenger 2010). They typically form around access to collective goods, such as institutionalized public culture (health care, education, social services, housing, transportation, parks, and gardens), which are common resources whose benefits accrue to the society at large (Smith-Nonini and Bell 2011). Civic networks and nonprofit organizations, based on voluntarism, social trust, and reciprocity, are forms of social capital that facilitate cooperation and communication in local-level communities of practice. These social formations were clearly needed to resolve the myriad dilemmas of collective action on behalf of common resource mobilization in relationship to state and corporate interests. Within them, experts and laypersons work together to both define issues and take action to promote equity and greater access to common resources, or public goods, despite vast disparities in knowledge and perspectives shaped by divergent occupational techniques, habits of mind, and world images. The chapter uses an extended case study of community-based participatory research, specifically reflecting on my partnership with various community and academic stakeholders to design and evaluate a research project on understanding and reducing toxic risks within an environmental justice framework.

The Community

Pacoima is a low-income, working-class community located in the northeast San Fernando Valley in the City of Los Angeles. It covers six square miles at the base of the San Gabriel Mountains and is encircled by three major freeways: Interstate 5, Highway 118, and the 405 Freeway. Of the 101,000 residents, 83 percent are Latino and 8 percent African American; 34 percent of the population has not completed a ninth-grade education; 19 percent of the population lives below the federal poverty level. Of the 22,000 housing units, 80 percent are single-family homes. Approximately 20 percent of inhabitants live in garages or rent rooms in single-family homes; many live in overcrowded conditions.

Pacoima is subject to emissions from numerous potentially toxic sources. Located just north of approximately thirty landfills (operating and non-operating), surrounded by three major freeways and diesel truck traffic, bisected by railroad tracks, and adjacent to a small airport with more than 300 flights per day, the community has long suffered from environmental neglect, which is likely to blame for the area's many sources of pollution and high rate of environmental health risks. In addition to the freeways, airport, and railway line, more than 300 industrial sites (large and small point sources) have left contaminants behind or continue to pollute the air, soil, and water. Observed conditions at 185 of these sites are likely problematic in terms of emission levels, improper storage of chemicals, contaminated runoff, and hazardous working conditions. In several areas in the community, residences are adjacent to industrial facilities.

Pacoima is home to five U.S. Environmental Protection Agency (US EPA) CERCLA/Superfund (toxic release) sites, two of which were being remediated at the time of the study. Community concerns focus on the cumulative impacts of contaminants such as lead in paint and in the soil; emissions from freeways, commuter planes, diesel trucks and machinery, and older "gross emitting" cars; landfills; and widespread use of toxic chemicals throughout the community.

The CARE Project

The work described in this chapter was supported by a grant from the US EPA through the CARE (Community Action for a Renewed Environment) program (Hansell et al. 2009; US EPA 2011). The CARE program is one of many EPA right-to-know initiatives enacted since Congress passed the Emergency Planning and Community Right-to-Know Act in 1986 after the industrial accidents at Union Carbide plants in Bhopal, India, and Institute, West Virginia. The CARE I project in Pacoima arose when the local environmental justice organization Pacoima Beautiful and its partners sought to identify sources of toxic substances and their health risks in the community and prioritize remediation of the sources (Maida 2011). Historically, few research projects were conducted in Pacoima, and even fewer involved environmental conditions. This changed as partnerships formed and sources such as US EPA made resources and expertise available to the community. Founded by locals in the mid 1990s to help residents clean up the town, Pacoima Beautiful grew to promote environmental education, leadership development, and advocacy skills for residents, eventually becoming the project's lead agency (Maida 2009). The organization partners with community-based organizations, residents and local high school students, university faculty, elected officials, businesses, and regulatory agencies to address environmental justice and environmental health issues in Pacoima and the northeast San Fernando Valley. These partners were the stakeholder groups for the CARE I project.

The CARE I grant, funded from 2005 to 2007, provided an opportunity to organize ideas, concepts, reports, and community knowledge into a cohesive set of risks that could be prioritized for future action.[1] The CARE I project ranked and prioritized broad-based community concerns about numerous toxic and other health risks. The risks were ranked as follows, in descending order of priority: diesel emissions, the airport, small point sources, the highway and major arterials, super emitters, lead, and secondhand smoke. Having successfully built a community of practice and produced the risk assessment, the partners received funding for a CARE II project, which specifically addressed two of these priorities: small point sources in Branford-Montague, an area with a concentration of industrial and commercial operations; and diesel emissions from trucks throughout the community.[2] The CARE II project, conducted from 2007 through 2009 at the onset of the "Great Recession" that affected the entire world economy, relied on a team-based approach that divided partners into research, business, education, diesel, and evaluation teams. Each team met regularly to discuss objectives, baseline data collection or educational material design strategies, timelines, and progress toward goals and objectives. Each team provided updates on their activities at a monthly partners meeting. The final report described the teams' progress on their core tasks, including data collection, methodology, analysis of findings, and lessons learned.

As a medical anthropologist, I was a member of a cross-disciplinary team of university-based researchers who collaborated for more than a decade to design a participatory evaluation approach to environmental justice research by combining the conventions of participant observation with the ethos of community-based participatory research (Minkler and Wallerstein 2008; Whitmore 1998). Guided by these principles, the university researchers served as the CARE II project's Evaluation Team, providing a framework for reporting progress; developing reporting guidelines; and providing critical readings of preliminary and final reports, suggestions for revisions, and editorial help to shape each report as a whole. For each team's project, rather than take the lead in summarizing a community-based research team's findings and conclusions, the evaluators always strove to maintain the integrity of each team's unique approach to attaining its own specific objectives and course of action as well as the project goals overall. Equally important was to stress each unique "voice" by explaining the study results and their meaning through a narrative about the research process, implementation, lessons learned, and moving forward.

Pacoima's community-based approach to the reduction of toxic risks — "manufactured risks," as Ulrich Beck (1992) put it—makes it a pertinent case study of resident engagement in both research and advocacy. By examining how a civic community of practice originated around the CARE II project in Pacoima and how well the partners accomplished project objectives as a result, we may gain a better understanding of how formal and informal organizations collaborate to mediate risks in urban locales, where hazards and insecurities of metropolitan life have sustained a turbulent landscape for more than a century (Kirby 1990; Lash et al. 1996).

Conducting Research with Regulatory Agency Stakeholders

At the start of the CARE II project, the Research Team set out to determine which businesses in the study area needed to comply with regulatory agencies' demands. It did so by compiling a baseline list of compliance data from these businesses and then focusing its research efforts on obtaining existing permitting records at nine agencies.[3] In addition, local university students and Pacoima Beautiful staff visited the study area several times to obtain information from owners, managers, and employees, using community-based ground-truthing techniques. The team synthesized the information obtained and entered it into a single database, allowing identification of businesses that had prior violations and had been cited by agencies' staff for various environmental conditions. The tasks of gathering baseline data and entering it into the database helped to inform outreach and education on improving environmental practices aimed at decreasing emission levels in the study area and within the businesses themselves. After conducting the research and cross-checking permits and addresses, the team members focused on 148 businesses in the study area that were not in compliance with at least one, but in some cases, multiple regulatory agencies.[4]

Research Implementation

To address the lack of permits in the study area, the team began to develop partnerships with various regulatory agencies to obtain information and data on the study area and begin discussions on reducing the impact of the environmental conditions. Many of the agencies supported the idea of working together to improve the permitting process and thereby prevent hazardous exposures. Consequently, agency partnerships enabled the team to focus on increasing permit compliance and developing educational materials that would be used to increase environmentally sound practices and facilitate the permitting process. In sum, the team members tracked and monitored permitting practices in the area through coordinated partnership efforts and were able to use their research findings to support the development of both Environmental Best Management Practices (EBMPs) and educational materials to communicate knowledge about environmental hazards to community residents and businesses.

Lessons Learned

Obtaining the information for the baseline was difficult because the agencies' data were sometimes inaccurate. For example, early in the project, university students were given a list of businesses to study. Once in the field, though, the students discovered that the list was outdated—many of the businesses were no longer in operation. Time was spent documenting the businesses currently in the area in another list, which itself was changed within a few months due to obsolete information. In this way the research was an economic index of the community, reflecting changes that clearly affected businesses' growth and formation. For instance, a business may ride out the economic downturn by "leasing" a portion of its place of business to another business to share the cost of rent.

Furthermore, ongoing research throughout the project highlighted outdated baseline data, necessitating revisions to educational material in light of business changes discovered through ground-truthing. For example, at the project's start the list named forty-nine auto dismantlers, but eventually only twenty-seven auto dismantlers remained in operation. The other businesses on the list dealt in auto parts, retail equipment, marble/granite cutting and polishing, chrome plating, and recycling, among other things. Meanwhile, the granite business seemed to expand from four granite shops to forty-seven and down to forty-four at the end of the project. The research showed a shift in businesses' land use in the study area that confirmed a high level of transience; however, this shift represented only the most recent economic transition. In the postwar decades, Pacoima's economy benefited from well-paid industrial jobs at the General Motors assembly plant in Van Nuys, the Lockheed aircraft plant in Burbank, and the Price Pfizer plumbing fixture plant in Pacoima, but plant closures and deindustrialization in the 1980s and early 1990s led to a proliferation of small service-oriented "shops" in recent decades. Such are the conditions of "postmodernity," characterized by shifts in the organization of late capitalism (Harvey 1990), and perhaps a "liquid modernity" (Bauman 2000) indicative of the fluidity of social formations accompanying recent capitalist development.

Moving Forward

At the outset of the project, the team contacted each agency to gain understanding of its permitting process. It found that "enforcement" was agency representatives' most frequent response to real and potential violations. The team found itself challenged to work with these agencies, not just to obtain information but also to discuss alternatives to their current methods. A standing goal was to influence agencies to use enforcement as one of several methods to reduce environmental hazards in environmental justice communities, in combination with a more collaborative approach that focuses on reduction, prevention, and restoration. To this end, an interagency collaborative was formed to work on reducing and preventing environmental contamination and restoring the community through healthy, environmentally focused businesses.

Community Ground-Truthing and Environmental Best Management Practices

The Business Team had the goal of developing and implementing (Environmental Best Management Practices (EBMPs).[5] Research Team members reviewed data from regulatory agencies to formulate a master list of businesses that would be the focus of the Business Team's outreach. University students also assisted in developing the master list. Because initial research showed that some of the data were outdated, ground-truthing was needed to correctly identify the businesses for outreach.[6] The Business Team members visited the area to compare and check the list developed by the Research Team by walking the study area, collecting names, addresses, and types of business through the entire corridor. This updated information helped the team determine the exact number of businesses to target regarding EBMPs. This ground-truthing exercise provided a more reliable picture of the most current and active businesses in the study area. Having done the ground-truthing, the team saw that most of the businesses in the master list were not auto dismantlers. In fact, there were only twenty-seven auto-dismantler shops, and the rest fit into the categories of auto-body paint shops, granite shops, and other types of industrial facilities. Moving forward, team members decided to proceed with the EBMP training for auto dismantlers, meanwhile noting the changes and transience in the business corridor. The revised business database built through ground-truthing was vital to the project because it lent accuracy to the outreach efforts.

During the ground-truthing phase, the Business Team also designed the EBMP curriculum, with reference to training materials from other organizations, such as the *Practical Guide to Environmental Management for Small Businesses* (US EPA 2002), *Best Management Practices for the Auto Salvage Outreach Program* (Vermont Department of Environmental Conservation 2005), and documents printed by Boston's Safe Shops Project (Shoemaker et al. 2007). Team members also visited Sonora Environmental Research Institute (SERI), a nonprofit organization based in Tucson, Arizona. Like Pacoima Beautiful, SERI works to enhance a community's ability to protect its environment by providing residents with the tools they need to advocate for environmental justice.

Research Implementation

Having carried out the research and ground-truthing, the team Business Team members decided to use the State of California Auto Dismantlers Association's *Partners in the Solution Guidance Manual* (SCADA, 2002) as the guide for the development of the EBMPs. They also reevaluated their outreach efforts, concluding that the best method for presenting the information was to visit door to door, distributing to each business a packet of educational materials containing basic, visual examples of how to prevent environmental exposure to risk.[7] To further extend the outreach efforts, the team sent two mailings to the twenty-seven auto dismantlers in the study area to invite shops to the workshops and notify them that the team would soon be visiting them with information. When two months had passed and the business owners had not responded, team members made phone calls. Most of the business owners refused to speak with them, perhaps due to lack of trust or the newness of the relationship.

In the end, four auto-dismantling businesses gave team members the chance to present the EBMPs to their employees. Each business allowed forty-five minutes to go over a printout of a PowerPoint presentation created as part of the EBMP curriculum. These trainings were interactive: employees could ask questions or comment throughout the presentation, as in a focus group. Going through the presentation, team members noticed that the employees demonstrated familiarity with all the proper procedures of the EBMP curriculum and solid knowledge about safety on the job and proper environmental procedures. From the presentation, participants said that they learned: (1) the importance of changing clothes before going home after work to keep from bringing chemicals into their homes and possibly contaminating their loved ones; (2) proper disposal of dirty towels used in the businesses; and (3) that airbags can be recycled and should be properly cleaned if they have been deployed because they contain dangerous chemicals.

Each of the four businesses that participated in the CARE II EBMP training was awarded a certificate of commitment to running a clean and healthy business that acknowledged the enterprise's participation in the workshop and genuine concern to be a better neighbor. In fact, the original four auto-dismantling business owners, by encouraging their peers to open their doors as they had, were key to the preparations for a community-wide auto-dismantler conference.[8] Team members interviewed the four business owners about their concerns and their views on significant challenges to their businesses' success. Each mentioned the frustration of the permitting requirements and miscommunications they had noticed among several regulating agencies. Acting as a cultural broker, Pacoima

Beautiful determined that, given the prominence of this auto-dismantler business concern, it was important to address frustration and miscommunication at the conference. The owners expressed excitement and gratitude at being able to convey a concern and hear it meaningfully addressed by the agencies. For the first time, their concerns were being heeded and action taken to resolve them. These business owners had often felt as though they were seen as "the enemy," and that the community considered them an "eyesore." In this regard, Pacoima Beautiful and the other CARE II stakeholders validated their work as vital to the local economy and helped them become better neighbors by working together with community residents.

The working conference for auto dismantlers, entitled "Auto Dismantlers: More than Just Spare Parts," was hosted by Pacoima Beautiful and SCADA in May 2009. It addressed loopholes in the permitting process for auto dismantlers and covered local and state solutions for handling the issue. Seventeen regulatory and local enforcement agencies statewide participated in the conference. The participating agencies' representatives at the conference agreed to work on forming a multi-agency task force to address the improper issuance of auto-dismantler permits. This partnership eventually led to the introduction and passage of AB 805, which requires the California Department of Motor Vehicles (DMV) to investigate all the information on an application submitted for an auto dismantler's original or renewed license. The bill amends the California Vehicle Code to ensure that persons procuring licenses to operate auto-dismantler businesses in California meet statutory requirements related to environmental protection and payment of taxes and fees.

During follow-up visits, auto-dismantling employees and owners complained that the granite shops in the area created too much dust, especially in the morning, which made it difficult to breathe, and that thick layers of dust particulate covered the cars in the auto-dismantling storage yards. Taking these comments into consideration, the team conducted ground-truthing to look into this industry more carefully and found that granite shops were discharging water dirtied in the granite-cutting process onto the street. Often, this used water did not run off but instead settled on the street, becoming a thickened substance and then dust that filled the air when heavy traffic in the area disturbed it. After learning about the potential health and environmental effects of granite shops, and noting that numerous granite shops had opened during the time frame of the CARE II project, the team members realized the need to develop a targeted EBMP training for granite shops, as well.

Team members met with significant difficulties in seeking published EBMPs for granite shops. However, with research and guidance from a local granite shop owner, they were able to develop step-by-step training for granite shops. Before bringing the training to local granite shops, team members gave a pilot presentation at a granite shop business in Los Angeles, where the audience provided feedback to improve the presentation. As with auto dismantlers, the team members took a door-to-door count of granite shops in the study area, finding a total of forty-seven businesses. They created a flyer and went door-to-door promoting a free EBMP workshop, but no one was ready to participate. Team members concluded that these small businesses were unfamiliar with the permitting process and the legal requirements of operating a granite business. For example, few of the granite shop employees and managers were familiar with "fictitious business name" filing guidelines. A fictitious name, also known as a DBA (Doing Business As), allows a person to legally conduct business under a particular name at minimal cost, and to accept payments, advertise, pay taxes, and generally present themselves under that name. Based on their conversations with granite employees, managers, and owners, team members found that the granite shops had little access to permitting information and hence were more likely to be out of compliance. In fact, the team was unable to identify a protocol for enforcement in the granite industry.

Lessons Learned

A challenge and subsequently a lesson of this project was finding out how best to work with local businesses. Through work with auto dismantlers, granite shops, and trucking firms, the team found that ground-truthing and outreach were key to uncovering these businesses' motives and concerns. Early on in the CARE II project, team members had focused on discussing the importance of a clean, improved environment during the outreach phase. Soon, however, they discovered that although many businesses were interested in working with them, their owners had concerns besides creating a clean environment, namely, meeting customers' demands to make a profit. As the economy worsened, businesses' interest in the team's efforts diminished as they struggled to stay open and survive the recession. Team members realized that in order to convince businesses to cooperate with them, their outreach efforts had to concentrate on educating owners about how environmental responsibility could save them money and actually be profitable. The team also learned that businesses in the study area did not necessarily have a "traditional" internal structure like other businesses. For example, a family-owned and -run business might only have temporary workers as employees. For employees and owners alike, taking time off to attend a workshop meant possible loss of sales, so EBMP trainings had very low priority.

At granite shops, the scenarios and circumstances were more difficult. Granite shops need a healthy economy to survive. In this industry, good economic times translate into work because people are more likely to repair, build, and remodel homes and businesses, creating high demand for granite and success for granite shops. Conversely, in an economic downturn many shops go out of business. Facing difficulty, many shops partner or combine with other shops to stay in business. For example, one granite shop owner may lease space to two or three other independent granite businesses to split the cost of rent. However, even after the business space is shared, the shop may have to close its doors upon experiencing insurmountable financial difficulties, whereupon three or four businesses may be going out of business even though only one shop appears to be closing. This scenario complicates identifying the owner and getting all the businesses to agree to EMBP training. Further, it illuminates the transiency of the granite business community in economic downturns.

Overall, the Business Team members identified two major problems in the research. First, the regulatory agencies had overlapping jurisdictions, so inspection systems were inconsistent and seemingly not coordinated. Moreover, given the lack of systematic reporting, follow-up, and perhaps resources too, issuing citations likely was not the solution to Pacoima's environmental problems. Second, many owners lacked permits because they were unaware of the permitting process or did not comprehend the permitting requirements. Building on the team's ground-truthing and outreach approach, Pacoima Beautiful focused on its collaborative efforts with various state and local regulatory agencies to develop EBMPs in auto-dismantler facilities. These efforts suggested a need for a task force to develop region-level EBMPs for auto dismantlers. The partnering agencies also agreed to continue meeting to work out a "road map" outlining ways that "environmental justice" communities and state agencies could work together to address issues of environmental hazards caused by auto dismantlers.

Despite collaborative activities on their behalf, auto dismantlers attending the EBMP trainings did not appear fully engaged, given the low priority business owners attached to EBMP in a sagging economy. Businesses were in crisis; as one owner stated, "[they] were just trying to survive this crisis." The recession caused one of the participating auto-dismantler shops to go out of business. The owner, who had committed to being in compliance, had also continuously stated that permits were becoming an expensive burden. Another owner indicated that he was considering closing down due to lack of sales. Team members observed that most auto-dismantler businesses had no clientele, and that both foot and vehicle traffic had diminished considerably since the onset of the project. Granite shops, for their part, were hit still harder: they were either closed or empty. Ongoing ground-truthing thus revealed the recession's drastic impact on these local businesses.

Moving Forward

Moving forward, the team planned to continue working with regulatory agencies, nonprofit partners, and businesses to develop policies to help increase compliance among auto dismantlers, and to push for stricter regulation of businesses that were not in compliance. To this end, the team would seek incentive opportunities to attract EBMP trainings and would continue to build and develop relationships with local auto dismantlers and businesses in the area, promoting EBMP trainings to reduce environmental emissions.

Community-Based Participatory Research to Document Diesel Exposure

The Diesel Team sought to reduce the health impacts of diesel exhaust on Pacoima residents with an ambitious community-based participatory research agenda. To establish the baseline data for diesel emissions, the team members first trained residents to measure truck traffic and document patterns of truck and bus movement in the study area. This project took a community-based participatory research approach similar to that employed in a multi-method case study of diesel air pollution in West Oakland by Gonzalez et al. (2011). Pacoima Beautiful staff and residents identified and targeted residential neighborhoods throughout Pacoima for further research and then, together with university interns and CARE II partners, conducted ground-truthing in the targeted neighborhoods. The data were used to map traffic volumes, businesses using diesel trucks, movement and idling patterns of diesel trucks and school buses, location of sensitive receptors, existing enforcement of anti-idling regulations, proposed areas for no-idling zones for trucks and school buses, and safe truck routes. The team elaborated a research plan specific to Pacoima in order to answer several research questions: What is the traffic volume? What are possible sources of the diesel exhaust? Do diesel trucks pass through residential neighborhoods? Are there problem areas that should receive special attention? What are sources of diesel emissions other than trucks? To create a baseline estimate of diesel emissions in Pacoima, the team then collected data on diesel sources based on traffic counting, a census of parked and idling trucks in residential neighborhoods, an assessment of trucking firms, and a resident community assessment of diesel truck traffic and idling in neighborhoods.

Truck traffic counting. Field research that university interns, Pacoima Beautiful staff, youth, and resident volunteers conducted jointly with environmental scientists from the University of Southern California (USC) measured diesel truck traffic volumes in "hotspot" areas of Pacoima. The team utilized existing research methods developed by Pacoima Beautiful and university scientists, leveraging knowledge and experience gained through previous community-based research partnerships.[9] Geographic Information System (GIS) maps created from the database illustrated truck traffic volumes. Traffic counting provided a baseline estimate of diesel emissions from trucks, as well as a way to engage residents in conducting community-based research to support their efforts to change policies in Pacoima. The process of collecting traffic data also proved a useful tool to Pacoima Beautiful: not only did it generate much more information about traffic patterns, but residents are now also trained in these methods and can repeat this study in the future.

Census of parked and idling trucks in residential neighborhoods. Pacoima Beautiful staff and university students also documented streets in the study area where residents had reported seeing truck violations. The information collected was presented in a map used in advocacy efforts—most recently at a meeting with the State of California Air Resources Board (ARB), the agency that gathers air quality data and sets ambient air quality standards for the state—to highlight the urgency and severity of the truck idling issue.

Assessment of trucking firms. The team conducted an assessment of the area's trucking firms using an online search of business records to identify trucking and transportation businesses with Pacoima addresses.

Resident community diesel assessment on truck traffic and idling. The diesel assessment was developed with locals to identify heavily traveled residential streets and pinpoint areas for diesel reduction measures. The area, selected for its population density, is a neighborhood that also houses industry and manufacturing.[10] Pacoima Beautiful staff members and volunteers then undertook to assess all the streets in the study area. Their findings showed that: (1) two-thirds of respondents were middle-aged (31–55), and their male-to-female ratio reflected the national average for gender breakdown; (2) 75 percent of the survey respondents said they had lived in Pacoima for 6+ years; (3) trucks passed through the neighborhood primarily in the morning and afternoon; (4) nine out of ten residents said they had seen diesel trucks pass through their neighborhood; (5) when asked how many times trucks passed in a day, the most common answers ranged between two and five trucks per day; (6) 30 percent of the respondents said that noise from truck traffic interrupted their sleep; (7) three-quarters of respondents said traffic was most noticeable in the morning and afternoon; (8) most respondents (65 percent) said they had seen diesel smoke; (9) almost half of the respondents said they had seen dust produced by diesel trucks in their neighborhood; (10) responses showed that truck idling was evenly distributed throughout the day; and (11) 90 percent of the respondents had seen trucks idling for longer than five minutes at a time, and 57 percent had observed idling for longer than ten minutes. These data were used to inform the areas of outreach and to identify where diesel advocacy needed to take place.

Community Characterization

The Diesel Team also collected qualitative information about the study area, including tests of ultrafine particle pollution, observation of other diesel sources, maps, and photos.

Ultrafine particle testing. Diesel exhaust contains a large amount of ultrafine particulate matter, which has serious health impacts. Working with USC environmental scientists, team members used a machine called a P-Trak to test pollution from local traffic exhaust. The P-Trak measures the tiny particles in ultrafine particulate matter (PM < 0.1 μ). Portable, easy to read, and designed to provide real-time data, the P-Trak is an excellent tool for community engagement dealing with air pollution. In four workshops led by the USC scientists, Pacoima Beautiful staff and volunteers received training in the P-Trak and used it to test for the presence of ultrafine particles in conjunction with traffic counting. Conducted for fifteen to twenty minutes each on a main truck route, tests showed average levels of 21,298 ultrafine particles per cubic centimeter (pt/cm^3) and peak levels of up to 133,200 pt/cm^3. At the time of the study, there were no federal or state standards for ultrafine particles, but other studies along major roadways have measured high concentrations of these particles, which can have serious health impacts (California Environmental Protection Agency and California Air Resources Board 2005; Ryan et al. 2007). The data have many limitations and cannot substitute for the quality of a long-term scientific analysis, but the snapshot provided by P-Trak measurements characterizes the air quality near roadways in Pacoima. The P-Trak is also a tool to engage residents and volunteers in the process of collecting data and documenting the issues in their community.

Other sources of diesel. Pacoima residents noticed other sources of diesel emissions, including trains, construction equipment, and other off-road vehicles used by nearby industries. Diesel emissions make freight and passenger trains an issue for the study area in Pacoima. State and federal regulation of locomotive emissions is looser than that for on-road vehicle emissions or stationary sources of pollution. Each day, twenty-four passenger trains and several freight trains pass through Pacoima. The team also examined buses as a source of pollution. The area's metro transit buses, which mostly use compressed natural gas, do not contribute to diesel exhaust volumes. School buses, however, are often older models and emit large amounts of diesel exhaust. The team counted an average of 13.8 buses (both transit and school buses) per hour on a main thoroughfare in Pacoima. Another significant air pollutant in Pacoima is exhaust from cars, even though they are not diesel-fueled. The team's traffic researchers counted an hourly average of 1,879 cars on the targeted thoroughfare.

Research Implementation

The team applied its research findings and took action, working with Pacoima Beautiful to organize *Corazones Unidos Por Un Pacoima Saludable y Sostenible* (United Hearts for a Sustainable and Healthy Pacoima), a group of thirty-five residents committed to advocating for diesel reduction in their community. These residents participated in training on diesel issues, assisted with the research and data collection, and met with elected officials, the police department, and air quality agencies. They prepared for community engagement by attending several training sessions the team conducted on diesel and traffic pollution, covering air pollution science, health effects, government agencies that regulate pollutants, and laws and guidelines on air pollution. The training also explained methods for doing community-based participatory research and elicited the group's discussion and feedback about how to proceed. Community members thus had input regarding the research and could understand its findings and discuss their uses for policy advocacy.

The Diesel Team's community-based research strengthened policy advocacy by promoting increased resident awareness of truck route ordinances. One way to reduce residents' diesel exposure is to ensure trucks use appropriate routes instead of driving near sensitive receptors. The diesel assessment and census of trucks revealed that many diesel trucks were passing through residential neighborhoods. Residents conducting truck counts documented trucks traveling on a residential street adjacent to industrial land uses. Pacoima Beautiful then persuaded city leaders to mark streets with traffic signs notifying truck drivers of route restrictions. Thanks to pressure from residents and Pacoima Beautiful, new signage on the residential street prohibited trucks over 6,000 pounds. Residents also met with elected officials to advocate for diesel reductions, using data collected through traffic counting, photos, ultrafine particle pollution tests, and their own experiences. At the meetings, the residents gave the officials background information about the hazards of diesel exhaust and the need to implement solutions to protect residents from this environmental health hazard. The advocacy efforts of Pacoima Beautiful, residents, and partners led the Los Angeles Department of Transportation (LADOT) to conduct a feasibility study in another neighborhood within the study area to implement new signage restricting truck passage.

The resident survey also recorded neighborhood concerns about trucks idling. California state law (California Regulation Code, Title 13, Section 2485) limits truck idling to no more than five minutes, but awareness and enforcement of this law are lacking. To address the issue, the team partnered with the ARB and the South Coast Air Quality Management District (SCAQMD), the air pollution control agency for the urban portions of Los Angeles, Riverside, and San Bernardino Counties and all of Orange County. On the enforcement side, the team met with SCAQMD, ARB, and the Los Angeles Police Department (LAPD) to bridge the gap between agencies for air quality and law enforcement. Thus the police department realized that it had authority to enforce the idling laws, and SCAQMD began facilitating resident calls to a bilingual phone hotline.

The team also pursued a strategy of education and outreach among truck drivers and trucking businesses, creating a flyer to educate diesel drivers about idling laws, the health effects of diesel, and the money drivers could save by shutting off their engines. To help truck drivers get needed upgrades, retrofits, and low-emission replacement trucks, the team created outreach materials to inform them about available public incentive funds. It also created an "incentive flyer," which was distributed with the diesel idling flyer to the businesses identified by the assessment of trucking firms. In collaboration with ARB and SCAQMD, the team also hosted a forum to help independent truck drivers in the community learn how to navigate the process of applying for funds for retrofits and replacement trucks. Ground-truthing to locate independent truck drivers in Pacoima produced eighteen addresses, residential and industrial, that housed fewer than four trucks. In addition, Pacoima Beautiful staff and residents successfully engaged the LAPD, meeting with them to emphasize community concerns about diesel and ways to work on an enforcement strategy. The police checkpoints, vehicle code standards that now address idling, and ongoing feasibility studies on more truck route signage are results of the combined efforts of city officials, LAPD officers, and staff from the LADOT, who meet bimonthly with the Pacoima team.

Lessons Learned

The Diesel Team found that engaging many diverse stakeholders—local law enforcement, city staff, elected officials, air quality agencies, universities—was an effective strategy for addressing a complex issue like air pollution. Through their community-based research, the team forged a division of labor: law enforcement, elected officials, and regulatory agencies enforced existing truck route signs and truck idling laws; universities helped with residents' research, education, and capacity building. The team saw reaching out to residents of the impacted area and engaging them through training and capacity-building opportunities as an effective way to get city hall to apply existing measures. By engaging local elected officials, the team secured the LAPD's willingness and ability to enforce existing laws and signage. The team also engaged local ARB and SCAQMD staff in enforcement efforts for a multipronged approach to enforcement.

Team members also came to understand how to use education and outreach strategies in work with truck drivers and local businesses. For example, providing drivers with opportunities to learn about incentives and funding for emissions-reducing retrofits for their trucks led to greater reductions in emissions than an enforcement-only strategy would have. For research and data collection, the team clearly found its community-based participatory research approach helpful in using community knowledge and engaging residents in the project. For instance, one of this project's successes was that its traffic counting locations were chosen based on residents' knowledge of hotspots or problem areas. Team members then observed firsthand how residents were able to validate their concerns and gain legitimacy in the eyes of city officials and regulatory agencies. The team's community-participatory research thus reinforced the advocacy component of the CARE II project while its community characterization information, such as photos and air pollution testing, was useful for education and outreach efforts. In the end, team members acknowledged that enlisting city officials to change truck routes was an effective way to reduce diesel exposure for residents and sensitive populations, and concluded that maintaining sustainable local change will require a committed group of involved community residents.

Moving Forward

The team has worked toward sustainability practices that will continue to reduce emissions in the long term. Sustainable partnerships created during CARE II include diesel team partners and local and state agencies. The team members are committed to future quarterly meetings with other

CARE II partners to sustain ongoing research and information dissemination activities and support Pacoima Beautiful's diesel reduction efforts. The LAPD, city officials, and LADOT have also committed to meeting quarterly to review the enforcement of truck idling limits. SCAQMD has committed to hosting a workshop to teach truck drivers and businesses about incentive funding for new and retrofitted trucks. These partnerships and commitments will help sustain diesel reduction efforts in the future. Most importantly, community residents have now engaged in the campaigns, received training, and conducted community-based research. The capacity-building activities conducted throughout the CARE II project gave residents the tools to continue to organize and advocate for reductions in diesel in Pacoima.

Educating Residents About Environmental Health Risks

The Education Team's objectives were to conduct research on health risk information and facilitate study area residents' access to that information. They did this by increasing residents' and communities' knowledge about environmental health risks. The team strove to establish comprehensive relationships with residents while promoting community awareness of environmental health risks. The team also helped residents make informed health decisions, which led to a sense of empowerment born of identifying their own concerns and solutions and making improvements in their own and their neighbors' lives. The team developed a curriculum to inform residents about the potential health impacts of living next to a high concentration of small point sources and diesel emissions, the two priorities of the CARE II project. Residents also received education on the hazards of auto dismantling and diesel exhaust, their potential health effects, and protective measures they could take. The materials created included a PowerPoint presentation, a brochure, a fact sheet, evaluation tools, and a display board.

The PowerPoint presentation covered the hazards of auto dismantling, diesel exhaust, and their potential health effects, emphasizing what residents can do to protect themselves and their families. A university-based expert on environmental and occupational health reviewed the communication of risk in this presentation to ensure that the message did not alarm or distress residents at the presentations. The team also produced a brochure alerting readers to the potential ill effects of diesel exhaust and outlining what individuals and the community can do to protect themselves, and a one-page fact sheet summarizing ways that community members can reduce their risk of exposure. A CARE II education display board for use at community events and meetings was created to highlight the team's results. In this way the team educated residents about the hazards and potential health effects of auto dismantling and diesel exhaust, and about what they could do to protect themselves.

Research Implementation

The team used a multipronged approach, focusing on schools, churches, and other community venues while also disseminating educational materials door to door and using presentations, leadership development training, and community meetings as opportunities to educate people living next to high concentrations of small point sources and diesel emissions. The team knocked on 417 doors in the study area and Pacoima Beautiful gave twenty-seven presentations, all to provide residents with the opportunity to sign up to receive more information on upcoming presentations and other activities that would teach them how to advocate for reduction of environmental health risks. These presentations were offered in parent centers, community centers, Head Start early education centers, churches, and any other venue where people at risk of diesel exposure might congregate. Attendance ranged from ten or twelve participants to several dozen people. Presentations were bilingual or conducted in Spanish as needed to ensure comprehension and access to the message.

Team members followed up with residents who expressed interest in the partnership's work of home visits. This strategy—a stepping-stone to provide more education and assess retention of the curriculum in a comfortable, safe environment—thus was also a way to develop meaningful relationships with potential resident advocates. The brochure and fact sheet likewise served as conduits to engage residents in peer-to-peer education. Pacoima Beautiful also used meetings and training sessions as a way to bring people together. The education imparted to residents inspired them to form two resident-led, diesel-oriented advocacy groups to further the work of the CARE II project in their respective areas. Thus, using the PowerPoint presentation and other educational tools too, the team ensured that residents had the opportunity to advocate for the reduction of environmental health hazards. Twelve of the thirty-five individuals involved in these groups were trained in entry-level advocacy efforts. In addition, more than 100 families attending presentations received reference information on health care resources in Pacoima.

Lessons Learned

The team's partnerships with Pacoima Beautiful and study area residents provided openings to learn about culturally appropriate information dissemination. For example, team members found that considerable work goes into creating educational materials of technical substance in linguistically appropriate and accessible formats. Collaboration with diverse experts helped the team ensure that the materials were comprehensive, accurate, and easy for residents to understand. Risk management review was an important quality control check ensuring that the materials the team developed fit their intended use and took into account the well-being of participants receiving the educational curriculums. The information, delivered in a non-threatening and productive manner, subsequently served to educate residents about potential hazards and protective measures. Presenting the curriculum thus provided not just education but opportunities for team members to develop ongoing relationships with residents, assisting them in identifying their own concerns and solutions for reducing environmental risks. The team's resident-focused training approach built a foundation for sustaining both the production of educational materials and the residents' capacity to continue disseminating them after the CARE II project.

Moving Forward

Looking forward with an eye to the sustainability of the educational tools developed, team members agreed to review and update educational curriculums annually. Pacoima Beautiful agreed to continue using the developed tools to educate residents of the study area, and to disseminate the information in schools, churches, and other places where residents live and work. The environmental justice organization has continued to train residents to disseminate educational materials in their neighborhoods and provide updates on legal and regulatory ameliorations of environmental health risks via community-based presentations, home visits, and organizational events.

Sustaining a Civic Community of Practice

The work and accomplishments of the CARE II project for developing strong environmental management practices to reduce environmental health risks in Pacoima hinged on collaboration between residents, organization and agency stakeholders, and elected officials. Diverse stakeholders demonstrated willingness to address core environmental justice issues across jurisdictions, boundaries, and departments. The teams learned that they had to push past the limits of comfort and tradition to make change happen. Beyond the CARE II project, a substantial amount of work remains to be done, and Pacoima Beautiful has committed itself to involving residents in decisions that affect their lives and their health. Moreover, the organization has learned many Pacoima residents may be monolingual Spanish speakers, but Pacoima's businesses are often owned and operated by members of non-Latino ethnic groups. Therefore, education and outreach materials developed for CARE II needed to engage various stakeholder groups, not just monolingual Spanish-speaking residents. Though Pacoima Beautiful has expanded its capacity to undertake and manage grants requiring data management and educational material development in languages other than Spanish and English, its growth in this direction was a challenge.

Besides learning how to grow and build on collaborative work, Pacoima Beautiful learned how complicated data management could be in its work with regulatory and enforcement bureaucracies. Early in the CARE II project, managing multiple lists from various public agencies proved difficult. Systems had to be developed to track the businesses' transiency and turnover. Furthermore, baseline measures had to correlate with the information the organization most needed to track. It was problematic to tell a story in data and numbers when the numbers were sometimes incomplete. Ground-truthing was an effective way to formulate the baseline, but the research was very time-intensive and multiple staff members were needed to manage the large pool of research data generated through this style of community-based research activity. By the end of the CARE II project, Pacoima Beautiful had improved its grasp of data management tasks by developing administrative processes and hiring staff with specific skills and backgrounds in research and policy development. The added staff eased the challenges of managing data and communications from complex administrative systems, such as regulatory agencies and research universities. For a grassroots environmental justice organization, the complexity of the system was overwhelming at times. However, in moving forward to continue the work of community-based participatory research and policy advocacy, Pacoima Beautiful advanced the capabilities of other community environmental organizations working on similar issues. Its efforts to reduce environmental risks have thus expanded in focus from the local to the regional.

Evaluating a Civic Community of Practice

Evaluating the Pacoima CARE II collaborative as a civic community of practice required a logic model—in this case, a theory-based approach that would help stakeholders, both professionals and residents, make explicit links between what might work best in the study community, strategies they planned to implement, and outcomes they hoped to achieve. According to Hernandez and Hodges (2001), a theory of change is an articulation of stakeholders' underlying beliefs and assumptions, which guide a local-level strategy. Such a theory incorporates an innovation and is critical to both making change and improving the knowledge of professionals and engaged residents, as well as other stakeholders within a system of care—in this case, the community of Pacoima. Hernandez and Hodges (2003) characterized a theory of change as having two broad components. The first involves conceptualizing and implementing the theory's three core elements: (1) the population's needs and strengths in the context of the environment where change will occur; (2) strategies stakeholders believe will accomplish desired outcomes; and (3) the outcomes, including the change desired by the population. The second component involves both understanding and expression of how stakeholders in the change process relate and articulate these three core elements. In sum, the theory of change approach envisions the shape of a system of community-based change, the necessary local service delivery and infrastructural changes, the nature of stakeholders' visions of the desired change, and the steps needed to build consensus among stakeholders for optimal engagement in the change process.

A central task of evaluation is to understand how diverse stakeholders engage in a change process around the adoption of innovative, community-based monitoring and educational approaches in a complex, urban multi-organizational milieu. In many professionally based systems, assessment and adoption of technology depends on sustained communities of practice encompassing scientists, public health practitioners, citizen scientists, governmental agency experts, and members of community-based organizations representing the broader population, as seen in this study. These diverse constituents' comprehension and expression of the ways the three core elements are related and articulated at each level of change—team, multi-agency stakeholders, environmental justice organization, engaged residents, community—were essential outcomes of the evaluation.

Toward Common Knowledge of Environmental Health Risks and the Quality of Life

This chapter focused on building communities of practice among laypersons and scientists engaged in community-based participatory research, a field where collaborative partnerships among researchers, practitioners, and consumers make for greater transparency in planning and implementing a broad-based, inclusive research agenda. A community of practice is comprised of individuals who share a common concern for a specific domain of knowledge. As collaborative peer networks based on a shared area of inquiry, communities of practice are voluntary and focus on both learning and building capacity. They share knowledge, develop expertise, and solve problems. Communities of practice break down communication barriers with open, informal, continuous exchanges of data, information, and knowledge, typically among those with clinical and research expertise. Recent discussions have centered on increasing public understanding of science through citizens' participation in producing scientific knowledge and assessing its technological applications. To sustain a "knowledge commons," communities of practice can work to diminish boundaries between the "expert" producers of research in the academic, public, nonprofit, and private sectors, and consumers across these sectors. In the case of the CARE II project, translating research into action promoted better decision-making by professionals and community residents alike, so that both could meaningfully engage in informed dialogues about their quality of life. Collaborative methods like community-based participatory research and citizen science insure a more socially responsive transfer of research findings across diverse sectors and constituencies.

Acknowledgments

I would like to acknowledge the ongoing support and critical judgment of Sam Beck, who continues to inspire my work in public anthropology. I would also like to thank Marlene Grossman, Barbara Yablon Maida, and Brian McKenna for their close readings of earlier versions of the manuscript, and to Jaime Taber for expert copy-editing of the final manuscript.

The following are the partners in the Reducing Toxic Risks in Pacoima, California (CARE II) Project: Linda Fidell, Thomas Hatfield, John Schillinger, Zeynep Toker, and Phyl Van Ammers, California State University, Northridge (CSUN); Tim Dagodag, Environmental Education and Communications, Inc. (EEC); Rita Mozian and Olga Vigdorchik, Los Angeles County Department of Public Health; Joseph Lyou, California Environmental Rights Alliance (CERA); Veronica Padilla, Initiating Change in Our Neighborhoods (ICON) Community Development Corporation; Deborah Rosen, Northeast Valley Health Corporation; Refugio Aguilera, Irma Galvan, Marlene Grossman, Maria Guzman, Sindy Lopez, Nury Martinez, Blanca Nuñez, and Patricia Ochoa, Pacoima Beautiful (PB); Carl Maida, University of California, Los Angeles (UCLA); Andrea Hricko and Carla Truax, University of Southern California (USC); Joni Novosel, Valley Care Community Consortium (VCCC); Brian Condon, Arnold and Porter; Mohsen Nazem, South Coast Air Quality Management District (SCAQMD); Steve Cain and David Bacharowski, California Regional Water Quality Control Board; Gale Filer, Florence Gharibian, Jessica Rodriguez, Ann Job, Department of Toxic Substance Control (DTSC); Gavin McHugh, State of California Auto Dismantlers Association (SCADA); Officer Carbajal, Los Angeles Police Department (LAPD) Foothill Division Transportation Control; Officers Walker and Mungia, Senior Lead Officers for LAPD in Pacoima. The project benefited from the participation of the following agencies: California Environmental Protection Agency; Los Angeles Department of Transportation, State of California Department of Transportation; State of California Air Resources Board; and the offices of Los Angeles City Council members Richard Alarcon and Tony Cardenas, State Senator Alex Padilla, and Assembly member Felipe Fuentes. The interns who worked on this project were Felipe Lopez (PB); John Darnell III, Chat Nguyen, Tony Doan, Firdousi Quaderi and Martha Tello (CSUN); Claudia Rodriguez (LA City Planning Department); Schuyler Thomas (VCCC). The following classes participated in the project: Winter 2008 Pacoima Beautiful Youth Environmentalists Institute; CSUN students in Urban Studies 490, Fall 2007 and Spring 2008, and Urban Studies 450: Urban Problems, Spring 2008. The partners are grateful to the US Environmental Protection Agency (US EPA) for guidance and ongoing support, and to Project Officer Karen Henry, who guided the work of the Pacoima CARE I and CARE II projects, providing sound counsel and resources throughout.

Carl A. Maida is a professor at the UCLA Institute of the Environment and Sustainability in the College of Letters and Science, where he teaches courses on action research methods and conducts community-based research on urban sustainability. His anthropological research in Los Angeles focuses on how various urban social formations—social networks, mutual aid groups, and associations based on ethnic, community, and voluntary ties—serve as arenas for making sense of atypical events and move into the vacuum to act as pathways through crisis, and will often form the basis of social movements on behalf of health and environmental quality of life. He also directs the UCLA Pre-College Science Education Program, and conducts studies of project-based and inquiry-based learning in schools and action research in community-based organizations funded by the National Science Foundation, National Institutes of Health, US Environmental Protection Agency, Robert Wood Johnson Foundation, Ford Foundation, Howard Hughes Medical Institute, and The California

Endowment. He is a Fellow of the American Association for the Advancement of Science, the American Anthropological Association, and the Society for Applied Anthropology.

Notes

1. CARE I goals: (1) identify all sources of toxic substances in Pacoima that may have negative health or environmental impacts; (2) work with community stakeholders (residents, community-based organizations, elected officials, etc.) to understand the health implications of potential hazards; (3) assist stakeholders in setting priorities for amelioration of those risks; and (4) create self-sustaining community-based partnerships that will continue to reduce risks and improve the local environment.
2. CARE II goals: (1) educate and mobilize local residents and businesses to voluntarily reduce toxic risks; (2) broaden the partnership base to include more residents, businesses, community and government partners, technical experts, and regulatory agencies in identifying and implementing risk reduction strategies within the CARE II grant time frame and beyond; and (3) develop indicators to track progress, measure results, and communicate knowledge to the Pacoima community and other communities facing similar circumstances.
3. These agencies were the Department of Toxic Substance Control (DTSC), Southern Regional Water Quality Control Board (Water Board), Los Angeles County Fire Department, Los Angeles County Unified Program Agency (CUPA), City of Los Angeles Bureau of Sanitation (Sanitation Department), South Coast Air Quality Management District (SCAQMD), Los Angeles City Board of Public Works Board Watershed Protection Division (WPD) and Industrial Waste Management Division (IWMD), and California State Department of Motor Vehicles (DMV).
4. The businesses had not complied with the DTSC, Water Board, or SCAQMD, had no US EPA ID number, or had storm water violations with WPD and IWMD.
5. The Business Team's four objectives were: (1) convene monthly meetings with residents, local businesses, and regulators to identify opportunities for voluntary pollution prevention and reduction; (2) develop best practices; (3) share best practice materials with fifty businesses; and (4) negotiate memoranda of understanding with 25 percent of the targeted businesses to implement EBMPs.
6. The Research Team's master list named 148 businesses in the study area, 12 of which were located outside of the area. The others consisted of 25 auto-body and paint shops, 4 granite shops, 46 auto-dismantling shops, 39 industrial facilities, and 22 businesses of unknown type.
7. The packet included information about Pacoima Beautiful and the Initiating Change in Our Neighborhoods (ICON) Community Development Corporation, a CARE II partner; a US EPA newsletter describing the CARE II program; an EBMP flyer offering free training and an informational sheet explaining what EBMP training covered; and a brochure outlining the EBMP training and the benefits of participating, together with a quick reference guide to four basic environmental practices.
8. To ensure that the other auto-dismantling facilities in the area would benefit from the EBMP training, the team delivered its packet to all auto-dismantling businesses and asked each to sign a letter affirming that they had received the package and supported

the CARE II goals and objectives. A total of twenty-six packets were delivered, seven to businesses that subsequently signed a Memorandum of Understanding (MOU) stating that they would follow EBMP practices.

9. The different groups' various methods of traffic counting were combined in a Pacoima Traffic Counting Database to analyze truck traffic. The database holds 54 separate field data collections from December 2007 through September 2009. For all locations, an average of 91.7 trucks passed by hourly. Follow-up counts completed in the second year of the CARE II grant were compared to the baseline data. The second-year truck counts showed reduced truck volume at two commercial intersections. At the first, truck traffic fell from 27 trucks per hour in 2008 to 18 trucks per hour in 2009. Similarly, at the second intersection, traffic dropped from 280 trucks per hour in 2008 to 112 trucks per hour in 2009. However, these results may not be generalizable to the entire study area. The sample size was small, and several confounding variables could have explained the results. Also, decreased trucking business and decreased truck volume in these areas could have resulted from Pacoima's declining economic activity. And time of day and season of the year—factors that may have influenced the truck volume at these locations—were not controlled as variables in the design of the truck counts.

10. The Philliber Research Associates (2006) Community Engagement survey, conducted in Pacoima from 2001 to 2005, was referenced because it was implemented through door-to-door residential interviews. The survey items touched on various everyday issues, including health and pollution. The assessment's design also borrowed from the format of the Pacoima Community Engagement resident questionnaire. The team also referred to the Sun Valley Air Quality Survey, which measured community residents' perceptions and knowledge about air quality issues in neighboring Sun Valley and documented demographics for each assessment, as well as the time of day, day of the week, and name of the person conducting the assessment. Finally, team members reviewed surveys developed for the Pacoima Beautiful Healthy Homes Program with an eye to their word choice and syntax.

References

Ash, Michael, and T. Robert Fetter. 2002. *Who Lives on the Wrong Side of the Environmental Tracks? Evidence from the EPA's Risk-Screening Environmental Indicators Model.* Working Paper WP50. Amherst: University of Massachusetts Amherst, Political Economy Research Institute.

Bäckstrand, Karin. 2003. "Civic Science for Sustainability: Reframing the Role of Experts, Policy-Makers and Citizens in Environmental Governance." *Global Environmental Politics* 3: 24–31.

Bauman, Zygmunt. 2000. *Liquid Modernity.* Malden, MA: Blackwell.

Beck, Ulrich. 1992. *Risk Society: Toward a New Modernity.* Thousand Oaks, CA: Sage.

Bonney, Rick, Caren B. Cooper, Janis Dickinson, Steve Kelling, Tina Phillips, Kenneth V. Rosenberg, and Jennifer Shirk. 2009. "Citizen Science: A Developing Tool for Expanding Science Knowledge and Scientific Literacy." *Bioscience* 59: 977–984.

Bouwes, Nicolass W., Steven M. Hasssur, and Mark D. Shapiro. 2001. *Empowerment Through Risk-Related Information: EPA's Risk Screening Environmental Indicators Project.* Working Paper WP18. Amherst: University of Massachusetts Amherst, Political Economy Research Institute.

Brossard, Dominique, Bruce Lewenstein, and Rick Bonney. 2005. "Scientific Knowledge and Attitude Change: The Impact of a Citizen Science Project." *International Journal of Science Education* 27: 1099–1121.

California Environmental Protection Agency and California Air Resources Board. 2005. *Air Quality and Land Use Handbook: A Community Health Perspective.* Sacramento: California Environmental Protection Agency and California Air Resources Board.

Gonzalez Priscilla A., Meredith Minkler, Analilia P. Garcia, Margaret Gordon, Catalina Garzón, Meena Palaniappan, Swati Prakash, and Brian Beveridge. 2011. "Community-Based Participatory Research and Policy Advocacy to Reduce Diesel Exposure in West Oakland, California." *American Journal of Public Health* 101, supplement 1: S166–S175.

Hansell, William H., Jr., Elizabeth Hollander, and John DeWitt. 2009. *Putting Community First: A Promising Approach to Federal Collaboration for Environmental Improvement. An Evaluation of the Community Action for a Renewed Environment (CARE) Demonstration Program.* Washington, DC: National Academy of Public Administration.

Harvey, David. 1990. *The Condition of Post-Modernity: An Enquiry into the Origins of Cultural Change.* Malden, MA: Blackwell.

Heaney, Christopher D., Sacoby Wilson, and Omega R. Wilson. 2007. "The West End Revitalization Association's Community-Owned and -Managed Research Model: Development, Implementation, and Action." *Progress in Community Health Partnerships: Research Education, and Action* 1, no. 4: 339–349.

Hernandez, Mario, and Sharon Hodges. 2001. "Theory-Based Accountability." In *Developing Outcome Strategies in Children's Mental Health*, ed. Mario Hernandez and Sharon Hodges. Baltimore, MD: Paul H. Brookes.

———. 2003. *Crafting Logic Models For Systems Of Care: Ideas Into Action.* Making Children's Mental Health Services Successful Series 1. Tampa, FL: University of South Florida, The Louis de la Parte Florida Mental Health Institute, Department of Child & Family Studies. http://cfs.fmhi.usf.edu.

Irwin, Alan. 2001. "Constructing the Scientific Citizen: Science and Democracy in the Biosciences." *Public Understanding of Science* 10: 1–18.

Kirby, Andrew, ed. 1990. *Nothing to Fear: Risks and Hazards in American Society.* Tucson: University of Arizona Press.

Lash, Scott, Bronislaw Szerszynski, and Brian Wynne, eds. 1996. *Risk, Environment, Modernity: Toward a New Ecology.* Thousand Oaks, CA: Sage.

Little, Peter C. 2009. "Negotiating Community Engagement and Science in the Federal Environmental Public Health Sector." *Medical Anthropology Quarterly* 23, no. 2: 94–118.

Maida, Carl A. 2009. "Expert and Lay Knowledge in Pacoima: Public Anthropology and an Essential Tension in Community-Based Participatory Action Research." *Anthropology in Action* 16, no. 2 (Summer): 14–26.

———. 2011. "Participatory Action Research and Urban Environmental Justice: The Pacoima CARE Project." In *Environmental Anthropology Today*, ed. Helen Kopnina and Eleanor Shoreman. New York: Routledge.

Minkler, Meredith, and Nina Wallerstein, eds. 2008. *Community-Based Participatory Research for Health: From Process to Outcomes.* 2nd ed. San Francisco: Wiley.

Morello-Frosch, Rachel, Manuel Pastor Jr., James Sadd, Carlos Porras, and Michele Prichard. 2005. "Citizens, Science, and Data Judo: Leveraging Community-Based Participatory Research to Build a Regional Collaborative for Environmental Justice in Southern California." In *Methods for Conducting Community-Based Participatory Research in Public Health*, ed. Barbara A. Israel, Eugenia Eng, Amy J. Schulz, and Edith A. Parker. San Francisco: Jossey-Bass.

Morello-Frosch, Rachel, Julia G. Brody, Phil Brown, Rebecca G. Altman, Ruthann A. Rudel, and Carla Pérez. 2009. "Toxic Ignorance and Right-To-Know in Biomonitoring Results Communication: A Survey of Scientists and Study Participants." *Environmental Health* 8. http://www.ehjournal.net/content/8/1/6.

Ostrom, Elinor, Joanna Burger, Christopher B. Field, Richard B. Norgaard, and David Policansky. 1999. "Revisiting the Commons: Local Lessons, Global Challenges." *Science* 284: 278–282.

Philliber Research Associates. 2006. *Pacoima California: A Comparison of Data on Businesses and Residents, 2001 through 2005. The Final Report.* Accord, NY: Philliber Research Associates.

Powell, Walter W., and Kaisa Snellman. 2004. "The Knowledge Economy." *Annual Review of Sociology* 30: 199–220.

Ryan, Patrick H., Grace K. LeMasters, Pratim Biswas, Linda Levin, Shaohua Hu, Mark Lindsey, David I. Bernstein, James Lockey, Manuel Villareal, Gurjit K. Khurana Hershey, and Sergey A. Grinshpun. 2007. "A Comparison of Proximity and Land Use Regression Traffic Exposure Models and Wheezing in Infants." *Environmental Health Perspectives* 115 (February): 278–284.

Shoemaker, Paul A., Tiffany Skogstrom, John Shea, and Leon Bethune. 2007. "The Boston Safe Shops Project: Preliminary Findings of a Case Study in Applying the 10 Essential Services of Public Health to Building Environmental Health Capacity." *Journal of Environmental Health* 70 (July/August): 22–28.

Smith-Nonini, Sandy, and Beverly Bell. 2011. "Operationalizing a Right to Health: Theorizing a National Health System as a 'Commons.'" In *A Companion to Medical Anthropology*, ed. Merrill Singer and Pamela I. Erikson. Malden, MA: Blackwell.

Snyder, William M., and Etienne Wenger. 2010. "Our World as a Learning System: A Communities of Practice Approach." In *Social Learning Systems and Communities of Practice*, ed. Chris Blackmore. London: Springer.

SCADA (State of California Auto Dismantlers Association). 2002. *Partners in the Solution Guidance Manual.* Sacramento: State of California Auto Dismantlers Association.

US EPA (U.S. Environmental Protection Agency). 2002. *Practical Guide to Environmental Management for Small Business.* EPA 233-K-02-001. Washington, DC: U.S. Environmental Protection Agency.

———. 2011. *An Update on Ongoing and Future EPA Actions to Empower Communities and Advance the Integration of Environmental Justice in Decision-Making and Research.* Washington, DC: U.S. Environmental Protection Agency.

Vermont Department of Environmental Conservation. 2005. *Best Management Practices (BMP) for the Auto Salvage Outreach Program.* Montpelier: Vermont Department of Environmental Conservation

Wenger, Etienne. 2000. "Communities of Practice and Social Learning Systems." *Organization* 7: 225–246.

Wenger, Etienne, and William M. Snyder. 2000. "Communities of Practice: The Organizational Frontier." *Harvard Business Review* 78: 139–145.

Whitmore, Elizabeth. 1998. *Understanding and Practicing Participatory Evaluation.* San Francisco: Jossey-Bass.

Chapter 4

POLITICAL-ETHICAL DILEMMAS
PARTICIPANT OBSERVED

——— ∞∞∞ ———

Josiah McC. Heyman

The literature on value-based, publicly engaged anthropology is domi-nated by the assertion, criticism, and defense of such commitments vis-à-vis putatively objective science (see D'Andrade 1995; Hale 2008; Heyman 1998; Scheper-Hughes 1995; and from an earlier generation Hymes 1972). The fine guide by Lassiter (2005) also advocates engagement but offers more of a how-to approach, as do key textbooks on applied anthropol-ogy (especially good is Ervin 2004). Here, I go beyond justifying partisan engagement in public issues to move to the stage of describing and ana-lyzing what actually happens in such activities. I propose that substantial involvement in public issues constitutes useful participant observation about the topic of engagement. Though I hope this chapter offers some useful practical insights, it is not simply a how-to guide. Rather, it criti-cally analyzes what happens in engagement and how its social process affects value choices and related political decisions. In this, I follow the excellent precedent of Fassin (2007).[1]

I begin by distinguishing radical from reformist politics. Both are ideal types that do not always constitute clear alternatives in reality, but they are useful in highlighting and thinking about certain important issues. Im-mediate reforms accept aspects of the status quo but attempt various "im-provements" (e.g., increased respect for human rights in border policing). Radical transformations emphasize struggle for fundamental changes in the actually existing order (e.g., pushing for open borders, ending border policing). Rather than advocate either approach as exclusively correct, I propose that explicit confrontation of such alternatives will produce better choices about engagement. Having mostly been engaged on the reformist side, I then move forward from this initial dichotomy to examine several aspects of the social and political process of engagement within the reformist frame. Here I review reformism critically while also paying more attention to it than in the initial section; whereas I state the radical position mainly for purposes of reflective contrast. My goal is not to build up one side and tear down the other, but to reflect on the choices between them and then within one of them.

I draw on my experiences as part of a reform coalition, the U.S.-Mexico Border and Immigration Task Force (and recently its successor, a still unnamed but very active border stakeholders coalition). Within these coalitions, I have had several roles, as described below in a brief narrative history. Most prominently, I have helped write and present (always as part of collaborative groups) alternative border and immigration policy language based on my social science expertise.[2] (I should emphasize that both my own engagement and the wider field of immigration and border politics are ongoing, but that to write this chapter, I stopped my narrative and analysis in December 2010.) In doing such work, I have approximated a classic anthropological participant-observer, learning within an ongoing stream of moral thinking and decision making over the preceding four years. For example, in recommending legal and organizational reform to the Department of Homeland Security or tinkering with legislative language in congressional bills that contain difficult compromises, do we accept the highly problematic frameworks of current border enforcement and national belonging? My goal is to identify such questions and dilemmas, and the sociopolitical contexts within which we confront them. While specific to the politics of the U.S.-Mexico border, the issues are of general import.

Difficult Choices in the Context of Recent U.S. Border and Migration Policies

The U.S. side of the U.S.-Mexico border has an enormous state apparatus for the detection, arrest ("apprehension"), detention, prosecution, and deportation ("removal") of unauthorized migrants, as well as for contraband commodities such as drugs. The enforcement apparatus there includes almost 20,000 patrol officers and a comparable number of port inspectors, a wall of roughly 700 miles, a vast web of electronic ground and air surveillance, a gulag of prisons ("detention centers"), and so forth. Many hundreds of thousands of people (and in the recent past, millions) are arrested and deported at or near the boundary annually, and uncounted numbers make the passage successfully but suffer practical and experiential effects. This enforcement does not take place in an empty zone but throughout a resident community, sometimes sparsely settled and sometimes dense, of about twelve million people, mostly of Mexican origin, holding a wide variety of citizenship and residency rights. An enormous literature can be consulted to deepen this brief summary (see Andreas 2000; Dunn 1996; 2009; Heyman 1998; Nevins 2010), but space limitations preclude any effort to explain why massive border enforcement occurs (see Heyman 1999; 2008).

Into this environment, first as an ivory-tower scholar and then as a combined scholar-activist, I have brought my own political-ethical framework. As discussed in Heyman (1998), I hold to a notion of unified humanity, for mutual moral recognition between people in different social positions across humanity, and for a vision of human rights based on such shared moral personhood. This would seem to imply a complete rejection of borders in favor of universal humanity, but I see that as a pointlessly abstract place to begin real moral reasoning; my principle concern is with actual migrants and actual hosts who create mutual moral reciprocities through their practical interactions (work, residence, etc.). My political work stems from that reasoning.

Several contexts particularly affect the sorts of engagement practices and political-ethical choices we face. First, the border is steadily subjected to waves of moral panic roiling the wider nation—about drugs, then undocumented (illegal) migrants, then possible terrorism, then immigration again, then violence in Mexico, and so on. This creates a strong political incentive structure favoring unrestrained, high-resource law enforcement and discouraging human or civil rights restraints on such enforcement. Second, immigrants to the United States are unpopular political figures—a highly varied and complicated topic—and Mexicans in particular are often viewed as subordinate outsiders with little to no social standing (e.g., as readily discarded and expelled from the nation). Third, the U.S. borderland with Mexico is politically marginalized, with limited recognition and voice in the larger society. Local society thus has little ability to guide and check the police operations of the central state. Meanwhile, opinions about such operations within the borderlands are significantly divided.

The combined effect of these contexts is that border human rights advocates face an uphill struggle. The situation is bad: even as an increment of positive change is achieved, or even comes into sight, other developments worsen. In a very bad situation, there is no one obvious best decision about how to bring about policy change. Conversely, many compelling things need to be done all at once, challenging our time, energy, and political resources. Numerous different interpretations of the situation and what to do are therefore justifiable. In making the basic (but again, not simple) choice between radical and reformist approaches, the implication of facing a bad context is that both perspectives are compelling. On the one hand, the relevant situations of human suffering, including death in crossing the desert, are virtually innumerable. Short-term, immediate actions to reduce these harms, such as advocating for local rescue operations by the Border Patrol, follow clearly from that assessment of the "bads" that face us. But at the same time, the radical approach points toward an equally compelling moral impulse, which is to identify and attack the root cause of the deaths: mass frontal enforcement operations that have pushed migrants from safer border-crossing corridors to more dangerous ones in the deserts and mountains. We thus should reject any argument that insists on one approach being correct and the other false or pernicious, when so much that needs to be done simultaneously concerns different issues, time horizons, and political arenas.

Choosing Reformist and Radical Options: Basic Considerations

The radical approach to alternative migration and border policy has three central components. First is to reduce migration-sending pressures through changes in the current capitalist system, including state and transnational policies supporting it, in favor of a more equitable pattern of development (Nevins 2007). Second is to reject the nation-state framework of belonging to society in favor of a wider, more flexible concept of membership, such as membership by activity (changing residence, working, community participation, etc.), and a related, vigorous rejection of invidious distinctions such as racism and citizenship-based inequality. Third is to apply a universal concept of human rights to all persons, not just nation-state insiders. These aims are variously exemplified by scholars such as Timothy Dunn (2009), Joseph Nevins (2010), Nandita Sharma (2006), and David Spener (2009). My own work has sometimes advocated for aspects of these values (Heyman 1998). The radical position is also exemplified on the ground by the work of various organizations and coalitions, such as Coalición de Derechos Humanos and No One Is Illegal.[3]

The point, rising above the specifics of borders and migration, is that radicals need a clear visionary agenda. That agenda includes, but also goes beyond, deep analysis of what is wrong with the status quo. It also involves a counterpart vision to the status quo—what I have called the "inverse of power" (Heyman 2003).

But an alternative vision alone is insufficient, for a coherent and meaningful radical position entails the work of transformation toward it. Here, radicals have two basic tasks. One is to pursue a long-term struggle for deep change in the political landscape (in Gramscian jargon, to change the balance of hegemony). The other task, closely related to the first, is to build a large, sustained community that acts on new social-cultural principles. In my judgment—which of course is debatable—words and action on the radical side must be evaluated vis-à-vis those tasks. To what extent does a particular analysis, display, protest, or expression of outrage advance some part of these two agendas for transformation?[4]

The foregoing offers a basis for some brief critical remarks about certain styles of radical practice (though not about the radical option as a whole, whose best performance I have carefully outlined above). Some radicals produce fierce, outraged responses or sharply negative analyses and critiques without linking them to a vision of transformation or political campaign to change the causes of the outrage. Outrage has a role. It brings an element of moral appeal into the political struggle: this law or social structure should change because it is wrong (deadly, inhumane, unjust, etc.). But negativity, without a path forward from it, is at best an expression of authenticity (but no more) and at worst a diversion of energy from meaningful transformative struggle.

The radical position sometimes involves rhetoric and performances, addressed toward an in-group, that provide satisfaction to the self in their speaking but do not help to construct a long-term political struggle. Actions that are visible but ineffectual (in radical terms as such) are a pitfall. Radical analyses that justify inaction are also troubling: they risk accepting the status quo while waiting for paradise to appear magically.

Finally, in the context of this chapter, it is particularly important to note how easily intellectuals can move into the radical position without critical reflection. Social science intellectual work attempts to reveal and understand the central processes of society and culture. Awareness of central processes readily leads to radical critique, and it also tends to increase awareness of the incompleteness and shortcomings of reformist tinkering (which is discussed below). Fair enough. But if this intellectual path to radicalism is not combined with meaningful involvement in transformative work (e.g., intellectual practice affecting the balance of hegemony over the long run), it is just a radical-seeming form of ivory-towerism.

The main difference between the radical approach and the reformist approach is the extent to which they intend action to change existing political frames rather than make changes within them (action concerns both political and economic frames, but because I focus on collective social action, I emphasize the political). A radical approach to migration change must be transnational in its diagnosis of the issue and thus in the character of its action frame, whereas the reformist approach largely accepts migration policy as made by nation-states or by agreements between nation-states. Likewise, the radical approach is fundamentally critical of the nation-state as an institution and seeks novel arrangements in keeping with the transformative character of migration. The reformist approach, however, takes any number of key political structures and actors for granted: the legislative process, aspects of the current legislative balance of power, key figures, discourses, forms of legality, modes of state action such as border administration. Reform may best be thought of as a countervailing power in an existing, badly unequal system.

As I will recount below, in most instances I have chosen a reformist practice, despite my scholarly work's focus on deep causes and radically distinctive visions of alternatives (Heyman 1998 is exemplary). My complex choice process, which involved many steps over many years, boils down to three main elements shaping my decision. The first, most purely political-ethical, is that I am unwilling to accept existing suffering while waiting for long-term, fundamental change. I want to reduce desert fatalities and terrorization of settled immigrant communities as soon as possible, even if in ultimately limited ways. This is an ameliorative ethic, and well justified in such terms. Second, I have come to understand that reformism needs to avoid simple window-dressing, but rather needs to envision how reforms can lead to meaningful, positive changes (though obviously not full transformations). In connection with that, it needs a political strategy for bringing about reforms. Minor, easy changes obtained for the sake of appearing to be doing something—when really doing nothing—cannot truly be called reformist any more than a utopia with no transformative capacity can truly be called radical.

Finally, I am influenced by the key organizations in the community (El Paso) that first recruited me. Their network subsequently expanded into wider, border-length coalitions. This influence is not just circumstantial, however: as a role player (discussed below), I have made the moral decision that effectiveness in a true struggle means avoiding perfectionist isolation. It follows that my scholarly strength (e.g., Heyman 1995; 2000; 2002) is analysis of the everyday operations of the repressive state apparatus (though I also do more fundamental critical analyses). This lends itself to a clear vision of how we might fruitfully be able to tinker (sometimes profoundly) with the system that actually exists. Indeed, much of my work has involved specific recommendations for administration of border enforcement from a human-rights perspective.

My moral choice can be described as engaging in reformist practices while being informed by radical ideals. Reform and radicalism can coex-

Table 4.1. Radical and Reformist Options

Radical
• Address deeper levels of causation of injustice and suffering.
• Go beyond fierce outrage and pointed critique.
• Move beyond strong analyses of deep systems issues to action.
• Envision a clear counterpart (alternative) to the status quo.
• Contribute meaningfully to long-term struggle for a changed political landscape.
• Build a large, sustained community that acts on new social-cultural principles.
• Produce longer-term effects that are also more encompassing in space.

Reformist
• Address injustice and suffering through specific changes.
• Abandon perfectionist isolationism for participation in change coalitions.
• Choose not to accept existing suffering while waiting for long-term, fundamental changes.
• Focus on amelioration.
• Work for meaningful, positive changes (not "window-dressing").
• Produce shorter-term effects that are sometimes less encompassing in space.

ist in this way because radical and reformist approaches differ in space, time, and causation. While weighing possible courses of action, it is useful to consider the following points. Issues are, of course, multiple in their levels. Radical approaches are longer-term; reformist approaches are shorter-term. Radical approaches tend to be more spatially encompassing than reformist approaches (e.g., reform is more tied to the nation-state, as mentioned above). Radical approaches tackle deeper levels of causation of human well-being and suffering; reformist approaches address more immediate needs and concerns. There is no universal correct choice, but only multiple, simultaneously necessary options. The main perils lie not in making a wrong commitment to one side or the other, but in committing ineffectually to a side or, alternatively, making no choice and doing nothing. Careful observation of and reflection on actual political ethical processes, then, diminish these perils.

Involvement with Border and Immigration Struggles: A Brief Narrative

The brief and schematic summary in the previous section may imply that my thinking about radical and reformist options was a unitary, comprehensive, rational process resulting in a single, cohesive decision. That was not the case. Unsurprisingly for an anthropologist, self-reflection shows the decision to have been a series of incremental steps, often unconscious, and substantially determined by immediate situations and social ties. The narrative that follows ends in December 2010, as noted above, but my involvement continues to evolve.

Table 4.2. Timeline of Involvement in Border Human Rights Struggle

- 1998: BNHR founded in El Paso, TX.
- 1998–2006: Community organizing, regional focus.
- 2005–2006: Initial formulation of national policy guidelines by BNHR and BAN.
- 2006: Formation of Border and Immigration Task Force, an intersectoral policy coalition. Heyman recruited into effort. Key initial decision toward reformist option.
- 2006–2007: Two trips with Task Force and one in community delegation to Washington, DC. Elements of recommendations included in House and Senate immigration reform legislation.
- Nov. 2007: Border Policy Conference in El Paso. Wide range of sectors and geographic locations represented.
- Early 2008: Heyman's first draft of long policy document based on Nov. 2007 conference discussions and earlier guidelines.
- Nov. 2008: "Effective Border Policy: Security, Responsibility and Human Rights" released in Washington, DC.
- Late 2008–early 2009: Border-region NGOs and related stakeholders undertake consultation process at four border sites.
- Spring 2009: Heyman and Michalowski use consultation notes to write new policy document with priority issues.
- April 2009: "Accountability, Community Security and Infrastructure on the U.S.-Mexico Border: Policy Priorities for 2009–2010" released in Washington, DC.
- 2009: Washington visits by border NGOs and community members involved in 2008–2009 consultations. Border and Immigration Task Force lapses into abeyance.
- Summer 2009: Heyman divides priority recommendations into legislative and administrative reforms.
- Nov.–Dec. 2009: Heyman, working with National Immigration Forum and Rep. Gutierrez's staff, converts recommendations into specific language in CIR-ASAP legislation; parts appear in 2010 Senate legislation.
- Dec. 2009, Jan. 2010: Meetings at border sites with CBP field and DC staff to discuss administrative recommendations.
- April, Sept. 2010: Follow-up on DC meetings with CBP staff to continue dialogue on administrative recommendations.
- Dec. 2010: Visit to Border Patrol Basic Academy in Artesia, NM; formulation of more detailed recommendations on training.
- Dec. 2010: Writing of chapter. Subsequent activities not included.

My scholarly work has long addressed U.S.-Mexico border migration enforcement. However, apart from a few moments when I was able to address some local and national publics, I did not engage in direct political action for most of that period—partly because I was living far from this border, and partly because of the ivory-tower academic leftism that pervaded my intellectual upbringing (see Roseberry 2002), despite my sporadic involvement in labor and anti-U.S. interventionism activism as a student. Ironically, although I had advocated for politically engaged, policy-oriented anthropology (e.g., as member and eventually chair of the Society for Applied Anthropology Public Policy committee, and in Heyman 1998), I had not really done it myself. But in 2002, I took a job at the University of Texas at El Paso, eliminating the first reason for my non-engagement. I became sporadically involved in border and immigration struggles, imparting short, accessible versions of my scholarly expertise locally and nationally. Still, these activities were not coherent or attached to a focused struggle for social change; nor had I started to clarify my political ethical frameworks.

Meanwhile, in 2005 and 2006 the Border Network for Human Rights (BNHR, an El Paso/Southern New Mexico community-organizing based immigration advocacy group) and the Border Action Network (BAN, a parallel Arizona group) formulated an initial set of alternative policy guidelines for border and migration policy. These recommendations mixed reform of current practices, such as oversight and accountability for border enforcement agencies' civil and human rights performance, with calls for radical change, such as ending the "operations" (large-scale deployments of border enforcement resources) that have increased migrant deaths at the border. The value choices and specific policy recommendations in these documents emerged from systematic discussions in organized immigrant base communities with BNHR and BAN.[5] My political choices followed the framework first created by community consultation, and I put my expertise at the service of that base.

In the summer and fall of 2006, BAN and BNHR assembled a coalition of elected officials, law enforcement officials, immigrant service providers, religious leaders, academics, and others from Texas, New Mexico, and Arizona to create the U.S.-Mexico Border and Immigration Task Force (see Heyman et al. 2009). I was a founding member of the Task Force. Some members of the Task Force are immigrants, but most are not; rather, they represent the immigrant-sympathetic members of border society by working toward goals that emerge from immigrant communities. The Task Force has three main strengths: it draws on considerable expertise in the formulation and statement of policy objectives; it maintains an extensive network of political contacts and public legitimacy in border and national arenas; and it encompasses a range of values, views, and skills conducive to thoughtful policy recommendations and tactics.

Deciding to engage in the Task Force was an important political-ethical act for me. I was sympathetic to the initial guidelines that mixed responses to immediate aspects of human suffering on the border with some demands for more far-reaching change, but I also recognized that the document neither offered comprehensive critical analysis of contemporary migration and border issues worldwide nor called for fundamental change. I had to think carefully about this. As an intellectual analyst of migration I saw the deeper vision as desirable, but I also recognized its great distance from actual political conditions in the United States and Mexico. The lengthy time horizon of even a well-envisioned radical political program seemed unresponsive to the immediate crisis at the border, where people die and are deported daily. The guidelines' strength seemed to lie in their identification of immediate measures.

I also was attracted to being part of a larger effort with a division of labor that fit my capacities. As a full-time teacher, researcher, and university administrator, I feel most useful in a part-time role outside of work. The skill set I bring to the struggle is not that of a radical political activist, but I could see that my scholarly expertise on border enforcement policy and my ability to synthesize and write could prove especially valuable. Finally, working with this document and the organizations behind it appealed to me because they were grounded in the participation of immigrant base communities. In other words, my political-ethical decision was partly conditioned by entry into a particular social structure of struggle, in particular the presence of the BNHR in El Paso.[6]

In November 2006, I traveled with the Task Force to Washington, DC, to present its policy recommendations to congressional offices and White House officials. During that trip, key congressional offices asked the Task Force to provide specific legislative language. We developed a full document with policy ideas and legislative recommendations and submitted it to congressional offices in December 2006. I helped with the writing. In March 2007, delegates from the immigrant base communities made a similar trip to emphasize the human experience of border realities, thus complementing the Task Force's policy-insider presentations. Both of these trips were closely coordinated with Washington, DC, immigration reform organizations, notably the National Immigration Forum, and included active outreach to the press.

In June 2007, approximately twenty Task Force members, led by co-chairs José Rodríguez (then county attorney, El Paso County, Texas) and Manny Ruíz (then supervisor, Santa Cruz County, Arizona), traveled again to Washington to reinforce the inclusion of the border policy guidelines in the immigration reform debate. The Task Force met with key congresspersons and staffers at a crucial moment in considering comprehensive immigration reform. They also met with high-level White House and Department of Homeland Security officials, and again with Washington advocates and the press. By mid June, several of the key Task Force recommendations had made it into the final version of both the House's STRIVE Act (a flawed but relatively progressive bill) and the problematic Senate compromise bill. These recommendations included creation of a U.S.-Mexico Border Review Commission to oversee and evaluate human rights in U.S. border enforcement, a report on border deaths, a border patrol training review, local community consultations, and an Office of Detention Oversight. Unfortunately, comprehensive immigration reform failed in the summer of 2007.

In fall 2007, facing an objectively frustrated situation, the Task Force turned inward. The year had demonstrated that national-level pro-immigration politicians and advocates would sacrifice the border (and enforcement reform in whatever location) to the wider agendas of immigration reform, such as legalization, by including harsh enforcement provisions to "sell" immigration liberalization. This pattern persists, indicating a need for a distinctive, powerful border and enforcement coalition in the political process. The Task Force recognized it was geographically limited by its concentration in El Paso/Southern New Mexico and Arizona. Meanwhile, the alternative policy guidelines were understood as a living document needing constant improvement based on a wider range of actors.

On 29 and 30 November 2007, more than 200 individuals representing diverse organizations and institutions from all along the U.S.-Mexico border convened in El Paso at a Border Policy Conference. After plenary presentations on border and immigration policy history, immigration and the global economy, and analysis of the current national immigration debate, participants formed small groups to discuss each of the main categories of the existing border guidelines, to improve or add to them, and to further develop a long-term vision of border policy.

After the conference, I assembled notes from the break-out sessions, reports from earlier BNHR and BAN abuse documentation campaigns, and my own knowledge of border issues. In early 2008, I synthesized from them a first draft of a new set of guidelines with considerably more background information and much more detailed policy recommendations. That draft circulated among key people in the Task Force, BAN, and BNHR, with considerable revisions being made; particularly important were a series of meetings during spring 2008. A version was finalized during early fall 2008.

On 19 November 2008, the Task Force unveiled the full report, "Effective Border Policy: Security, Responsibility and Human Rights" (Border Network for Human Rights et al. 2008) during a visit by coalition members to Washington, DC, to meet with congresspersons, staff, transition committee members from the Obama team, DC advocacy groups, and the press. They timed the report's release to impact the administrative and legislative agenda early on in the incoming Obama administration and new Congress. The report made more than sixty recommendations, all relatively immediate and concrete. By the standards of current U.S. politics, some were radical—for instance, removing the military from all border enforcement roles, including support roles. Others involved narrower reforms, such as improved flows through ports of entry. But none of them posed fundamental challenges to the territorial nation-state, unequal rights to be in that space, the state's overall administrative role in regulating borders or territories, or the contemporary capitalist system.

Feedback from Washington advocacy organizations, Obama transition team staff, and congressional staff pointed out further steps beyond the report. One—obviously reflecting an impulse toward political pragmatism—was to prioritize the sixty guidelines. The other was to distinguish the broader, more fundamental guidelines best implemented via legislation from changes in specific practices that could be administratively implemented within executive branch agencies. Of course, in either case, implementation depended on continuous political pressure and struggle.

The Task Force, aware that it lacked involvement of major organizations from the two important border regions of San Diego County and South Texas, arranged four consultations late that winter and in spring of 2009 with border stakeholders, one each in South Texas, El Paso (attended by representatives from Southern New Mexico), Arizona, and San Diego. It had two goals: to add new recommendations from additional stakeholders, and to get stakeholders to prioritize among policy guidelines in terms of the short, medium, and long term. Using detailed notes from these four meetings, I composed an overall list of priorities (which reflected considerable consensus) and added some new policy suggestions in response to changing conditions, particularly the increased violence in Northern Mexico. Raymond Michalowski and I then used this to compose a short-term document focused on concerns of early to mid 2009, titled "Accountability, Community Security and Infrastructure on the U.S.-Mexico Border: Policy Priorities for 2009–2010" (U.S.-Mexico Border and Immigration Task Force 2009).

In April 2009 these were carried to Washington on another trip in which I participated. At this point, the group designation Border and Immigration Task Force lost currency because of the influx of important newcomers who had not been in the Task Force. Since then, the active group has not had a formal name but is generally referred to as the border stakeholders (more on this below). These recommendations were reinforced during visits to DC by stakeholders in September and then immigrant community members in October 2009. In the summer of 2009, I undertook the task of dividing the whole set of guidelines (2008 and 2009) into ordered priorities and also into two categories, legislative goals and administrative goals (completed on 10 September 2009).

Two activities flowed from this. From 28 November to 15 December, I worked closely (from home, and on my own time)[7] with National Immigration Forum staff to write actionable legislative language, which we shared in turn with the staff of Representative Luis Gutierrez. Much of that language, with alterations, was combined with language from many other sources (some very problematic) in Title I, the border enforcement title, of the proposed 2009 Comprehensive Immigration Reform ASAP Act of 2009 (Library of Congress 2009). Though introduced in December 2009, this bill, as expected, did not go anywhere, though it did set patterns for future legislation. Parts of the suggested border language were then included in Title I of the Comprehensive Immigration Reform Act of 2010 (Library of Congress 2010). Both bills combine fundamentally troubling elements with important ameliorative reforms. Given my intimate role in writing some of those ameliorative passages, I am deeply ambivalent about this legislation. The political-ethical considerations are discussed below.

The border stakeholders have entered into a lengthy negotiation process with Customs and Border Protection (CBP) and the Office of Civil Liberties and Civil Rights, both under the Department of Homeland Security (DHS). They met on December 2009 in Brownsville, Texas; January 2010 in San Diego; and April and September 2010 in Washington, DC. At these meetings, we presented our suggestions for administrative change and the rationale for them. For example, we requested that DHS systematically tabulate and analyze complaints to identify management and training issues, patterns of misbehavior, and so forth. The border stakeholders and DHS came away from these meetings with further agendas of supplying each other with concrete information and suggestions, such as field-tested complaint forms from immigrant service providers working at the border.

This process of presentations, criticisms, and defenses posed difficulties for both sides. Some progress has been made on complaints in particular, and important recommendations have been made more meaningful and specific, but much remains to be done. Moreover, considerable distance still separates advocates and government officials. The discussion is ongoing, the process has been made more effective, and CBP has appointed a liaison to border stakeholders. I have been deeply involved in many aspects, especially training, complaints, evaluation, and management. This involvement hinged on my political-ethical choice to acknowledge the centrality of the territorialized membership-state and to then tinker with its implementation.

The Task Force gradually faded away. Its replacement—the unnamed coalition of border stakeholders—emerged in 2009 and was fully active by that December. At an organizational meeting in San Diego in June 2010, it became the Southern Border Communities Coalition (SBCC). As an active member,[8] I co-coordinate the working group on CPB training, complaints, conduct, evaluation, and management. Extensive dialogue has shaped the detailed recommendations stakeholders formulate for CBP to improve officer conduct on issues such as respect for human and constitutional rights, appropriate use of force, community relations, cultural sensitivity, and handling of vulnerable populations—all ameliorative concerns within a wider law enforcement–oriented framework. Of course, this is the administrative track, where changes are less fundamental than on the legislative track.

The Task Force became the SBCC via two changes: a geographical expansion from Arizona/El Paso (and Southern New Mexico) to include California (especially San Diego), South Texas, and a wider range of groups within Arizona; and a shift toward being a coalition of nongovernmental organizations (NGOs) as such, rather than a task force of diverse civil society and local political actors. It retains its helpful array of civil society allies, but the NGOs have more organizational capacity than individuals to call meetings, pay for trips, and so on. The various NGOs fall roughly into two clusters: ground-level humanitarian activists, and community-organizing immigrant entities. The stakeholders embody considerable local knowledge and energy from the borderlands, a marginalized (i.e., poor, stigmatized, heavily Mexican-origin) region that often lacks a political voice. The development of an active coalition across the whole West-East length of the U.S. side of the border is a historical accomplishment that defies huge structural obstacles, especially fragmentation by states and by clusters of separated population concentrations.[9]

The 2006–2008 Task Force and the subsequent 2009–2011 stakeholders have been energetic and creative. Our recommendations have become more comprehensive, better phrased, and more usefully focused, and have garnered national attention. We have forged connections to the legislative and administrative arenas, and mobilized inside politics as well as community and media pressure. Nevertheless, as of this writing (December 2010), we have achieved few goals. The administration of immigration enforcement is little changed (though small victories have largely eliminated local law enforcement involvement in immigration law in El

Paso County, Texas, and Otero County, New Mexico). Reform legislation, including our suggestions or not, has not passed. Highly anti-immigrant politics at the national and state levels has limited our reformist approach, and we have not achieved the more radical objective of changing the overall balance of struggle (then again, neither have the immigration radicals). And most important in human terms, the border migration situation is as bad as ever.[10]

The Politics and Ethics of the Reformist Path, Participant-Observed

Whatever the characteristics, strengths, and weaknesses of the reformist path, the final criterion is maintaining a constant political struggle for change. When reformers stop struggling even for incremental change toward a more humane world, they lose touch with all that makes their engagement effective and meaningful. Pressure on key actors in the dominant system is essential (see Piven and Cloward 1977). Two deviations threaten this task of constant struggle. One is thinking that "correct" analysis and recommendations by themselves will bring about change. Far from it: change comes out of discussion, debate, pressure, and political impact. The other deviation is self-satisfying play that does not strive for tactical efficacy. Playing at the forms of tactical politics can mask failure to actually make an impact (e.g., issuing recommendations without seeing them get into legislation).

But direct political struggle affects value commitments. Concrete, actionable policy recommendations shape the sorts of political-ethical choices we make. Throughout the narrative above, our coalition moved toward increasingly concrete policy recommendations. For example, we went from being broadly against a vague "militarization" of the border to recommending specifically that the military neither conduct armed immigration enforcement operations nor engage in such operations within twenty-five miles of the border, while still generally stating that immigration enforcement should not involve the military at all. We did so because legislation requires specific language that moves beyond feelings and attitudes.

Concrete recommendations are specific, positive instructions: do this particular thing; don't do that one. Such recommendations must be actionable within the existing sociopolitical framework (e.g., the territorial nation-state), even if they would represent great changes to existing policy. So the political-ethical frame is necessarily narrowed or, better said, focused. We are constantly in conversation—within the coalition, with political allies and counterparts, and in inward dialogues—with what we envision as "practical" and "implementable," and whether it reflects our values. Of course, as Marshall Sahlins (1976) demonstrated, "practical" logic is socially and culturally shaped. Border ports of entry are practical places for the state to stop movement for inspection: we accept that practical logic and then recommend concrete ways to improve civil and human rights performance at such ports. Yet this does not mean limiting ourselves to what is likely to be politically acceptable, an issue I will address below. Some of our recommendations (e.g., anti-militarization measures) are politically quite unlikely, even if they would be practical to implement. I draw attention, then, to the value implications of specificity and concreteness within the actually existing frame.

A related concern is our emphasis on ameliorative recommendations. Some of our recommendations are far-reaching, especially in legislation. But many respond to the surface manifestations of human suffering, consistent with my (and evidently others') value choice in favor of immediate effect. For example, several of our administrative recommendations about conditions in short-term detention would ameliorate suffering after immigration arrests; however, they would not reduce or eliminate such arrests, detentions, and removals. Reformism, then, tends toward this particular value choice with its consequent strengths and limitations.

A key Task Force and stakeholder recommendation is to institute an oversight and accountability commission for border immigration enforcement. This is ameliorative in that it aims to detect, critique, and thus reduce specific human rights abuses in extant border control. At the same time, it makes border enforcement realities visible and public, potentially helping to transform the broader hegemony within which such activity occurs. Amelioration is ambiguous in political-ethical terms. It accepts much of the current, troubling system and may even increase its efficiency and public acceptability. But amelioration's immediate, forthright treatment of human suffering also gives it a powerful ethical appeal.

Both legislation and administrative reform interact with the current power order. Legislation can be the more transformative of the two, as illustrated by the imperatives in the two main forms of legislative action: legal statutes (e.g., "you will legalize people," "you will build 700 miles of border wall") and appropriations (e.g., "you will spend money on a study of deaths at the border"). However, legislation inherently requires involvement in the existing political process. Whereas the climate for legislation may be shaped, sometimes profoundly, by hegemony-transformative radical political movements, actual legislation requires negotiation of specific language with specific politicians and their staffs, in an immediate context of their coalitions with other politicians and, more broadly, their need to win elections. Obviously, then, legislative action is compromised and constrained by existing political conditions. This political-ethical reality manifests itself via a constant self-reflective balancing of ultimate values and political viability. Values achieve little if they cannot ultimately be enacted, yet they can also be sacrificed in the game of political maneuver.

Our coalition has experienced this in two moments of political-ethical challenge. First, before we even enter the political arena, our imagination is constrained by our vision of what is possible politically. Our coalition exercises ample political-ethical imagination, so our guidelines envision profound changes in border and immigration policy. Nevertheless, we have tried to imagine how each guideline could be implemented through a full political process (unlike, say, the approach of the No One is Illegal coalition). We have not succumbed to the worst of this risk, but it does exist in the potential for self-censorship—that is, not seeking to realize values, in anticipation of rejection in the political process.

The second challenge concerns the necessary but also deeply problematic tradeoffs and compromises within the political process itself, memorably termed "sausage-making" for its mix of diverse, sometimes unsavory ingredients. These compromises occur when legislative staffs write initial bills with input—often, specific language—from various partners like our coalition, and when elements are added to or removed from legislation in the various steps from bill to law. A fundamental political-ethical question is what sorts of elements we should allow (by maintaining our support) to coexist in legislation with our own chosen initiatives. For example, the CIR ASAP bill paired provisions based closely on our guidelines (e.g., ways of removing the military from border enforcement, ending "Operation Streamline," and strong language about officer misconduct) with enforcement-first provisions, such as studies and funding for high-technology surveillance of the border. A closely related question is which elements of our agenda we are willing to let drop while maintaining our support. Such a choice is obviously on the horizon, and we have privately discussed some of the relevant issues. The trade-off between accomplishing the good and accepting the bad is a fundamental issue that never permits a uniform or simple solution.

Unlike comprehensive, radical visions of change, reformism tends to involve a narrowing or fragmenting of goals.[11] This is not inherently good or bad; rather, its evaluation depends on the play of political struggle and the values at stake. For example, a diverse package of elements, such as a political coalition or an item of legislation is first a matter of deciding what is included and what is excluded. Once a variegated whole is assembled, several political-ethical tasks arise as actors engage in the politics needed to insert, promote, and preserve specific elements (e.g., specific legislative provisions within a larger bill)—or to embrace a position for or against the whole package, and carry on the attendant struggle. In both cases, but especially the former, fragmentation of vision is a real consequence that can become politically and ethically problematic even though it is not wrong per se.

Political struggle requires effective movements and coalitions. Coalitions are based on mutual networks of recognition, communication, and reciprocity, both political and symbolic. This means that political-ethical decisions are not just abstract but are (and must be) conditioned by their social environment. The goals of the Task Force and SBCC were first conditioned by immigrant communities. The initial guidelines grew out of base community consultations, and immigrant-community based organizations later carried out the guidelines, and the politics of the struggle for them, via organizational structures giving leaders and staff considerable ability to shape the applications of those values and goals. In both radical and reform politics, the nature of a constant tactical struggle dictates that decisions be made by specific individuals or groups in a division of labor, and for that reason are not easily subjected to constant, pure participation. For example, I composed recommendations for legislation and administration by drawing on base community principles, but only the leadership of the Task Force reviewed the specific language. Clearly there is need for a social analysis of the political-ethical implications of the relationship between activists/staffs and bases, and among activists/staffs themselves.[12]

Importantly, key activist members of the coalition condition each other. We have different backgrounds, needs, and agendas. For example, one goal of the Task Force was to involve a range of sectors across border society in building a strong political voice for this usually ignored region. At the 2007 border summit that elaborated the 2008 guidelines, we examined how conditions at land ports of entry affect the flow of legal trade and cross-border visits. This occasioned some disagreement between radicals whose fundamental critique of the "free trade" relationship between the United States and Mexico led them to oppose measures serving trade, and reformers who saw improvement of trade and other movement through ports as a need and desire of border society, given the regional economy and society's utter dependence on these transactions. Because of the vast economic importance of the affected sectors, improvement of the flow of trade and visiting through ports of entry is the single most important item on the border commercial and political elites' agenda. Such key border actors are a desirable part of our coalition and help us pursue other goals (e.g., human and constitutional rights in port enforcement). This is not only a rational trade-off—such mutual conditioning emerges constantly from social interactions. My value decisions have been conditioned by being part of a coalition.

Another, related concern is that actors allied in coalitions share many important values and policy choices, but not all of them. Richard Wiles, currently sheriff of El Paso county and formerly police chief of the city of El Paso, has been crucial to our political coalition. He is an important leader, locally and nationwide, in the push to keep local law enforcement out of immigration enforcement. Yet his sheriff's department still turns records of some pre-conviction immigrant arrestees (those with violations higher than Class C misdemeanors, a relatively progressive approach) over to Immigration and Customs Enforcement, initiating the process of removal, as part of the Secure Communities program. This follows the logic of local law enforcement, which sees jailing as a huge expense, thus favoring the diversion of some people into the immigrant removal process. Several other coalition members disagree with this policy and value choice, though we continue to respect and appreciate the sheriff. This poses a broader political-ethical question: When should political alliances within a struggle be prioritized over specific policy principle, and vice versa?

Finally, various relationships with people in government condition our policy and value decisions. Political allies, such as key legislators and staff, cannot easily be considered opponents in a policy struggle, even when they try to guide us politically (see the remarks above on legislative compromise). We sometimes find ourselves critiquing and wanting to change the policies and practices of people who are our direct counterparts—for example, some key administrative figures in DHS. Yet we also need to forge and retain relations with them, even when our agenda is to present vigorous critiques of and alternatives to their work. This is a delicate dance on both sides. The key question is whether maintaining needed relationships with counterparts results in changes to practical proposals and deeper political-ethical values.[13]

Social processes also condition political-ethical choices through interactions over time. Broadly, our decision making is not one-time, complete, and coherent but instead involves considerable path dependency. This is illustrated, in a positive way, by the underlying persistence of the basic 2006 guidelines that emerged from immigrant community consultations held by BNHR and BAN. In deepening, widening, and modifying them, we have always worked from their earlier versions. Path dependency connects to another set of dilemmas that confronts all struggle processes, radical and reformist alike. Issues and opportunities emerge over the short term, an example being our concern with violence in Mexico and related law enforcement in the United States in our 2009 report. The challenge is to address immediate political opportunities and challenges while maintaining long-term vision and direction. In some sense, we have balanced immediate opportunism (in a positive sense, addressing real needs of po-

Table 4.3. Lessons of the Reformist Path

• Correct social analyses and policy recommendations are never self-enacting.
• Ameliorative needs often shape reform priorities.
• Unlike radicalism's comprehensive visions of change, reformism is prone to a narrowing or fragmenting of goals.
• Constant self-reflection is needed to balance ultimate values against political viability.
• Path dependency strongly influences moves from activity to activity. An important question is, how does one maintain direction within a fluid and pragmatic path?
• To bring about change, constant political struggle must be maintained; details of immediate reformist politics must contribute to change rather than becoming ends in themselves.
• Direct political struggle within the status quo conditions policy choices, vocabulary, compromises, etc.
• Frameworks of "practical" reason (e.g., current state institutions) shape policy choices.
• Coalitions condition choices that, as a social product of a network of persons and groups, are not analytically pure.
• Relatively conservative groups may be key allies on some issues.
• Even key counterparts (e.g., government officials) condition reformist activities in the debate/dialogue process.
• Beware the "legitimation trap": being heard is insufficient if it does not effect real change.

litical struggle) with the long-term value choices embodied in enduring policy themes in our documents and presentations.

When interacting with counterparts who represent the dominant power system, reformists are vulnerable to "legitimation traps," whereby such counterparts deflect their attention from their struggle with the status quo by exciting their hopes of improvement via possible legislation and administrative reforms, and "dialogues" more generally. Fear that dialogues will be broken off then deters direct attacks. More generally, the feeling of "being heard" by politicians and other authorities has a seductive allure, even if no action ensues. A related effect is a change in language to render terms friendly, or at least less offensive—in other words, restraint from honestly critical analysis.

Arguably, the Democratic Party and the Obama administration have encountered this since 2009. Apparent legitimation traps that have kept immigration and border reformers patient and quiet include the introduction of comprehensive immigration reform legislation in general (with some of our suggestions as language in the bills) and certain features of the new DHS's administration of immigration law (e.g., prioritizing removal of supposedly criminal aliens over indiscriminate removal). Ameliorative reforms, no matter how ethically justified, are particularly vulnerable to legitimation traps. But even if we are aware of the risk of legitimation traps, what are our alternatives? Careful, case-by-case political analysis is needed to weigh the possible opportunities for meaningful action against the risks of co-optation and seduction.

Conclusion

Political engagement is processual, complex, and replete with difficult choices. This reality warrants serious reflection on the part of enthusiasts of public anthropology and other public social sciences. We can apply careful participant observation — a tool we already possess — to discover, delineate, and analyze the various complications in the action process itself. In so doing, we strengthen our political engagement with our enhanced ability to discern issues and choose among possible actions. We need to build up and use a substantial literature on case studies of political engagement, above and beyond critical analysis of the status quo. Thus I advocate for a reflexive, case study–based social science of scholarly public engagement.

Tension between radicalism and reformism inheres in the struggle for social change. Radicals are oriented to the systematic quality of injustices; reformists seek opportunities for change. Admittedly, it is overly rigid to state them as a dichotomy (a shortcut I am guilty of taking here for communicative purposes). Rather, they are two ever-present potentials in the process of change. In this view, the choice between them (or complicated blends of them) never fully disappears, even given a basic tendency toward one option, like my mostly reformist stance. The key point is that at any given historical moment, actors make judgments as to whether there is a possibility of real contribution to long-term change via the political path of struggle — a possibility mainly grounded in the radical option. Absent that possibility and meaningful actions toward it, reformist amelioration becomes more compelling in view of the terrible intensity of present human suffering.

The most important lesson of reformism has been the continuous process of political-ethical reflection. The reformist path is never a pure ethical or political choice but rather a social process, part of a movement for change to promote human rights and social justice. It involves assessing — with ultimate values and goals in mind — one's own capabilities; opportunities to act; fellow coalition members' visions, skills, and interests; and counterparts in media, law, legislatures, and bureaucratic state apparatuses. And unlike radical projects, which have relatively coherent visions of alternative social orders, reformism emphasizes a variety of ameliorative needs, practical opportunities, and diverse actions. Adding to this complexity are the various compromises required for action within the status quo, and the often quite short timelines involved in reform opportunities. Thus, in this process that lends itself to loss of vision, a sense of human justice—maintained by reinforcing equalities such as rights, and reducing unnecessary suffering—is crucial as a guiding compass.

My own reformism is best understood as an exercise in strategic pessimism (possibilities for fundamentally progressive border and migration politics are currently remote [Heyman 2008; 2012]) combined with tactical optimism (pushing for particular legislative or administrative suggestions in determinate time frames) based on compelling need for amelioration. Were the strategic situation more optimistic, the case for pursuing more fundamental transformations would be more compelling. Yet even in this difficult time, we struggle on. People die in the desert, suffer rights violations, face racial profiling in their home communities, and so on. The ultimate political-ethical challenge is to not lose hope and direction. How do we maintain energy and direction throughout the process? In my case, the answer is dedication to the struggle and the process as such. The reformist's motivation is nourished by the radical ideal. The struggle and the process are what (little) we can do, in and of ourselves.

Josiah McC. Heyman is Professor of Anthropology and Director of the Center for Inter-American and Border Studies at the University of Texas at El Paso. His work focuses on borders, states, power, public issues, and engaged social sciences. He is the author or editor of three books and more than one hundred forty scholarly articles, book chapters, and essays. He is President of the Board of Directors of the Border Network for Human Rights and coordinator of the Training, Complaints, and Operations Task Force of border NGOs. Previously, he was a member of the Border and Immigration Task Force, and did much of the drafting of their two policy reports. He is currently working on specific legislative and administrative suggestions concerning human rights accountability and performance for border agencies.

Notes

1. I acknowledge and sincerely thank John Symons, Fernando Garcia, and Anna Ochoa O'Leary for their important contributions to this chapter. All responsibility for errors remains my own.

2. I have been the social scientist most involved in the Task Force/Stakeholders, but I also should recognize Raymond Michalowski, Zoe Hammer, Rebecca Orozco, Louie Gilot, Robin Hoover, Timothy Dunn, Kathleen Staudt, Maria Cristina Morales, and Guillermina Gina Núñez-Mchiri. Moreover, social scientists are not unique bearers of sociopolitical data and analysis, for activists—many with political, legal, human rights, immigrant community, and other kinds of expertise—also possess vast knowledge and sharp analysis. On social science as part of such coalitions, see Heyman et al. (2009).

3. See www.derechoshumanosaz.net/; http://nooneisillegal-montreal.blogspot.com. Right-libertarian open-borders radicalism (e.g., by the Cato Institute) favors a decreased role of borders in constraint of movement as somewhat coherent with free investment/trade neoliberalism. The radical left immigration and border position, on the other hand, attends mainly to liberating the movement of people (e.g., Hing 2010). Although the latter stance addresses the inequitable treatment of people versus capital, its radical thrust involves difficult contradictions that are poorly explored on the left. For example, the role of the anti-capitalist component as opposed to the universalist/human rights perspective merits more exploration.

4. Obviously, I draw on Alinsky's *Rules for Radicals* (1971) but do not necessarily associate the entirety of the radical option with his specific approach, which contains elements that are closer to my reformist option.

5. The roots of the policy priorities in grassroots consultations are described as follows: "In the summer of 2005, the Border Network for Human Rights (BNHR) and the Border Action Network (BAN) launched an unprecedented consultation within border communities in Texas, New Mexico, and Arizona, placing border policies and practices at the center of the discussions. As a result of those community dialogues, it became clear that border communities critically questioned the content and form of U.S. border policies and the process by which they are shaped by Congress, the Administration, and Washington-based institutions, who essentially have left out the voices, opinions, and perceptions of border communities. … By the spring of 2006, the BNHR and BAN, with the support of the Latin America Working Group, had translated the results of the community consultations into a series of nearly 40 policy recommendations. These recommendations, which dealt with issues such as border operations, fencing, military involvement at the border, law-enforcement misconduct, community security, and detention and deportation, became known as the Guidelines for Alternative Border Enforcement Policies and Practices" (Border Network for Human Rights et al., 2008: 8).

6. A useful comparison is the opportunity I had to pursue a radical option by serving at Annunciation House, a local shelter for travelers (including many undocumented people) that clearly rejects the dominant state order and its control over people and their mobility. The shelter enacts an alternative social order, but it remains a service provider because this alternative order cannot spread under current political conditions. I respect this, but recognition of the nation-state is explicit in my work with the Task Force and successor groups struggling for increased practical human rights in enforcement and reduced border deaths.

7. As part of the University of Texas system, the University of Texas, El Paso, adheres to regulations that imply limits on university employees' direct lobbying on public time or with public resources. I am careful to follow these guidelines.

8. I changed my status from academic member to member via the BNHR.

9. Parallel coalitions have tentatively developed within Mexico to work on human rights of migrants, including Central Americans in transit through Mexico. Any fundamental analysis of migration necessarily sees it as a transnational phenomenon. The distinctly

national approach of the Task Force and stakeholders, then, indicates the impact of national political frames on a reformist approach. The two groups have many binational members and even more bicultural/bilingual members, and they often switch between Spanish and English in their internal work. Formal political activities, however, accept the cultural-linguistic dominance of English in the U.S. state.

10. For simplicity's sake, this participant-observation narrative omits mention some of my other work on, e.g., activities aimed at fending off Arizona-style legislation in the Texas state legislature; the summit of opponents to the border wall in El Paso on 2–3 December 2008, and follow-up activities; testimony on the militarization of the border given at the Universal Periodic Review (of U.S. human rights performance) in El Paso on 8 March 2010; and many appearances and interviews in local, national, and international media. Nor does it discuss important activities that I support only behind the scenes, e.g., through my role as member, and most recently president, of the BNHR Board of Directors.

11. Likewise, insiders in political struggles usually are highly aware of and sensitive to specific units of policy, whereas outsiders generally emphasize feelings about overall legislation.

12. My own role as a writer merits some attention as having some degree of power over others, in that I interpret comments collected at meetings and synthesize their coherent statements. I never simply dictate final results; rather, I work with collective input to produce drafts for review by other members of the Task Force. Still, I have power over one synapse in the process of making political-ethical decisions.

13. One entirely useless stance is a sense of being contaminated by interaction with those holding opposing views, even in pursuit of an admirable goal. E.g., although I am fundamentally uncomfortable with the full frontal border enforcement model embodied in the Border Patrol, I have not hesitated to present recommendations on training, complaints, and many other issues to Border Patrol decision makers. I do not feel contaminated by my relationship to them; I am, after all, promoting socially just values. This sort of symbolic contamination thinking is, in my experience, quite widespread on the left.

References

Alinsky, Saul. 1971. *Rules for Radicals: A Pragmatic Primer for Realistic Radicals.* New York: Random House.

Andreas, Peter. 2000. *Border Games: Policing the U.S.–Mexico Divide.* Ithaca, NY: Cornell University Press.

Border Network for Human Rights, the Border Action Network, and the U.S.-Mexico Border and Immigration Task Force. 2008. *Effective Border Policy: Security, Responsibility and Human Rights.* El Paso: Border Network for Human Rights, and Tucson: Border Action Network. http://cdm15029.contentdm.oclc.org/utils/getfile/collection/p266901coll4/id/1842/filename/1732.pdf.

D'Andrade, Roy. 1995. "Moral Models in Anthropology." *Current Anthropology* 36: 399–408.

Dunn, Timothy J. 1996. *The Militarization of the U.S.–Mexico Border, 1978–1992: Low-Intensity Conflict Doctrine Comes Home.* Austin: CMAS Books, University of Texas at Austin.

———. 2009. *Blockading the Border and Human Rights: The El Paso Operation that Remade Immigration Enforcement.* Austin: University of Texas Press.

Ervin, Alexander M. 2004. *Applied Anthropology: Tools and Perspectives for Contemporary Practice,* 2nd ed. Boston: Pearson Allyn & Bacon.

Fassin, Didier. 2007. "Humanitarianism as a Politics of Life." *Public Culture* 19: 499–520.

Hale, Charles R., ed. 2008. *Engaging Contradictions: Theory, Politics, and Methods of Activist Scholarship.* Berkeley: University of California Press.

Heyman, Josiah. 1995. "Putting Power into the Anthropology of Bureaucracy: The Immigration and Naturalization Service at the Mexico-United States Border." *Current Anthropology* 36: 261–287.

———. 1998. *Finding a Moral Heart for U.S. Immigration Policy: An Anthropological Perspective.* Washington, DC: American Anthropological Association.

———. 1999. "Why Interdiction? Immigration Law Enforcement at the United States–Mexico Border." *Regional Studies* 33: 619–630.

———. 2000. "Respect for Outsiders? Respect for the Law? The Moral Evaluation of High-Scale Issues by US Immigration Officers." *Journal of the Royal Anthropological Institute* (N.S.) 6: 635–652.

———. 2002. "U.S. Immigration Officers of Mexican Ancestry as Mexican Americans, Citizens, and Immigration Police." *Current Anthropology* 43: 479–507.

———. 2003. "The Inverse of Power." *Anthropological Theory* 3: 139–156.

———. 2008. "Constructing a Virtual Wall: Race and Citizenship in U.S.-Mexico Border Policing." *Journal of the Southwest* 50: 305–334.

———. 2012. "Constructing a 'Perfect' Wall: Race, Class, and Citizenship in U.S.-Mexico Border Policing." In *Migration in the 21st Century: Ethnography and Political Economy,* ed. Winnie Lem and Pauline Gardiner Barber. New York and London: Routledge.

Heyman, Josiah M., Maria Cristina Morales, and Guillermina Gina Núñez. 2009. "Engaging with the Immigrant Human Rights Movement in a Besieged Border Region: What Do Applied Social Scientists Bring to the Policy Process?" *NAPA Bulletin* 31: 13–29.

Hing, Bill Ong. 2010. *Ethical Borders: NAFTA, Globalization, and Mexican Migration.* Philadelphia: Temple University Press.

Hymes, Dell, ed. 1972. *Reinventing Anthropology.* New York: Pantheon.

Lassiter, Luke E. 2005. *The Chicago Guide to Collaborative Ethnography.* Chicago: University of Chicago Press.

Library of Congress. 2009. H.R.4321 – Comprehensive Immigration Reform ASAP Act of 2009. 111th Congress (2009–2010). Washington, DC: Library of Congress. http://thomas.loc.gov/cgi-bin/query/z?c111:H.R.4321:.

———. 2010. S.3932 — CIR Act of 2010. 111th Congress (2009–2010). Washington, DC: Library of Congress. http://thomas.loc.gov/cgi-bin/query/z?c111:S.3932:.

Nevins, Joseph. 2007. "Dying for a Cup of Coffee? Migrant Deaths in the US-Mexico Border Region in a Neoliberal Age." *Geopolitics* 12: 228–247.

———. 2010. *Operation Gatekeeper and Beyond: The War On "Illegals" and the Remaking of the U.S.–Mexico Boundary,* 2nd ed. New York and London: Routledge.

Piven, Frances Fox, and Richard A. Cloward. 1977. *Poor People's Movements: Why They Succeed, How They Fail.* New York: Vintage Books.

Roseberry, William. 2002. "Political Economy in the United States." In *Culture, Economy, Power: Anthropology as Critique, Anthropology as Praxis,* ed. Winnie Lem and Belinda Leach. Albany: SUNY Press.

Sahlins, Marshall. 1976. *Culture and Practical Reason.* Chicago: University of Chicago Press.

Scheper-Hughes, Nancy. 1995. "The Primacy of the Ethical." *Current Anthropology* 36: 409–420.

Sharma, Nandita. 2006. *Home Economics: Nationalism and the Making of 'Migrant Workers' in Canada.* Toronto: University of Toronto Press.

Spener, David. 2009. *Clandestine Crossings: Migrants and Coyotes on the Texas-Mexico Border.* Ithaca, NY: Cornell University Press.

U.S.-Mexico Border and Immigration Task Force. 2009. *Border Policy Priorities for 2009–2010: Accountability, Community Security and Infrastructure.* Washington, DC: U.S.-Mexico Border and Immigration Task Force. http://shapleigh.org/system/reporting_document/file/349/2009.Border.Policy.Report.Final.pdf.

Chapter 5

PUBLIC ANTHROPOLOGY AND STRUCTURAL ENGAGEMENT
Making Ameliorating Social Inequality Our Primary Agenda

————— ∞∞ —————

Merrill Singer

By way of lending a hand to ushering in the twenty-first century for an-thropology—a discipline that still struggles with the burden of its nine-teenth-century colonial heritage—I authored an essay in the *Anthropology Newsletter* entitled, "Why I am Not a Public Anthropologist" (Singer 2000). My intention in that and several subsequent papers (Rylko-Bauer et al. 2006; Singer 2008; also see Rylko-Bauer 2000) was something akin (if less political) to what Jim Hightower (2008) had in mind with his book, *Swim Against the Current: Even a Dead Fish Can Go With the Flow,* namely that there may be good reasons to challenge seemingly unstoppable social trends and robust conceptual flows. At the time I wrote the initial essay, the rush to create a "public anthropology"—both because of an increasing concern about the future of the field and the undeniable appeal of a well-chosen trope—had gathered momentum and was beginning to surge downhill, remaking in its path, so it was hoped, the mission and public face of our discipline. Today, public anthropology can claim an established space within the broader disciplinary domain of anthropology (and a parallel enterprise exists in sociology, suggesting something about the very public nature of our contemporary era). It has achieved frequent appearance in anthropological discourse, a Wikipedia listing, graduate programs, a book series, a journal, a review section within the *American Anthropologist,* blog discussions, an annual conference, frequent listing in the titles of anthro-pology conference sessions, the American Anthropological Association's

Solon T. Kimball Award for Public and Applied Anthropology (which, as irony would have it, I have been one of the recipients), and much more. When Borofsky in 2007 carried out a search for "public anthropology" on scholarly/academic databases using Google Scholar he was provided with 475 links. Three years later, the same search produced 4,570 items.

Despite this notable success, just what public anthropology is remains in dispute. As Borofsky (2007) observes, public anthropology has "developed a life of its own ... with different people using it in different ways for different ends." So too in this volume, which asserts an alternative activist and engaged strategy for public anthropology as the most promising path for gaining public acquaintance with the usefulness of anthropological insight about emergent social developments, world-shaping events, and intense civic controversies.

Within the conceptual space provided by Sam Beck and Carl Maida in the opening essay of this volume, the purpose of this chapter is to contribute to the further development of a socially conscious anthropology, guided by critical social theory, that publically engages contemporary human problems that contribute to profound human suffering. Paul Farmer (1999: 6) has argued that "A blindness to inequality and structural violence ... has long marred anthropology," a consequence, adds Scheper-Hughes and Bourgois (1999: 6), of "the bourgeois identity of most of its practitioners." Thus, in a famous example, Clifford Geertz (1995), for many years the most recognized and honored voice in anthropology, admitted that he consciously avoided paying attention to the coming government-sponsored (and U.S.-supported) slaughter in Indonesia of between half a million and one million communists (real and suspected) in 1965 following a failed uprising (of uncertain origin). At the time (following recent independence from colonial Dutch rule and Japanese war-time occupation), Indonesia was organized by a rigid class hierarchy topped by traditional aristocracy and emergent elite that resisted the creation of more equitable social conditions for the impoverished majority population of the country (Geertz 1963; van der Kroef 1956). Asked about his lack of commentary on the massacre at his Russell Sage Foundation presentation in 1991, Geertz stressed that he preferred a scholarly focus on theoretical issues in human life to both the swirl of a public media controversy and participation in the politics of advocacy. Unaddressed in this defense, and of great relevance here, are the no less important academic politics of inattentional blindness to inequality and the exercise of power in the creation and enforcement of disparity. A meaningful and creditable publically oriented anthropology, it is argued here, cannot avoid "seeing" and providing critical social assessment of inequality and power as central world-shaping forces.

Existential Disciplinary Dilemmas

Entrée into these issues begins by addressing two questions: Why have a public anthropology? Why now? The appeal of developing a broader public face for anthropology stems in part from growing recognition of real threats to the survival of anthropology as a distinct discipline and the need for developing an acknowledged relevance for the field within and beyond the academy, including in the imaginaries of diverse publics and even subaltern counterpublics (Fraser 1990; Warner 2005).

It should be recalled that the issue of contemporary relevance has itself been one of controversy within the history of the discipline. Gerald Berreman (1968: 391), in alluding to a critical moment in this debate (although one that was not as decisive as he might have liked, as seen in post–Vietnam War efforts to cleanse the discipline of its embrace of social consciousness), comments:

> The notion that contemporary world events are irrelevant to the professional concerns of anthropologists was laid neatly to rest when, at the meeting of Fellows of the American Anthropological Association in Pittsburg in November, 1966, Michael Harner rose to challenge the ruling of the president-elect that a resolution introduced by David and Kathleen Gough Aberle condemning the United States' role in the war in Vietnam was out of order because it did not "advance the science of anthropology" or "further the professional interests of anthropologists." Harner suggested that "genocide is not in the professional interests of anthropologists." With that, the chair was voted down and the resolution was presented, amended, and passed.

A few decades after the heady days Berreman describes, with dramatic shifts and (from the vantage of 1968) unforeseen developments in the world that we seek to comprehend (and influence), anthropological confidence in its relevance—and, more so, in the discipline's future—is an issue of uncertainty. There are several components to what might be termed anthropology's contemporary existential dilemma.

First, there is the problem of loss of mission. In a sense, this is a revisiting of an old problem in anthropology. In the introduction to *Argonauts of the Western Pacific*, for example, Malinowski (1922: xv) argued that anthropology was in a "sadly ludicrous, not to say tragic position" in the world because "at the very moment it begins to put its workshop in order, to forge its proper tools" the "native" populations that constitute the "material of its study" are melting away "with hopeless rapidity." Subsequently, at the Sixth World Congress of Sociology, Peter Worsley (1968) presented a paper entitled "The End of Anthropology" in which he argued that the "tribal" societies of traditional anthropological interest were withering away, and so too the discipline that studies them unless it changes its focus. Having survived the loss of the "primitive," anthropology now confronts the asserted loss of cultural diversity all together (Friedman 2005). In a globalizing world, it is clear, for example, that there have been vast changes in the original micro-populations of historic concern to the discipline. Today, as we know, a traditionally somewhat isolated, semi-nomadic, rainforest-dwelling horticulturalist/foraging group like the Waorani of Ecuador now wear western clothes, pray in Christian churches, trade for soccer balls and packaged noodles, and must contend with the encroachments of the multinational oil companies, logging companies, and the global epidemic diseases brought to them by outsiders. As a result, the Waorani cannot fairly be studied any longer as a remote people with a distinct and unique culture, however great the need for "lost tribes" in the Western imaginary. While they have not lost key components of their traditional lifestyle, the Waorani are citizens of far broader social and economic worlds than in the past, as signaled by events like their public march in 2005 on the Ecuadoran Congress chanting "We don't want more drilling in our land. We don't want to disappear. We want our rights to be respected" (Survival International 2005).

In this assertion of identity politics, the Waorani echo other groups around the world that have begun to formulate their concerns in a common, globally circulating language of human rights. Consequently, the issue is raised about the restructuring capacity and fast-paced nature of globalization and the consequent demise of cultural diversity. Various observers have noted the potential source of such loss. Thus, multinational corporations, whose reach is seemingly limitless (and endlessly restless), promote the development of a consumerist culture and the thirst for manufactured commodities in the far-flung corners of the world (a process aptly titled either the Coca-Colonization or McDonaldization of humanity). At the same time, global electronic communication promotes the rapid global flow of ideas and understandings, values and lifestyles, primarily of Western origin, that imperially overrun local traditions and lead arguably to the homogenization of human social life and the emergence of a global monoculture. In light of these changes, some believe, we now inhabit a world in which an "onrush of economic and ecological forces ... demand integration and uniformity ... that mesmerize the world with fast music, fast computers, and fast food—with MTV, Macintosh, and McDonald's, pressing nations into one commercially homogenous global network: one McWorld tied together by technology, ecology, communications, and commerce" (Barber 1992: 53). While the Waorani, and all of the other diverse groups "tribal" and otherwise that have been studied by anthropologists certainly can be re-imagined as local actors on a shifting global stage, in this kind of world what is the distinctive disciplinary domain and public rationale of anthropology? While anthropologists have certainly grappled with this dilemma (e.g., Watson 1997), turning their sights to indigenization, macro/macro processes, and localized reactions to globalization, this turn has hardly been integrated into the public face of the discipline, nor even our own definition of the field.

Related to this is the fact that questions have been asked (e.g., of Geertz) about our effectiveness in recognizing social consequences of globalization and other expressions of contemporary change in the world as well as our willingness and preparedness in assessing social change even as it transpires all around us. Well known in this regard is Orin Starn's (1991: 63) example from Andean anthropology, and the failure of "hundreds of anthropologists ... working in the Andes" to realize that a major insurgency by Shining Path was brewing in the communities they studied. More recently, Didier Fassim (2006) expressed dismay that anthropologists in France failed to foresee the uprising that took place in poor neighborhoods of the country's principle cities in October and November of 2005. Additionally, he laments that "even afterwards they had nothing to say about [these events]" (Fassim 2006: 1). Examples like these magnify worries about the relevance of anthropology in the modern, ever more complicated and intertwined world.

Secondly, even within the academy various forces threaten anthropology's professional role including the emergence of other claimants (like cultural studies) to anthropology's key concepts and defining methods. As notes Howell (1997: 104), "from an academic power-politics point of view, [anthropologists] may have to fight for a recognition of our unique contribution to the study of social and cultural institutions and processes, a contribution whose disciplinary roots are largely unacknowledged by exponents of cultural studies who seem to claim for themselves concepts, theories and methodologies which have long been integral to social anthropology." In short, there is concern that "the discipline has lost its brand" (Comaroff 2010: 525). Related to this is fear, especially in a time of economic crisis, shrinking state budgets, and re-thinking of university structures and missions, of the downsizing, merging, or even loss of departments of anthropology. Witness the decision to close the department of anthropology at Howard University in December 2010 (Bugarin et al. 2010). More broadly, there is concern that as universities ever more "aggressively embrace corporate values, corporate management practices, corporate labor-relations policies, and corporate money" (Turk 2010) anthropology may slide off the standard curriculum of what, in a corporatized world, is considered a "well-rounded" college education.

Thirdly, at least some anthropologists claim that anthropology suffers from severe intellectual insulation. In Eriksen's assessment: "Since the Second World War, anthropology has shrunk away from the public eye in almost every country where it has an academic presence. Student numbers grow; young men and women are still being seduced by the intellectual magic of anthropology, ideas originating in anthropology become part of an everyday cultural reflexivity—and yet, the subject is all but invisible outside its own circles" (2006: 26). Adds Chambers: "We are engaged in a struggle to demonstrate our worth in a world that seems disinterested if not hostile" (1987: 329). As a result, this perspective suggests, anthropologists have circled their wagons and talk primary to each other, as no one else seems to be interested in listening anymore.

Finally, anthropology's contemporary dilemma, in fact, is greater still, as most anthropologists no longer (can) talk much to most other anthropologists, especially those who inhabit other subdomains of specialized inquiry. As Nugent (1997: 3) observes, "Anthropology … has largely forsaken the idea of a central theory and is now comprised of a number of sub-fields or specialisms." As a result, the discipline "has become decentered and [is] unable to articulate as clear a sense of purpose as was the case in earlier periods" (Nugent 1997 4). Narrowing of research careers has led to departments of anthropology in which faculty have little, beyond simple pleasantries (perhaps), to say to their colleagues down the hall who intellectually inhabit other corners of the multifarious anthropological project (assuming that angered internal debates about issues like science vs. postmodernism have not shut down all peer communication already). Yet, as Comaroff (2010: 533) avows, for a discipline to survive participants must "continue to argue with one another," as it is debate over issues like theory, method, ethics, application, and direction that engages members, builds commitment, and pushes a field forward.

As a consequence of challenging developments like these, the kinds of work that gained anthropology its initial place in academia and in public discussions of the nature of our species are withering away. As a result, the relevance of anthropology and the rationale for its continued existence as an independent discipline (and all the paraphernalia, stages, customs, titles, events, and whatnot that goes with it), are in question. In fact, in the view of some anthropologists the demise of academic anthropology would not be a bad thing. Thus, Maurice Bloch (Bloch and Kaaristo 2007) asserts, "It's very possible that anthropology departments will disappear, there's no reason why they should continue existing. … It may well be that they just disappear; it wouldn't bother me very much."

It is here that public anthropology as a "new" forward thrust within the discipline has gained cache. While it would not be hard to find examples of public-oriented anthropology that long pre-date more recent efforts (e.g., Eddy and Partridge 1978) to address "important social concerns in an engaging, non-academic manner" (Borofsky 2008), the current initiative has helped both to heighten awareness of the risks of insular patterns within what had come to be seen by many as anthropology's core (i.e., the academy and scholarly exchange), and to draw attention to the important questions of what, in a rapidly changing world, are to be the discipline's place and value beyond the ivory tower.

How are Anthropologists Applying Anthropology?

Yet, from its inception, public anthropology has had to contend with those who question its distinctiveness relative to already existing and labeled subfields of the discipline, most notably practicing and applied anthropology (a dual naming that reflects a now largely moribund debate among those in and out of the academy concerned with putting anthropology to use in the wider world). The older of these two terms, "applied anthropology," has been part of the discipline's vernacular and practice for more than a century. In an oft-cited passage, E.B. Tylor (1871: 453) captured this aspect of early anthropology noting that by being "active at once in aiding progress and in removing hindrance, the science of culture is essentially a reformer's science."

Tylor's era, of course, in its (still disputed) relationship with colonialism, has haunted anthropology ever since. The discipline has sought to free itself of this irksome thorn in part by making applied anthropology stand-in like the whipping boys of sixteenth-century England princes. Thus, in their condensed history of the field, Scheper-Hughes and Bourgois (1999: 7–8) assert not only is applied anthropology the singular heir to anthropology's colonial legacy, the subfield continues to err on the side of inequity in one guise or another: "So called 'applied anthropology' is especially tainted by history. Born as a stepchild of colonialism ... it came of age during the Cold War ... only to find itself maturing into a partisan of neoliberal globalization in the name of a kinder, gentler cultural sensitivity and sometimes more openly as cost-effective market-based research."

But theirs is a peculiar reading of the history of the discipline, one in which applied anthropology is reduced to its own or the broader discipline's worst features (Rylko-Bauer et al. 2006). Fuller histories of applied work within the discipline paint a different, far more complex, and, at times, more virtuous picture (Ervin 2000; Singer 2008; van Willigen 2002). Certainly a balanced reading of the relationship of applied anthropologists and their work to groups and systems of social dominance would have little difficulty finding numerous examples that complicate the stigmatizing understanding offered by Scheper-Hughes and Bourgois. Moreover, the relationship of anthropology with colonialism extended to the whole discipline and was not the peculiar misadventure of applied anthropology. Additionally, anthropologists—applied and otherwise—in and out of colonial service have counted among their number committed opponents and critics of colonialism, neoliberal globalization, anthropology as a marketing strategy, and, more recently, the involvement of anthropologists in cultural mapping in combat zones through the army's $40 million Human Terrain System (HTS) program. With regard to the later, while it has been noted in the mass media that the American Anthropological Association in October 2007 denounced the use of anthropologists in such army operations as unethical, it has been less publicized that the Society for Applied Anthropology published a thorough critique of anthropological involvement in human terrain mapping in its newsletter (Rylko-Bauer 2008) and that its Board of Directors subsequently passed a critical resolution on the HTS.

Thus, while notions of cultural progress and colonial regime colored Tylor's perspective on the reformer's science, the social mission that drives contemporary applied anthropology is that of solving human problems through the application of anthropological methods, theories, and insights. Chambers, for example, defines applied anthropology broadly as "the field of inquiry concerned with relationships between anthropological knowledge and the uses of that knowledge in the world beyond anthropology" (1987: 309). Although definitional construction is almost always, sooner or later, contested, it is likely that Chambers's language would be acceptable to many if not most of those who are regularly engaged in applied work.

However defined, it can fairly be said that applications of anthropology have been wide-ranging, complicated, and undertaken in the service of disparate (and conflicting, and certainly not always admirable) agendas, collectively constituting "some of the best and some of the worst work carried out in the name of anthropology" (Singer 2008: 326). While the issues addressed by applied anthropologists are far too numerous to itemize, to cite just those topics addressed in a single recent issue of *Practicing Anthropology* (Fall 2010), these would include: working as an expert witness in death penalty mitigation, interviewing Latina girls in child research, evaluating a youth-oriented drug use prevention program, protecting endangered cultures, working in a community hospital, addressing food insecurity, and collaborating with an African American history project. Moreover, applied anthropologists have played a diverse array of social and institutional roles, seeing application as including advocacy, information development, organizational analysis, mediation, brokerage, cultural marketing, product design, organizational operation assessment, resource management, evaluation, impact assessment, needs assessment, cultural appraisal, and much more, including, of note, engagement with issues of broad public concern that move us "beyond disciplinary defined problems to the problems of the world — the problems that interest others, rather than the problems that interest us as anthropologists" (Borofsky 2008). Exemplary of this longstanding (although far from universally supported, e.g. Cowlishaw 2003) theme is the work of Walter Goldschmidt, whose obituary underlines that he was (in the view of its authors) "the finest example of an applied anthropologist" (Durrenberger and Thu 2010). Expressing his views on the assortment of anthropological roles, in his American Anthropological Association Presidential nomination statement Goldschmidt emphasized the "need to develop a climate where anthropologists will find their way into policy-making positions and where their voices will be heard in public debate" (cited in Durrenberger and Thu 2010).

The Public Anthropology Narrative

As a result of the wide array of topics and types of engagement among applied anthropologists, and the stigmatized task they promote, since its advent public anthropology has danced "an ambiguous minuet with applied anthropology" (Borofsky 2008), resulting at times in stepped upon toes and edgy exchanges. Admits Borofsky (2008), perusing "the Society for Applied Anthropology's mission statement, one is hard pressed to differentiate" public from applied anthropology. However, in selecting a title for what came to be called the University of California Press's Studies in Public Anthropology book series, Borofsky (2008) concedes he and co-editor Naomi Schneider did not choose "applied anthropology" for a reason: "It had — in my view, however unfairly–acquired negative connotations. What we were seeking was a new term that had a certain 'pizzazz' that would draw anthropologists into rethinking their connections to the broader society."

Claiming a sector of the work that would seem to fall already into the domain of an existing subfield, advocates of public anthropology have sought to differential public and applied anthropology. Borofsky (2008) has made two arguments in his (evolving) definitional statement about the distinctions of public anthropology. First, public anthropology emphasizes public accountability in its work. This approach, it is argued, allows broad access to understanding how and why anthropological projects and the knowledge that they generate are undertaken. By implication, this is not or not always the case with applied anthropology initiatives, and this is indeed the case in some instances. For example, applied anthropologists who work for corporations in marketing or other tasks may be restricted by proprietary rules from fully revealing their methods or findings. As van Willigen (1995) comments, "publication of technical reports and disposition of primary-data records may be influenced by the proprietary interests of the client. It is not unusual for applied anthropologists to be denied the opportunity to publish freely from the data following their collection and primary use." But, as noted, this is only the case in a few of the many arenas of applied anthropology (e.g., work carried out for corporate or specific government clients, for example); it is hardly a blanket rule that covers the field. Quite commonly, as the pages of *Human Organization, Practicing Anthropology, Anthropology in Action,* and other journals indicate, applied anthropologists seek to publish their work in open venues and to have their methods and findings be subject to peer and (potential) public review. Moreover, the Statement on Professional and Ethical Responsibilities of the Society for Applied Anthropology (1983) stresses that "while respecting the needs, responsibilities, and legitimate proprietary interests of our sponsors we should not impede the flow of information about research outcomes and professional practice techniques ... We shall not condone falsification or distortion by others." Consequently, lack of accountability, while it is sometimes the case, is not an inherent feature of work conducted under the broad banner of applied anthropology and is therefore not an adequate basis for differentiating applied anthropology from public anthropology (in which degree of accountability is controlled primarily by the individual researcher's personality, disclosure decisions, or other, often unrevealed, factors).

Secondly, public anthropology claims distinction on the grounds that it is concerned with "understanding the hegemonic structures that frame and restrict solutions to problems as a way of more effectively addressing these problems" (Borofsky 2008). This is a worthy objective but again scarcely a distinctive feature of public anthropology. It is, for example, a framing principle of critical medical anthropology, including applied work guided by that theoretical framework (e.g., Singer 1994).

In the end, after attempting at some length to define public anthropology and to make the case for its distinctive features, Borofsky (2008) abruptly announces: "Public anthropology, applied anthropology, whatever. Who out there, beyond the discipline, really cares? The important issue, whatever we call ourselves, is doing whatever it takes—short of the unethical—to solve the social problems at hand. ... From my perspective, the distinction between public and applied is not something that should take up a lot of energy." This comment is noteworthy because, at the most shallow level, of course, labels do not matter (they are all arbitrary social constructions) and, indeed, few beyond the discipline are much interested in such issues. But, at a deeper level, words do matter, precisely because they serve the ends of social structure. Building on the work of Silverstein (1979), linguistic anthropologists have thus analyzed the "social situatedness" of linguistic devices, and how they help construct both communication practices and social lives (Kroskrity 2000; Schieffelin et al. 1998). Consequently, academic debates over labels are not always trivial affairs; they may well be channeled contestations over hierarchies of social relationship and veiled conflicts over regimes of control over social access. As implied above, not only is there an enduring (if always shifting) hierarchy within anthropology, traditionally applied anthropologists have tended to fill rungs on lower (and social stigmatized) levels of our discipline's internal social structure. As van Willigen (2002: ix) comments: "It is important to recognize that names matter and that the use of the term applied anthropology is in some contexts contentious." The historic tainting of applied anthropology "limits competition and protects vested intellectual interests" (van Willigen 2002: xi).

Traditional inequalities notwithstanding, perusal of the websites of the American Anthropology Association and the Royal Anthropological Institutes (which, respectively, claim title as the world's largest organization of individuals interested in anthropology and the longest-established scholarly association dedicated to the furtherance of anthropology) affirms we are clearly in a period in which the role and inclusion of applied anthropology within the broader discipline is being revisited. Public anthropology, it is argued below, has a role to play in this transformative process.

Positioning Public Anthropology: A Disciplinary Rationale for Social Criticism

In his book *Interpretation and Social Criticism*, political philosopher Michael Walzer (1987) argues that social criticism, the "educated cousin of common complaint," involves a reflective comparison between the normative beliefs shared within a society and the actual behaviors and institutions found therein. Identifying and analyzing the nature of the gaps between what anthropologists traditionally have called "the ideal and the real," in other words, is part of the work that drives the critical agenda. Social critics are effective, Walzer suggests, not simply because of their persuasive ability, but because they are committed and involved locally. Much like ethnographers engaged in participant observation, they stand in close proximity to the social practices and structures of concern to them. In short, in both social criticism and anthropology, understanding and theory are grounded in an "experience-near" methodology.

Despite this shared attitude toward knowledge, much ink has been spilled over the legitimacy of marrying anthropology or any social science to social criticism. Usually debates in this arena involve questions of objectivity, responsibility, and partisanship. The argument, often played out in the meeting rooms and corridors of anthropology conferences and at fractious departmental meetings, was the centerpiece of an oft-cited 1995 issue of *Current Anthropology*. On one side, representing the pure science or positivist perspective, what might be called the "'knowledge as enlightenment' orientation," Roy D'Andrade dispassionately maintained that anthropologists must avoid all forms of moral bias and cleave instead, however slim our foothold, to the objective path to understanding. The engagement of anthropologists, he argued, should be in the construction of falsifiable models of human behavior. Accordingly D'Andrade (1995: 404) maintained, "Science works not because it produces unbiased accounts but because its accounts are objective enough to be proved or disproved no matter what anyone wants to be true." In this vein, Hastrup and Elsass (1990) have argued that anthropological involvement in the advocacy of a particular moral stance cannot be legitimized in anthropological terms (an assertion critiqued in Singer 1990). On the other side of the debate was Nancy Scheper-Hughes, who proposed a view of knowledge as a means to a moral end. Asserting the subjectivist view that because all data are inherently biased by the social origins and structural position of science and scientist alike, true objectivity, although socially useful in making claims for authority, is ultimately unattainable, scientific methodology notwithstanding. Consequently, anthropologists, she said, should engage in moral criticism and advocacy based on an "explicit ethical orientation to 'the [ethnographic] other'" (Scheper-Hughes 1995: 418). Thus, Scheper-Hughes called for the development of "an active, politically committed morally, engaged anthropology" (Scheper-Hughes 1995: 415). This orientation, keenly aware of moral ambiguities within the discipline, past and present, is characterized by a burdensome sense of regret and foreboding, as well as a belief in scholarly accountability in troubled times.

As noted in the introduction to the 1963 inaugural issue of the journal *Transaction* (now *Society*), those who embrace engaged anthropology believe that "The social scientist studying contemporary problems and the complex relationships among modern [peoples] knows that he/[she] can no longer discharge his[/her] social responsibilities by retreating from the world until more is known" (quoted in Marx 1972: 1).

As numerous studies, including the literatures on globalization, global warming, unnatural disasters and ecocrises, the sixth global species extinction, nuclear proliferation, social emiseration, and physical violence make clear, human problems are urgent, divisions between social strata are growing, the contradictions of the global economy are multiple, dominant political economies in the world today are unsustainable on planet Earth, and current and pending health and social consequences are ominous (Baer et al. 2013; Bodley 2007; Farmer 2004; Scheper-Hughes 1993). Hence, the anthropological lexicon has, in recent years, added terms like social suffering, structural violence, disempowerment, and resistance, while some traditional topics of disciplinary focus (e.g., kinship) have moved off of the center stage of disciplinary discourse. In an earlier era, before the debates between the scientific and humanistic sides of anthropology acquired an acrimonious tone, involvement in pubic social criticism was not unknown within the discipline, indeed it was not uncommon (Low and Merry 2010; Susser 2010; Johnston 2010). Elsie Clews Parsons, for example, was publishing anthropological books with a distinct critical orientation, such as *The Family* (1906), *Religious Chastity* (1913), and *Fear and Conventionality* (1914), early in the twentieth century. Others like Franz Boas, Margaret Mead, Ruth Bennedict, Gene Weltfish, and Ashley Montagu followed suit. By the 1930s a number of anthropologists were "searching for ways to address issues of social justice emerging from the Great Depression, and many … worked for transformative changes" (Susser 2010: S230). These efforts were redoubled during the 1960s and 1970s, triggered in part by anthropology's lead role in the launching of the anti–Vietnam War teach-in movement on college campuses.

Yet, as the contemporary public anthropology discourse makes clear, the result of anthropology's somewhat cloistered development within academia after the Vietnam War era has left twenty-first-century anthropologists unprepared and untrained to act as effective social critics. Noted progressive historian Howard Zinn: "The university traditionally is supposed to be a place for independent thought and a place that teaches critical thinking. … But when it comes to really critical matters of life and death, of war and peace, you do not find that the educational system prepares young people to be … critical thinkers about American society" (quoted in Barsamian 2005).

One might think that anthropologists, as students of the world, as people who are better traveled than most, and as researchers who, as a result of their approach to knowledge, have often seen the most adverse effects of social inequality, the egregious exercise of power, the gross violation of human rights, and hazardous environmental degradation up close, might naturally be social critics of the dominant socioeconomic and sociopolitical structures and processes that oppress the subjects of their research and threaten the environments they inhabit. And to greater or lesser degree many are. But, as the recent debate about anthropologists participating in data collection for the U.S. military suggests—data which the military admitted might be used to target individuals for elimination (Beyerstein 2007)—even anthropologists can be poorly trained as critical thinkers, speakers, writers, and actors on the public stage. In part, as Zinn (quoted in Barsamian 2005) also argues, the problem is one of ideological hegemony: "If information is withheld from the public by government secrecy, the public is misled by government lies, if the media do not report these lies, and if the media do not investigate what the government is doing and watch very carefully what the government is doing, then we do not have a democracy."

In this light, it can be argued that a major contemporary role for public anthropology is that of teaching the field the methods of social criticism. Such an undertaking would extend our discipline's evidence-based recognition of the social utility of omission, diverted focus, and falsification, as Zinn suggests. Outright lies, convenient misrepresentations, obscuring of known information (sometimes including anthropological and other research findings), official forgetting and not knowing, conscious ideological slanting of social realities, and similar distortions are all significant contributors to the maintenance of social inequality (Gordon 1988). Without falsification, in the form of authoritative pronouncements by politically or socially privileged public figures and pundits (e.g., Rector 2007), policy decisions (Ryan 2004), mass media reports and advertisements (Bullock et al. 2001), educational materials and classroom communications (Sleeter 1992), and similar "reality-defining" hegemonic "webs of mystification" (Keesing 1987), the existing structure of social inequality might be far more troublesome than it is for many potential publics of anthropological social criticism.

Demystification, as award-winning author Toni Morrison (1993: xi) points out, entails an anthropological examination of "Frustrating language, devious calls to arms, and ancient inflammatory codes deployed to do their weary work of obfuscation, short circuiting, evasion and distortion."

Based on the growing body of research pointing to the fundamental importance of structural factors in health and social disparities, it appears that the most effective, long-term way to significantly improve the health and well-being of the global population (including the so-called "bottom billion" and those who are not much above the bottom), as noted by the British social epidemiologist, Peter Townsend (1986: 29), "is to restrict the power and wealth of the rich, to dismantle the present structures of social privilege, and to build social institutions based on fair allocation of wealth and social equity." Unwillingness to consider such an approach as thinkable, realistic, or valid, and in fact, unwillingness to implement any policies and programs that do much (for long) significantly narrow prevailing disparities and injustices while representing a compelling challenge to the Western equity narrative. This challenge, however, is muted and managed through the spinning of webs of mystification about the causes of and solutions to the enduring problem of social inequality. In calling attention to this cultural spin work, and in analyzing its nature and social functions in the maintenance of existing social orders at local, regional, and global scales, as well as in providing detailed accounts of the social realities, experiences, and voices of disparity populations, the anthropologist can serve at once as rigorous scientist and public social critic. Engagement in community struggles for equity, that is to say anthropological involvement in knowledge-based assaults on the causes of social suffering and structural violence, respond to anthropology's core epistemological dilemma: "knowledge for what?" with Gavin Smith's applied reply: "the practical transformation of the real world" (1999: 238). Here then, in standing as a bridge between research-informed social criticism and action-oriented applied social change, looms a role for a praxis aptly named public anthropology.

Merrill Singer, PhD, a medical and cultural anthropologist, is a Professor in the departments of Anthropology and Community Medicine, and a Senior Research Scientist at the Center for Health, Intervention and Prevention at the University of Connecticut. Additionally, he is affiliated with the Center for Interdisciplinary Research on AIDS at Yale University. The central issue in his work is the social origins of health inequality. Over his career, his research and writing have addressed HIV/AIDS in highly vulnerable and disadvantaged populations, illicit drug use and drinking behavior, community and structural violence, and the political ecology of health including the impacts of climate change. In recent years, his research has focused especially on the nature and impact of both syndemics (interacting epidemics) and pluralea (intersecting ecocrises) on health. Dr. Singer has published more than 265 articles and book chapters and has authored or edited 29 books. He is a recipient of the Rudolph Virchow Professional Prize, the George Foster Memorial Award for Practicing Anthropology, the AIDS and Anthropology Paper Prize, the Prize for Distinguished Achievement in the Critical Study of North America, the Solon T. Kimball Award for Public and Applied Anthropology from the American Anthropological Association, and the AIDS and Anthropology Research Group's Distinguished Service Award.

References

Baer, Hans, Singer, Merrill and Susser, Ida. 2013 *Medical Anthropology and the World System.* Westport, CT: Greenwood Publishing Co.

Barsamian, David. 2005. "Critical Thinking: An Interview with Howard Zinn." *International Socialist Review* 39 (Jan/Feb). http://www.isreview.org/issues/39/zinn.shtml.

Barber, Benjamin. 1992. "Jihad Vs. McWorld." *Atlantic Monthly* 269: 53–65.

Berreman, Gerald. 1968. "Is Anthropology Alive? Social Responsibility in Social Anthropology." *Current Anthropology* 9, no. 3: 391–396.

Beyerstein, Lindsay. 2007. Anthropologists on the Front Lines. In These Times. http://inthe setimes.com/article/3433/anthropologists_on_the_front_lines.

Bloch, Maurice, and Maarja Kaaristo. 2007. "The Reluctant Anthropologist: An Interview With Maurice Bloch." http://www.eurozine.com/articles/2008-02-28-bloch-en.html.

Bodley, John. 2007. *Anthropology and Contemporary Human Problems.* Lanham, MD: AltaMira.

Borofsky, Rob. 2007. "Defining Public Anthropology: A Personal Perspective." http://www .publicanthropology.org/Defining/publicanth-07Oct10.htm.

Bugarin, Flordeliz, Eleanor King, Mark Mack, and Arvilla Payne-Jackson. 2010. "An Impending Death for Anthropology at Howard University." *Anthropology News* 51, no. 8: 28.

Bullock, Heather, Karen Wyche, and Wendy Williams. 2001. "Media Images of the Poor." *Journal of Social Issues* 57 no. 2: 229–246.

Chambers, Erve. 1987. "Applied Anthropology in the Post-Vietnam Era: Anticipations and Ironies." *Annual Review of Anthropology* 16: 309–331.

Cowlishaw, Gillian. 2003. "Euphemism, Banality, Propaganda: Anthropology, Public Debate and Indigenous Communities." *Australian Aboriginal Studies* 1: 3–18.

Comaroff, John. 2010. The End of Anthropology, Again: On the Future of an In/Discipline" *American Anthropologist* 112, no. 4: 524–538.

D'Andrade, Roy. 1995. "Moral Models in Anthropology." *Current Anthropology* 36: 399–408.

Durrenberger, Paul, and Kendall Thu. 2010. "In Memory of Walter Goldschmidt: Exemplary Anthropologist." *Society for Applied Anthropology News.* http://192.163.234.187/~sfaanet/ news/files/5313/7493/9949/21-4.pdf. .

Eddy, Elizabeth, and William Partridge, eds. 1978. *Applied Anthropology in America.* New York: Columbia University Press.

Eriksen, Thomas Hylland. 2006. *Engaging Anthropology: The Case for a Public Presence.* Oxford: Berg.

Ervin, Alexander. 2000. *Applied Anthropology: Tools and Perspectives in Contemporary Practice.* Boston: Allyn and Bacon.

Farmer, Paul. 1999. *Infections and Inequalities: The Modern Plagues.* Berkeley: University of California Press.

———. 2004. *Pathologies of Power: Health, Human Rights, and the New War on the Poor.* Berkeley: University of California Press.

Fassim, Didier. 2006. "Riots in France and silent anthropologists." *Anthropology Today* 22, no. 1: 1–3.

Fraser, Nancy. 1990. "Rethinking the Public Sphere: A Contribution to the Critique of Actually Existing Democracy." *Social Text* 25, no. 26: 56–80.

Friedman, Thomas. 2005. *The World Is Flat: A Brief History of the Twenty-First Century.* New York: Farrar, Straus and Giroux.

Geertz, Clifford. 1963. *Peddlers and Princes.* Chicago: University of Chicago Press.

———. 1995. *After the Fact: Two Countries, Four Decades, One Anthropologist.* Cambridge, MA: Harvard University Press.

Gordon, Robert. 1988. "Apartheid's Anthropologists: On the Genealogy of Afrikaner Anthropology." *American Ethnologist* 15, no. 3: 535–553.

Hastrup, Kirsten, and Peter Elsass. 1990. "Anthropological Advocacy: A Contradiction in Terms?" *Current Anthropology* 31, no. 3: 301–311.

Hightower, Jim. 2008. *Swim Against the Current: Even a Dead Fish Can Go With the Flow.* Malden, MA: Wiley.

Howell, Signe. 1997. "Cultural Studies and Social Anthropology: Contesting or Complementary Discourses," in *Anthropology and Cultural Studies*, ed. Stephen Nugent and Cris Shore, 103–125. London: Pluto Books.

Johnston, Barbara. 2010. "Social Responsibility and the Anthropological Citizen." *Current Anthropology* 51, Supplement 2: S235–S248.

Keesing, Roger. 1987. "Anthropology as Interpretive Quest." *Current Anthropology* 28: 161–176.

Kroskrity Paul, ed. 2000. *Regimes of Language: Ideologies, Polities, and Identities.* Santa Fe, NM: SAR Press.

Low, Setha, and Sally Merry. 2010. "Engaged Anthropology: Diversity and Dilemmas." *Current Anthropology* 51, Supplement 2: S203–S226.

Malinowski, Bronislaw. 1922. *Argonauts of the Western Pacific.* London: Rutledge.

Marx, Gary. 1972. *Muckracking Sociology: Research as Social Criticism.* New York: Transaction Publishers.

Morrison, Toni, ed. 1993. *Race-ing Justice, En-gendering Power: Essays on Anita Hill, Clarence Thomas and the Construction of Social Reality.* London: Chatto and Windus.

Nugent, Stephen. 1997. "Introduction: Brother, Can You Share a Paradigm." In *Anthropology and Cultural Studies*, ed. Stephen Nugent and Cris Shore, 1–10. London: Pluto Books.

Parsons, Elsie. 1906. *The Family: An Ethnographic and Historic Outline with Descriptive Notes.* New York: G.P. Putnam's Sons.

———. 1913. *Religious Chastity: An Ethnological Study.* New York: Macaulay Co.

———. 1914. *Fear and Conventionality.* New York: G.P. Putnam's Sons.

Rector, Robert. 2007. Edwards's poverty "plague" examined. *National Review.* http://www.nationalreview.com/article/221932/poor-politics-robert-rector.

Ryan, James. 2004. *The Perverse Incentives of the No Child Left Behind Act.* New York University Law Review 79: 932–989.

Rylko-Bauer, Barbara. 2000. "Toward a More Inclusive Relevant Anthropology." *Society for Applied Anthropology Newsletter* 11, no. 2: 6–7.

———. 2008. "Applied Anthropology and Counterinsurgency." *Society for Applied Anthropology Newsletter* 19, no. 1: 1–5.

Rylko-Bauer, Barbara, Merrill Singer, and John van Willigen. 2006. "Reclaiming Applied Anthropology: Its Past, Present, and Future." *American Anthropologist* 108, no. 1: 178–190

Scheper-Hughes, Nancy, and Philippe Bourgois. 1999. "Introduction: Making Sense of Violence." ed Nancy Scheper-Hughes and Philippe Bourgois. In *Violence in War and Peace: An Anthology*, 1–31. Malden, MA: Blackwell.

Scheper-Hughes, Nancy. 1993. *Death Without Weeping: The Violence of Everyday Life in Brazil.* Berkeley: University of California Press.

———. 1995. "The Primacy of the Ethical." *Current Anthropology* 35: 409–420.

Schieffelin, Bambi, Kathryn Woolard, and Paul Kroskrity, eds. 1998. *Language Ideologies: Practice and Theory.* Oxford: Oxford University Press.

Silverstein, Michael. 1979. "Language structure and linguistic ideology." In *The Elements: A parasession on linguistic units and levels.* ed. R. Clyne, W. Hanks & C. Hofbauer, 193–247. Chicago: Chicago Linguistic Society.

Singer, Merrill. 1990. "Another Perspective on Advocacy." *Current Anthropology* 31, no. 5: 548–549.

———. 1994. "Community Centered Praxis: Toward an Alternative Nondominative Applied Anthropology." *Human Organization* 53, no. 4: 336–344.

———. 2000. "Why I am Not a Public Anthropologist." Anthropology Newsletter 41, no. 6: 6–7.

———. 2008. "Applied Anthropology." In *A New History of Anthropology,* ed. Henrika Kulick, 326–340. Malden, MA: Blackwell.

Sleeter, Christine. 1992. "How White Teachers Construct Race." In *Race Identity and Representation in Education,* ed. Cameron McCarthy and Warren Crichlow, 157–171. New York: Routledge.

Smith, Gavin. 1999. *Confronting the Present: Towards a Politically Engaged Anthropology.* Oxford: Berg.

Society for Applied Anthropology. 1983. "Ethical and Professional Responsibilities." http://www.sfaa.net/about/ethics/...

Starn, Orin. 1991. "Missing the Revolution: Anthropologists and the War in Peru." *Current Anthropology* 6, no. 1: 63–91.

Survival International. 2005. "Waorani Indians march against oil drilling." http://www.survivalinternational.org/news/864.

Susser, Ida. 2010. "The Anthropologist as Social Critic: Working Toward a More Engaged Anthropology." *Current Anthropology* 51, Supplement 2: S227–234.

Townsend, Peter. 1986. "Why are the Many Poor?" *International Journal of Health Services* 16: 1–32.

Turk, James. 2010. "The Canadian Corporate-Academic Complex." *Academe* 96, no. 6. http://www.aaup.org/AAUP/pubsres/academe/2010/ND/feat/turk.htm.

Tylor, E.B. 1871. *Primitive Culture,* Volume 2. London: John Murray.

van der Kroef. 1956. "The Changing Class Structure of Indonesia." *American Sociological Review* 21, no. 2: 138–148.

van Willigen, John. 1995. "The Records of Applied Anthropology." In *Preserving the Anthropological Record,* ed. Sydel Silverman and Nancy Parezo. New York: Wenner-Gren Foundation for Anthropological Research, Inc. http://copar.org/par/index.htm.

———. 2002. *Applied Anthropology: An Introduction.* 3rd ed. South Hadley, MA: Bergin and Garvey.

Walzer, Michael. 1987. *Interpretation and Social Criticism.* Cambridge, MA: Harvard University Press.

Warner, Michael. 2005. *Publics and Counterpublics.* Cambridge, MA: Zone Books.

Watson, James, ed. 1997. *Golden Arches East: McDonald's in East Asia.* Stanford, CA: Stanford University Press.

Worsley, Peter. 1968. "The End of Anthropology." In *Transactions of the Sixth World Congress of Sociology,* vol. 4. Louvain, Belgium: International Sociology Association.

Chapter 6

PUBLIC ANTHROPOLOGY AND THE TRANSFORMATION OF ANTHROPOLOGICAL RESEARCH

Louise Lamphere

By 1962, when I entered graduate school in social anthropology at Harvard University, anthropology had become a "social science." The United States' place in the world was expanding as Europe declined after World War II, and many new independent countries were emerging. The social sciences—economics, political science, sociology, and now anthropology—had all adopted the scientific method and turned their attention to research on a wide range of human problems: economic development, modernization, poverty, urban renewal, and the future of democracy, among others. Whereas anthropology in the United States had previously been preoccupied with American Indian populations and Mexican indigenous groups, post–World War II research targeted new locations in Latin America, Africa, India, Southeast Asia, the Pacific, and the Middle East. Rather than "salvage anthropology" or broad ethnographic descriptions of whole cultures, we were taught a "problem-oriented" approach. Our dissertation topics emerged from a careful reading of the literature that led the way to an unexplored issue—often even a hypothesis—that could be illuminated or tested by further research.

This social-science orientation shared many traits with applied anthropology, the focus of anthropologists who had broken away from the American Anthropological Association in 1941 to found the Society for Applied Anthropology. The split separated academic anthropologists from some anthropologists in academic departments, along with other

---

social scientists in governmental agencies, research institutes, and NGOs, who wanted to apply research knowledge (gained via social science methods) to human problems that directly impacted communities.

Fifty years later, the discipline of anthropology (including biological anthropology, archaeology, linguistic anthropology, and applied anthropology, as well as cultural and social anthropology) has been radically transformed. As I have argued elsewhere (Lamphere 2004), applied, practicing, and "public" anthropology have converged in terms of the communities studied, the topics researched, our relationships with these communities, and the dissemination of anthropological knowledge. Like other contributors to this collection, I do not distinguish applied anthropology from public or "engaged" anthropology.

This chapter's first section will trace my own evolution from a distanced social scientist into someone committed to the continued growth of public or engaged anthropology. I still consider myself a social scientist and have no wish to exclude science from anthropology. However, it is important to acknowledge recent transformations in the way we construct relationships with our "research subjects" — the people we study. These changes, through which subjects become consultants and collaborators in the research process and readers or even co-authors of conference papers and publications, have altered how anthropological knowledge is acquired.

My own trajectory led me to team research on what I call "critical social issues," topics that also concern the populations we study: work/family balance, poverty and homelessness, access to health care, water rights, environmental impact and sustainability, economic development, immigration, language revitalization, the maintenance of ethnic identities, and heritage preservation. The midsection of this chapter will draw attention to recent projects addressing critical social issues. I will primarily focus on research and dissertation projects conducted mainly by colleagues and students at my home institution, the University of New Mexico in the U.S. Southwest.

Two once-distinct approaches to the study of critical social issues have tended to merge in the past two decades. The first derives from what Meredith Minkler and Nina Wallerstein (2003) label the Northern tradition (based on the work of Kurt Lewin and later action anthropologists) and the second evolved from the Southern tradition based on the work of Paulo Freire (1970). In the Northern tradition, researchers are experts who set out to solve practical problems by planning, acting, and investigating the results of action. They use the research process to make recommendations that will generate new scientific knowledge and contribute to social progress. In the Southern tradition, communities are not subjects of inquiry but catalysts and supporters of change emanating from the community, and researchers are not experts so much as facilitators who help plan research, train cadres, and carry out the projects along with community members. Formulated around critical pedagogy, this research has an egalitarian orientation. Recently, these two approaches have converged somewhat. Participatory action research (PAR) stems from the Northern tradition but includes participation from and collaboration with community or organization members at every step, including definition of the need for research and the problems to be investigated. PAR resembles the community-based participatory research (CBPR) developed by public health researchers influenced by the Southern tradition (Butterfoss 2007; Minkler 1997; Wallerstein 1992). CBPR emphasizes a collaborative equitable partnership between researchers and community members, co-learning, and capacity building as part of the research process. It also involves all partners in the dissemination process.

The projects I will discuss involve degrees of collaboration, but a distinction remains between projects where researchers or a research team define the problem and obtain the permission and sometimes the studied community's help, and those projects where the research questions emanate from the community, whose members help carry out the study and disseminate information. In the former case, university-based researchers conduct the study and then disseminate the findings back to the community or organization. The latter case involves community members at all stages, including planning, research, and dissemination.

Finally, I feel strongly that U.S. Ph.D. programs do not fully train students to engage in publicly focused research that involves collaboration with communities and organizations. Academic jobs are scarce (partly because the recession of 2007–2009 set off a crisis in state-funded education), and this training is crucial for students interested in working outside academia. To round out this chapter, I will offer suggestions for training and supervising students in graduate programs so that the next generation of public anthropologists will flourish.

Becoming a Social Scientist

The Social Relations Department at Harvard prototypically exemplified the trend toward social science (with emphasis on "science"). Unhappy with their home departments, sociologist Talcott Parsons, anthropologist Clyde Kluckhohn, clinical psychologist Henry Murray, and social psychologist Gordon Allport joined forces and combined four degree programs (sociology, social anthropology, clinical psychology, and social psychology) to found the department. Faculty members in the new department were united in their efforts to improve human relationships through combining theory with careful empirical research. We Ph.D. students were required to take a statistics class and at least one course from one of the other subfields in social relations. I was exposed to research on international development in a seminar given by Alex Inkeles, to the literature on personality and social structure in a seminar taught by Daniel Levinson, and to the work of Jean Piaget through a class taught by cognitive psychologist Jerome Bruner. All these courses considered the scientific method applicable to human behavior and strove to build an objective understanding of personality, small groups, cognition, society, and culture.

In the fall of 1962, I was one of six students entering social anthropology. Along with students in sociology, social psychology, and clinical psychology, we took a year-long theory course (Soc Rel 263). In the first semester, Talcott Parsons and Thomas Pettigrew introduced us to sociology and social psychology, and in the second we learned about clinical psychology from David McClelland and social anthropology from Frank Cancian. Other faculty from the four social relations subdivisions also gave lectures in the course. The class was about half women, a much stronger representation than in the medical and law schools, where two of my Stanford classmates were among a handful of female students in each entering class. However, the anthropology faculty had the only woman, the Samuel Zemurray, Jr. and Doris Zemurray Stone-Radcliffe Professor of Anthropology Cora Du Bois (in the Anthropology Department located in the Peabody Museum, not in the Social Relations Department) (Seymour 2015).

In the summer of 1963, I took part in a field school based in Santa Fe, New Mexico, at the Laboratory of Anthropology. A joint effort of the Anthropology Departments at Harvard, Columbia, and Cornell, it was directed by Benjamin "Nick" Colby with Alfonso Ortiz (then a graduate student at the University of Chicago) as assistant director. Most of the seven students were placed in the Navajo Community of Ramah, New Mexico, which had been the location of the Harvard Values Project. I lived with the family of a Navajo Blessingway singer who had worked with several anthropologists and remembered Clyde Kluckhohn. I returned to Ramah the next summer with Terry Reynolds, another student of the field school, and worked with the allotment records and a census to construct a genealogy and map of the Ramah Navajo community, which had grown to more than 1,000 members. My experiences these first two summers were enough to give me sense that I felt very comfortable with Navajo life and the Navajo way of doing things. It was also wonderful to be in New Mexico—not far from Denver, where I grew up—in a beautiful, inspiring natural environment.

As an undergraduate I had admired Clyde Kluckhohn's work on values, and several of my sociology professors at Stanford were products of the Social Relations Department. I had hoped to study values when I came to Harvard, but upon arriving I realized that the Values Project was "passé" and Evon Vogt, who was from Ramah and had done his dissertation on the Navajo, had moved on to do research in the Mayan indigenous population of Zinacantan, Chiapas, Mexico. A National Science Foundation (NSF) grant financed a large project that attracted many of my fellow graduate students. Frank Cancian, my Social Relations 263 professor and an early researcher in Zinacantan, taught a small seminar that I took in my second year at Harvard. Social anthropologists in the Social Relations Department and the Anthropology Department located in the Peabody Museum had moved away from studying American Indians and were launching research projects in Brazil among the Gé (David Maybury-Lewis), Chiapas, Mexico (Evon Vogt), India (Cora Du Bois), the Pacific (Douglas Oliver), and six cultures around the world (John and Bea Whiting). We who worked with Native American populations in this period considered ourselves a marginalized group outside the discipline's main trajectory.

In anthropology, values were "out" and the work of Levi-Straus was "in," as was "ethnoscience," a more rigorous set of methodologies for studying culture by analyzing cognitive maps, taxonomies, and paradigms. Harvard had recently hired David Maybury-Lewis and Tom Beidelman, who were trained at Oxford in British social anthropology. I took several courses with each and found the societal analysis of British Social Anthropologists to be both more structured and clearer than the cultural and values approach of most American anthropologists. I read studies of the developmental cycle of domestic groups, theoretical work on social structure and social organization, and case analyses of matrilineal societies, which all influenced my approach to Navajo social organization.

I wrote my dissertation proposal intending to study residence patterns among the matrilineal Navajo, something unclear in previous studies, which had produced contradictory results. Not all couples after marriage lived with the wife's family as was the case in other matrilineal societies, but they often lived with the husband's family or neolocally in their own separate residence. How to account for this variability seemed an appropriate problem for investigation. A woman we met in the Ramah area introduced Terry Reynolds and me to the community of Sheep Springs, New Mexico, where we spent the summer of 1965 in a borrowed, empty winter hooghan (round log-cabin-like traditional Navajo house), improving our Navajo language skills. Over the course of the next year, I lived with five different Sheep Springs families. Once in the field, I realized that issues of postmarital residence seemed relatively unimportant to the daily lives of these Navajo families. I began instead to see myself as studying everyday patterns of cooperation, such as when kin collaborated to shear sheep; plant fields; travel to distant hospitals, schools, or towns; or help with Navajo traditional ceremonies or Native American Church meetings.

In my dissertation-based book *To Run After Them: Cultural and Social Bases of Cooperation in a Navajo Community* (1977), I set forth two "observer's models": one oriented to the cultural ideals surrounding cooperation and reciprocity, and the other attuned to social structure (i.e., the residence group and wider network of kin and clan relations). Both were needed, I argued, to understand how cooperation was organized. I used the concepts of "set" and "network" (then very popular among urban anthropologists and several mathematical sociologists) along with an analysis of the developmental cycle of domestic groups (derived from British social anthropology). The text presented abundant case material from the lives of the families I lived with. I took the role of the observer, however, and my distanced descriptions held little in the way of Navajo voices. By comparison, my more recent life history of three women in one of these families, *Weaving Women's Lives* (2007), relies on taped interviews, participant observation, and informal conversations, and has a very different "feel." *To Run After Them* was very much a product of a scientific approach to ethnography and the study of social structure.

Social Movements and the Beginnings of Transformation

For many anthropologists who came of age as professionals in the late 1960s and early 1970s, participation in the social movements of that time created a desire to engage in a different kind of anthropology. My first demonstration was a march through the streets of Rochester (where I held a one-year appointment in 1967–1968) after the death of Martin Luther King. In the spring of 1970 at Brown University (where I taught from 1968 to 1975), students responded to the shootings at Kent State by organizing a university-wide strike and an alternative graduation. At community meetings and dinners over the following summer, students and faculty worked to increase anti-war awareness. I joined a consciousness-raising group, like many women in the anti-war movement who were attracted to the growing feminist movement and saw consciousness-raising as a way to explore the new feminist principle, "the person is political."[1] Meanwhile, feminists in Rhode Island were beginning to mobilize on several women's issues. I recall attending a hearing at the Rhode Island State House in April 1970 to support an abortion rights bill that had little chance, in this very

Catholic state, of being reported out of the House Education and Welfare Committee and then voted on in the Rhode Island House and Senate, the next steps if it were to become law. Still, more than forty witnesses testified to a packed room. Later, women faculty at Brown protested the all-male membership rules at the private University Club where the Brown president was an honorary member and university business was routinely conducted over lunch.[2]

In the spring of 1971, several Brown faculty and staff reached out to women in the larger community around Brown with a series of forums on issues of women's inequality. Returning to school or finding a profession was an important goal for many women in our upper middle-class audience. The forums became an important step toward the formation of the Pembroke Center for Research and Teaching in 1981.

Within anthropology, numerous young graduate students, faculty, and faculty wives wanted to relate their newfound interest in women's situation to their teaching and research. By 1971, Michelle Zimbalist Rosaldo (Shelly), Jane Collier, and several other women at Stanford offered a quarter-long course on women. They presented papers drawing on their lecture notes at the American Anthropological Association (AAA) Meetings in New York City. After hearing the session and seeing the notes from the class lectures, I suggested to Shelly that we co-edit a collection. We each saw a connection between our own personal and political situation and our academic work. As we eventually said in our introduction, "Along with many women today, we are trying to understand our position and to change it." We also felt that middle-class feminists were urging anthropologists to answer some of the "big questions." Why is Woman "The Other?" Were there matriarchies where women ruled? Or are women universally the "second sex?" For their part, women anthropologists influenced by the feminist movement were also examining their own fieldwork and thinking about how to focus on women in particular societies.

We wrote to thirty-five women who had given talks on women at the AAA Meeting in 1971 as well as those who had participated in the Stanford course. We struggled to find a framework, as we knew few women besides Simone de Beauvoir and Margaret Mead who had addressed the position of women worldwide. We jettisoned an outline of the usual topics (women in the economy, politics, religion) in favor of three initial essays (by Michelle Rosaldo, Nancy Chodorow, and Sherry Ortner) that argued that women are universally subordinated. We eventually selected thirteen additional essays that emphasized the variety of women's lives in several cultural contexts. After almost three years spent writing the introduction, shaping the contributions, finding a publisher, and getting a revised manuscript accepted, we published *Woman, Culture, and Society* with Stanford

University Press in April 1974. Like Rayna Reiter's edited volume *Toward an Anthropology of Women* (1975),[3] the collection became a feminist classic (see Lamphere et al. 2007). Bringing our feminist politics into our research, we felt, gave us the potential to change the face of a discipline that had largely ignored women's role both ethnographically and theoretically.

In 1971–1972, I was on leave at the London School of Economics, attempting to turn myself into an urban anthropologist. At Brown, much of our work targeted upper middle-class students and residents of Providence's East Side. Attaining their goals might improve women's position in the professions, but combining marriage and career was much easier for these women than for working-class women in ordinary jobs whose salaries could not cover expensive day care, housecleaners, an additional car, and private schools. Meanwhile, although I saw balance between work and family as an important social issue, I also felt the situation of working-class and immigrant women was being ignored. My NSF postdoctoral fellowship in London allowed me to pursue these issues and augment my interest in kin and social networks. Working with Robert and Rhona Rapoport, who had published a study of dual-career families, I adapted their interview guide and conducted some pilot interviews with dual-worker families in North London.

On returning to Brown, I taught my first class on "Women in Cross-Cultural Perspective," using some of the essays we were developing for *Woman, Culture, and Society*. I also collaborated with several women faculty and graduate students on a Group Independent Study featuring material from several different disciplines (history, sociology, anthropology, biology); students could also participate in one of several discussion sections (e.g., on women and the body or women and culture). In 1973, I moved into a collective house with Ed and Sue Benson, Peter Evans, and several others. Over a dozen years, this group — mostly historians and social scientists (with the occasional literature teacher, social worker, or union organizer in the mix) — led me to appreciate the new social history and the importance of combining academic work with social activism. My housemates also constituted a support network of friends and part-time collaborators. From 1970 to 1974, I participated in a socialist-feminist group of women from New York and Rhode Island that met periodically to discuss women's issues. Rayna Rapp was also a member of this group, and we continued to discuss what anthropology could contribute to the broader analysis of American society and working-class women.

My nascent feminism began to drive a wedge between my department's male faculty and me. I was teaching about women, working on a feminist collection, lecturing for colleagues on women's issues, and spending fewer leisure hours with my male colleagues. The Anthropology Faculty split from the larger Sociology Department in 1971 and moved to its own building in 1972. The new department had six tenured males; I was the only untenured female, until Jane Dwyer was hired as head of the Haffenreffer Museum in 1972. In November 1973, when Department Chair Phil Leis went over the details of the tenure process and indicated that there had been complaints about my teaching, I became nervous about my impending tenure review. There were no teaching evaluations at the time, so I spent the next several months obtaining letters of support from graduate students, putting together my research publications, and compiling a list of potential outside reviewers that together would make a strong case for tenure, I thought. I was anxious to hear the department and administration's decision, and my concerns deepened as the days in May passed without word of a decision. I clearly remember sitting across from Phil Leis at his desk on 24 May 1974, when he told me I would not be getting tenure. I asked him why the department had not recommended me to Provost Merton Stolz, who had ratified their decision. The faculty, he said, had been "evenly divided." Some found my teaching "poor but not so much worse than others"; also, my essay in *Woman, Culture, and Society* revealed "an extremely weak theoretical orientation." On graduation day, I asked Phil to meet with me in his office after our Departmental reception. I told him hat I had hired a lawyer and intended to sue.

My last year at Brown, 1974–1975, was spent going through an internal grievance procedure that only allowed me to raise procedural issues, although I brought up the issue of sex discrimination. The outcome was a pro forma review of my case by the Academic Council, which ratified the department's original decision. The Grievance Committee forwarded its report (which found procedural irregularities) to the Brown Corporation, which accepted the report but not its findings. On May 9, 1975, my lawyers, Milton Stanzler and his nephew Jordan Stanzler, and I filed a class-action suit under Title VII of the Civil Rights Act. Over the next two and a half years I pursued this case, which was finally settled out of court with a consent decree in September 1977. It provided tenure for me and two other women, and a cash settlement for a fourth plaintiff. It also set up a procedure whereby women whom Brown had discriminated against could claim damages, and set aside $400,000 for such claims. An Affirmative Action Monitoring Committee was created to monitor hiring, tenure, and promotion at Brown, and new procedures were instituted for hiring, annual reviews, and the tenure process. Most importantly, through a series of goals and timetables, the university committed itself to achieving a faculty with 100 women of whom 57 would be tenured by 1987. I returned to Brown in 1979 as a full-time associate professor of anthropology. My initial academic interest in understanding women's subordination and strategies for empowerment had grown into a full-scale public struggle to change women's position at a major university.

Team Research, Urban Anthropology, and the New Immigration

Losing my job at Brown was a traumatic experience, but I pulled myself together, applied for jobs, and submitted grant proposals. I was able to continue pursuing my research on working-class women through a semester at the Radcliffe Institute and a grant proposal to study dual-worker families in Central Falls, Rhode Island. I became affiliated with the Center for Policy Research at Columbia University and applied for funding from the National Institute for Mental Health (NIMH) Center for the Study of Metropolitan Problems. I submitted the grant proposal in 1975 but did not receive funding until 1976. When I went on the job market in 1975, I was offered a position at the University of New Mexico (UNM). After a semester commuting from Providence to Cambridge to be at the Radcliffe Institute, I drove out to New Mexico in January 1976 to begin teaching at UNM.

I returned to Central Falls in June 1976 to begin research on Azorean and Colombian immigrants who had recently arrived in this small factory town to work in the textile mills, wire plants, and a large apparel factory. The project continued over the next eighteen months. Three Brown undergraduate students who were fluent in Portuguese or Spanish helped me conduct interviews, and a Brown graduate student collected information on the wider community and administered the project. This was my first experience with working with a research team. After my undergraduate research assistants graduated, I hired two Portuguese community members (a teacher and a social worker) to conduct interviews. I was on hand all of 1977 and spent most of my research time working in an apparel factory in order to understand the work lives of Central Falls working-class women. Another Brown graduate studied the Franco-American community, and a Polish graduate student from Johns Hopkins conducted excellent interviews and carried out participant observation in the Polish American community. Several of my historian friends helped me work with Rhode Island Census data, historical documents, and oral histories that greatly enriched my sense of the community's history. What had started out as a study of dual-worker immigrant families became *From Working Daughters to Working Mothers: Immigrant Women in a New England*

Industrial Community (1987), a historical and contemporary study of women's work in a mill town over 170 years.

Toward a Public Anthropology

My ability to coordinate team research and my interest in critical social issues expanded with my next two projects, on Sunbelt working mothers and on the Ford Foundation Project on Changing Relations. The research on dual-worker families in Albuquerque focused not on immigrants, but on Hispano and Anglo working-class families. The new Sunbelt apparel and electronics plants employed women who, despite having excellent factory jobs in the low-wage Albuquerque economy, still faced difficulties juggling different shifts, often without day care. Husbands helped more than their fathers had, especially with child care, but women still handled a "double day," relying on a network of kin (particularly the Hispana interviewees, who had many relatives in Albuquerque) and work friends. This time I had greater success assembling a research team, which included Patricia Zavella and Felipe Gonzales, two Ph.D. students from the University of California, Berkeley, who were living in Albuquerque while working on dissertations. Pat interviewed Hispanas, I interviewed the Anglo women, Felipe interviewed many of the Hispano men, and Gary Lemons, a graduate student in sociology, interviewed Anglo husbands. Three other graduate students also participated. Pat, Felipe, and I worked together on the book manuscript, and Peter Evans contributed a chapter based on his interviews with plant managers. The result was *Sunbelt Working Mothers: Reconciling Family and Factory* (1993).

In 1987 Roger Sanjek asked me to be a member of the advisory board for a Ford Foundation project on relationships between new immigrants and established residents in six American cities. The Immigration Reform and Control Act (IRCA) was just taking effect, and I leapt at the chance to research immigration in a team effort that might have some policy implications. However, the project was large and complex, with six differently structured teams working on different topics in six different cities. We learned that on many teams the researchers were of uneven quality; one team had to be replaced with a completely different project in another city. As a member of the advisory board, and later project co-director, I concentrated on putting together two collections from the project: *Structuring Diversity: Ethnographic Perspectives on the New Immigration* (1992) and *Newcomers in the Workplace: Immigrants and the Restructuring of the U.S. Economy* (1994).

The project report summarized our major findings, but we were unable to forge any policy initiatives. We did, however, create the PBS documentary *America Becoming* (aired in September 1991), which showed a broad audience how America was diversifying and how new immigrants in Chicago, Philadelphia, Miami, Houston, Los Angeles, and Garden City were integrating into these communities. The Changing Relations Project depended on collaboration among anthropologists and social scientists, but did not involve collaboration with the research subjects and interviewees. Soon, however, a shift in ethnographic writing increased my chances for collaboration with research subjects in the context of the life history.

The Ethnographic Revolution

With the publication of *Writing Culture* (Clifford and Marcus 1986) and *Anthropology as Cultural Critique* (Marcus and Fischer 1986), several male anthropologists pointed the way toward a more dialogical type of ethnographic writing that included authors as actors rather than invisible observers. Rooted in Clifford Geertz's "Thick Description" (Geertz 1973), this shift to "ethnography as text" went hand in hand with increased attention to postmodern theory and the work of Foucault and Bourdieu. I learned much more about postmodern theory by attending seminars at the Pembroke Center under the guidance of Joan Scott, who became its first director.

Although I remained committed to empirical research, new approaches to ethnographic writing and life history as developed by feminists like Dorinne Kondo (*Crafting Selves,* 1990), Lila Abu-Lughod (*Writing Women's Worlds,* 1993), and Ruth Behar (*Translated Woman,* 1993) opened up new avenues for my own writing. I was, of course, dismayed that Clifford, Marcus, Fischer, and others ignored feminist ethnography, and that their books' popularity further spread the notion that men were at the forefront of more dialogical approaches. But soon feminist research on the contributions of Elsie Clews Parsons, Zora Neal Hurston, and Gladys Reichard illuminated the long history of women's innovative ethnographic writing, and the collection *Women Writing Culture* (Behar and Gordon 1996) brought together both historical and contemporary examples of feminist ethnographic contributions.

I began collaborative work with Eva Price, her daughter Carole Cadman, and her granddaughter Valerie Darwin in the mid 1990s. Initially this was to be the life history of Eva, who wanted to write a book about her life for her grandchildren and great-grandchildren. Soon, though, it was clear that Carole and Valerie's narratives would add richness to the book and emphasize the changes experienced by each generation as well as their attempts to preserve Navajo language and traditions. Moreover, the older women's life histories did not include the experiences of young college-age Navajos who often struggled with education, jobs, marriage, and children. Including Valerie's narratives filled this gap. Working with each woman, I taped and transcribed several loosely constructed interviews in which I encouraged the women to extend and elaborate on questions. I drafted and redrafted the manuscript eventually removing many references to Navajo history, social structure, feminist theory and oral history in order to allow the women's narratives to carry the story forward.

I vetted the chapters I wrote with each, reading them to Eva, reviewing them with Carole, and letting Valerie make her own deletions. I came to respect their decisions to present certain aspects of their lives rather than others. They often surprised me with their candor and willingness to share important events, each in her own voice. I also began incorporating events from my own life into the book, illustrating our common participation in the same regional economy, despite divisions of race/ethnicity, class, and family history. This new way of writing (incorporating my experiences rather than removing myself from the interaction) was a challenge, but it made for a much more dialogical ethnography that more clearly explicated points of cultural difference. The outcome, *Weaving Women's Lives: Three Generations in a Navajo Family* (2007), chronicles changes from 1928 to 2005 and clearly positions these women within American society while also emphasizing the continued importance of Navajo language, culture, religion, and traditions in women's lives.

My experience writing *Weaving Women's Lives* informed a more recent oral history project in the Grants/San Rafael area of New Mexico. A collaboration between the Alfonso Ortiz Center in the Department of Anthropology at UNM and the Cibola County Arts Council, the project involved interviews conducted over five years with older residents (mostly Hispanos) from San Rafael, San Mateo, and other communities in the Grants area (eighty miles from Albuquerque). We documented economic changes since the 1920s, the transformation of family networks through immigration, and efforts to preserve Hispano traditions (food ways, religious feast days, family gatherings, etc.). Stephanie Sanchez, Jara Carrington, Anna Cabrera, and several other students worked on the project, conducting and transcribing interviews, constructing genealogies, and digitizing photos and documents. CDs prepared for each interviewee hold the digital recording, transcriptions, photos, and genealogy. These materials will be archived at UNM and other locations in the Grants area.

Since the 1980s I have slowly evolved a process of collaboration in my projects that focus on critical social issues, and many students and colleagues have followed my lead, some only taking tentative steps. Others, however, have recently taken on more fully collaborative research.

Critical Social Issues and Collaboration

In the discipline as a whole, practicing and applied anthropologists increasingly emphasize collaboration. This interest has led to more efforts to work with communities and populations where research is being conducted. Institutional Review Board (IRB) approval for research on human subjects is now mandatory for all cultural anthropology projects using participant observation, interviews, oral histories, and other qualitative methods. This provides a framework for taking informed consent seriously and working more closely and transparently with individuals and communities.

However, many anthropologists have forged a wide range of collaborative relationships beyond what is required by the IRB process. At one end of a continuum are anthropology students who begin crafting a dissertation proposal based on their own interests and then conduct preliminary field research, usually volunteering with an organization. Often collaboration emerges when the researcher's service efforts lead the organization's staff to decide to support the research, hoping it will dovetail with some of their own needs. Members of the organization often receive feedback or a written report about research findings. They may also review chapters of a dissertation or give their own interpretations of the data.

Other anthropologists (students, faculty, practicing anthropologists) do not work with organizations but develop their own networks of contacts through preliminary research. They often provide interviewees with transportation, translations of documents, help in navigating a bureaucracy, or small payments. Such individually oriented support often cements relationships beyond the formal consent process. This becomes a limited kind of collaboration in which interviewees provide a sounding board for ideas, are asked to review their own transcripts, or give feedback on formal presentations. In both of these cases, collaboration develops after the research is conceptualized. It often takes place during fieldwork or during the dissemination phase, when results are presented or feedback requested.

At the other end of the continuum are projects that develop through conversations and dialogue between the researcher and members of an organization or community. In some cases (usually involving Native American pueblos or tribal entities) the anthropologist works for a community-run institution and develops projects explicitly for it.[4] Many of these researchers, both archaeologists and cultural anthropologists, have adopted PAR or CBPR approaches. Native American tribal governments often set up their own IRB processes, hire their own archaeologists, and encourage cultural anthropologists who want to conduct research in a reservation community to work more collaboratively.

As a way of illustrating these differences, in the next sections I examine the critical social issues that UNM students, colleagues, and Southwest archaeologists have approached over the last decade. These include issues of immigration, health, economic development, water rights and sustainability, language preservation, cultural resource management, and heritage or cultural preservation.

Research on Immigration

Several students at UNM have produced dissertations on immigration since 2005 Deborah Boehm taught English classes for new immigrants from Mexico though a local Albuquerque NGO. She made contacts with immigrants from a rancho near San Luis Potosi and, by working in both the rancho and Albuquerque, she was able to compose a dissertation on the role of gender in the creation of a transnational community (Boehm 2005; 2012). Through her connection with Catholic Refugee Services in Albuquerque, Nancy Burke made a documentary film aimed at dislodging stereotypes of new Cuban immigrants to Albuquerque. She went on to conduct a series of interviews focusing on Cuban Santeria and new immigrants' maintenance of their rituals and connections to Cuban practitioners, even at a distance (Burke 2001).

More recently, between 2011 and 2013 Jara Carrington studied binational same-sex couples, examining their political and everyday struggles to allow the non-U.S. partner to remain in the United States. Up until the Supreme Court struck down parts of the Federal Defense of Marriage Act on June 26, 2013, marriage was not an avenue to citizenship as it was for a heterosexual couple. Jara volunteered with an NGO that advocated for legal changes in immigration law to broaden the definition of marriage and create a path to citizenship for foreign-born partners of U.S. citizens. The NGO supported her research, and asked her to analyze their data on binational same-sex couples and write a report. These three students put time and effort into working with NGOs and engaged in activities that benefited the organizations and often the participants in their dissertation research, but the students formulated and carried out their research without input from either.

A project led by Christina Getrich, "Investigating Cultural Citizenship Among Second-Generation Mexican Immigrant Youth," exemplifies a more fully collaborative approach to research on immigration. Christina conducted research in San Diego at the Barrio Logan College Institute (BLCI), an NGO organized to help children of Mexican immigrants qualify for college admission. Christina volunteered at the organization as a tutor and formulated her project to fit both its needs and her interests. Her sister was its director at the time, and BLCI was glad to have her volunteer and analyze its program because her evaluation might prove helpful in obtaining grant funds. Christina was interested in understanding how immigrant teenagers conceptualize citizenship, national belonging, and nativist racism (i.e., verbal attacks and prejudice directed against immigrants both documented and undocumented). She was also interested in family and peer influence on identity formation and in whether, and how, students displayed forms of what anthropologists call cultural citizenship (a sense of belonging separate from legal status).

Christina was exploring these topics in 2006, the year massive of demonstrations in California over immigrant rights (Getrich 2008). Using a technique called photovoice, she had the students photograph their neighborhoods and the BLCI. The resulting exhibit of photos and accompanying narratives expressed the students' ideas about belonging, community, and identity. Despite the wide range of experiences that Christina uncovered in terms of migration, documentation issues, and transnational experiences, many students indicated that they were both Mexican and American rather than choosing one identity over the other. Christina also provided parents, staff, and students with a report on the program, its success in getting students into college, and their growing senses of binational identity. During portions of the research and all of the dissemination phase, the project was collaborative in that Christina worked closely with the students to get them to express their own ideas (in addition to what they had told her in interviews). In demonstrating that holding two national identities does not compromise students' loyalty to the United States or their full participation in society, the project results could have broad implications for U.S. immigration policy. However, actually impacting public policy in California typically requires working closely with legislators, school board members, or local colleges around particular policies.[5]

Economic Development

In 2004 Nicole Kellett went to Andahuaylas, Peru, where her husband was pursing archaeological research, to develop her own Ph.D. dissertation project. In this rural high-altitude valley devoted to subsistence farming, the issue of economic development was pressing. Women's empowerment through increased access to economic resources seemed like a potential path to families' financial betterment. Nicole initially cultivated ties with Asociación Para el Desarrollo Empresarial en Apurímac (ADEA), an NGO that provided small loans to rural women in the communities surrounding Andahuaylas. In 2005 she began a collaborative relationship with ADEA. First she interviewed the staff and participated in many of their meetings, activities, and training sessions. However, the main portion of her research was conducted in Sacclaya, a small community outside of Andahuaylas where she lived with a family, engaged in extensive participant observation, and conducted forty formal interviews.

Nicole discovered that although the women in the Sacclaya area and the employees of ADEA shared similar views of women's empowerment, ADEA was unintentionally disrupting gender relations and pushing an ineffective leadership-training program. Nicole found a huge gap between the middle-class, urban, Spanish-speaking ADEA workers and the rural, indigenous Sacclaya women, and traced it to microfinance program administrators. These middle-class women failed to understand the kinds of power and autonomy indigenous women held, the gender division of labor, and the economic constraints under which Sacclaya women labored (Kellett 2009). Concluding her research, Nicole wrote an extensive report for ADEA outlining this disjuncture and providing recommendations for future action. Nicole's research went beyond measuring the financial success of microfinance programs—the predominant subject of previous research—to assess how these programs may or may not be changing gender relations and women's ability to make decisions and participate more broadly in community affairs. She was also able to make concrete policy recommendations at a local level.

Health Care Issues for Native Americans

Of all our department's recent Ph.D. students, Sean Bruna has gone the farthest in building collaborative relationships. His dissertation research with the Ysleta del Sur Pueblo near El Paso used principles from PAR and CBPR and became collaborative when he realized that the tribe was uninterested in extending the topic of his MA research at the University of Chicago—namely, the court battle over the tribe's casino (a topic he had pursued without conducting fieldwork). After becoming a Ph.D. student at UNM, he visited the pueblo often, attending meetings and getting to know tribal members. He moved to El Paso and spent a year volunteering with the tribe's after-school program and diabetes program. These placements, he learned later, served as a form of "researcher vetting." Tribal members were interested in having Sean conduct research on diabetes because, they said, "we need to find something that is good for you and good for us." As an unpaid staff member, Sean was able to work with elders, youth, and adults, acquiring "a feel for the community." He helped create a community garden, assisted in grant writing, and, as his ideas for the dissertation developed, met with elders and tribal leaders. Only then did he write his dissertation proposal. By this time he had managed to assemble the local research team necessary to get the Tribal Council's approval for his project. Most importantly, his attitude was he did not have all the answers to issues of diabetes, and that enhanced diabetes prevention was a puzzle everyone was engaged in solving.

The local research team was involved in formulating the goals of the research, developing the questionnaires and survey instruments, conducting interviews, and assessing the feasibility and appropriateness of the research methods. Once Sean was in the writing stage of the project, he began co-writing papers for public presentation with individuals from the Ysleta diabetes program. He shared his completed dissertation with tribal leadership, health staff and community members who wanted a copy. It is also available on his web-site. Finally, after defending his dissertation, he returned Ysleta del Sur and presented his findings at a community meeting and had been involved in consulting with the community to design a "Wellness Roadmap to guild health programs for 2015–2025.

Language Preservation and Water Rights

Two of my colleagues at UNM are involved in long-term collaborative research with New Mexican Hispano and Native American communities. In both cases the community participants (an association and a pueblo) set the parameters of the research, participate in it, and control the resulting products in a collaboration much more thoroughgoing than in the cases discussed above.

In 2003 Erin Debenport, then a Ph.D. student at the University of Chicago, joined the education committee of a pueblo she calls San Ramon[6] to collaborate with them in building a Keiwa community dictionary (2010). Over a nine-year period they worked closely to build a dictionary and teach pueblo youth the Keiwa language and hone their literacy skills. She has adhered to the pueblo's rules of privacy and secrecy, using a pseudonym for the pueblo's name and withholding her collaborators' and students' identities. The dictionary is for internal use only. She does not use Keiwa words in her publications, and at least one member of the education committee reviewed her talks and presentations before she gave them. Her presentations and publications discuss theoretical issues of language preservation, innovations in written texts, and generational differences in text making, while her collaborative efforts have meaningfully helped advance the dictionary and produce a new generation who are familiar with their language and increasingly literate in it.

Sylvia Rodriguez, a native of Taos, has worked closely first with the Taos Valley Acequia Association (TVAA) and, more recently, with the New Mexico Acequia Association (NMAA). Both are regional associations that serve and are made up of local community ditch or acequia associations. Her book *Acequia: Water Sharing, Sanctity, and Place* (2006), based on collaboration with the TVAA, describes the Taos Valley's complex irrigation system, its importance to local agriculture, and the religious traditions that sustain it. Her work with the NMAA began in late 2008 with an initial three-hour consultation with the executive director about major issues facing acequias and how her skills as a researcher might be of help. The association's chief concern was its "mayordomo crisis": knowledge loss, attrition, and inadequate replacement of the mayordomos or "ditch bosses" who manage the allocation of water in the ancient local village ditch systems.

Sylvia used the PAR model, organizing extended conversations with NMAA members to formulate a methodology and set of activities that might reverse this potential loss of knowledge. Through these early meetings a core team of participants emerged, including local acequia commissioners, NMAA staff members, Sylvia, and a graduate student. The team met on a monthly basis for the next four years to design and oversee the project and bring its final products to fruition. The original idea was to interview current mayordomos and document their practices in order to create a handbook or practical everyday guide to use in the training of a new generation of mayordomos. The project evolved through several stages: conceptualization, design of interviews, selection of interviewers and interviewees, recording of interviews, identification of themes, and the production of a handbook and recruitment video. In the process of conducting, transcribing, and reviewing approximately forty interviews, the team decided to implement a pilot internship to document the teaching of knowledge to a new mayordomo. They took field trips to observe and video acequia-related activities and document the ongoing internship for a thirty-minute recruitment video about the art of mayordomia. The project culminated in 2013 with the production of the handbook and video, compiled into a "Mayordomo Toolkit" subsequently disseminated by the NMAA. The handbook was intended to be maintained online as a living document, periodically revised and updated on the basis of feedback from its users.

Cultural Resource Management and Heritage Preservation

Archaeologists in the Southwest have actively developed collaborative relationships with Native American groups because these groups have demanded it and because cultural resource management is a top priority for both Native American tribal governments and archaeologists. Tribes have established their own preservation departments, developed museums, and actively pursued the return of human remains and cultural items through the Native American Graves Protection and Repatriation Act (NAGPRA). In just one example, T.J. Ferguson and Chip Colwell-Chanthaphonh used a collaborative model, consulting with elders from four groups (Zuni, Hopi, Western Apache, and Tohono O'odham) to understand the archaeology of the San Pedro Valley. They outlined this process in their book, *History Is in the Land: Multivocal Tribal Histories in Arizona's San Pedro Valley* (Ferguson and Colwell-Chanthaphonh 2006). In an *American Anthropologist* article, they discussed consultations they held with Zuni and Hopi elders, some-times on trips to archaeological sites and museum collections, in order to construct parallel histories (Colwell-Chanthaphonh and Ferguson 2006). These excursions changed the archaeologists' analysis of the sites' mean-ings. The researchers came to understand these places' sacred living status for Zuni and Hopi elders and their connection to oral traditions. For their part, the Zuni and Hopi consultants were happy to visit sites far from their home villages and identify pottery designs, petroglyphs, and structural features of sites that were parallel or similar to their own.

This collaborative approach has expanded to other areas. For exam-ple, research teams from Acoma, Hopi, Laguna, and Zuni visited sites in west-central New Mexico's Largo-Creek-Carrizo watershed, including the Zuni Salt Lake, in the summer of 2006. The visits complemented the research of Andrew Duff of Washington State University, attracting an-thropologists Susan Bruning from Southern Methodist University and Peter Whiteley from the American Museum of Natural History (Duff et al. 2008). Members of the Zuni and Acoma teams shared important infor-mation about the religious significance of the Zuni Salt Lake, the home of Salt Woman, a key figure in the oral tradition of both tribes.

At a two-day meeting in Acoma in the summer of 2007, all four teams discussed the cultural importance of this landscape and recent threats, in-cluding a controversial coal mine that, after much controversy, was not de-veloped. Tribal members were able to meet archaeologists from the New Mexico State Lands Department and the Bureau of Land Management, which have responsibility for large parts of the area. Having discussed their differences, the participants agreed that they all shared the common goal of protecting sites and traditional cultural properties, and they com-mitted their organizations and communities to continued communication in the future.

Collaboration between archaeologists and tribal governments has be-come much more common in the Southwest over the past twenty years.

Robert Preusel's research with Cochiti Pueblo and Matthew Liebmann's position as tribal archaeologist for the Pueblo of Jemez Department of Resource Protection are just two additional examples (see Liebmann and Preusel 2007).

Research on Mental Health and Health Reform

Research on health care, particularly in the United States, has focused on critical social issues such as access, health disparities, and privatization of Medicaid in addition to examining tobacco use, substance abuse, cancer, hypertension, and a host of other diseases whose sufferers, as patients and "consumers," would benefit from lower rates and more successful treatment regimens. However, I suspect that forging collaborative relationships in research is easier among professionals (anthropologists, epidemiologists, physicians, nurse practitioners, and medical researchers) than between professionals and the communities they serve. Andrea Lopez, for example, studies health and institutional engagement among poor women with addiction, mental health, and chronic health issues in San Francisco. Individuals in this unstably housed population (many of whom live in Single Room Occupancy Hotels (SROs) can be hard to maintain consistent contact with. They face numerous acute crises daily, so drawing them in as "collaborators" would be challenging and logistically complicated. On the other hand, Nancy Burke has studied a support group of Filipina breast cancer survivors and maintained a relationship with them for several years. She has worked with the group to develop a peer navigation program to address linguistic and navigational challenges new patients experience in accessing treatment. Importantly, this program also meets the needs of family members and caregivers.

Developing large-scale medical anthropology projects, especially those focusing on health care reform, entails dealing with both state bureaucrats and administrators in private for-profit managed care corporations. These professionals often have very different goals for medical programs, and priorities that conflict with those of clinic administrators, support staff, and direct service providers (nurses, social workers, case managers). I was involved in a five-year multi-method assessment of behavioral health reform in New Mexico. The reform pooled funds from sixteen different departments into the Interagency Behavioral Health Purchasing Collaborative and contracted with a for-profit corporation to administer the funds. The reform was intended to maximize access to care and enhance quality, increase the use of evidence-based treatment, improve efficient use of disparate public funds, and incorporate client and family input into service delivery. In addition to a statewide survey of providers, our research team conducted research at fourteen rural and small-town sites, interviewing providers, staff, clients, and family members at three different times over a five-year period. We were interested in how well the new reform was realizing its goals and in whether and how it better served Hispano and Native Americans in rural areas.

Cathleen Willging, the principal investigator, initially established supportive relations with both the CEO of the Purchasing Collaborative and certain key cabinet secretaries who were members of the Purchasing Collaborative (Willging et al. 2007). However, bureaucratic turnover and several years of observing the reform's ups and downs made those in charge warier of the team's findings and less willing to listen to analysis of missteps. Meanwhile, interviews with providers (clinic administrators and direct service providers) often revealed details of how programs had been poorly implemented or how changed billing policies had stretched their finances (Willging et al. 2009; 2014). When preliminary papers presented this point of view, providers were enthusiastic about having the results disseminated, but those in charge of the reform felt the findings were biased. At one point, Purchasing Collaborative officials requested that we post all papers and potential publications on a secure website for vetting before presentation or publication. Once the website was set up, though, they rarely used it.

Native American officials also required the team to submit papers before publication as a condition of IRB approval. However, obtaining their approval was comparatively easy because the interviewees (Native American participants in the reform, both providers and consumers) were generally critical of state programs. Papers advancing this point coincided with the views of tribal professionals who reviewed our work (Willging et al. 2012). This example demonstrates the frustrations of collaboration across different levels in a hierarchically organized reform, where those at the top are empowered to make decisions that impact professionals as well as consumers and clients. Getting those who can change the course of a program to listen to our policy recommendations was difficult at best.

Training Graduate Students

Despite the above examples of various collaborative dissertation projects, many students at UNM and in other Ph.D. programs still seem on track for writing run-of-the-mill proposals that devote little thought to collaboration. Making public anthropology more central to MA and Ph.D. programs is thus one of the next steps in creating a public anthropology focused on critical social issues and based in collaborative research. In the

United States there are several well-developed applied anthropology MA programs represented by the Coalition of Practicing and Applied Anthropology (COPAA). These programs teach students the ethical orientation and methodological skills needed in applied or practicing work. However, "traditional" Ph.D. programs must do more to orient students to the broader goals of public, applied, and practicing anthropology and introduce them to recent collaborative research.

More seminars and courses are needed to introduce undergraduate students to a range of critical social issues involving immigration, human rights, health, education, environmental issues, and local economic development. Besides examining anthropological approaches, such instruction can introduce more interdisciplinary research and policy issues, as well as examples of anthropologists who have written for broader publics and engaged in advocacy at the state and local levels. Our students need to see case studies that show how anthropological research can dovetail or critically engage with NGOs or social movements working in a particular policy area. PAR and CBPR approaches can be studied, and local scholars who have conducted collaborative work or are employees of government, museums, NGOs, or other local institutions can talk or lecture on their work and its relationship to anthropology. More departments should institute a graduate seminar in public anthropology, giving students the chance to listen to public anthropologists and read their work, and also to launch collaborative pilot projects of their own that could lead to dissertation research. A seminar that included archaeologists, linguists, and biological anthropologists as well as cultural anthropologists could enrich a department's graduate curriculum and promote discussion about making collaboration part of each subfield's practice.[7]

Field schools are another avenue for introducing students to collaborative approaches. Ethnological field schools seem to have declined over the last decade, although Sam Beck's semester in New York (see Beck's chapter in this volume) provides the kind of training in critical social issues and collaboration that could help undergraduate (and graduate) students understand the connection between conducting research and working for change.

Archaeologists focused on issues of historic preservation have much more actively utilized field schools to engage students in collaborative research. For example, Barbara Mills (Murray et al. 2009) conducted an NSF-funded summertime field school in collaboration with the White Mountain Apache tribe from 2002 to 2004. The White Mountain Apache Tribe Historic Preservation Program helped design the projects and had ownership and control of all information and materials collected on the reservation. Tribal members participated in a series of discussions on archaeologists' legal and ethical obligations in studying Native American cultural materials, and shared their personal views with students over meals and on visits to sites where students were working (Murray et al. 2009: 67). Two students (Murray and Laluk) went on to design and carry out collaborative dissertation research with two Native American tribal groups: the Mandan, Hidatsa, and Arikara tribal government and the White Mountain Apache (Murray et al. 2009: 70–81).

Students should be encouraged to consider collaborative strategies for crafting dissertation topics and proposals. Not all students want to work with an organization, but most will need to consider serving communities or building networks of interviewees and participants through some sort of volunteer activity. Seminars on proposal writing should include examples of anthropological research that uses PAR and CBPR approaches. Most importantly, students should learn how to explore a potential topic with a community or group, so as to craft an appropriate topic and work out ways to enhance the capacity of an organization and/or its members. To gain entrée and approval for their research, researchers working with Native American communities may need to adopt a PAR approach, which often is key to IRB approval or success in obtaining funding. Depending on the context, students might also consider research incorporating activities that enhance the skills of those they work with, such as training interviewers, helping participants learn computer skills or utilize archival materials, or developing expertise in writing grant proposals. At a minimum, students should be asked to describe how they will communicate their research results to the collaborating community or organization, or to interviewees and research participants. This might include translating their dissertation or placing it with some appropriate organization or library near the fieldwork site.

These steps could be built into the proposal writing and approval process. Close work with dissertation committee members would help students evolve strategies for making their research more collaborative, even after fieldwork has begun or while they are writing dissertations. Also worth considering is how students can work with their interviewees or project participants to elicit feedback and comments during the write-up phase of the dissertation research or on papers for academic conferences. Depending on the context, students should consider co-authorship with some of their research participants, even if their capacity in the actual writing of the paper or chapter was primarily advisory.

Collaboration can also be built into the dissertation defense. In presenting their research, students could discuss their efforts to collaborate with organizations or communities. This might include discussion of how they asked participants to give feedback on chapters or public presentations and incorporated participant commentary in their analysis. They can also outline steps that they have taken or will take to present their findings to a relevant community group or the public (e.g., public talks, magazine features, websites, op-ed pieces). Particularly when students' research concerns a critical social issue such as immigration, health care, or education, the policy implications of the research can be stressed in the dissertation and discussed during the defense.

This is usually the most difficult step for anthropologists. Few of us have worked in the policy field, so we lack experience translating research into concrete policy recommendations, changes in programs, or legislation. Sandra Morgen's research on welfare policy in Oregon (Acker and Morgen 2001) could serve as a model. Morgen and Joan Acker presented their report to the state agency that funded them, posted it on their website, made brief "cameo" reports on issues to legislators, and got the press to publicize their research. In 2004 Morgen's team helped change Oregon state policy so that some recipients of Temporary Assistance for Needy Families (TANF) can count postsecondary education as part of their work requirement.

The generation of anthropologists in their forties and fifties needs to carve out more room in their departments for public/engaged/applied anthropology. This means rethinking the way positions are advertised and stating expectations about public anthropology in job offers and contracts. Departments need to revise guidelines for tenure and promotion so that documents like policy briefings, white papers, and even newspaper articles, website content, and magazine articles can be included in a faculty member's dossier. Many departments already count museum exhibits, museum catalogues, and documentary films as evidence of scholarly research. Documentation of community consultation and organizational consultation relating to scholarly research should also be brought into the mix. Aspects of teaching that entail outreach to broader publics—such as service learning projects, study abroad programs, educational programming, and training programs—should potentially contribute to a candidate's teaching record. Such efforts should be evaluated by external reviewers with expertise in public anthropology in the candidate's research area (see COPAPIA 2011). Public anthropology will continue to expand and become part of graduate degree programs only if younger anthropologists in major anthropology departments keep teaching engagement, public policy, and collaboration while also serving as role models for this kind of researcher.

Conclusions

Public anthropology—particularly public anthropology oriented to studying critical social issues, maintaining collaboration with communities, and shaping public policy—has become a significant part of cultural anthropology and archaeology. For many in the generation that completed Ph.D.s in the late 1960s and 1970s, participation in social movements (feminism, the anti-war movement, the civil rights movement, the Chicano and Native American movements) provided the initial catalyst for changing the kinds of anthropological research and teaching we did and still do. These movements led to new topics and opened up research on an array of critical social issues. Developing collaborative research and writing dialogically is, I think, much slower than the traditional process. NAGPRA and Native American and minority communities' demands for more collaboration in formulating research and giving feedback upon its completion have pushed us along. Many of us lack the experience or will to bring collaborators to presentations in public venues and offer them co-authorship of articles and books. But as young anthropologists increasingly engage in critical public anthropology, this approach to research, collaboration, and public advocacy will spread.

Louise Lamphere is a Distinguished Professor of Anthropology Emerita at the University of New Mexico and Past President of the American Anthropological Association. During 2001–2002 she was a Visiting Scholar at the Russell Sage Foundation in New York City and was a Visiting Fellow in the Department of Anthropology at Princeton University in Fall 2007. Her first major publication was *Woman, Culture, and Society* co-edited with Michelle Zimbalist Rosaldo (1974), and her book on Navajo family life, *To Run After Them: Cultural and Social Bases of Cooperation in a Navajo Community*, was published in 1977. She has studied issues of women and work for more than forty-five years, beginning with her study of women workers in Central Falls, Rhode Island industry in 1976, *From Working Daughters to Working Mothers* (1977). She also co-authored a study of working women in Albuquerque entitled *Sunbelt Working Mothers: Reconciling Family and Factory* (1993) with Patricia Zavella, Felipe Gonzales, and Peter Evans. She co-edited with Helena Ragone and Patricia Zavella a collection of articles entitled *Situated Lives: Gender and Culture in Everyday Life* (1997). Finally, her 2007 book *Weaving Women's Lives: Three Generations in a Navajo Family* employs some of the collaborative research and dialogical writing strategies advocated in this chapter.

Notes

1. On the East Coast, the movement started in New York City. *Notes from the Second Year,* published in 1970, declared that "the personal is political" and set out the parameters of consciousness-raising (Radical Feminism 1970).
2. For many of us, adopting the notion that "the personal is political" may have been the first step in taking our personal interests and concerns into the public sphere. Women were not only interested in revamping their personal lives and their relationships with men but also aimed to address a host of critical issues, particularly rape and sexual abuse, discrimination in the workplace, male dominance in political life, and the control of women's bodies through advertising, popular culture, and the medical establishment. Among the many books on second-wave feminism, Linda Nicholson's collection (1997) and Sara Evans's (1979) and Ruth Rosen's (2000) histories provide a good overview.
3. Rayna Reiter returned to using her maiden name Rayna Rapp in the late 1970s, and some of her best-known publications appeared under this name.
4. Of course government agencies and corporations have a long history of employing anthropologists (see David Price 2008). Such cases (particularly the historical ones) often present difficult ethical issues because the subjects of study are subordinate to hierarchical, bureaucratic organizations where power is exercised from the top. Examples range from anthropologists employed during World War II to study Japanese internment camps (Leighton 1945), to research connected to counterinsurgency efforts in the Vietnam War (Wakin 1992). In a more recent example in 2007, the AAA received a report from a commission appointed to examine ethical issues involved in anthropological research with the armed services (American Anthropological Association 2007). This article primarily concerns research that is independent of such bureaucracies, mainly with local community groups, tribal groups, or NGOs.
5. In contrast, Claudia Anguiano, a UNM Ph.D. in journalism and communication, conducted dissertation research that does have important policy implications for students like those studied by Christina Getrich. Claudia studied activism around the Dream Act, which will enable undocumented youth to attend college and receive federal financial support. Several of the students Christina interviewed, or their relatives, were barred from attending college because they were undocumented, but Christina did not take her research in that direction, and make suggestions for policy changes. Rather, she focused on what she could do for the program she was studying.
6. Debenport has used a pseudonym for the name of the village and also for the language.
7. Sylvia Rodriquez instituted such a seminar at UNM in 2009–2010, but she retired and it has not been given since. Such seminars should not depend on an individual faculty member but be offered on a regular basis as part of the department's core curriculum.

References

Abu-Lughod, Lila. 1993. *Writing Women's Worlds: Bedouin Stories.* Berkeley: University of California Press.
Acker, Joan, and Sandra Morgen. 2001. *Oregon Families Who Left Temporary Assistance for Needy Families (TANF) or Food Stamps: A Study of Economic and Family Well-Being from 1998–2000.* Eugene: Center for the Study of Women in Society, University of Oregon.

Anguiano, Claudia. 2011. "Determined Dreamers: Rhetorical Strategies of the Undocumented Immigrant Youth Social Movement." Ph.D. diss. University of New Mexico.

American Anthropological Association. 2007. "Final Report of the Commission on the Engagement of Anthropology with the U.S. Security and Intelligence Communities (CEAUSSIC)." http://www.aaanet.org/cmtes/Commission-on-the-Engagement-of-Anthropology-with-the-US-Security-and-Intelligence-Communities.cfm.

Behar, Ruth. 1993. *Translated Woman*. Boston: Beacon Press.

Behar, Ruth, and Deborah A. Gordon. 1996. *Women Writing Culture*. Berkeley: University of California Press.

Boehm, Deborah. 2005. "'De Ambos Lados/From Both Sides': Gender, Family and Nation among Transnational Mexicans." Ph.D. diss., University of New Mexico.

———. 2012. *Intimate Migrations: Gender, Family, and Illegality among Transnational Mexicans*. New York: New York University Press.

Burke, Nancy. 2001. "Creating Islands in the Desert: Place, Space and Ritual Among Santeria Practitioners in Albuquerque, New Mexico." Ph.D. diss., University of New Mexico.

Butterfoss, Frances. 2007. *Coalitions and Partnerships in Community Health*. San Francisco: Jossey-Bass.

Clifford, James, and George E. Marcus. 1986. *Writing Culture: The Poetics and Politics of Ethnography*. Berkeley: University of California Press.

Colwell-Chanthaphonh, Chip, and T.J. Ferguson. 2006. "Memory Pieces and Footprints: Multivocality and the Meanings of Ancient Times and Ancestral Places among the Zuni and Hopi." *American Anthropologist* 108, no. 1: 48–162.

Committee on Practicing, Applied and Public Interest Anthropology (COPAPIA). 2011. "Guidelines for Evaluating Scholarship in the Realm of Practicing, Applied and Public Interest Anthropology for Academic Promotion and Tenure." American Anthropological Association, unpublished. http://www.aaanet.org/cmtes/Commission-on-the-Engagement-of-Anthropology-with-the-US-Security-and-Intelligence-Communities.cfm.

Debenport, Erin. 2010. "'Listen So You Can Live Life the Way It's Supposed to Be Lived': Literacy, Lexicography, and Pueblo Propriety." Colloquium presentation, University of New Mexico, February.

Duff, Andrew J., T.J. Ferguson, Susan Bruning, and Peter Whiteley. 2008. "Collaborative Research in a Living Landscape: Pueblo Land, Culture and History in West-Central New Mexico." *Archaeology Southwest* 22, no. 1: 1–23.

England-Kennedy, Elizabeth Sara, and Sarah Horton. 2011. "'Everything That I Thought That They Would Be, They Weren't': Family Systems as Support and Impediment to Recovery." *Social Science and Medicine* 73, Issue 8, 1222–1229.

Evans, Sara. 1979. *Personal Politics*. New York: Knopf.

Ferguson, T.J., and Chip Colwell-Chanthaphonh. 2006. *History Is in the Land: Multivocal Tribal Traditions in Arizona's San Pedro Valley*. Tucson: University of Arizona Press.

Freire, Paulo. 1970. *Pedagogy of the Oppressed*. New York: Continuum.

Geertz, Clifford. 1973. "Thick Description: Toward an Interpretive Theory of Culture." In *The Interpretation of Culture*. New York: Basic Books.

Getrich, Christina. 2008. "American by Birth, Mexican by Blood: Cultural Citizenship and Identity among Second-Generation Mexican Youth." Ph.D. diss., University of New Mexico.

Kellett, Nicole. 2009. "Empowering Women: Microfinance, Development and Relations of Inequality in the South Central Peruvian Highlands." Ph.D. diss., University of New Mexico.

Kondo, Dorinne. 1990. *Crafting Selves: Power, Gender, and Discourses of Identity in a Japanese Workplace*. Chicago: University of Chicago Press.

Lamphere, Louise. 1977. *To Run After Them: Cultural and Social Bases of Cooperation in a Navajo Community*. Tucson: University of Arizona Press.

———. 1987. *From Working Daughters to Working Mothers: Immigrant Women in a New England Industrial Community*. Ithaca, NY: Cornell University Press.

———, ed. 1992. *Structuring Diversity: Ethnographic Perspectives on the New Immigration*. Chicago: University of Chicago Press.

———. 2004. "The Convergence of Applied, Practicing and Public Anthropology in the 21st Century." *Human Organization* 63, no. 4 (Winter): 431–443.

———. 2007. *Weaving Women's Lives: Three Generations in a Navajo Family*. Albuquerque: University of New Mexico Press.

Lamphere, Louise, Alex Stepik, and Guillermo Grenier, eds. 1994. *Newcomers in the Workplace: Immigrants and the Restructuring of the U.S. Economy*. Philadelphia: Temple University Press.

Lamphere, Louise, Patricia Zavella, and Felipe Gonzales, with Peter B. Evans. 1993. *Sunbelt Working Mothers: Reconciling Family and Factory*. Ithaca, NY: Cornell University Press.

Lamphere, Louise, Rayna Rapp, and Gail Rubin. 2007. "Anthropologists Are Talking about Feminist Anthropology." *Ethnos* 72, no. 3: 408–426.

Leighton, Alexander H., *The Governing of Men*. 1945. Princeton, NJ: Princeton University Press

Liebmann, Matthew, and Robert Preusel. 2007. "The Archaeology of the Pueblo Revolt and the Formation of the Modern Pueblo World." *Kiva* 73, no. 2 The Rio Arriba (Winter): 195–217.

Marcus, George, and Michael M.J. Fischer. 1986. *Anthropology as Cultural Critique: An Experimental Moment in the Human Sciences*. Chicago: University of Chicago Press.

Minkler, Meredith. 1997. *Community Organizing and Community Building for Health*. New Brunswick, NJ: Rutgers University Press.

Minkler, Meridith, and Nina Wallerstein. 2003. *Community-Based Participatory Research for Health*. San Francisco: Jossey-Bass.

Murray, Wendi Field, Nicholas C. Laluk, Barbara J. Mills, and T.J. Ferguson. 2009. "Archaeological Collaboration with American Indians: Case Studies from The Western United States." In *Collaborative Anthropologies*, ed. Luke Eric Lassiter. Lincoln: University of Nebraska Press.

Nicholson, Linda, ed. 1997. *The Second Wave: A Reader in Feminist Theory*. New York: Routledge.

Price, David H. 2008. *Anthropological Intelligence: The Deployment and Neglect of American Anthropology in the Second World War*. Durham, NC: Duke University Press.

Radical Feminism. 1970. *Notes From the Second Year: Major Writings of the Radical Feminists*. Radical Feminists: Box AA Old Chelsea Station: New York, New York.

Reiter, Rayna, ed. 1975. *Toward an Anthropology of Women*. New York: Monthly Review Press.

Rodriguez, Sylvia. 2006. *Acequia: Watersharing, Sanctity, and Place*. Santa Fe, NM: SAR.

Rosaldo, Michele Zimbalist, and Louise Lamphere, eds. 1974. *Woman, Culture, and Society*. Stanford, CA: Stanford University Press.

Rosen, Ruth. 2000. *The World Split Open: How the Women's Movement Changed America*. New York: Penguin Books.

Seymour, Susan C. 2015. *Cora Du Bois: Anthropologist, Diplomat, Agent*. Lincoln and London: University of Nebraska Press.

Wakin, Eric. 1992. *Anthropology Goes to War: Professional Ethics and Counterinsurgency in Thailand*. Monograph no. 7. Madison: University of Wisconsin Center for Southeast Asian Studies.

Wallerstein, Nina. 1992. "Powerlessness, Empowerment, and Health: Implications for Health Promotion Programs." *American Journal of Health Promotion* 6: 197–205.

Willging, Cathleen E., David Sommerfeld, Gregory Aarons, and Howard Waitzkin. 2014. "The Effects of Behavioral Health Reform on Safety-Net Institutions: A Mixed-Method Assessment in a Rural State." *Administration and Policy in Mental Health and Mental Health Services Research*, 41, no. 2: 276–291.

Willging, Cathleen E., Jessica Goodkind, Louise Lamphere, Gwendolyn Saul, Shannon Fluder, and Paula Seanez. 2012. "State Behavioral Health Reform in Native American Communities: A Qualitative Assessment." *Qualitative Health Research* 7: 880–896.

Willging, Cathleen E., Howard Waitzkin, and Louise Lamphere. 2009. Transforming Administrative and Clinical Practice in a Public Behavioral Health System: An Ethnographic Assessment of the Context of Change, *Journal of Health Care for the Poor and the Underserved* 20, no. 3: 866–883.

Willging, Cathleen E., Leslie Tremaine, Richard Hough, Jill Reichman, Steve Adelsheim, Karen Meader, and Betty Downes. 2007. "'We Never Used to Do Things This Way': Behavioral Health Reform in New Mexico." *Psychiatric Services* 58, no. 12: 1529–1531.

Chapter 7

PUBLIC ANTHROPOLOGY AND ITS RECEPTION

———— ꧁꧂ ————

Judith Goode

Since 1970 , I have been engaged in a series of team ethnographies in the city of Philadelphia. These projects took place alongside the development of new poststructural theoretical frameworks, methodological modes emphasizing historical formation processes and exploring the relationships between multiple, multi-scaled sites. As research subjects shifted from populations of "others" to ourselves and ethnography involved encounters between people differentially situated in the sociopolitical order, and as the call for more public engagement between anthropology and the public sector intensified, the possible audiences for anthropological knowledge production and related action roles for anthropologists broadened. Yet at the same time, critical theories of power and knowledge, essential to analyzing both structural and cultural forms of neoliberalism, generated new ways of framing research that complicated communication with publics by creating complex, often critical views of professional "expertise."

Here I intend to use my experience of data collection, analysis, and communication to different publics in Philadelphia to examine how power relations affected different audiences' willingness to take up research results. I will explore contested interpretations of economic decline, race, class, and other axes of difference within the research projects, and discuss how the findings were taken up or rejected by different publics, including the mass, popular, or "public" sphere as well as variously positioned funders, collaborators, and participants.

I will address four cases of how an analysis was or was not taken up and why different parties challenged or ignored it, focusing especially on

---

Notes for this chapter begin on page 218.

political agendas and epistemological hierarchies of value attributed to forms of data and modes of interpretation. After examining the different reception and uptake of research results, I will argue that as research becomes increasingly framed by critical political analysis, anthropologists must identify the most salient publics for our research, whose positions are less constrained or particularly dispose them to "hear" and "get" our interpretations. These include those who already affirm our critiques, as well as those in positions to be potential listeners. Meanwhile, experiences with many publics illustrate various ways of rejecting unwanted, discomforting research messages.

The Philadelphia Context

In postwar Philadelphia, poverty rates rose as redlining, deindustrialization, white flight, and suburbanization produced a middle-class exodus. Activism in poor neighborhoods for civil rights, welfare rights, and local Alinskian organizing often conflicted with the city's technocratic, optimistic practices. Based on the assumptions and practices of mid-twentieth-century postwar U.S. development policy and social engineering, urban planning and economic development practices guided citywide efforts to restructure and rebrand the city, first in terms of regional and national standing and then as a competitive node in the global economy.

More recently, neoliberal policies aimed at privatizing public space and schooling, and forging public-private partnerships for local land use and workforce development policy (Hackworth 2007; Goode 2010) were expected to achieve an imagined future in which people and spaces formerly perceived as unkempt, unproductive, and ungovernable could be transformed into "governable," "economically productive" people and places. In Philadelphia, the city with the largest proportion of people living in poverty among the ten largest U.S. cities, these policies have dire implications for the poor. Three of the four projects discussed below targeted people and spaces seen as "obstacles" to future development. Intentionally or not, such projects often displace individuals and erase community social support networks and social capital.

The projects also revealed differently positioned institutional interests and different preferences for data types and interpretive strategies, and each held different appeal to the broader public. In retrospect, we were able to provide analysis that, like the models developed in critical policy studies (Ferguson 1994; Kingfisher 2013; Shore and Wright 1997; Shore et al. 2011), showed how actions were based on misdiagnoses of problems, and how interventions changed upon encountering political and economic realities to produce contradictions and unintended consequences or "instrument effects" (Ferguson 1994).

The projects yielded complex analyses that linked actual postindustrial development trajectories in the city to the racial, ethnic, and class restructuring of localities and in turn linked these processes to very different "discourses of blame" generated by the professional middle classes. Embedded in institutions governed by the city and the middle class (e.g., schools, officially recognized NGOs) and spread by citywide print and electronic media, such discourses contrasted with those heard in more locally governed institutions in poor neighborhoods, where "race," national identity, and citizenship status were also invoked, but through different understandings of who "caused" local problems and what needed to be done about them.

Unintended Public Anthropology

The first ethnographic project, the Philadelphia Food Project, did not focus on the poor and downwardly mobile. It was a rather traditional analysis of a food system in one ethnic community over four generations. Yet this research easily found a popular audience as two publics read unintended messages into the results. Though initially enticed by the self-promotional aspects of publicity and attention, I soon learned to be wary of loss of control over the message as the research was too enthusiastically taken up by "family values" lobbyists and then by status-seeking "foodies" and commercial food producers.

The intent of the project was academic. Using food as a marker of ethnic identity and group boundaries, we looked at how a transplanted Southern Italian food system had been reproduced and changed over four generations within two differently structured local communities in the Philadelphia metropolitan area. The differences concerned class mobility and shifts in the way that ethnicity was used to mark difference within the Philadelphia region.

The first encounter with the mass public occurred when the Associated Press (AP) reported on a paper presented at a regional anthropology conference (Goode et al. 1977). Its coverage zeroed in on an ancillary point: that families in the study had family dinners together every day. This fit into a widespread narrative that positioned family dinners as central to transmitting moral values and linked the loss of this practice to working mothers, divorce, and dysfunction. More than 300 U.S. newspapers ran the AP article under the headline "Family dinner survives in the United States." This experience aptly demonstrated how editors cherry-pick anthropological information that supports dominant middle-class beliefs.

One of the family values think tanks even contacted me to write a piece for them (I declined).

The research also drew attention from the American Institute of Wine and Food. Founded by Julia Child and Robert Mondavi, this national organization strove to promote gastronomy as a new field of academic study, equal to studies of the traditional academic Arts and thus eligible to be an officially recognized marker of taste and social distinction à la Bourdieu. Local chapters of this membership-supported organization included people with commercial interests, such as industrial producers; local food professionals like specialty food purveyors, chefs, food writers, and restaurateurs; and dues-paying, status-seeking "foodies." Ethnic food traditions, valued for their anti-modern authenticity, attracted great interest. The institute enticed researchers to bolster this authenticity through presentations at both national and local meetings in elegant venues alongside celebrities in the world of food. We also were asked to endorse the nutritional value of a locally produced conglomerate product (we declined). In sum, media and institutional actors ignored our central research questions about food systems and identity, but sought our official "expertise" to promote other interests.

A final lesson harks back to the project's outset, when I asked an outreach nutritional educator who worked with Italian American families about their diet. She responded, "I don't know what they eat, but I know what they should eat." This was my first experience with professionals charged with changing behavior who were oblivious to the significance of people's own experience and prior knowledge. Faulty practices and ignorance were assumed, as was the value of expert knowledge. This theme of "talking down" to policy targets without inquiring or listening threaded through all the projects.

Intentional Change Programs

The three projects discussed below all observed the progress of programs designed to change structures, beliefs, and practice. Access to research populations involved agreements with gatekeepers in most cases. Each project incorporated a dissemination plan to communicate its relevance, both for the designers and implementers of changes and for the target populations.

In keeping with urban ethnographic practice, actual political economic policies and the culturally constructed narratives about them were studied in small-scale, face-to-face interacting groups (micro level) and through the linkages between these local social fields and relevant larger-scale institutions (macro level) citywide, regionally, nationally, and globally. At each of these scaled levels, processes of historical sociocultural formations were an important feature of the research.

The projects together represent a broader ethnographic project to explicate the linkages between actually shifting political economic structures, situated sociocultural narratives of "diversity," and discourses of blame for "social problems" in Philadelphia. In each case, the middle-class professionals who designed the projects from a distance and/or were embedded in distinct matrices of institutional interests had little opportunity for what Donald Schoen has called "reflective practice" (Schoen 1983) However, many street-level professionals who implemented projects for deliberate sociocultural change through local interaction were more open to experience-based reflection.

In retrospect, all these change projects are examples of a dominant theme in critiques of development policy (Edelman and Haugerud 2005), namely, that such policies define populations and problems to fit a priori techniques in change toolkits, resulting in faulty diagnosis. Each project assumed that a technical, mechanical process would fix a problem through "training" focused on changing dysfunctions assumed to be "inside" individuals. But as the nutrition educator's remarks above demonstrate, even the best-intentioned agents of change overlooked actual historically and structurally produced life experiences and practices, thus failing to recognize actual needs.

Supermarket Job Saving Strategies 1975–1980

A project to preserve supermarket jobs allowed the team to observe how audiences situated in different institutions differed in their interests and ideologies, as well as their definitions of empirical "proof." This affected what they chose to pay attention to or ignore. The particulars illuminate the obstacles inherent in public anthropology's central project of cultivating publics.

Emerging from an interdisciplinary urban studies working group on plant closings and job loss in Philadelphia, this project developed when a national supermarket chain, A&P, threatened to close its operations and eliminate 2,000 jobs in southeastern Pennsylvania. A group of anthropologists and social psychologists interested in deindustrialization and plant closings in Philadelphia set out to examine a yearlong attempt to save supermarket jobs by creating two new types of store: worker owner collectives and a new corporate chain with more worker "participation."

Locals of the United Food and Commercial Workers responded to the looming closures by activating a preexisting plan for creating union subsidies to promote collective worker ownership. They proposed to help members buy and reopen stores, to be called "Owned and Operated" (O&O). The second alternative, offered later by the chain, was a new wholly owned subsidiary to be called Super Fresh (SF), to be staffed by union call backs of laid-off workers from the chain. O&O workforces were entirely full-time, whereas former workers called back to SF found a continuing chain practice of predominantly part-time positions. The new chain stores were branded and advertised as having innovative participatory labor management relations, which suggested new rights and power. In fact, the SF contract involved givebacks in wages and benefits in exchange for rights of participation in decisions about a limited range of work procedures. Interviews and conversations showed that SF workers saw the thin veneer of "empowerment" as an inadequate trade-off for material concessions. While shopping in one of the study stores one day, I heard one cashier ask another, "Did you go to the QWL [quality work life] meeting last night" Her colleague said she had, but as usual it was a waste of time. "They make you talk about silly things and won't let you talk about what's important, like hours and schedules."

The research working group developed a project to comparatively examine why workers chose O&O or SF, and observed the processes of training for new roles, start-up, and first-year operations in both types of store. We then secured funding from the Upjohn Institute for Employment Research (Upjohn). This set up a varied set of interested publics to match the diversity among the interdisciplinary research team, discussed below. Audiences for research included Upjohn, SF, the union, and members of a consulting nonprofit organization embedded in the worker ownership movement who took charge of O&O workers' training and the workers themselves.

Upjohn and SF distinguished decisively between economic and social variables, and were only interested in two economic outcomes: worker productivity (Upjohn) and profit-increasing management practices (SF). These were to be measured through data manipulations that communicated "truth" in compressed formats using precise measurements of decontextualized variables. They strongly disdained the social as irrelevant. Upjohn initially stated that it already knew all it wanted to know about "social issues" and preferred economic data in the customary form of mathematical equations. Its award of the grant was contingent on our hiring an economist. We hired a feminist economist with policy experience who was concerned about the intersection of work and social reproduction as well as the redesign of work for important social outcomes.

SF classically and radically distinguished between market logic and morality and generally dismissed any social responsibility. After our oral presentation, its CEO responded: "We are not a social welfare agency. We are a business. Our job is to make money for our stockholders and nobody should expect to support a family with a supermarket job."

Meanwhile, the academic researchers, the union, and the worker ownership consultant-trainers were primarily interested in the social: saving jobs in a time of escalating layoffs, and even improving job quality and flattening workplace hierarchies. Yet each of these groups also had more instrumental stakes in the research, such as advancing academic careers within specific disciplines, retaining union members, or maintaining a good reputation as trainers for worker ownership.

This group had little knowledge of, and assigned little value to, ethnographic knowledge. The O&O consultants and two research team members were positivist social psychologists. Like Upjohn and SF, their ideas of data and "proof" were based on a universal (decontextualized) human subject and the use of predetermined discipline-standardized variables selected for their measurability and tested for validity as the best proxies for grounded reality. Using systems models, they undertook to measure inputs into the transition and subsequent outputs (i.e., productivity and job satisfaction). The O&O consultants were primarily interested in a standardized way to identify personalities suited to worker ownership through personality tests.

Positivism requires scientific, distanced neutrality, and our survey-using research colleagues took pains not to visit (contaminate) any study store before presenting our report. They did not think about the ways in which power relations in the stores contaminated the data collection—for example, store managers pressured workers to fill out individual surveys quickly, and shop stewards, whose personal assessment of store morale was used as a "measurement," had intertwined relationships within the union, a major player with a stake in store success. These implications were never examined.

Ethnography, through continuous, direct fieldwork and elicitation of meaning, became critical to the project since our initial work rapidly identified several contradictions embedded in actual events. Through participant observation, we documented union meetings to recruit laid-off workers to both store types, the processes of selecting and being accepted by a store, and operations over the first year. We also interviewed the relevant corporation, O&O consultants, and union leaders, as well as all study store workers to examine why workers chose to participate, their work histories, and their aspirations.

Early ethnographic data revealed mismatches among the union's, chain's, and O&O consultants' cultural constructions of their targets. Rapid changes in transnational ownership and management policy over recent decades had produced numerous crucial differences between workers, most notably a highly gendered division based on male control and women's deference, which was reflected in assignments to rare full-time positions and to important departments. We found that the new stores reproduced the same hierarchy.

Contrary to the sponsors' expectations of change, the main reason both men and women joined O&O stores was not their risk-taking, collective psychologies but their desire for full-time jobs, which remained limited at SF. Women and part-time male workers saw O&O as the only way to become full-time. Men indicated that they had chosen O&O not because of worker ownership but despite it.

Men and women generally had different goals for the new store. Men were aspiring entrepreneurs who shared the chain's interest in the bottom line. They regarded worker ownership as "too close to socialism" but thought it would give them an opportunity to be their own boss. They were unimpressed by the training, which relied on readings and films about the Basque worker ownership movement in Mondragon, Spain, a distant place they saw as exotic and not modern. They looked forward to dressing like owners, talking to bankers, and acquiring the "paperwork" skills the chain had monopolized. They shared the same gender, racial, and age biases as the chain.

Women, though, imagined different outcomes for the change. They liked the idea of a cooperative. Their limited departmental locations had enabled close-knit relationships, and they often spoke of the stores as families. They believed that their undervalued social skills with customers kept the stores afloat. Women did much of the voluntary invisible work in the O&O team-building activities, maintaining committee meetings and the minutes of the monthly owners' meetings, and celebrating birthdays and other events. Most of their former store roles had made them deferential clients to male supervisors, and they really bought into the promise of empowerment in an egalitarian workplace (Goode and Simon 1994).

The original research design was a four-cell comparison of two O&O and two SF stores at different points of being "treated" or "trained." A corporate-union data sheet listing the dates for store training was the source for the classifications involved. It soon became apparent that this schedule did not reflect actual training and that no training had been monitored. This revealed the distance between what "corporate" and the union knew and what had actually happened within the "black box" of each store. Workers told us what had happened. In the O&O store, a series of weather- and illness-related cancellations had postponed the trainings; at the SF store, only a handful of workers were officially trained. Moreover, all trainers differed in their selection, emphasis, and presentation of thematic material.

This ethnographic data was immediately used to reclassify the stores for comparison based on the degree of observed teamwork, worker engagement, and shared information in each. Differences among them all traced back to earlier relationships between individual workers in the old stores. Clearly, these preexisting relationships were key to the new stores' composition and the best source of insight into collective operations.

As indicated above, the surveys of job satisfaction were collected quickly, as store managers mandated compliance. Shop stewards were responsible for much of the store-level data, which was simplified to rating scales and overlooked the workers' narrative of a complicated age- and gender-related dynamics that had recently escalated anger and hostility toward the chain. Luckily, by the time the survey numbers were "crunched," we had enough interview data to reveal the SF workers' narrative of actual experience, enabling a reality-based re-categorization.[1]

The ethnography revealed that workers were not the passive, trainable people envisioned by the innovators. They were agents with aspirations, embedded in work experience that reproduced preexisting cultural constructions and sociopolitical relationships with decisive influence on the course of events.

Store Outcomes

Unsurprisingly, after the first year of operation the majority male workers of one O&O store, believing the store was not as profitable as expected and salary increases were too slow, voted to use their shared capital to buy out the other workers. Simultaneously, some women who spoke of disillusionment about the possibility of equality in communal governance accepted buyouts, and the smaller group of remaining owners undermined their capital, defaulted on loans, and closed their co-op. The other O&O store used its profits to buy additional stores and hire part-time workers, thereby turning a worker collective into a developing mini-chain dependent on the profit-enhancing use of part-time labor.[2]

Within the first year, the majority of the SF workers had left their mostly part-time jobs and been replaced by workers hired at lower wages under a two-tier contract that paid new hires lower wages than former A&P employees. Many workers, especially women, understood that they were marked for phase-out.

Receiving Knowledge and Taking it Up

Our findings, in various formats, all reached their intended audiences, only a few of which took them seriously. We made two key points. First,

O&O stores with all full-time workers were at least as productive (as measured in a way legible to economists) as SF stores with mostly part-timers. The survey data on job satisfaction supported this finding, which was further explained by ethnographic work histories in which workers' accounts linked full-time work to satisfaction. Second, the contradictions between change agents' cultural construction of workers and workers' actual experiences and skills revealed a need to involve workers more centrally in the design and implementation of change.

We presented our research and findings to the corporation, union, O&O consultants, and each store. Despite our concentration on the social, Upjohn published a monograph (Hochner et al. 1988). SF received the information pleasantly but had already made clear its view that workers were units of labor to be used efficiently for the bottom line. The union, facing many simultaneous threats of job losses, moved on to the next case and in fact negotiated a contract with another chain that, like SF's, stipulated both an exchange of givebacks for illusory worker empowerment and a two-tier wage system that incentivized elimination of former chain workers. These parties ignored the links between economic indicators of productivity and workers' actual sociopolitical experiences.

Promoters of worker ownership learned how ethnographic knowledge of earlier experiences and attention to workers' goals could make ideal candidates more legible. The information about gender and the significance of past experience and preexisting social relationships helped them understand the necessity of knowing about context and listening to perspectives and knowledge. They shifted from thinking like the nutrition educator who assumed that experts (or in this case, motivated progressives) knew what was good for people and should and could successfully motivate them to embrace "best practices" without any knowledge about them. Workers in the four stores, as targets of change by the other actors, and as our most intimate ethnographic research subjects were the source of our knowledge production rather than the beneficiaries. Worker's reactions to presentations depended on their initial aspirations and current positions. Male would-be entrepreneurs paid little attention and the disappointed women had anticipated the outcome.

We tried to create a mass public audience through a series of conversations with business section writers and a few news stories, but it was impossible to spread the word that Super Fresh stores were not worker owned. I often asked students and friends what they knew about the stores, and they always said they liked shopping at Super Fresh because the workers owned the stores. In short, the chain's marketing ploy worked.

Changing Relations Project: New Immigrants and Established Residents (late 1988–1992)

The Philadelphia Changing Relations Project (CRP) was one site in a six-city national project comparing the nature of relationships between post-1965 immigrants to the United States and the established residents who dominated the neighborhoods and institutions they entered, which were divided by class, racial, and ethnic identities. Ethnographic data was used to identify discourses and actions that brought populations together or kept them apart.

In three poor and working-class neighborhoods, the Philadelphia site examined everyday race and ethnic relations in schools, shopping strips, and city-sponsored collective local activities focused on addressing conflicts and promoting improved human relations through multicultural programming.[3] For two years we observed everyday public and private life and interviewed households, local organizations, clergy, representatives of city-governed agencies, and NGOs that worked in the neighborhoods. We observed nonacademic activities in schools and public life in shopping strips. Over the period we also followed critical events, including vandalism and murders, to tease out the differences in the ways these were analyzed by middle-class professionals charged with developing strategies to bring people together.

At the same time, we observed local place-based actions of protest and demand. Rooted in the earlier civil rights and welfare rights movements as well as Alinsky-influenced neighborhood organizing, these were now led by a loosely affiliated network of clergy and grassroots leaders with earlier movement experience. Many whites participated in local place-based, interracial neighborhoods through groups organized to reverse the effects of redlining and gentrification through actions to promote self-help and activism to control and rehabilitate abandoned housing stock, aggregate empty land into land trusts, or work for the passage of the Community Reinvestment Act. Many whites alongside newcomer people of color were active in antiracist organizations, even as others took part in overtly racist activities.

When incipient gentrification stalled for a time in the 1980s, the presence of collective action was key to these community groups' success, allowing new immigrants and established residents to develop intimate and trusting relationships in neighborhood institutions in several areas of the three localities studied. We observed many budding cross-racial coalitions working on class-based projects on schooling, jobs, and housing. Still, a significant color line persisted. Violent incidents that occurred when it was crossed interrupted these collaborative projects. The standard media coverage of these events oversimplified the narrative of blame, emphasizing white working-class racism or innate adolescent violence. For a period, middle class–governed city agencies, schools, churches, and a growing network of NGOs increasingly offered interventions to heal or prevent such incidents. These interventions involved a new group of human relations experts who were contracted to either train organizational staff or run diversity programs for them.

Middle-class professionals, including diversity trainers, blamed white ethnic parents for teaching racism to their children out of "fear of the other." They encouraged prevention and healing events that taught appreciation of "other cultures" through the consumption of commodified aspects of culture like musical performances, food, and handicrafts. These events reproduced what they themselves enjoyed in leisure time at downtown festivals where they consumed "authenticity" as "internal tourists" marking their cosmopolitanism. As one middle-class resident said, "I get an adrenaline rush when I go out into the neighborhood and hear so many languages spoken."

We encountered such middle-class "diversity seekers" throughout the research. At one event, middle-class organizers rejected two performances in which Puerto Ricans and South Asians respectively performed English-language songs. The performers were exhorted to "sing songs in your language" even after they explained that they were English speakers in their homeland. Commodified diversity was also seen as a way to handle inequalities between middle-class benefactors and residents of declining neighborhoods. One high-level clergyman, trying to assuage congregants angered by news that the diocese could not help with a crucial building repair, emphasized that the parish and church hierarchy were in a mutually equal relationship. "We have a reciprocal relationship," he stated. "You share your culture with us and we share with you the resources we can." This attempt to sound un-patronizing implied that the only resource the congregation had was its exotic culture, to be offered as delectable to elites. Afterward, moreover, several local board members challenged the notion of equivalent exchange. One said, "He says it's equal, but we know it's not and it's so obvious."

Reliance on techniques of "enjoying other cultures at a distance" also denied the significance of historical power relations and structural racism in producing tensions. Residents saw such events as lacking reference to the politics of cultural identity, in which inequalities in political economic power explained local issues. Nevertheless, local organizations staging prescribed cultural festivals often accepted the funding that one middle class–run NGO granted if performances and food events were included. Local groups hoped to defray the costs of their mostly volunteer or semi-volunteer staff (part-time pay for full-time or overtime work), who found themselves spending much time planning and carrying out events whose premises did not fit their experience and in fact strongly reified the very intergroup differences that their everyday cross-racial activism was diminishing.

Many local organizations that accepted such grants were in fact very inclusive sites for multiracial immigrants and established residents. One unintended consequence of multicultural funding was the disruption of various political campaigns for housing, jobs, and better schools. These required daily activity to identify abandoned homes by tracing tax and utility statuses, participate in school and school district organizations, form coalitions, visit local politicians, and attend city council meetings. Planning for what seemed to be programming that missed the mark was seen as a diversion from important goals.

Multiple Channels, Scales, and Obstacles to Reception

After the analysis, our task was to convey the complex messages of the research to variously situated publics: local residents' grassroots organizations, locally based institutions and professionals (teachers, clergy, NGO staffs), and institutions and diversity specialists who prescribed solutions from a distance or provided one-size-fits-all diversity programming. The two core messages were that (1) the middle class misdiagnosed the source of intergroup problems as depoliticized "fear and ignorance" and prescribed consumption of commodified performances in an oversimplified, uncritical multiculturalism that erased the political history of structural racism and avoided discomfort; and (2) such events actually reified differences and diverted attention from already developing political actions that spanned boundaries.

We planned to transmit both these messages through two highly structured formal events: a national project film and a formally structured local conference of research participants. Both formal productions failed to transmit the central findings. The CRP funders had allocated a budget equal to that of the entire six-site ethnographic study to produce the film *America Becoming* (Kim-Gibson 1991), which held six 25-minute narratives, one from each city. Yet even teams of highly competent, well-known filmmakers with high production values found it impossible to compress the nuanced, counterintuitive narratives about race, class, citizenship, and the historical particularities of each site, especially under the pressures of brief location time. The Philadelphia ethnographic research team saw our findings as revealing a narrative about how Philadelphia's specific history had produced a local black-white dyad that in turn shaped the way Asian and

Latino immigrants positioned themselves in the city (Goode and Schneider 1994). The filmmakers instead used the Philadelphia segment to tell a more generalized media story of racism and the civil rights movement in a highly segregated deindustrialized city. They used footage of industrial work never present in Philadelphia to establish the industrial past. Almost all people of color in the film were professional citywide civil-rights activists previously known to the filmmaker, and they represented groups and spaces not included in the study because they were still tightly segregated rather than mixed. Virtually no new immigrant residents or white working-class leaders spoke, and no mention was made of the middle-class professional assumptions that local narratives contradicted.

Unlike the film, the local CRP conference was planned and controlled by the research team itself. Yet it too did not accomplish its goals. We sought to assemble locally embedded research participants, from residents to local representatives of grassroots organizations, street-level professionals (teachers and social service workers), and citywide "policy makers." To avoid seeming like an event for telling people what *we* thought they should know, we created space for them to assert their understandings using the ubiquitous format of keynoters and breakout sessions. This format was a common experience for people in the growing citywide networks of local organizations and institutions. The format was adapted from the conferences of academics and professionals where knowledge is exchanged. In Philadelphia, such local community events had come to be seen more as "fairs," or trade shows that is, vehicles for individual and group self-promotion, public relations, and networking with a dollop of marketing services and packaged technical information (booklets and training tapes) for professionalizing organizations. We had intended to present ideas and engage in discussions about the research findings, but this did not happen.

In contrast, less formal presentations to small groups of street-level professionals — teachers, providers of immigrant services and literacy and ESL programs, grassroots organizations — often enjoyed greater success, as these people lived and worked daily in the community, facing such issues head-on.

A noteworthy case arose upon publication of an op-ed column we wrote (Schneider and Goode 1989) to show how planning and producing multicultural festivals created more division than solidarity. The next day, a priest with whom we had worked closely called and said, "Hey, why didn't you tell us?" The parish staff had recognized themselves in an ethnographic vignette. This led to a meeting and later to restructuring for a more successful festival the following year, as well as new patterns of relationships in the parish schools and congregation. We also realized that we had goofed. In avoiding the discomfort of a direct critique, we had failed to meet our obligation to communicate with the parish before going "public" as experts.[4]

Meanwhile, other locally embedded service workers often challenged ethnographic authority, feeling that their interpretations of daily experiences in the community were equally authoritative. It was difficult to convey how people in different sociopolitical positions with different experiences see situations differently, and how class-positioned master narratives such as the culture of poverty operated in the cultural constructions of clients by professionals, or of students by teachers. We often cited examples of how we, the ethnographers, had come to realize that we must deal with our own unexamined biases.

More difficult were communications with higher-level citywide professionals who funded and designed programs. Our findings demonstrated that their dominant class beliefs and practices channeled and limited contact, reifying difference. Operating out of downtown offices, these practitioners had no experience with the local life their programs targeted. The greatest resistance came from emerging professionals in diversity training. These itinerant trainers passed through social spaces with a toolkit of packaged techniques in which their careers were vested, but their messages did not fit with local experience. Rightly seeing the research as a challenge to their practices, they withdrew from such knowledge-dissemination workshops.

Large public lectures in venues like museums and libraries drew educated middle-class audiences that attended presentations to enrich their knowledge with new research. They were drawn to topics of race, ethnicity, and immigration, which were *interesting* in the same academic way that ethnic food or travel were, that is, as a way to experience the "other." Discussions revealed that many challenged our findings or were disappointed by them. They had come to learn about people set apart from themselves, and seeing their own middle-class views implicated (albeit diplomatically) as problematic made them feel uncomfortable or complicit. Rather than change the message in exchange for larger audiences, we concentrated on targeted groups with more at stake in the research, expecting to later consider new approaches for broader audiences.

Local media turned to us when local conflicts arose or race and immigration became central in city politics. Our contributions included several hour-long interviews on three local news programs and three appearances on a popular NPR local interview show, as well as one feature and two op-ed columns in metropolitan dailies. Features in major ethnic and place-based weeklies also provided a platform for targeted messages. We learned to be wary of providing "expert" sound bites that could be used to validate popular narratives that did not fit local realities, as had occurred in the CRP film production. Many of these media pieces yielded follow-ups such as calls from city agencies, local politicians, and organizations interested in specific findings.

Considering all channels of dissemination—differently scaled media and in-person public events—the messages resonated best with those who needed them: community residents and the street-level professionals in regular direct contact with them. The messages in our episodic, more distant, public media events were likely to be misunderstood or ignored, unless examined through different frameworks. Audiences who actively rejected the ideas because of significant institutional or personal stakes in what was being criticized could tune out—or simply walk out, which happened occasionally. The next section covers research on the local social processes in one study neighborhood as the onset of a new city development regime turned an area of stalled gentrification into a hot spot once more.

Civic Engagement in Three Poor Neighborhoods 1999–Present

My role in this three-locality study was to return to the poorest neighborhood studied in the CRP, to look at how public and private interventions were shaping civic participation, and to compare this area with two other low-income neighborhoods in the city. Between the CRP and the civic engagement (CE) studies, I served on three nonprofit boards and maintained contact with key informants to keep up with trends from a distance.

Under the Rendell mayoralty in the 1990s, Philadelphia began a campaign to attract serious private investment and realize its decade-long aspiration to raise its global-scale position. Borrowing from the neoliberal playbook for urban development and popular ideas such as Richard Florida's argument (Florida 2005) that successful urban development relied on "creative knowledge workers" in arts and culture or in the academy, the city built its hopes for the future on Rendell's Avenue of the Arts project[5] and the expansion of its leading industry, "meds and eds"—shorthand for universities and their health care institutions. Both were imagined as global magnets that would attract capital investment and cosmopolitan populations.

Northern Liberties (NL), a space adjacent to Kensington in which gentrification had stalled in the 1980s, soon became a residential hot spot for creative knowledge workers. When the CE project began, the study neighborhood, which was located just north of NL, was seen as a poor neighborhood whose people needed to be reformed. It was in its third year as a site of Bill Clinton's central urban policy experiment, the Empowerment Zone Program (EZ). Prior to that, it had been a major target for antipoverty and industrial economic development interventions since the 1970s.[6]

Under the new neoliberal regime, which channeled declining public monies into private development, the EZ transformed. Once a local program to promote poor people's civic engagement and link their participation to setting priorities for local development, it was now oriented to developers' goals of producing space to serve the needs of new, northward-moving upscale residents. To the west at the same time, expanding Temple University became a major player in the development of Greater North Philadelphia by developing Temple Town for student residences and consumption, and extending the downtown Avenue of the Arts northward. As the university took over more space, substantial investments supported student engagement in local service organizations through a community learning network (CLN). Even as the EZ and Temple expansion projects squeezed the space of the study neighborhood, its locally run organizations and leadership networks were increasingly, and via different processes, being incorporated into networks of city and university agencies and activities.[7]

At this time, city agencies and foundations generally cultivated deeper involvement in local organizations, garnering significant influence through selective funding, auditing, and regulatory surveillance. Local grassroots organizations had to upgrade their professionalism, credentials, and computer skills to handle the constantly shifting demands for audit data on their activities, "deliverables," and budgets.

Organizations became arrayed in an implicit reputational hierarchy (Kromer 1999) that often judged professionalism by surface appearance—especially dress and speech, which accounted for big differences in performance evaluations. For example, a foundation head called me to ask whether one local organization's executive director was "okay" before they renewed her funding. An older member of a religious order, she bore few professional speech and clothing markers, although she had gone to college and ran a successful organization. Her writing of correspondence by hand added to concerns. Over three years of acquaintance, I had observed her uncanny ability to garner funding from a wide variety of political and philanthropic sources. She used her social capital (kin and church connections) and was an expert recruiter of volunteer staff. Her organization was very successful in terms of both head count and retention. I assured the foundation director that she had not misrepresented her accomplishments and was far from "losing it."

Gender-, age-, class-, and race-based biases were not unusual and had funding implications. In grassroots organizations, they especially affected refunding judgments based on data compliance, where class markers (speech, dress) and racial biases were evident. At an open meeting of a well-funded public program, staff presented a report on compliance (i.e., prompt submission of "deliverables"). A grassroots organization dependent on donated, used computers that broke down often was sanctioned for data sloppiness (appearance-based lack of professionalism), which seemed to call into question the legitimacy of the well-kept numbers themselves.[8] At the same time, another program run by more formally trained middle-class people in the arts had failed to submit head counts or any other data, even after several reminders. The agency director suggested that they be given a pass rather than sanctioned, saying, "You just have to watch them in action to see that they are doing a good job." The statement went unchallenged.

Paid staff soon replaced local women volunteers. Because of the ratcheting up of the new "audit culture" (Strathern 2000), constant changes in required formats for submitting data required constant new training. Two local organizations were forced to close when they lost track of their actual cash flow during a period when new national nonprofit accounting procedures were taking effect.

These changes affected local leaders' responses to such new rules. During the CRP, these mostly voluntary community action groups had grown out of local mothers' concerns about their children's futures in what Naples (1998) called "activist mothering" (see also Mullings 2001; Mullings and Wali 2001. Organizations operated through non-hierarchical, informal networks, and mothers often brought their children to work, rotating childcare responsibility. Now that such jobs could mean salaries, possible career mobility, higher status, and connections to elites, leaders positioned themselves variably. Some groups and individuals remained oppositional, continuing protest and demand tactics. Others, like those who accepted funding for multicultural programming during CRP, changed their stance to cooperate and maintain a good reputation because it was the only way to get support at the time. One such leader stated: "It's the best we can do. We get what we can." Still other leaders internalized neoliberal ideas of "personal responsibility," taking on the appearance, language, and behavioral propriety of the professional middle classes. Their commitment to collective concerns lessened, and their speech came to reflect discourses of blaming the victim: the culture of poverty, underclass culture, and moral divisions between the "deserving" and "undeserving" poor (Goode and Maskovsky 2001), which neoliberal understandings had reintroduced and reinforced (Goode and O'Brien 2006).

Finally, the new gentry moving northward from NL took over governance of many community development corporations to represent the different neighborhood desires of creative knowledge workers. The array of community-based groups became more complex in terms of their relationships with local residents as well as with city and developer interests, further complicating assumptions about the nature of the fictional universal, homogenous "community."

The Empowerment Zone

Our observation of the EZ coincided with shifts between the first and second years of the Community Trust Board (CTB). In its first year, the elected CTB was mostly long-term grassroots actors serving one-year terms, during which they set priorities for future project spending through a locally governed financial services structure. The program money banked in this new organization was supposed to be allocated in the second year according to priorities set by the first CTB. Its wish list, which emphasized long-standing priorities of investing in human capital (jobs and quality education) and protecting local social capital from displacement by developing local housing stock, centered on education for social mobility and job skill training programs.

In the EZ's second year, John Street was elected mayor on a platform of fighting urban blight by improving the local physical infrastructure. Once in office, he developed the Neighborhood Transition Initiative (NTI), an anti-blight program. By this time, the plans once laid for Kensington had shifted from those of the CRP decade or even those envisioned by the original EZ program. No longer did interventions in Kensington focus on reforming residents through anti-violence programs (such as multiculturalism) or anti-drug programs like those developed in the 1980s and early 1990s to create a safety buffer between stigmatized poor communities and the gentry further south. The jobs and education programs envisioned by local leaders on the CTB were also sidelined. The NTI redirected the EZ program to create a space to serve the expanding gentrification in nearby NL, a space that downtown planners now saw as a future recreational and entertainment zone for new knowledge workers in the resurging residential hot spot.

As the EZ entered its second year, Street's first act was to appoint a new, unelected CTB. He was slow to select the full prescribed quota for resident members. To meet the numerical requirements for residents, he appointed residents who were also staff in city agencies and thus were hostage to their careers. Over time, the new CTB members who had been close to the first year CTB lost trust in the process. Elsewhere (Goode and O'Brien

2006) we have documented the many mechanisms used to blunt the effect of increasingly dissenting local voices as unofficial resident watchdogs began to attend every meeting and the network of groups that the first CTB had represented called a large emergency meeting.

Finally, it was announced at a CTB meeting that the EZ was thenceforth linked fiscally and administratively to the NTI. The activist residents on the CTB, accustomed to hearing developers' pitches for local residents' high-priority projects like the creation of a community-directed Lifelong Learning Center, now began hearing and seeing a plan to develop an arts, crafts, food, entertainment, and recreation consumption zone for the upscale new neighbors from further south. The human capital investments envisioned by the EZ's first CTB were replaced by financial capital investment in spaces to be used by residents outside the EZ. Many community leaders had experienced decades of promised job generation that never materialized; now, questions about the number and nature of possible jobs in the new consumption zones were regularly sidelined. Furthermore, an array of carefully produced visuals—architectural designs, overlay maps, and statistics—clearly showed residents' representatives that this project had been in the planning stage for a long time. The second-year CTB had been meeting and planning in good faith for five months in hopes of allocating funds to their preferred projects. This was their first knowledge of behind-the-scenes activities.

As the EZ became the NTI, we documented the increasing divergence between residents' goals and the actual allocation of capital to projects. During CRP, we had observed much sweat-equity, volunteer-dependent investment of individual and collective labor in local community projects that turned abandoned empty lots into community gardens, playgrounds, and pocket parks. Now, large grants went to the Philadelphia Horticultural Society, which in turn outsourced gardening jobs to nonlocal firms that brought in labor crews from New Jersey and New York, thereby bypassing the local labor market and the well-developed skills it had acquired through self-help projects. The society justified this by citing a need for speedy and "efficient" labor management.

Most of these beautification projects focused on diverting land use from housing to the middle-class consumption zone. As contracts were let for new streetscapes, signage, sidewalk removal, and driveways, it became clear that the need for truck access for deliveries trumped local pedestrians' use of sidewalks to traverse local space for their social and consumption needs. One resident CTB member who had never been part of an activist network and previously had always enthusiastically supported the EZ staff finally joined more oppositional members (and watchdogs) who had begun to protest the loss of walking paths and attendant dangers for children. Like the activists, she defined this space as home and as the locus of social support, and recognized that her local interests were rapidly losing ground.

Soon after, a rash of development-related eminent domain displacements ("takings") and the promise of more once again spurred campaigns of unified local action until changes in the mayoral regime and the economy slowed development once again.[9]

University Expansion

West of the study community, Temple University is expanding in line with the city's plans to use universities as engines of development. As a leading force in the northward expansion of the Avenue of the Arts and a main actor in the related North Philadelphia Cultural Alliance, it is part of a project for beautifying local spaces and dissolving the often-evoked invisible race line north of the downtown that middle-class arts and recreation consumers will not cross. The university is also space-hungry as it tries to upscale from a commuter to a residential campus.

Temple's role in restructuring of development in North Philadelphia is visible in its building programs and coalitions, but also through a host of projects that, like the early EZ, promise a commitment to empowerment programs for poor residents. These programs use students as learners and volunteers within a CLN.

Who benefits most from these activities whose goals demand control of space, like the later EZ/NTI projects. Such projects strongly imply displacement of local social capital, support networks, and grassroots organizing. For example, Temple's mortgage lending program, which is based on creating communities of local faculty and staff, could be potentially dislocating. New malls for student consumption are also space-hungry. Attempts to make the physical locale more attractive to students, their parents, and investors work to displace any people and parts of the built environment perceived as "blight."

University engagement programs also have implications for politics, either demobilizing or reenergizing opposition. Schools and departments mount programs in the CLN to offer local residents direct services such as health care, after-school mentoring and tutoring to enhance upward mobility, and the "leadership" skills seen as missing from local civic structures. Often a disconnect separates this assumption about local resident capacities from the leadership networks, sociality, and social capital that actually exist in communities around the university (Hyatt 2003.) The students who man generic mentoring and tutoring programs have little training, and the way their schedules are structured means their presence is inconsistent throughout a short fourteen-week semester punctuated by midterms and finals.

This is not to deny that many good things happen as people cross the formerly closed boundaries of school and neighborhood social fields. But the benefits accrue more to students than to local residents. Many short-lived new relationships develop. Some students are gratified by relationships made and lessons learned through one-on-one service delivery that humanizes formerly stigmatized people. Many professional training programs are enhanced by opportunities to learn through practice. In the end, though, students reap rewards for their volunteerism, have new, socially satisfying experiences with people from different backgrounds, and advance their credentials without learning about the structural and cultural production of poverty and inequality. They leave with their middle-class privilege intact and face no intervention in their blame discourses and beliefs in the "deserving" and "undeserving" poor. Their need to believe in their efficacy as change agents renders the history of leadership and action that has sustained local social relations even more invisible to them.

What Is the Story and Who Is the Audience?

Like Ferguson's famous Lesotho case (1994), this research addressed issues of interventions that are meant to "develop" communities but rely on faulty assumptions about problems and solutions and at the same time produce "instrument effects" that bring the city government (EZ) and university into close, often co-opting relationships with local organizations. The EZ and CLN presented social change interventions as technical programs using "best practices," standardized so that one size fits all contexts. Such practices are praised as neutral and apolitical. However, regardless of their intent, their actual effects often concern the power relationships more than the economic development of poor neighborhoods or their residents. Once community leaders are incorporated into powerful institutions and grassroots organizations are demobilized, the class interests of the powerful, the economically advantaged, and capital accumulation ultimately trump everything else.

EZ resources were incorporated into the NTI by simply ignoring the first-year CTB's recommendations and getting experts from the city's economic development office to recommend a new development path using an array of maps, charts, and photos that promised a new future. These goals were antithetical to the goals set out by the first, locally representative CTB. Community residents—especially after the eminent domain takings—protested loudly and collectively, to no avail. In this case, the politics were discernible to the parties inside, who responded using their prior political activism skills.

City governments' applying direct power to take over federal programs is not a new story. It goes back to Model Cities, the first major federal anti–urban poverty program in the 1960s. Many ethnographies concern social mobilizations that persisted and won small battles, only to encounter powerful demobilizing practices (Beck 1992; Checker 2005; Gregory 1998; Lyon Callo 2004; Paley 2001). Nonetheless, more cases' particular trajectories and possibilities need to be specifically documented.

How seriously can we expect our findings to be taken up by those with much at stake in top-down governance schemes? Ours is an uncomfortable message for credentialed experts and development managers, who must summon willful ignorance to successfully overlook the facts: interventions' actual effects on those with little power contradicted the social justifications for these programs; false notes of equality complemented acts of paternalism; promises to provide skills were only minimally honored; and the mistaken cultural constructions of the "community's" capacities and residents were egregiously insulting.

How did knowledge from this project travel to different publics, and how was it received? Although virtually no local news media covered the eminent domain abuse in North Philadelphia, the activism that mobilized protests against eminent domain abuse in North Philadelphia was publicized on film. Two progressive filmmaker teams drawn to the case[10] made two films, screened mostly in academic circles. Attempts at broader public impact were less successful.[11]

Junior-level EZ staff were open to new frameworks. One anthropology Ph.D. student conducted a qualitative process evaluation of one of the most active local groups. Their formal deliverables often looked sloppy due to poor equipment, frequent forced relocations from one donated space to another, and reliance on volunteer activist mothers. The assessment documented all the activities—meetings, household visits, work with local politicians and city agencies—that took place over a year. The EZ administrator responsible for monitoring recipients dismissed the report as unscientific and meaningless.[12]

Still, one novice EZ staff member involved in evaluation data management became very interested in qualitative process evaluation as a technique that dug below the surface. Her experiences with the group being evaluated allowed her to see the advantages of observing actually unfolding processes. She had not seen anything similar in her MA program and knew that her boss, the audit enforcer, took measurability very seriously and disdained information that did not conform to formal data formats based on numbers and standardized measurements. However, seeing value in knowing what was actually happening within the "black box," she asked the researcher to teach her how to do such qualitative evaluations. New to the field, she thought she might be job-hunting soon and saw this as a useful skill.

Others closely involved in university outreach programs were disinclined to reflect on their programs. Many had material (livelihood and career) and symbolic (fame and awards) stakes in such activities. Moreover, many individuals who invested their time generously, often volunteering or working overtime, felt their hard, earnest work should be above reproach and validated their sincere commitment to doing ethical work. Warmed by their successful interpersonal engagements, they did not want to know about the downsides.

Finally, ethnography is expected to be about "the other," but when subjects and publics are one and the same, interpretive authority is easily challenged by audiences' own experience. Once, during a graduate student's presentation of dissertation research accumulated over two years of continuous ethnographic fieldwork framed by social theory, an audience member took issue with the analysis, disagreeing with the findings about one of the organizations. Seemingly unaware of the type of data or analysis used in the research—rigorous in-depth participant observation and interviews coupled with analysis that included reflexivity—she staked her authority on the fact that she walked by the storefront organization daily and could see the kind of people there. Thus she equated her own surface observations with rigorous study, unconscious of her own position and biases. If we fail to illuminate our methodology, our work will continue to be challenged by the situated cultural constructions of others.

Agendas, Epistemologies, and Power

In the supermarket project, the ethnographic narrative was irrelevant to the chain's focus on profit. Amid massive layoffs, the union could not entertain issues of job quality and the lack of substance in "participation." Upjohn's interest was limited to what could be measured through what they defined as meaningful data formats. Those interested in a sociopolitical justice agenda, the O&O trainers and the women who worked against gender inequity, however, accepted the message about the importance of looking underneath the superficial official chain data on who had been "treated" with innovation training, what training was, and how and why the intervention played out the way it did in this specific context. They located the false assumptions embedded in the original treatment design.

In the CRP, even though historical experiences had produced clear boundaries and worldview differences between local residents and change agents, even newcomers like racialized immigrants and native-born minorities often became insiders. Many shared views on what needed to be done and saw through the discourses of blame that initially informed many street-level, middle-class professionals' diagnosis of local problems. Yet many were open to our ethnographic messages because they resonated with their experience. Communicating to more distant social engineers, diversity trainers, and "the public at large" was a mixed bag, depending on their stakes in the diversity seeking or diversity training agenda.

In the case of the CE project, elites were particularly resistant to research results. As powerful institutions' development agendas shifted toward a "spatial fix" (Lefevbre 1991), new projects carried out by the EZ/NTI staff and dispersed university actors threatened the social supports of the incumbent local residents, who organized to remain in the localities where they had invested their savings and developed social capital. Individuals—among local leaders and program directors (EZ staff, university staff and faculty)—became differently incorporated into these projects. Both their stakes and their epistemological views of objective science and "proof" were obstacles to hearing and believing the ethnographic narratives, especially when they hit so close to home, implied complicity, and contradicted their ideas about their efficacy and benevolence.

These cases show us how corporate management, the development arm of the city, and universities maintain the upper hand in dealing with workers and community residents. They easily ignore critical research by withdrawing to arguments based on the logics of economics or law while seeing the softer realm of the sociocultural as trivial or non-authoritative knowledge. They refuse to take up results on the grounds that the evidence is not "scientific," that is, objectively neutral, and capable of predicting universal human subject behavior using standardized instruments. Ethnographic knowledge which is produced through analyzing empirical data about social context, processual contingency, accounts of lived experience, and the effects of race, class, gender, or power is rendered useless on these grounds.

Whereas critical ethnographic research often proves useful to street-level professionals trying to deal with difficult situations (O&O trainers, the priest who read the op-ed piece on multiculturalism, the junior EZ staff member), it most threatens experts who are well situated in careers and strongly committed to particular techniques and toolkits for their career success.

The broader middle-class public, which often uncritically consumes topics of interest to gain more cultural capital, tends to avoid knowledge about poverty and inequality that renders it uncomfortably complicit in these problems. Most of its members prefer a knowledge "marketplace" that limits consumption to what is fun, entertaining, or useful in upscaling one's erudition or cultural capital.

As the CRP film project showed, people outside of research projects — in this case, the filmmakers — often misread important, nuanced, counterintuitive research findings. The films made to spread the word about eminent domain abuse made the case, but they failed to develop audience appeal for the broader Philadelphia public, which remained ignorant of this episode.

At this critical moment, however, neoliberal urban solutions have been ratcheted up and inequality is increasing. Large-scale institutional planning has also expanded in the rush toward global upscaling and has increasingly demobilized local grassroots activists, displaced local residents, destabilized support networks, and fragmented formerly unified alliances of local leaders. There is little time to cultivate those most politically unreachable. Given the urgent need for activism, the people most directly concerned with poverty and inequality remain our work's most receptive audiences. In past research, they were women supermarket workers, grassroots leaders furthering efforts to develop skills and housing stock through political action, and their allies among street-level workers. In 2013 , some of these activists began to campaign in a new coalition to re-establish land trusts and other progressive projects. It is a time for a sustained activist anthropology that works to reverse neoliberal excesses. To this end, addressing narrower, more receptive "niche" publics and collaborating with groups in an activist agenda works best.

Judith Goode is a Professor of Anthropology and Urban Studies at Temple University. She is an urban anthropologist who uses ethnography to explore the production of unintended consequences in policy domains such as economic development, social provisioning, multiculturalism, and immigration. She seeks to identify the specific contingent events, structures, and cultural constructions at the local, national, and global scale which produce these outcomes. Her ethnographic projects in Philadelphia are framed by the political economic trajectory of the city in the late twentieth century, especially in relation to the production of local space, social movements, and the shifting fault lines of the key axes of social differences as she seeks to demonstrate how the shift from the Keynesian welfare state to neoliberal privatization played out in this specific city and the consequences of this for governance, politics, political subjectivities , and action. She has co-authored four books and co-edited a fifth, as well as publishing many articles. She is a past-president of the Society for Urban, National, and Transnational Anthropology (SUNTA) and The Society for Anthropology of North America (SANA).

Notes

1. The team initially assumed that survey work was cheaper than labor-intensive ethnography, but in the end the costs of printing professional surveys and subcontracting computer time eliminated any difference.
2. It should be noted that the part-time workers reported strongly preferring their work and bosses in these stores over those in the chains they had worked for before.
3. The following synopsis is drawn from several sources: Goode 1990; 1998a; 1998b; 2001; 2005; Goode and Schneider 1994.
4. Though we had protected their identity by not naming specific institutions, we had ignored more meaningful obligations.
5. After South Broad Street became a development zone for the arts, political action garnered public resources for the construction of new performance venues in the Kimmel Center, an expanding University of the Arts, and new theater construction for two relocating repertory theaters, all aspects of a new zone of arts and culture consumption. Part of this development was the implosion of the Martin Luther King housing projects, whose residents received just two months' notice of eviction and little relocation help, despite having an active tenants' association.
6. During the CRP, we worked with businessmen who had benefited from an earlier federal economic development policy orchestrated by Reagan's Secretary of HUD Jack Kemp. Enterprise zones granted tax breaks to relocating and new businesses and imposed no requirement to hire local labor. The views of the entrepreneurs in the local communities are described in Ninivaggi (1994). The EZ program claimed to have fixed the Kemp enterprise zone loopholes.
7. For an expanded analysis of the effects of neoliberalism in Philadelphia, see Maskovsky (2006).
8. We had been working with this organization for six months, and one team member had compiled an inventory of their projects and daily activities.
9. Although many of the taken homes were demolished, no private developers were interested in the parcels, no projects were built, and the land is still vacant.
10. The two films were *I Choose to Stay Here* (Dornfield 2004), produced collaboratively by the Philadelphia Folklore Project and Community Leadership Institute, both non-profits, and *All for the Taking: 21st Century Urban Renewal* (2005), produced by George McCullough as a critical examination of the NTI and eminent domain in Philadelphia.
11. A showing to a very small audience at the Free Library of Philadelphia provoked little discussion, much of which refuted the narrative based on personal experience.
12. At one EZ meeting, the regulator asked me to have a "sidebar" conversation about the status of such ethnographic process evaluations. I told him about their frequent use in educational and medical anthropology and offered to provide him with an overview, but he was only interested in their federal standing as data sources.

References

Beck, Sam. 1992. *Manny Almeida's Ringside Lounge.* Providence, RI: Gavea-Brown.
Checker, Melissa. 2005. *Polluted Promises: Environmental Racism, Power and Public Life in America.* New York: New York University Press.

Dornfield, Barry. 2004. *I Choose to Stay Here*. Film documentary produced by the Philadelphia Folklore Project and the Community Leadership Institute, Philadelphia.

Edelman, Marc, and Angelique Haugerud, eds. 2005. *The Anthropology of Development and Globalization: From Classical Economy to Contemporary Neoliberalism*. Oxford: Blackwell.

Ferguson, James. 1994. *The Anti-Politics Machine: "Development," Depoliticization, and Bureaucratic Power in Lesotho*. Minneapolis: University of Minnesota Press.

Florida, Richard. 2005. *Cities and the Creative Class*. London: Routledge.

Goode, Judith. 1990. "A Wary Welcome to the Neighborhood: Community Responses to the New Immigration." *Urban Anthropology* 19: 125–153.

———. 1998a. "Becoming Insiders: Factors Affecting the Creation and Maintenance of Boundaries for New Immigrants." In *The Tribal Basis of American Life*, ed. Murray Friedman and Nancy Isserman. New York: Praeger.

———. 1998b. "The Contingent Construction of Local Identities: Koreans and Puerto Ricans in Philadelphia." *Identities* 5: 33–64.

———. 2001. "Let's Get Our Act Together: How Racial Discourses Disrupt Local Social Relations." In *The New Poverty Studies: The Ethnography of Power, Policy and Impoverished People in the United States*, ed. Judith Goode and Jeff Maskovsky. New York: NYU Press.

———. 2005. "Dousing the Fire or Fanning the Flames: The Role of Human Relations Practice in Inter-Group Conflict." *Transforming Anthropology* 13: 1–18.

———. 2010. "The Campaign for New Immigrants in Philadelphia: Imagining Possibilities and Confronting Realities." In *Locating Migration: Global Immigration and Urban Scale*, eds. Nina Glick Schiller and Ayse Calgar. Ithaca, NY: Cornell University Press.

Goode, Judith, and Jeff Maskovsky. 2001. "Introduction." In *The New Poverty Studies: The Ethnography of Power, Policy and Impoverished People in the United States*, ed. Judith Goode and Jeff Maskovsky. New York: NYU Press.

Goode, Judith, and Robert T. O'Brien. 2006. "Whose Social Capital? How Economic Development Programs Depoliticize the Urban Poor." In *Social Capital in The City*, ed. Richardson Dilworth III. Philadelphia: Temple University Press.

Goode, Judith, and JoAnne Schneider. 1994. *Reshaping Ethnic and Racial Relations in Philadelphia: Immigrants in A Divided City*. Philadelphia: Temple University Press.

Goode, Judith, and Elaine Simon. 1994. "Women's Work Culture and the Transition to Leadership in the Supermarket Industry." *Frontiers: A Journal of Women's Studies* (Winter): 143–168.

Goode, Judith, Janet Theophano, and Karen Curtis. 1977. "Ethnic Persistence: Assumptions and Reality." Paper presented at the annual meeting of the Northeastern Anthropological Association. Providence, RI.

Gregory, Steven. 1998. *Black Corona: Race and Politics of Place in an Urban Community*. Princeton, NJ: Princeton University Press.

Hackworth, Jason. 2007. *Neoliberal City: Governance, Ideology and Development in American Urbanism*. Ithaca, NY: Cornell University Press.

Hochner, Arthur, Judith Goode, Cheryl Granrose, Elaine Simon, and Eileen Appelbaum. 1988. *Job-Saving Strategies: Worker Buyouts and Quality Work Life*. Kalamazoo, MI: The W. E. Upjohn Institute for Employment Research.

Hyatt, Susan Brin, and Paula Peebles, eds. 2003. "The Death and Rebirth of North Central Philadelphia." Philadelphia: Renaissance Community Development Corporation.

Kim-Gibson, Dai Sil. 1991. *America Becoming*. Film documentary produced by the Ford Foundation and WETA/PBS, Washington, DC.

Kingfisher, Catherine. 2013. *A Policy Travelogue: Tracing Welfare Reform in Aotearoa/New Zealand and Alberta, Canada*. New York: Berghahn Books.

Kingfisher, Catherine, and Jeff Maskovsky. 2008. "Introduction: Limits of Neoliberalism." *Critique of Anthropology* 28, no. 2: 115–126.

Kromer, John. 1999. *Neighborhood Recovery: Reinvestment Policy in the New Hometown.* New Brunswick, NJ: Rutgers University Press.

Lefebvre, Henri. 1991. *The Production of Space.* Oxford: Blackwell.

Lyon Callo, Vin. 2004. *Inequality, Poverty and Neoliberal Governance: Activist Ethnography in the Homeless Sheltering Industry.* Orchard Park, NY: Broadview Press.

McCullough, George. 2005. *All for the Taking: 21st Century Urban Renewal.* Produced and directed by George McCullough, Philadelphia.

Maskovsky, Jeff. 2006. "Governing the New Hometowns: Race, Power and Neighborhood Participation in the New Inner City." *Identities* 13: 73–99.

Mullings, Leith. 2001. "Households Headed by Women: The Politics of Class, Race, and Gender." In *The New Poverty Studies: The Ethnography of Power, Policy and Impoverished People in the United States,* ed. Judith Goode and Jeff Maskovsky. New York: NYU Press.

Mullings, Leith, and Alaka Wali. 2001. *Stress and Resilience: The Social Context of Reproduction in Central Harlem.* New York: Kluwer Academic/Plenum Press.

Naples, Nancy. 1998. *Grassroots Warriors: Activist Mothering, Community Work and the War on Poverty.* London: Routledge.

Ninivaggi, Cynthia. 1994. "Who Benefits from Federal Enterprise Zones in Philadelphia?" In *Newcomers in the Workplace,* ed. Louise Lamphere, Guillermo J. Grenier, and Alex Stepick. Philadelphia: Temple University Press.

Paley, Julia. 2001. *Marketing Democracy: Power and Social Movements in Post-Dictatorship Chile.* Berkeley: University of California Press.

Schneider, JoAnne, and Judith Goode. 1989. "Bringing People Together or Keeping Them Apart." *Philadelphia Inquirer,* 15 March, A18.

Schoen, D. 1983. *The Reflective Practitioner: How Professionals Think in Action.* New York: Basic Books.

Shore, Cris, and Susan Wright, eds. 1997. *Anthropology of Policy: Critical Perspectives on Governance and Power.* London: Routledge.

Shore, Cris, Susan Wright, and Davide Pero, eds. 2011. *Policy Worlds: Anthropology and the Analysis of Contemporary Power.* New York: Berghahn Books.

Strathern, Marilyn, ed. 2000. *Audit Culture: Anthropological Studies in Accountability, Ethics and the Academy.* London: Routledge.

Chapter 8

ANTHROPOLOGY FOR WHOM?
Challenges and Prospects of Activist Scholarship

⌒⌒⌒

Angela Stuesse

When I stumbled upon anthropology in college, I was drawn in because I found that it troubled my conceptions about the world and my place in it. My first anthropology course, taken when I was an exchange student at the *Universidad Autónoma de Yucatán* in Mérida, México, focused on the legacies of a colonialist and racist "science" that sought to justify European and North American global dominance by categorizing "the other." It challenged me to think about others in new ways, but more importantly, it pushed me to understand myself—and my privilege as a white, middle-class, U.S.-born college student—in a new light. This critical self-reflection laid the foundation for my continued study of the discipline.

As a graduate student at the University of Texas in the late twentieth century, I found sustenance in a new brand of anthropology that my mentors dubbed "activist." A small cohort of faculty there had begun training students, recruiting faculty, and carving out institutional space for an anthropology that drew on the field's critical history and moved it in new directions. Driven by a politics of liberation, the "Austin School" espoused a deep ethical commitment to decolonization of both the discipline and the world more broadly. It did so by asking, "Anthropology for whom?" and answering in explicit political alignment with "people organizing to change the conditions of their lives" (Gordon and Hale 1997).

The Austin School teaches that activist research "begins with an act of political identification and dialogue with collective subjects in struggle for

Notes for this chapter begin on page 242.

relief from oppression, for equality and betterment" (Gordon 2007: 95–96). I was drawn to its radical reconception of anthropological research as a tool that marginalized peoples could wield to effect social transformation toward greater equality and justice. In the years that followed, I designed and carried out a research project that sought to put these ideas into practice. Conducted over six years in rural Mississippi's chicken processing towns and factories, the research aimed to understand how the recent influx of Latin American immigrant labor was transforming communities and influencing workers' ability to organize in one of the most dangerous, dehumanizing industries in the country. It was carried out in collaboration with a fledgling workers' center dedicated to advancing workers' political mobilization through education, organizing, access to services, and legal advocacy.

The experience gave me much food for thought about the promises and pitfalls of activist research. Perhaps most transformational was the realization that my research complicated one of the fundamental principles of activist anthropology as taught by the Austin School—that of sustained collaboration with an organized collective. Somewhat problematically, I found, it presupposes a concrete, bounded, organized group of individuals or organizations with whom one works throughout the various stages of research, when in fact, the "communities in struggle" with whom we align ourselves are often amorphous and transitional, at times even metaphorical or imagined.

In this chapter I reflect on my research collaboration in Mississippi to illuminate this complication of the Austin School's proposition of activist research. This case, in dialogue with other research experiences that also challenge the notion of research in collaboration with an "organized collective," allows consideration of potential alternative conceptions of politically engaged research that can produce more varied configurations of ethically grounded, mutually fruitful collaboration. It also abundantly exemplifies how anthropologists are "put to use" by our partners and can contribute to their goals in different phases of the research process. Ultimately, it illustrates that the Austin School's core notions of "communities in struggle" or an "organized collective" can elide the complexity of relationships and allegiances that activist research must negotiate. I argue for reconceptualizing these terms with a more nuanced understanding of their intersecting parts—the individual people, the institutions, and a set of (mutually shared?) political ideals.

Before elaborating on the Mississippi experiment, however, I will consider some of activist anthropology's historical genealogies and the contemporary contours of its relationship to the idea of public anthropology in a borderless world.

Activist Anthropology

Activist anthropology has a multi-stranded genealogy. This section aims to first delineate some of its roots and, later, more fully operationalize the teachings of the Austin School. One vital predecessor of today's activist anthropology can be located in efforts to create an "action anthropology" in the 1950s. This work grew out of Sol Tax's research and teaching with the Fox (Mesquaki) Indians, sought to create an anthropology that was more dialogic and practical approach than its predecessors (Tax 1952). Tax and his many students strove to involve community members in identifying problems that social science research might solve, conducting studies, and generating more useful community-centered research products. Critics disagree about the extent to which Tax achieved these ideals, but they concur that his ideas were groundbreaking for their time (Blanchard 1979; Foley 1995; 1999). They influenced a subsection of American anthropologists and marked the early formalization of the U.S. field of applied anthropology in the United States (Bastide 1973; Rylko-Bauer et al. 2006).

In the wake of independence movements around the globe in the late 1960s and early 1970s, a critical mass of anthropologists and those affected by their work caught the discipline's attention. With biting critiques of anthropology's role in bolstering colonialism and furthering the empires of the United States and its European Allies, these voices set the stage for anthropology's "critical turn" (Asad 1973; Deloria Jr. 1969; Hymes 1972; Lewis 1973; Nader 1972; Symposium on Inter-Ethnic Conflict in South America 1973 [1971]; Willis 1972). Around the same time, in South America Paolo Freire's critical teachings on popular education as a tool of resistance inspired social scientists to conceive new collaborative research methodologies as pedagogical tools for social transformation, giving rise to Participatory Action Research (Fals Borda 1979; Freire 1970; 1982 [1972]; Kassam and Mustafa 1982).[1] By the end of the 1970s, these entwined efforts, in tandem with other crucial global and domestic events of political significance (movements for civil rights, racial justice, and gender equality; politics of war and peace; U.S. foreign policy, etc.), had politicized a growing number of U.S. anthropology departments. Among students and newly-minted faculty, the concept of "radical anthropology," a critical theory-based Marxist approach seeking to align its aims with those of the "oppressed," began to emerge (Polgar 1979).

In the 1980s, these critiques prompted anthropology to turn its gaze upon itself and begin to grapple with questions of ethnographic authority and the politics of representation (Clifford 1988; Clifford and Marcus 1986; Rosaldo 1989). Feminist scholars' scathing critiques of long-held ideas about objectivity and positivism in science had far-reaching impacts on the field (Haraway 1988; Harding 1987; 1993). Around this time, increasing numbers of women, people of color, queer writer-theorists, and other scholar-activists on or outside the margins of the discipline deepened the "critical turn," engendering intense discussions over anthropology's (and the academy's) role and relevance in society and its complicity in sustaining unequal relations of power in the world.[2]

As works in this vein have multiplied in recent decades, the discipline has witnessed an increased interest in an "engaged" anthropology that "gives back" to the communities where we work and seeks relevance with broader publics. Several edited volumes and articles on the topic have emerged in recent years, the present volume being a fine example of this trend.[3] In 2010, *American Anthropologist,* the discipline's leading U.S. periodical, dedicated a new section to anthropologists' public engagement (Checker et al. 2010). The term "engagement," however, has as many meanings as it does users. Some focus on putting anthropology "to use," reclaiming the moniker "applied" in its broadest sense (Rylko-Bauer et al. 2006). Others seek to alter understandings of important social issues via their scholarly critiques (which some dub "cultural critique") (Hale 2006). Still others strive for a broader impact on social change by writing for a more general audience, sometimes using new means of communication (Borofsky 2010; Lende 2013; Scheper-Hughes 2009).

The Austin School's approach to "activist anthropology" grows out of this diverse scholarly and political lineage and intersects variously with these contemporary inclinations, yet it proposes something qualitatively distinct. Its defining feature is its emphasis on long-term collaboration with "communities in struggle" in each phase of the research process. "To be an anthropology which no longer serves the interests of the oppressors it must be one which actively serves those of the oppressed," wrote Edmund T. Gordon, one of the founders of the Austin School (Gordon 1991: 153). Certainly, an important foundation of activist research is its explicit political positioning, though some might argue that the move toward a values-driven anthropology embodied in the Austin School is but a logical conclusion reached by taking seriously the thoroughgoing critiques of some of anthropology's earlier forms of engagement in the world. Overt political alignment enables us and our interlocutors to more directly consider how our positioning is always situated and how this shapes our research and results. Failure to do so is itself a political act that may well be read as complicity with the status quo.

Activist anthropology attempts to address longstanding power inequities in the relationship between anthropologists and their research "subjects"—in essence, democratizing our practice—while simultaneously putting anthropology to use in ways that advance struggles for justice more broadly. However, calls for a more "militant" anthropology (Scheper-Hughes 1995) that enables some of us to be anthropologists while staying true to our deepest beliefs about the world and our role in it only partially address the advantages proffered by activist research.

Charles R. Hale asserts that activist anthropology offers the potential for at least two (other) significant scholarly contributions to our discipline, those of enhanced methodological rigor and theoretical innovation (2008). In terms of methodology, because activist research demands a more horizontal, collaborative relationship between the anthropologist and her interlocutors from the conception of the research questions to the dissemination of its final products, it offers fertile ground for improving rigor. Moreover, because our collaborators often have use for positivist, objectivist findings to inform their struggles, these needs require sound, defensible methodologies. By exploring new or creative ways to internally validate our data, and by positioning ourselves in the most transparent ways possible, Hale argues, activist researchers can enhance the precision and accuracy of our claims, reclaiming notions of strong objectivity in the process.

He also suggests that activist anthropology is positioned to enrich our discipline by offering new analytical insights into social processes and relations. The argument here is quite simply that deeply engaged and collaborative research provides the researcher with a *different* partial perspective from which to examine the problems under study. This alternative vantage point can provide novel understandings to help us complicate and advance theories of power, inequality, and social change. Shannon Speed makes a similar claim, and her work on how discourses of human rights have been wielded in the Zapatista struggle for indigenous rights in Chiapas offers a prime example of how activist research positioning can enrich anthropological theory (2008). In sum, activist research produces qualitatively different findings.

The activist research process begins with collaborative design of the research project. As Gupta and Ferguson pointed out, "The political task is not to 'share' knowledge with those who lack it, but to forge links between different knowledges that are possible from different locations, and to trace lines of possible alliance and shared purpose between them" (Gupta and Ferguson 1997: 48). The exchange of ideas among differently positioned social actors, including the researcher, becomes a fieldwork process in which methodologies, data, and analyses remain in constant dialogue with one another. Their simultaneity makes it possible—and essential—to continually reappraise and revise project questions, methods, and theoretical assertions throughout the research.

Depending on the work context, the processes of fieldwork and data collection may be directly relevant to our collaborators, particularly when they entail building networks or training local partners in research methods. More often, however, activist researchers combine data collection with fulfillment of other roles—fundraiser, organizer, educator, director, interpreter, cartographer, logistical coordinator, phone answerer, coffee maker—deemed more immediately relevant by the organizations or movements we work with. I will elaborate on these roles and the attendant political commitments below, but they merit note here because they are key to the activist researcher's privileged perspective and insight into the social processes under study. Through precisely this positioning, politically engaged research offers the promise of deeper, more nuanced—"better"—analyses and results (Hale 2001; Holland et al. 2010; Speed 2006). In active partnership with the people central to the analysis, one learns not only more but differently, having gained access to distinctive and collaborative theoretical insights.

Activist research also takes particular approaches to the process of writing and dissemination of knowledge. How does one write against inequality? What are the political stakes of publicly sharing our analyses? How do we balance accountability to our political commitments and collaborators with self-reflexivity, honesty, and critical attunement to our topics of study? Who "owns" the knowledge produced by collaborative, politically engaged projects, and who should control and benefit from its dissemination? To start, activist research requires us to dialogue with our collaborators throughout analysis, writing, and dissemination, and work out ways to incorporate their critiques and concerns into the research products. This increases the research's accountability, accuracy, and usefulness to our closest collaborators (Bernard 2002; Foley 1990; Hale 2001; Scheper-Hughes 1995; Sudbury 1998). Meanwhile, validation, popular consumption, and critique of our (often shared, collective) analyses force us to seriously consider who will benefit from the knowledge we produce and its utility in the struggle on the ground.

Having described the Austin School's forerunners, its positioning within a larger movement toward engaged and public anthropologies, and the ways in which a commitment to activist scholarship challenges and transforms the research process, I will now show how my first experiment in activist research complicates the teachings of the Austin School.

Collaborative Beginnings: Founding the Poultry Worker Justice Research Project

I spent more than six years, from 2001 to 2008, experimenting with the Austin School's model of activist research. As indicated earlier, my ethnographic inquiry took place in rural Mississippi's chicken processing plants and communities. Since the mid-1990s, hundreds of Latin American migrants from across the continent had moved to the area in response to chicken plants' recruitment of foreign-born laborers. As a result, during that decade poultry communities' "Hispanic" population grew by more than 1,000 percent, dramatically altering neighborhoods' and workplaces' dynamics and demographics. My research was fundamentally interested in how these changes were impacting poultry processing workers' ability to organize for higher wages, improved working conditions, and basic human dignity.

To comprehend how recent and ongoing transformations might impact workers' strategies of political mobilization, however, I needed to grasp how old and new Mississippians of different backgrounds—white and Black as well as "Hispanic," representing a diversity of cultures and nationalities—understood and experienced the ongoing changes in their communities and workplaces. The research revealed that interpretations of the escalating globalization of rural Mississippi are conditioned by people's positioning vis-à-vis whiteness and Blackness, as well as by their relationship to the poultry industry. Moreover, it showed that the industry adeptly wields these diverse relationships to race and labor (along with other forms of difference) to keep workers from recognizing potential mutual self-interest. These findings led me to conclude that the region's complicated historical and contemporary political economies of race seriously impede poultry workers' organization across difference in the newly transnational U.S. South. Having elaborated elsewhere on these results, here I mention them as background to contextualize the subsequent methodological discussion of activist research (Stuesse 2003; 2009; 2010; forthcoming; Stuesse and Helton 2013).

The project began in 2001 as a dialogue with the Equal Justice Center (EJC), a newly formed nonprofit legal advocacy organization in Austin, Texas, which advocated for worker justice in the poultry industry.[4] Decades of representing migrant farm workers in employment law cases in Texas had piqued EJC Director Bill Beardall's interest in the growing immigrant communities in other parts of the U.S. South, particularly their participation in emerging forms of industrial agriculture like poultry processing. My academic advisor introduced me to Beardall and encouraged us to discuss potential activist research collaboration. After a series of conversations on the goals of politically engaged scholarship and its potential contributions to social justice movements generally and recent inflections of the poultry justice movement particularly, Beardall invited me to participate in a National Poultry Justice Alliance convening in Washington, DC, in early 2002. The alliance brought together individuals and organizations interested in poultry justice from a diversity of perspectives, including workers' rights, growers' (farmers') interests, the environment, and public health. As I began to learn about the issues and actors, I asked myself and potential collaborators how politically engaged ethnographic research could contribute to their work and enhance ongoing struggles for poultry justice. The initial meeting suggested potential for partnership between an activist anthropologist and poultry justice stakeholders, but particulars remained vague. Where and with what organization(s) or collective(s) might I collaborate? Around what research question(s)?

In the following months, dialogue continued with the EJC and others I had met at the national convening. Beardall's connection to a Southern labor organizer led to a conversation with a local union representative and former poultry worker in Mississippi. He had witnessed the operators of the production lines change from predominantly African American workers to, increasingly, Latin American immigrants. "I need someone who can help me speak Mexican!" he implored. He had fought the changes at first, even calling federal immigration agents to demand deportation of "illegal" workers, but by early 2002 he was working to incorporate them into the union's membership. Further discussions with poultry worker organizers and advocates in Mississippi revealed that a small, diverse, multiracial group of people were grappling with the recent phenomenon of Latin American migration into the area's poultry processing plants and communities. Along with fellow graduate student Anita Grabowski, I agreed to spend the summer of 2002 in Mississippi meeting the actors, learning about the issues, and further exploring possibilities for activist research in alignment with poultry justice efforts there.

Besides identifying key problems faced by poultry workers and their advocates, this preliminary research established relationships with religious leaders, union organizers, immigrant and civil rights advocates, and poultry workers of diverse backgrounds. It revealed their commitment and perseverance, as well as a staggering lack of resources and information with which to improve conditions in chicken plants and communities. To address this limitation, Grabowski and I, working with the EJC and our new Mississippi-based collaborators, began offering "know your rights" workshops for poultry workers and advocates in the area. These efforts built rapport and seeded key research relationships between me, Grabowski, and our Mississippi partners, and also helped solidify the nascent ties between each of these actors and the EJC, whose legal expertise in workers' rights and employment justice filled a significant void in local capacity. As our collaboration developed, advocates expressed interest in opening a workers' center to help them address continuing obstacles to poultry worker justice, and worker participants in the workshops supported this idea. This early coalition between local actors, the Equal Justice Center, and University of Texas–based activist researchers was soon dubbed the Poultry Worker Justice Research Project.

In fall of 2002 and throughout 2003, I traveled frequently to Mississippi, where Beardall, Grabowski, and I, along with colleagues from Southern Migrant Legal Services and other legal advocacy organizations, continued supporting local activists and the poultry workers they represented. We expanded and refined the popular education workshops and participated in formulating preliminary plans for a workers' center. At the time I was also focused on meeting key requirements of my doctoral program: studying for and passing qualifying exams, writing and defending a dissertation research prospectus, applying for research funding. The political process moved forward despite periods of my own diminished engagement compelled by my program of study.

Establishing Ownership: Becoming a Project of the Equal Justice Center

By January 2004, when I arrived in Mississippi with my U-Haul and moved into my rented home, Grabowski had finished her MA program and Beardall had hired her to work with him in Austin coordinating the EJC's collaboration in founding a workers' center in Mississippi. To oversee and guide its creation, a diverse group of our closest collaborators since 2002 formed a Mississippi-based advisory committee. I struggled to determine what, precisely, my role should be within this structure. I was neither EJC staff nor a member of the advisory committee, and formal affiliation with the workers' center was not possible at this preliminary stage of its existence. Still, my participation was vital to the project. My presence "on the ground" in Mississippi lent credibility to the Texas-based EJC, and my daily engagement with poultry workers and their allies made me a crucial gatekeeper of "local" knowledge that fueled the EJC's continued involvement. Likewise, my collaboration with the EJC helped me build relationships with workers, union representatives, and other allies; facilitated my repeated entry into several chicken plants as a union interpreter; and boosted my credibility with allies such as the Mississippi Immigrant Rights Alliance in ways I couldn't have achieved as an independent researcher or graduate student. Moreover, interaction with Beardall provided me with ongoing education in employment law, and his mentorship greatly improved my ability to help Mississippi-based activists and workers troubleshoot issues as they arose. Thus, in mutually constitutive fashion, my relationship with the EJC provided me with vital tools and research access while also enabling the organization to deepen its relationships and engagement in Mississippi.

I communicated with Grabowski almost daily and joined in weekly conference calls with her and Beardall. Drawing on what I was learning from our collaboration with local actors, my participation was integral in laying the groundwork for the workers' center. I devoted much of my time to planning and conducting activities and campaigns in Mississippi in collaboration with the EJC and local advocates, and also participated in monthly advisory committee meetings. However, I was not invited to the EJC staff meetings in Austin or made privy to many other key organizational conversations, which limited my power to influence EJC's strategic planning. After more than two years of collaboration, I found I was both an insider and an outsider in the processes I was studying. Moreover, our mutual consideration of the potentialities of activist research often felt reduced to the (considerable) value of intelligent, eager, exploitable free labor.

As the spring of 2004 advanced, I realized that what had begun as a collaborative project between Mississippi-based advocates, university-based researchers, and the Texas-based Equal Justice Center to facilitate the creation of a locally owned and run workers' center was now becoming a "project" of the EJC. Despite the loose alliance supporting the work, decisions came largely from Beardall and Grabowski in Austin. Their nominal creation of a regional Poultry Worker Justice Project housed the Mississippi initiative and helped to justify non-local control over its development.

Local people were certainly integral to and supportive of the work, but their sense of ownership over the center's creation was minimal. The advisory committee members willingly offered guidance to the project, but their more-than-full time commitments to their own work, often involving intensive advocacy or service provision, left them unable to take on the burden of running a workers' center. Their comments in meetings suggested that they saw the EJC's expertise, resources, and dedication as vital to the center's development, and they generally supported its position of ownership over the initiative. Poultry worker organizing—one of the center's key objectives—was barely nascent, so those whom the proposed work most directly affected were poorly positioned to opine.

I wrestled with the complexities of political alignment in this context. I was conducting research in collaboration with loosely affiliated actors with overlapping political commitments and social justice goals, including most obviously the EJC, but I (idealistically) envisioned being a partner in a locally sustainable project led by Mississippi advocates, community members, and especially poultry workers. Where did I stand as an activist researcher, seeing this political commitment and vision jeopardized by the very organization I was most closely affiliated with? And what could I do about it? My field notes from this time reflect the unease I felt. I repeatedly raised my concerns with Beardall and Grabowski, but my insistence did not have the desired effect. I began to suspect that instead of stimulating greater impulse to contribute strategically to a locally owned and driven program, my outspokenness was resulting in my exclusion from key planning and relationship-building meetings. Ownership of the project had passed tacitly to the EJC, which dedicated considerable resources to fundraising and making the workers' center a reality.

We continued to work toward building the center without resolving this point of contention. My relationship with the EJC was at times strained, but reflection on these early months of effort reveals that the collaboration was mutually beneficial — in fact, quite necessary — for all involved. Moreover, despite the tensions, all parties shared a deep political commitment to achieving greater justice in the poultry industry, and this ideological glue held us together in difficult times. My formal relationship to the project as both activist researcher and volunteer remained nebulous throughout 2004, and ambiguities about my positioning and political alignment persisted but also changed as the year wore on.

A Conflicted Labor Movement: Conducting Activist Research with Unions

Throughout my time in Mississippi, we worked to gain the confidence of the various unions representing poultry workers there. Since the project's outset, the union local representatives on the advisory committee had expressed varying degrees of skepticism about the concept and role of the projected workers' center. Aware of concerns raised by the growing national workers' center movement, unions justifiably wanted to know how the workers' center would support their efforts to organize workers without compromising their work or competing with them (Fine 2006; Fink 2003). We therefore trod softly while trying to establish trusting relationships with union representatives and convince them that by working together, we could do more to help poultry workers.

Distressingly, the longer we worked with the unions and with poultry workers of diverse backgrounds, the more we questioned the unions' (general) business-model approach to organizing and representing workers. This approach consists of short bursts of intensive effort by local, regional, and international staff to mobilize workers during National Labor Relations Board elections and union contract negotiations, followed by long periods in which local representatives struggle to keep up with "servicing" their contract. Local representatives' time is often split between several plants, towns, and even states, and their limited capital is spent mediating between workers and plant management and representing workers with grievances. Mississippi's status as a Right to Work[5] state — coupled with other state-level anti-labor policies, its intense rurality, the historic presence of a disempowered, low-wage workforce with few options, and an increasingly undocumented pool of immigrant workers — means union locals must struggle to maintain the resources they need to pay salaries and stay in business. This greatly limits their ability, and sometimes willingness, to adequately represent their members, let alone focus on workers' political education, organizing, and empowerment.

While I fully recognized the structural conditions that severely circumscribe unions' potential to grow a movement in a place like Mississippi, in 2004 I began to question the EJC's decision to stand with the unions despite what at times appeared to be union locals' negligence or lack of good-faith effort in representing their members. I agreed with the EJC's argument that a troubled labor movement is better than none at all, but I often ruminated over questions of worker (dis)empowerment and worried that the project was sacrificing standing with workers in order to build the trust of the unions. These concerns — part of a larger set of ethical questions about the project's approach — again raised doubts about my relationships and allegiances as an activist researcher. I saw the EJC as the closest thing to an organized collective with which I could continue formal collaboration on this work. Yet I acutely felt the tensions between my methodological and political alignment with an organization whose interests did not always align with those of the people it sought to empower, and the poultry workers with whom I was gradually building political and personal alliances over time.

Becoming Staff: The Founding of the Mississippi Poultry Workers' Center

By the end of 2004, the workers' center we had worked to build could claim initial success. It now had a name — the Mississippi Poultry Workers' Center — and a small office in a central poultry town. More importantly, Grabowski's fundraising efforts had borne fruit, enabling the workers' center (via the EJC) to hire its first full-time Mississippi-based community organizer, an African American woman from the nearby state capital of Jackson who boasted deep roots as an advocate for social justice in the state. I benefited too from the newly acquired funding when the EJC hired me as part-time staff with the title Community Outreach and Education

Associate. I had sought this formal role for several reasons. First, lacking external funding to support my research, since arriving in Mississippi I had taken on two part-time jobs—one as a teacher of English as a Second Language to recent immigrants and the other as a contract researcher for a Jackson-based nonprofit agency—and compensation from the EJC would let me focus more exclusively on issues central to the research. Second, I expected a title and clear affiliation with the EJC to bolster my credibility with local Mississippi advocates—particularly certain unions that I saw as vital to my research and to the worker justice movement. Finally, I hoped that a "staff" role on the project would strengthen my ability to guide the development of the workers' center in directions I deemed promising. Emerging implications of the research pointed to leadership development, political education, and relationship-building efforts with African American and Latin American poultry workers as key components of this vision.

Throughout 2005 we continued to respond to worker justice crises as they arose and cultivate relationships with unions, while also endeavoring to consolidate a mission, vision, and clearly defined areas of work for the workers' center. Meantime, several of the EJC's other projects grew rapidly and Beardall focused most of his energies on the issues before him in Texas. His diminished engagement in the Mississippi work opened space for Grabowski and the Mississippi-based staff, guided by the advisory committee, to craft the center's foci according to our vision. We downgraded the role legal advocacy and technical expertise would play in the organization and privileged community organizing and popular education work. This shift in focus reflected our areas of interest and training (none of us had legal education beyond what we had learned from Beardall), but more importantly it suggested an alternative theory of social change, one that centrally involves the people most affected in advocating their own interests. During this time the advisory committee dissolved to make way for a leadership council, at least half of whose members would be poultry workers. This focus on making the work more locally run and accountable felt promising, even though the project remained under the auspices of the EJC.

In collaboration with a Peruvian educator and former poultry worker, I developed a pilot curriculum to bring Latino and Black worker leaders together to build a critical analysis of the political, social, and economic conditions that affect their lives and keep them divided. *Solidarity*/Solidaridad: *Building Cross-Cultural Understanding for Poultry Worker Justice,* inspired by the pedagogies of popular education, encouraged participants to draw on their life experiences as both learners and teachers in a nonhierarchical setting. The classes offered tools for practicing basic communication in

English and Spanish, upholding workers' rights, and understanding the realities of immigration and the struggle for civil and immigrant rights in the United States. By learning about each other's histories and cultures and identifying how their experiences as raced, gendered, classed beings keeps them from recognizing common problems and seeking collective solutions, participants began to recognize their mutual self-interest in building strategic alliances for social change. The urgent need for this popular education course emerged from the principal findings of the collaborative research — that people's life experiences as raced, gendered, and classed beings, and their positioning vis-à-vis whiteness and Blackness, inhibits the formation of a collective vision whereby people of different backgrounds can build strategic alliances for social change.

The curriculum offered a modest glimpse of the prospects for politically engaged research as well as one strategy that might begin to contest the racialized and other identity-based divisions that uphold industry power and white supremacy in the newly transnational South. It emerged from the conviction that whereas common oppression as workers does not naturally unite diverse groups of individuals, "coalitions within and across identity categories can be built by open and honest discussion of the ways in which all of us have been differently racialized, gendered, and infused with complex and composite identities and interests" (Lipsitz 1998: 232). The curriculum acknowledged the structural and institutional nature of power and oppression exercised via neoliberal globalization and confronted it head-on, seeking to build solidarity not by silencing difference, but by embracing diversity as both a lived social "problem" and a resource to be leveraged in building a more just world. It taught that any sustainable worker movement must be rooted in experiences of culture, history, and identity, and that this approach is vital to the "emancipation of the whole" (Kelley 1997: 110). To this end, it began building a common language and points of connection through which poultry workers might begin to forge coalitions with co-workers and community members who are different from them, a notion Black feminist Barbara Smith deemed "truly radical" (Smith 2000: 232).

In my formalized role, I sensed throughout 2005 that collaborators, including those at the EJC, began to see me less as "teacher," "researcher," or "volunteer" and more as an integral part of the organization. I, too, felt more a part of the team building the workers' center. As I became further integrated, some of my earlier concerns about the center's leadership diminished. In hindsight, I have often pondered the extent to which assuming a position of greater leadership moderated my critical lens. At other times I've wondered if the EJC had the foresight to recognize that my new role might help to quell my critiques. In any case, my reflections on this period of collaboration are also somewhat sunnier because this was when our shared dreams about the potential of activist research began to bear fruit.

As the research suggested potential paths toward worker education and organizing and the workers' center eagerly sought to incorporate these lessons in its work, I felt renewed hope for the constructive possibilities of activist research. Not only was the collaborative relationship mutually beneficial from a methodological and utilitarian perspective (or as one of my graduate students recently put it, "mutually exploitative"), but my positionality was now simultaneously giving me a privileged perspective on the issues I was studying *and* letting me apply that insight in ways that developed the workers' center and strengthened poultry workers' political consciousness. The popular education initiative discussed above is but one of the key examples of the contours of our activist research efforts during the worker center's heyday.

Leaving the Field: The Creation and Decline of MPOWER

As I prepared to leave Mississippi in early 2006, my formal relationship to the EJC changed again when I became an "independent contractor." I continued to work with the workers' center while in Mississippi and after I left on a project basis. I trained new instructors to continue the political education and language courses we had developed, and I coordinated this and another workers' center program as I focused on writing my dissertation back in Austin (and later, Santa Fe). Shortly before I left, we hired a Salvadoran woman who had previously worked in the chicken plants to be the center's second full-time community organizer. Grabowski continued to direct the workers' center as an EJC project, traveling regularly between Texas and Mississippi.

As the year progressed, tensions escalated within the EJC over the organization's decision-making processes, the activities staff should spend their time on, and the most effective ways to bring about social change. The disputes involved a cross-section of the EJC staff and were not unique to the workers' center project, but they both fed off and deepened earlier divisions surrounding the mission and work of the workers' center. These fissures grew increasingly urgent, as did tensions concerning perceived gender, age, and race inequalities within the EJC. Grabowski involved the leadership council, the Mississippi staff, and me in conversation as she weighed the potential paths forward in light of these developments. After months of painful discussion, the council authorized Grabowski to negotiate the center's separation from the EJC. By the end of 2006 the workers' center had formally spun off with high hopes of becoming its own community-based nonprofit organization.

Under this new structure, the leadership council was poised to become the governing board of directors and the workers' center changed its name to MPOWER (Mississippi Poultry Workers for Equality and Respect). The activist research relationship that began as a collaboration with local advocates and the EJC and grew over time into a close, if complicated, partnership with EJC, now shifted into a third phase in which I was most closely affiliated with a new organization, MPOWER. Throughout 2007, while focused on completing my dissertation, I continued to support MPOWER from afar. Spatial distance and my divided attention made it increasingly harder to engage with the changes the organization was undergoing. Meanwhile, turnover within MPOWER's leadership council and staff presented the activist research relationship (and, much more acutely, the organization itself) with additional challenges.

The shift to local ownership compromised Grabowski's ability to lead the organization, both logistically and ideologically. She agreed to remain for a one-year transitional period devoted mainly to board training, organizational development, and the hiring of MPOWER's first executive director. This turned out to be a very tall order. The commitment to growing a board of directors composed mostly of poultry workers required equipping the leadership council with the tools it needed to successfully govern a nonprofit organization. However, many of its members were unfamiliar with nonprofit management, and irregular meeting attendance (poultry plants often operate six days a week) and the need to conduct gatherings in English and Spanish at once also proved problematic. That summer, Grabowski, the leadership council, MPOWER's staff, and I interviewed three candidates for the directorship and offered the job to the most promising individual. Despite his enthusiasm, a family crisis delayed his decision and ultimately prevented him from starting work. By late 2007 the board faced the prospect of another director search. With Grabowski's departure looming, they appointed the board chair, who had been involved in the organization for approximately the past year, interim director.

Under her direction, MPOWER's staff increasingly approached their work through a lens of service and Latino immigrant rights, all but abandoning the organization's mission of building worker power through cross-racial organizing and education. As before, I faced an internal conflict between accountability to an organization and commitment to an increasingly divergent set of political goals. On a practical level, I was immersed in writing across the country, and because my work had principally involved coordinating and supporting a pool of independent contractors (*Solidarity*/Solidaridad instructors and Workplace Injury Project interpreters), I had not worked closely with MPOWER's interim director and barely knew many of the newer board members. Confusion about my role repeatedly surfaced, and my shifting and under-defined relationship to the organization generated more questions than answers.

I invited MPOWER staff, board, and collaborators to read and critique drafts of my dissertation, and some took up the challenge. Grabowski commented on multiple drafts of the complete manuscript; others reviewed, critiqued, and clarified sections in which they figured prominently; and impressively, a few for whom English was a new, third language gave me painstakingly detailed feedback. The EJC's Beardall, with whom relations had been strained since MPOWER's spin-off, never responded to my invitations. Others at MPOWER, puzzled, asked what they could possibly contribute to an academic paper. Many of the individuals with whom I had for years discussed furthering the goals of poultry worker justice through activist research had moved on, and I found myself at the end of a six-year road starting new conversations about the politics, methods, and goals of politically engaged research. However, our geographic distance, the newcomers' unfamiliarity with MPOWER's history and my role within it, and a healthy skepticism of outsider academics made these conversations difficult and, at times, impossible.

As I put the finishing touches on the dissertation in early 2008, MPOWER was in decline. Grabowski's overly ambitious plan to transform the workers' center from a professional legal advocacy organization's project into an independent, community-led nonprofit organization in the span of one year encountered more challenges than successes. The time allotted proved insufficient to build the capacities and cultivate the local ownership needed to sustain the organization. By summer MPOWER was broke and insolvent, and the interim director had vanished. Amid rumors of her financial impropriety, the frustrated, defeated leadership council ceased to meet. All programming ended, and MPOWER never received formal nonprofit recognition from the state. Ironically, as I successfully defended the dissertation and my academic career began to bloom, the organization at the heart of my ethnographic narrative—and which the activist research relationship had helped to grow—was withering.

Since then, a small group of Latin American women poultry workers has continued to meet irregularly, utilizing MPOWER's popular education and workers' rights materials. Organized by the last MPOWER staff person standing at the time of its collapse, these women gather to support one another and confront issues of sexual harassment, discrimination, workplace injuries, and domestic violence while learning to defend their rights at work and at home. They benefited briefly from affiliating with STITCH, a transnational organization that supports leadership development among women workers in Latin America and the United States, but by the time of this writing, STITCH, too, had gone under.

Reflections

Throughout my research and writing, I was repeatedly troubled by dissonance between my relationship to a shifting group of individuals and organizations, and the ethics, methods, and theory taught by the Austin School. As the project moved from the hands of a loose local coalition to the EJC to the Mississippi Poultry Workers' Center and later to MPOWER, I struggled with questions of responsibility and allegiance in the activist research context. What were my ongoing responsibilities to individuals no longer involved in the workers' center, such as my initial collaborator and mentor, Beardall? What responsibilities did I have to organizational newcomers, and how could I make activist research "real" for them after my involvement in day-to-day activities had waned? Were my primary alliances with individuals or the organization? Moreover, how could I reconcile my forging of an activist research relationship with institutions (mainly the EJC but also the unions) that at times seemed at odds with the very politics I thought myself aligned with? As a new initiative founded by a coalition of people who themselves were not poultry workers, the Mississippi Poultry Workers' Center/MPOWER had experienced its share of growing pains, which made my relationships and potential contributions as an activist researcher more fluid and more complex.

In the dissertation I speculated that activist research with a more established organization—one with a clear constituency, vision, and strategic plan—would likely entail a different type of negotiation between researcher and organization, resulting in a more defined relationship, specific responsibilities and/or deliverables, and clear lines of accountability. I did not write about one lingering question: Had I fundamentally failed to operationalize the Austin School's approach to activist research by not allying myself from the start with a bounded group of individuals organizing to change the conditions of their own lives? Did I misstep by unwittingly selecting a project that early on vested power in individuals who were not poultry workers? Then again, MPOWER's later leadership reminded me that worker control did not necessarily translate into commitment to a progressive political vision. Would there have been fruitful ground for collaboration if my initial contact had been with a largely service-oriented (albeit worker-led) organization? Revealed over time, the project's many complexities muddied the notion of activist research with which I identified.

Regarding the lessons my fieldwork experience in Mississippi holds for the practice of activist research, I have devoted much thought to what I might do differently in crafting future collaborative projects. Should I be more intentional about identifying potential organizational collaborators that not only share my political vision but also meet a particular threshold of institutional stability and democratic organizational culture? It is very difficult to assess an organization's internal politics from the outside looking in, and gathering this information before beginning a dialogue about the potentialities of activist research would be impractical and perhaps unethical. More importantly, subsequent experience in activist research endeavors has taught me that all organizations are fraught with contradictions, like any product of human relationships. The idea that careful selection of an organization could elide all the conflicts and contradictions that might arise is naive and unrealistic.

I have also considered and experimented with ways of more explicitly delineating the contours of the activist research relationship early on, though this has proven difficult in practice. Specifying precisely how the activist research relationship will benefit collaborators through particular outcomes jeopardizes our ability to respond to needs and opportunities as they arise. And by focusing too much on research products, we risk overlooking the immediate benefit (and accompanying research opportunities) that our labor—used as our collaborators see fit—often provides. Corroborating this cautionary note are the experiences of several engaged researchers whose collaborators "put them to use" in tasks as mundane as making coffee and copies and as high-stakes as representing the organization in meetings with prospective international funders or helping it build strong legal arguments (Checker 2005; Duneier 1999; Hemment 2007; Johnston and Barker 2008; Speed 2008; Vargas 2006; Vine 2009). Flexibility and willingness to be "put to use" are often key components of the activist research relationship.

Yet I have begun to question what I have long accepted as a cornerstone of the Austin School. Is alignment with an organized collective imperative? Should activist research not partake in building something new, helping to forge political consciousness and organize a loosely defined group with potentially overlapping interests, even if it has not yet been constituted as such? Feminist anthropologist Julie Hemment did precisely this by joining a budding organization of politicized women in post-Soviet Russia (Hemment 2007). Her self-reflexive ethnography frankly considers the benefits and challenges this collaboration brought to her as a researcher and to the group. The organization was fragile (as is, Hemment concluded, the sustainability of the "third sector" in contemporary Russia), and as with the workers' center in Mississippi, the focus of its work and particular individuals' active participation within it changed over time. By the time her book came out, the organization was no longer active, but she maintained relationships with its former members, who continued to work for women's empowerment (Hemment 2007: 149–151). Indeed, she and the organization's founder continue to collaborate on engaged research projects of mutual interest. In Hemment's case, the organization she collaborated with dissolved over time, but its people continued the work in other forms, guided by the same political principles they had held when she met them. Her text gives no intimation that her collaborators' politics ever shifted in ways that required her to choose between the organization and its people.

Anthropologist and engaged scholar of the African diaspora Jemima Pierre offers another case that complicates the Austin School's insistence on partnership with an organized collective. Her chapter in Charles R. Hale's edited volume *Engaging Contradictions: Theory, Politics and Methods of Activist Scholarship* attempts to carve out space for academics engaged with a progressive politics located in spaces *other than* an organized collective (Pierre 2008). Despite her predisposition to engaged research, when studying racialization in postcolonial Ghana Pierre found no organized group struggles around matters of racial disparity in which to participate. Reflecting on how her positionality as a Black woman studying Blackness in Africa opened transformative spaces for Africans to rethink their relationships to global political economies of race, the essay advocates a reconception of the relationship between activism and research. Ultimately, Pierre argues, it is her commitment to the ideals of "global Black emancipation" in all areas of life, including the relationships she forges with research participants in Ghana and the spaces she occupies within the academy, that makes her scholarship fundamentally activist (Pierre 2008:127). The myriad ways she lives her politics, she insists, make her academic encounters transformative.

Hemment's and Pierre's discussions help me think about how my experience in Mississippi might encourage us to broaden our notion of activist research. Like Pierre, I based my relationships with collaborators in Mississippi on a particular vision—a more just life for Mississippi's immigrant and U.S.-born poultry workers, but more broadly, a world where power is more equally distributed in ways that move us closer to the goals of social, racial, and economic justice. Like Hemment, I had and retain concrete accountability to a collaborating organization and to particular individuals.[6] Thus, enmeshed in the idea of activist research collaboration with an organized collective are at least three identifiable overlapping commitments: (1) to individuals, (2) to an institution (formal or informal), and (3) to a politics of liberation. In the Austin School's ideal type, the individuals, the group, and the politics exist in harmony within "communities in struggle," but in light of this chapter they might be better understood as three strands that at times become tightly interwoven but can also loosen and fray. To further the analogy, the longer a fabric is worn, the more likely it is to unravel.

Activist research calls for long-term commitment to all three strands. Given the privileged perspective the collaborative relationship typically enables, the passage of (more) time associated with activist research likely allows us to witness fabric unraveling (through personality conflicts, ideological disagreements, organizational collapse, etc.) more often than do ethnographers of other inclinations. Most often, however, we forbear to write about it, concerned with protecting our research participants, our future research access, or the social movements we support. In reflecting on my own experiments in activist research, I have taken pains not to harm any of the above. I have used deliberate language, exercised caution with revelations, and narrated the story with my purpose in mind.

My aim is to refine the teachings of the Austin School and illustrate the importance of its framework for an anthropology in collaboration with broader publics. Crucially, sustained engagement with the question "Anthropology for whom?" ensures that we consider the impacts, contributions, and relevance of our work. Meanwhile, although the notion of research aligned with "communities in struggle" works as a theoretical tool to guide our research methodologies, it implies an overly idealistic conflation of "communities" and "struggle," eliding the complexities involved in simultaneous commitments to people, institutions, and a shared politics. When these diverge, the relative weight given to each often depends on situational particularities and the stakes involved in the decision. This chapter has shown how I struggled to come to this realization, privileging political/ethical commitments and, to a lesser extent, the personal relationships these politics helped forge, over obligation to any one organization or group. My deliberations also demonstrate some of the many possible inflections of activist research and their potential contributions to publics beyond the academy. The realities of carrying out politically engaged research are always more complicated in practice than in theory, and considering the challenges that emerge from on-the-ground scholarship aligned with political struggle enables us to further refine the analytical frames through which we conceive our work. One of my mentors, Charlie Hale, has suggested that engagement with the contradictions of engaged research can cultivate new ground for debate, broaden the community of scholars conducting relevant work, and further map out the field of activist anthropology (Hale 2008: 26). In this spirit, and with these goals, I offer my reflections for consideration.

Angela Stuesse (Ph.D. University of Texas, Austin 2008) is Assistant Professor of Anthropology at the University of South Florida. Her research and teaching interests include neoliberal globalization, migration, race, human rights, and methodologies of activist research. She has conducted research in the U.S.-Mexico borderlands and in the newer borderlands of the U.S. South. Her book manuscript, *Globalization "Southern Style": Immigration, Race, and Work in the Rural U.S. South,* explores how new Latino migration into Mississippi's poultry industry has impacted communities and prospects for worker organizing. It is based on six years of activist research engagement with poultry workers and their supporters. Her more recent work investigates the intensification of immigrant policing in Atlanta, Georgia, with an emphasis on racialized effects and community responses. She has published in the journals *American Anthropologist, City & Society, Latino Studies, Southern Spaces,* and *Human Organization,* among others.

Notes

1. For discussion of the development of participatory action research and its contemporary uses, see, for example, Hemment 2007; Nabudere 2008.
2. See, for example, Anzaldúa 1999; Behar and Gordon 1995; Crenshaw 1991; Enslin 1994; Fox 1991; Harrison 1991; Lorde 1983 [1980]; McIntosh 1997 [1986]; Moraga and Anzaldúa 1981; Narayan 1993; Sandoval 2000; Scheper-Hughes 1995; Smith 1983; Trouillot 1995; Visweswaran 1994.
3. See, for example, Beck and Maida 2013; Benmayor 1991; Craven and Davis 2013; Field and Fox 2007; Hale 2008; Holland et al. 2010; Hyatt and Lyon-Callo 2003; Juris and Khasnabish 2013; Low and Merry 2010; Sanford and Angel-Ajani 2006.
4. For more on the Equal Justice Center's current work, see http://equaljusticecenter.org.
5. The federal Taft-Hartley Act of 1947 empowered states to determine whether employees at unionized workplaces would be required to join the union. Under "Right to Work" legislation, currently enacted in twenty-three states located mostly in the South and West, individual workers choose whether or not to pay union dues and become a member. In such "open shops," the collective bargaining agreement protects all workers, whom unions are required to represent equally, but often only a fraction of these workers are dues-paying members. As a result, unions in Right to Work states typically lack resources, crippling their ability to sustainably organize and represent workers.
6. Despite the passage of time, I invited both Beardall and Grabowski to comment on the present piece.

References

Anzaldúa, Gloria. 1999. *Borderlands/La Frontera.* San Francisco: Aunt Lute Books.
Asad, Talal. 1973. *Anthropology and the Colonial Encounter.* London: Ithaca Press.

Bastide, Roger. 1973. *Applied Anthropology*, trans. A.L. Morton. London: Croom Helm.

Beck, Sam, and Carl A. Maida. 2013. *Toward Engaged Anthropology*. New York and Oxford: Berghan Books.

Behar, Ruth, and Deborah A. Gordon, eds. 1995. *Women Writing Culture*. Berkeley: University of California Press.

Benmayor, Rina. 1991. "Testimony, Action Research, and Empowerment: Puerto Rican Women and Popular Education." In *Women's Words*, ed. Daphne Patai and Sherna Berger Gluck. New York: Routledge.

Bernard, H. Russell, ed. 2002. *Handbook of Methods in Cultural Anthropology*. Walnut Creek, CA: AltaMira Press.

Blanchard, David. 1979. "Beyond Empathy: The Emergence of an Action Anthropology in the Life and Career of Sol Tax." In *Currents in Anthropology: Essays in Honor of Sol Tax*, ed. Robert Hinshaw. New York: Mouton.

Borofsky, Rob. 2010. "Public Anthropology: A Personal Perspective." http://www.publican thropology.org/Defining/publicanth-07Oct10.htm.

Checker, Melissa. 2005. *Polluted Promises: Environmental Racism and the Search for Justice in a Southern Town*. New York: New York University Press.

Checker, Melissa, David Vine, and Alaka Wali. 2010. "A Sea Change in Anthropology? Public Anthropology Reviews." *American Anthropologist* 112, no. 1 (March): 5–6.

Clifford, James. 1988. *The Predicament of Culture: Twentieth-Century Ethnography, Literature, and Art*. Cambridge, MA: Harvard University Press.

Clifford, James, and George E. Marcus. 1986. *Writing Culture: The Poetics and Politics of Ethnography*. Berkeley: University of California Press.

Craven, Christa, and Dána-Ain Davis. 2013. *Feminist Activist Ethnography: Counterpoints to Neoliberalism in North America*. Lanham, MD: Lexington Books.

Crenshaw, Kimberlé. 1991. "Mapping the Margins: Intersectionality, Identity Politics, and Violence against Women of Color." *Stanford Law Review* 43, no. 6 (July): 1241–1299.

Deloria Jr., Vine. 1969. "Anthropologists and Other Friends." In *Custer Died for Your Sins: An Indian Manifesto*. Toronto: The Macmillan Company.

Duneier, Mitchell. 1999. *Sidewalk*. New York: Farrar, Straus and Giroux.

Enslin, Elizabeth. 1994. "Beyond Writing: Feminist Practice and the Limitations of Ethnography." *Cultural Anthropology* 9, no. 4 (November): 537–568.

Fals Borda, Orlando. 1979. "Investigating Reality in Order to Transform It: The Colombian Experience." *Dialectical Anthropology* 4, (March): 33–55.

Field, Les W., and Richard G. Fox, eds. 2007. *Anthropology Put to Work*. Oxford: Berg Publishers.

Fine, Janice. 2006. *Worker Centers: Organizing Communities at the Edge of the Dream*. Ithaca: ILR Press/Cornell University Press.

Fink, Leon. 2003. *The Maya of Morganton: Work and Community in the Nuevo New South*. Durham: University of North Carolina Press.

Foley, Douglas E. 1990. *Learning Capitalist Culture: Deep in the Heart of Tejas*. Philadelphia: University of Pennsylvania Press.

———. 1995. *The Heartland Chronicles*. Philadelphia: University of Pennsylvania Press.

———. 1999. "The Fox Project: A Reappraisal (with replies)." *Current Anthropology* 40, no. 2 (April): 171–192.

Fox, Richard G., ed. 1991. *Recapturing Anthropology: Working in the Present*. Santa Fe: School of American Research Press.

Freire, Paulo. 1970. *Pedagogy of the Oppressed*. New York: Herder and Herder.

———. 1982 [1972]. "Creating Alternative Research Methods: Learning to Do It by Doing It." In *Creating Knowledge: A Monopoly? Participating Research in Development*, ed. Budd Hall. New Dehli: Society for Participatory Research in Asia.

Gordon, Edmund T. 1991. "Anthropology and Liberation." In *Decolonizing Anthropology*, ed. F.V. Harrison. Washington, D.C.: American Anthropological Association.

———. 2007. "The Austin School Manifesto: An Approach to the Black or African Diaspora." *Cultural Anthropology* no. 19 (March): 93–97.

Gordon, Edmund T., and Charles R. Hale. 1997. *Activist Anthropology Concept Statement*. http://www.utexas.edu/cola/depts/anthropology/activist/concept statement.html.

Gupta, Akhil, and James Ferguson. 1997. *Anthropological Locations: Boundaries and Grounds of a Field Science*. Berkeley: University of California Press.

Hale, Charles R. 2001. "What is Activist Research?" *Items (Social Science Research Council)* 2, no. 1–2: 13–15.

———. 2006. "Activist Research v. Cultural Critique: Indigenous Land Rights and the Contradictions of Politically Engaged Anthropology." *Cultural Anthropology* 21, no. 1 (February): 96–120.

———. 2008. *Engaging Contradictions: Theory, Politics and Methods of Activist Scholarship*. Berkeley: University of California Press.

Haraway, Donna. 1988. "Situated Knowledges: The Science Question in Feminism and the Privilege of Partial Perspective." *Feminist Studies* 14, no. 3 (Autumn): 575–599.

Harding, Sandra. 1987. *Feminism and Methodology*. Bloomington: Indiana University Press.

———. 1993. "Rethinking Standpoint Epistemology: 'What Is Strong Objectivity?'" In *Feminist Epistemologies*, ed. Linda Alcoff and Elizabeth Potter. New York: Routledge.

Harrison, Faye V., ed. 1991. *Decolonizing Anthropology*. Washington, DC: American Anthropological Association.

Hemment, Julie. 2007. *Empowering Women in Russia: Activism, Aid, and NGOs*. Bloomington: Indiana University Press.

Holland, Dorothy, Dana Powell, Eugenia Eng, and Georgina Drew. 2010. "Models of Engaged Scholarship: An Interdisciplinary Discussion." *Collaborative Anthropologies* 3, no. 1: 1–36.

Hyatt, Susan Brin, and Vincent Lyon-Callo. 2003. "Introduction: Anthropology and Political Engagement." *Urban Anthropology* 32, no. 2 (July): 133–146.

Hymes, Dell, ed. 1972. *Reinventing Anthropology*. New York: Vintage Books.

Johnston, Barbara Rose, and Holly M. Barker. 2008. *Consequential Damages of Nuclear War: The Rongelap Report*. Walnut Creek, CA: Left Coast Press.

Juris, Jeffrey S., and Alex Khasnabish. 2013. *Insurgent Encounters: Transnational Activism, Ethnography, and the Political*. Durham: Duke University Press.

Kassam, Yusuf, and Kamal Mustafa, eds. 1982. *Participatory Research: An Emerging Alternative Methodology in Social Science Research*. New Delhi: Society for Participatory Research in Asia.

Kelley, Robin D.G. 1997. *Yo' Mama's DisFUNKtional!: Fighting the Culture Wars in Urban America*. Boston: Beacon Press.

Lende, Daniel H. 2013. *Anthropology: Growth and Relevance, Not Popularity*. Neuroanthropology PLOS, September 12. http://blogs.plos.org/neuroanthropology/2013/09/12/anthropology-growth-and-relevance-not-popularity/.

Lewis, Diane. 1973. "Anthropology and Colonialism." *Current Anthropology* 14, no. 5 (December): 581–602.

Lipsitz, George. 1998. *The Possessive Investment in Whiteness: How White People Profit from Identity Politics*. Philadelphia: Temple University Press.

Lorde, Audre. 1983 [1980]. "The Master's Tools." In *This Bridge Called My Back: Writings by Radical Women of Color*, ed. Cherríe Moraga and Gloria Anzaldúa. Vol. 2. New York: Kitchen Table: Women of Color Press.

Low, Setha M., and Sally Engle Merry. 2010. "Engaged Anthropology: Diversity and Dilemmas: An Introduction to Supplement 2." *Current Anthropology* 51, no. S2 (October): S203–S226.

McIntosh, Peggy. 1997 [1986]. "White Privilege and Male Privilege: A Personal Account of Coming to See Correspondences through Work in Women's Studies." In *Critical White Studies: Looking Behind the Mirror*, ed. Richard Delgado and Jean Stefancic. Philadelphia: Temple University Press.

Moraga, Cherríe, and Gloria Anzaldúa. 1981. *This Bridge Called My Back: Writings by Radical Women of Color.* Latham, NY: Kitchen Table Press.

Nabudere, Dani Wadada. 2008. "Research, Activism, and Knowledge Production." In *Engaging Contradictions: Theory, Politics, and Methods of Activist Scholarship*, ed. C.R. Hale, 62–87. Berkeley: University of California Press.

Nader, Laura. 1972. "Up the Anthropologist — Perspectives Gained from Studying Up." In *Reinventing Anthropology*, ed. Dell Hymes. New York: Pantheon Books.

Narayan, Kirin. 1993. "How Native is a 'Native Anthropologist'?" *American Anthropologist* 95 (September): 671–686.

Pierre, Jemima. 2008. "Activist Groundings or Groundings for Activism? The Study of Racialization as a Site of Political Engagement." In *Engaging Contradictions: Theory, Politics, and Methods of Activist Scholarship*, ed. C.R. Hale. Berkeley: University of California Press.

Polgar, Steven. 1979. "Applied, Action, Radical and Committed Anthropology." In *Currents in Anthropology: Essays in Honor of Sol Tax*, ed. Robert Hinshaw. New York: Mouton.

Rosaldo, Renato. 1989. *Culture and Truth: The Remaking of Social Analysis.* Boston: Beacon Press.

Rylko-Bauer, Barbara, Merrill Singer, and John Van Willigen. 2006. "Reclaiming Applied Anthropology: Its Past, Present, and Future." *American Anthropologist* 108, no 1 (March): 178–190.

Sandoval, Chela. 2000. *Methodology of the Oppressed.* Minneapolis: University of Minnesota Press.

Sanford, Victoria, and Asale Angel-Ajani. 2006. *Engaged Observer: Anthropology, Advocacy, and Activism.* New Brunswick, NJ: Rutgers University Press.

Scheper-Hughes, Nancy. 1995. "The Primacy of the Ethical: Propositions for a Militant Anthropology." *Current Anthropology* 36, no. 3 (June): 409–440.

———. 2009. "Making Anthropology Public." *Anthropology Today* 25, no. 4 (August): 1–3.

Smith, Barbara. 1983. *Home Girls: A Black Feminist Anthology.* Latham, NY: Kitchen Table Press.

———. 2000. *The Truth that Never Hurts: Writings on Race, Gender, and Freedom.* New Brunswick, NJ: Rutgers University Press.

Speed, Shannon. 2006. "At the Crossroads of Human Rights and Anthropology: Toward a Critically Engaged Activist Research." *American Anthropologist* 108, no. 1: 66–76.

———. 2008. *Rights in Rebellion: Indigenous Struggle and Human Rights in Chiapas.* Palo Alto, CA: Stanford University Press.

Stuesse, Angela C. 2003. "Hablando Mexicano: La restructuración industrial y los desafíos para la organización a través de la diferencia en un Mississippi transnacional." *Estudios Migratorios Latinoamericanos* 17, no. 52: 603–626.

———. 2008. "Globalization "Southern Style": Transnational Migration, the Poultry Industry, and Implications for Organizing Workers across Difference." Ph.D. diss., University of Texas at Austin.

———. 2009. "Race, Migration, and Labor Control: Neoliberal Challenges to Organizing Mississippi's Poultry Workers." In *Latino Immigrants and the Transformation of the U.S. South*, ed. Mary Odem and Elaine Lacy. Athens: University of Georgia Press.

———. 2010. "What's "Justice and Dignity" Got to Do with It? Migrant Vulnerability, Corporate Complicity, and the State." *Human Organization* 69, no 1: 19–30.

———. Forthcoming. *Scratching Out a Living: Latinos, Race, and Work in the Deep South.* Berkeley: University of California Press.

Stuesse, Angela, and Laura E Helton. 2013. "Low-wage Legacies, Race, and the Golden Chicken in Mississippi: Where Contemporary Immigration Meets African American Labor History." *Southern Spaces.* http://southernspaces.org/2013/low-wage-legacies-race-and-golden-chicken-mississippi.

Sudbury, Julia. 1998. *'Other Kinds of Dreams': Black Women's Organizations and the Politics of Transformation.* London: Routledge.

Symposium on Inter-Ethnic Conflict in South America. 1973 [1971]. "The Declaration of Barbados: For the Liberation of the Indians." *Current Anthropology* 14, no 3 (July): 267–270.

Tax, Sol. 1952. "Action Anthropology." *America Indígena* 12, no 2: 103–109.

Trouillot, Michel-Rolph. 1995. *Silencing the Past: Power and the Production of History.* Boston: Beacon Press.

Vargas, João H. Costa. 2006. *Catching Hell in the City of Angels: Life and Meanings of Blackness in South Central Los Angeles.* Minneapolis: University of Minnesota Press.

Vine, David. 2009. *Island of Shame: The Secret History of the U.S. Military Base on Diego Garcia.* Princeton, NJ: Princeton University Press.

Visweswaran, Kamala. 1994. *Fictions of Feminist Ethnography.* Minneapolis: University of Minnesota Press.

Willis, William S. Jr. 1972. "Skeletons in the Anthropological Closet." In *Reinventing Anthropology,* ed Dell Hymes. New York: Random House.

Chapter 9

"WE ARE PLUMBERS OF DEMOCRACY"

A Study of Aspirations to Inclusive Public Dialogues in Mexico and Its Repercussions

———— ⌾⌾⌾ ————

Raúl Acosta

When Ciro opened the door to greet a local successful businessman, Jacinto exchanged his relaxed, joking tone for a more serious, professional demeanor. He was in the living room, explaining a slide to a small audience made up of activists, entrepreneurs, academics, and Ciro's colleagues at a small consultancy firm. The meeting was the result of months of negotiations to bring together various social movements, independent associations, and individuals that had never worked with each other before. Their objective was to improve urban life for all in Guadalajara, Mexico's second most populous city and a thriving commercial and industrial hub. Those gathered in Ciro's house intended specifically to stop government plans to build an express toll road through the city. Jacinto was explaining the details of a study on local newspaper coverage of the toll road debate that found that compared to the official viewpoint, critical opinions based on technical knowledge had received minimal exposure. This, he said, indicated the inadequacy of public dialogue on a decision that would affect the city in many ways. Afterward, Ciro opened debate on how to convince members of the local state parliament not to approve the governor's plan. One major issue was the need for a proper public dialogue, with expert opinions, to publicize the social, spatial, and economic repercussions of building the road.

This chapter tells the story of a public anthropology research project on dialogue and civil society in Guadalajara. It offers an account of the underlying tension between an academic project and activists' expectations regarding its analyses and proposals. Ciro exemplifies a new breed of activists that has gained ground in Mexican public life over the last few years. A middle-class, university-educated, well-traveled professional, he invests time and money in his activism. He and his activist friends are "reasonable radicals" (Werbner 2004) engaged in "cosmopolitan activism" (Morgan 2004). "There is a piping problem between citizens and government in Mexico," Ciro told me in an interview, "and we are a sort of plumbers of democracy."

Mine was not a militant approach, but members of the network that was the main object of my research constantly appropriated the reflections and concepts I used to analyze efforts like his for their own purposes. The focus on dialogue as an essential concept to explain their political aspirations influenced some of their actions and strategies, and some cases, analyses "went public" before being academically processed and written up. During the research and later writing-up stages, I had to wonder whether this haste affected the quality of further analyses or limited the reach of reflection. Would more distance enable deeper scrutiny on my part? Often an anthropologist will leave the fieldwork site, process the information over a few months, and then return to share the results. My experience with this project was nothing like that: the field was the city I lived in, and I continued observations while writing up the results. Blurred boundaries between the field and the desk could produce controversial results (Mosse 2006). Just how public is public anthropology supposed to be? In this chapter, I will reflect on how the key concept of my research project—dialogue—pervaded my fieldwork, leading to mixed results.

Dialogue is a type of social interaction in which each participant is willing to listen to what the others want to say. In this meaningful symbolic exchange dominated by, but not limited to, language (Surrallés 2003), all parties have the opportunity to let others' opinions, ideas, and expressions influence their own. Dialogue does not imply that one's own psyche immediately appropriates such external elements, but rather that one is inclined to be open and attentive to what the other communicates. Anthropological studies have regarded dialogue as part of various ceremonies and as a distinctive characteristic of human relations (van Meijl 2006). These reflections in our discipline derive partly from the influence of the literary theorists Bakhtin and Volosinov (Bakhtin 1981; Gurdin 1994; Shotter 1999) and from work on the "dialogical self" within the field of psychology (Hermans 2001). Recently, however, dialogue has also come to be considered a feature of the discipline itself. This process, initially spurred by critiques of anthropological representation in the 1970s and consideration of the dialogic nature of anthropological research (Dwyer 1977; 1979), resulted in "dialogical anthropology" (Tedlock 1979; 1987).

It continues to arouse interest, especially since the authoritative role of the anthropologist has come into question and new ways of dealing with collaborators, formerly called informants, have been advanced (Hendry 2007). Clifford (1983) even suggested including "plural authorship" in our endeavors. Some current reflections on public anthropology have refocused on the dialogical character of anthropological research, shedding light on its relevance in a research process useful to all participants (Butler 2009).

Taking a more critical stance, Handler argues for a cautious approach to the matter (Handler 1985). Leaving aside the value of the dialogical process of sociability, he questions the extent to which the anthropological venture can include it, asking how much dialogue a research analysis can involve without losing its critical edge. It could happen that "dialogue will amount to little more than mutually confirming, rather than critically examining, each other's beliefs" (Handler 1985: 182). He makes his point in light of his own research on nationalist or ethnic ideologies and identities. If analytical categories were left up to negotiation with research subjects, then the resulting analysis would risk simply repeating the assumptions and common sense of those interviewed or observed. My own caution with the project at hand resembles Handler's, but with a twist. Originally, I was interested in dialogues about the observed network, especially since the individuals in webs within it yearned for more inclusive, democratic public dialogues. But this led to further scrutiny of situations in which government officials enacted dialogues with individual citizens or independent associations, during which my own dialogues with participants seemed to become part of the network's ongoing work. My inquiries about dialogue seemed to generate interest in the concept and lead to a certain "branding" of aims. This, however, did not cause a significant shift in relations, as a couple of examples in this chapter will show.

Public anthropology strives for relevant applications of knowledge as perceived through a disciplinary lens. This does not mean that its work is not academic. In fact, the ethical guidelines of two preeminent professional academic associations of the discipline, the American Anthropological Association and the Association of Social Anthropologists of the UK and the Commonwealth, state that contributing somehow to the community one is studying is good practice. It combines gathering data with informing those being observed about the nature of the research project to provide something in return for the time and attention given. But just how public should all processes of public anthropology be? Any type of social research requires different stages, each with its own set of characteristics and challenges. Allowing everything to be public may prove problematic. Likely stages include planning, data collection during fieldwork, reflective notes on fieldwork, analyses, write-up, publication, and debate on the results via channels such as seminars or workshops. Each of these activities is probably divisible into three phases: preparatory, investigative, and expositive. Some definitions of public anthropology emphasize the need for public engagement in the expository phase. Wider dissemination of a given research project's results, this argument goes, will lead more people to understand the value of anthropological research (Eriksen 2006). Others claim that the second, investigative phase of work should necessarily be public, so that constant feedback between researcher and research subjects will achieve a result relevant to the latter (Butler 2009). I found no text to support such openness during the first, preparatory phase of activity, probably because the work would risk straying too far from academic interests or becoming some sort of informed journalistic endeavor. Anthropology, as an academic discipline, applies analytical depth and conceptual rigor to the process of understanding social phenomena.

These last reflections imply limits on what can be public in anthropological analyses. Deep reflections and examinations also take time. It is difficult to convince activists in a hostile environment to wait a few months for a text that is probably most useful now. In such a situation, it is perhaps fruitful to advance a few concepts and reflections while taking time to conduct deeper analyses. The following text concerns a research project carried out between 2008 and 2010 in Guadalajara, Mexico. The names of the people involved and their organizations or activities have been changed. The first of the chapter's two parts describes the formation of the network of activists and organizations that was the project's main focus of research and attests to the way in which this investigation intertwined with the network's development. The second part analyzes the narratives that pervaded the coalition and discusses the risk of new projects inheriting old structures that contradict the ideals behind the projects.

The Birth of a Network

Early in 2008, a series of meetings were held in the headquarters of a local NGO in Guadalajara. Ciro was one convener; the other was Holger, who presided over a coalition of neighborhood associations. The two had discussed the need for a new association that would unite organizations struggling to get public authorities' attention and response. Their own experience and stories told by friends and acquaintances in other citizens' groups had led both to notice a pattern in different government offices' handling of these independent efforts: officials commonly disregarded organized citizens' critical opinions of government projects, policies, or plans, and discredited these views openly and harshly. They even managed to criminalize key members of each group by accusing them of petty crimes, thus diverting attention from their criticism and arousing fear among individuals disposed to be critical. In earlier times, these strategies sufficed to deter most organized criticism against a corrupt government.

Abuses committed during seventy-two years of authoritarian single-party government (1929–2000) lingered in memory. Yet after a few years of "transition" to democracy, many independent, critical citizens' groups had sprouted not only in Guadalajara but also throughout Mexico. These groups, including the one portrayed in this text, brought together affluent individuals and poorer grassroots activists who would not have collaborated before. The self-assurance of the better off boosts such groups' resilience. When some members are comparatively well informed about their legal situation and articulate in denouncing abuses, the group is unlikely to back down as easily as many grassroots groups once did.

Initially, I attended these meetings intending to design a research proposal to follow the formation of the network. For my doctoral research, I had investigated the internal politics of similar networks in the Brazilian Amazon and the Mediterranean (Acosta 2007). That study's main conclusion was that the webs managed dissent by coming together in networks that crossed ideological, class, institutional, ethnic, and other boundaries. The effort of joining in a larger network compelled all organizations to find common ground so as to better negotiate with governments or other institutions. In Guadalajara, however, I wanted a different issue as a guiding concept to help me understand the complex dynamics among individuals and organizations. My first few weeks of preliminary observations and conversations revealed a fundamental objective underlying the efforts of all those involved: to improve public dialogue on governmental policies and projects. Thus I designed a project to assess the "quality of public dialogues" as civil society organizations in Guadalajara saw it, which secured funding from the Mexican Council for Scientific Research.

Most of the network's activity centered on meetings that at first aimed to build trust among all those convened—a logical step for Ciro and his wife, who, as leaders of a small consultancy firm working with neighborhood associations, were used to facilitating group dynamics. For all their experience, however, they had not expected the level of difficulty they confronted in forming this network. Most of the problems were due to the contrasting backgrounds and profiles of the convened organizations. "We chose seven organizations that would represent various socioeconomic levels and issue areas," Ciro told me. "We" meant Ciro and Holger, a German businessman who owns a small manufacturing company in Guadalajara. Resident in Mexico since the 1970s, he has a Mexican wife and children, and is now a Mexican citizen. In 2008 Holger headed a coalition of neighborhood associations.

Other organizations convening to form the network included an environmental grassroots group from a marginal area of the city affected by extreme pollution; an environmental association conducting various campaigns to improve urban life; a social movement to keep woodlands from being razed to build housing estates; a political association to promote government accountability and defend the secular state; an urban rights association working to protect pedestrians and public transport; a small organization defending a woodland area within the city from encroaching urban development; and an established NGO boasting decades of work in popular education. Each convened organization had its own agenda and was limited by shortages of volunteers and resources. Networks they had previously partaken in usually centered on a single issue or had members with similar organizational profiles. The range of interests and backgrounds was a challenge for all participants.

At the first few meetings, Holger, emphasizing the need for clarity about the new network, asked all those present to help develop a mission statement, a vision, and objectives. "We need to agree on these issues to move forward," he insisted. This business-language strategic planning discomforted several participants, whose left-wing ideological stances made them distrust anything businesslike. His slight German accent did not help either. "I felt a strong resistance to my proposals, even offensive, and I realized what people feared most was that I would seek some sort of prominence within the network," he told me in an interview two years later. Holger left the network after a few months of heated debates and disagreements. It took the remaining members over a year to agree that the elements Holger had insisted on had been necessary from the start. In the first months, most meetings were dedicated to debating what the network was for and how it could best achieve it. These discussions presented contrasting idealized visions of democracy, romanticized aspirations, and exasperated denunciations of wrongdoing by politicians and government officials. Some sessions seemed to be a space for like-minded people to share their thoughts, away from their daily routines. Often, the official aim was to produce a series of documents establishing the network's profile and thus clarifying its purpose for other independent organizations and civil servants. Some sessions were devoted to reaching a (seemingly impossible) consensus on texts in progress. Usually one of the conveners would open a document on a computer, project it onto a screen, and modify it based on other attendees' comments. Many suggested word changes uncovered underlying ideological differences, prejudices, alliances, and other characteristics.

The network initially portrayed itself as fundamentally both open to a wide range of citizens' groups and nonideological. It was stated several times that the network sought to unite all independent citizen groups in the state of Jalisco (of which Guadalajara is the capital). To this end, Ciro repeatedly insisted on a nonideological stance, regardless of groups' affiliations or preferences. Both core qualities, however, suffered radical alteration over the course of a few months. Despite the goal of inclusiveness, there was no strategy to increase membership or even invite other groups to participate. Furthermore, the number of organizations represented at the first meetings gradually declined; two years later only three of the initial seven remained active in the meetings. Meanwhile, the attendees' ideological discourse shifted to the left. From insisting that "[we] must be un-ideological and focus on being open to all citizens" at the first meetings, Ciro ended up saying two years later that "reason lies on the left wing of political ideologies, as right-wingers just obey and do not think by themselves or consider the common good." Both transformations seemed to result from ongoing identification among some of the most voluble participants in the meetings.

A common activity at the gatherings was to criticize the latest foolish action or declaration by a government representative. With insights from local media and their own personal contacts, they would point to the politician's lack of competence, disdain for public opinion, or outright corruption. At the time, politicians from the conservative party headed all three levels of government—municipal, state, and federal. While constant reports documented government officials' harassment of left-wing movements or organizations, the state government was funding conservative causes and groups without any transparency or accountability. Such revelations fueled a sense of outrage that in turn strengthened a sense of belonging "to the left." It also seemed to limit the network to the few participating members, as distrust grew toward outsiders.

The location, timing, and weekly ceremony of the meetings also reflected the route the network followed. It held its first meetings in the headquarters of the oldest member group: a well-known, thirty-year-old local NGO focused on popular education. For the first few months, a weekly meeting was scheduled from 8 P.M. to 10 P.M. on a weekday, usually Tuesday. The NGO provided a meeting room, a data projector, some material to work on, a coffeemaker, and cups for all. The conveners slated someone to bring coffee and biscuits, and someone to chair each meeting. The NGO staff members were very helpful, but after a few sessions it was clear that they were pressed for time, as they had deadlines to meet for other projects, reports, and activities. Their participation in the network was more an expression of solidarity with its aims than an official part of their organization's work. People also found it hard to meet so late after a full day of work. Furthermore, a conflict arose between the organization based in the marginal, highly polluted area, and NGO staff who worked on internationally funded projects in that area. The former accused the latter of collaborating with local government and neutralizing their efforts to realize public works that would reduce contaminants in their suburban town. This conflict sparked debates that derailed the network's discussions and produced discomfort in the room.

All these factors prompted a decision to change the time and location of the meeting to Saturday mornings at a school managed by Sandra, one of the participants. Some members who had to work on Saturday mornings were forced to drop out at this point. In the new setting, Sandra ensured that food and drink were always available just outside the room. The remaining participants seemed invigorated by the change of place, day, and time. Morning debates were more energetic than those in the evening, when everyone was clearly tired. Attendees commonly remarked that they found inspiration for their ongoing activism in these meetings.

Whereas the network profited from its consistent routine of weekly meetings, it also faced harsh criticism. The discontented founding member Holger was among the most fervent critics. "It has become another organization," he told me in an interview, reflecting on his early departure. "I think those who remain have the best of intentions and do think creatively ... but we needed a structure that would not be a burden on organizations that already have many activities and few resources." Holger had insisted on an agile association capable of providing resources and support to organizations facing difficulties or requiring assistance. The network that was taking shape differed from this vision. The meetings I witnessed seemed to be hammering out an ambitious roadmap for redesigning statewide structures of democratic governance. For example, participants constantly referred to the institutionalization of direct democracy as a key aim. This shift toward a more institutional aim was due partly to the involvement of several academics and intellectuals who were close friends of some members. These guest scholars were invited to lead workshops on political analysis and contestation, activities that took up numerous Saturday mornings and shaped a common ideological stance from which to criticize the government and plan the network's activities.

From the outset, my analysis held that the network's main interest was to improve public dialogue about government policies and projects. Javier, an architect who clearly enjoyed the meetings and constantly related his candid, striking reflections, told me that he owed his enthusiasm to the learning process that participation involved. He was a good example of the new generation of activists, as his participation in social movements had begun only a few weeks before the network was convened. Over the course of the meetings, his interventions and opinions were increasingly well regarded and useful. In an interview at the end of my fieldwork, Javier explained that "over the last almost two years I have been involved in this movement, I have learnt that it is not enough to just have a better rhetoric style, but that information is key." As an architect interested in urban planning, his participation more and more concerned creative ways to motivate people to engage in political debate. "I am now much more aware of political issues," he told me.

Javier's individual learning process mirrored the greater one sought by the network. This pedagogic aspiration was clear, once the participants got around to defining the network's name and purpose. The network named itself Platform 39 (henceforth P39) after Article 39 in the Mexican Constitution, which reads: "National sovereignty is vested in the people in essence and origin. All public power derives from the people and is instituted for their benefit. The people have the inalienable right at any time to alter or modify the form of government" (my translation). "Platform" referred to the aim of providing a common discourse that would encompass all citizens' groups involved in their individual causes. P39's mission statement is as follows: "[We seek to] share the skills, knowledge and proposals of citizens' and neighborhood organizations in order to join hands in a learning process to enact our citizenship, and to activate and motivate more citizens in the ongoing creation of concrete options to enforce the provisions of Article 39 of our Constitution" (my translation).

To achieve their aims, attendees of the meetings planned actions to disseminate their message, encourage other organizations and individuals to join their cause, and assist member organizations. Among the ideas for events that took weeks of planning and debate, two stand out, both with the purpose of publicizing cases of criminalization or repression of critical movements in Jalisco. The first was a one-day seminar reviewing some cases that had surfaced in 2008; the second was a smaller, follow-up public meeting. A human rights legal advocacy group and a few specialized academics helped guide the events, which centered on testimonies by individuals who had been arrested, harassed, or accused of criminal activity because of their activism. Both events had media coverage, mainly in local newspapers. These were the only high-profile activities that took take place during my fieldwork. Their fewness was due partly to the limited number of activists involved, but also to a side effect of the network: its splinter webs. Participants in P39 meetings were creating new networks—in many cases inspired by conversations about ideas outside of P39's agenda—and some P39 members were devoting more time and energy to the splinter groups than to the original network during the weekly meetings.

The two most notable splinter webs were two coalitions, one to promote vote annulment at elections, and one to improve urban life in Guadalajara. Use of new communications technologies, particularly through the Internet, was a key component of campaigns and activities in both cases. For instance, both used videos on YouTube, Facebook pages with information and lists of events, and messages and calls for action on Twitter. They also benefited from P39's debates on many topics.

The vote annulment coalition emerged as a small local group seeking similar initiatives in other countries and cities and preparing to publicize its arguments. Its premise was that politicians, regardless of their political party or supposed ideology, were unwilling to act for the public good within government; therefore, it was best to annul one's vote as a clear message of discontent with the political class. This message found fertile ground in many small groups around the country, and the movement snowballed into a national one. Ciro, Javier, and Sandra actively participated in this splinter group, organizing press conferences and different multimedia products to spread its message. The movement's timing a few months before the July 2009 federal elections filled the atmosphere with expectations stoked by the media frenzy around political campaigns. The coalition's activities and messages thus had considerable media coverage. Sandra was adamant about the importance of organizing gatherings at which activists from different parts of the country could meet each other. Five meetings were held in different cities, and live streaming of debates via the Internet enabled the virtual participation of many activists who could not attend in person. On election day, more than 5 percent of votes were annulled nationwide, and twice that in Mexico City.

The second notable network, driven by several P39 members, took longer to establish. This broad web of organizations and individuals seeking to improve life in Guadalajara first coalesced around opposition to an elevated toll road to be built on top of a railway. The scene portrayed at the start of this chapter was from a meeting held in December 2010. A few months thereafter, the network succeeded in stopping what appeared to be a construction project that the incumbent governor had taken for granted. Several environmental and urban rights groups had pointed out that this public work would not only divide the city but also stimulate growth in the number of cars. By managing to assemble a far-reaching coalition including professional guilds and influential independent politicians, this network established a clear need for public dialogue on urban policies. Both splinter webs seemed to apply much of the learning gained from P39, even though this original network had apparently fallen into oblivion after three years of existence.

During my fieldwork within P39, my contributions to the network and its many projects constantly raised questions about my role as an observer. In most sessions dedicated to analysis and debate, my participation was limited to providing a basic analysis of situations or giving my opinion on current situations. I also helped organize the first meeting to denounce the criminalization of protest. When pressed to take part in on-the-ground protests or activism, I refused, explaining that my contribution was more analytical than practical. At the end of my fieldwork, I wrote an article about P39 and sent it to all the participants involved (Acosta 2012). It emphasized the basic contradiction I found in apparently aspiring to improve public dialogue while also dismissing government officials as appropriate interlocutors. Such a radical position, I argued, reduced the chances of dialogue that could achieve the network's aims. The lesson of this critique was that merely criticizing was not enough — it was also necessary to try to engage government officials in dialogue. Moreover, the dialogue P39 had achieved was restricted to a small circle of activists who were the most assiduous participants in meetings and seemed closed to other viewpoints. These lessons seemed to prove useful to the new splinter networks created after P39.

Further analyses led me to reflect on the performative character of dialogue. Dialogue cannot consist of mere statements of intent. It is a practice that takes time to improve (Weigand 2008). Should I have allowed for a more balanced analysis with this in mind? When used as a brand, the concept of dialogue risks being used in a sense different from its intended meaning, as happened with the concept of democracy in Mexico. The next part of this chapter considers this possibility in the light of a sociocultural context dominated by patron-client relations and lies.

Contested Discourses of Democracy

The Mexican public sphere is swamped with references to democracy. Often used to ascribe political legitimacy to government, the concept also functions as an adjective akin to "fair treatment" or "justice" in other spheres of life. Though its meaning is both elusive and contested, it has come to symbolize moral conduct. The difference between the concept's use in Mexico and elsewhere is that Mexico has had very little experience of anything close to democracy. Though one of the earliest legally formed modern states, it underwent a violent period in the nineteenth century, followed by a dictatorship at the turn of the twentieth and then a single-party authoritarian regime until the turn of the millennium. Only in the year 2000 did an opposition party win the federal presidency, despite competitive elections taking place around the country since the late 1980s. Throughout this difficult history, little effort has been expended to develop a mature institutional democracy. Yet for more than a century, "democracy" has been part of the official discourse of government functionaries and political parties. Their use of the concept seems to show a need for legitimacy on the one hand, and for creation of ongoing uncertainty among the national population on the other. The former use seems designed for foreigners' and historians' eyes; the latter, for a local population characterized by low levels of open criticism.

Lately, numerous independent groups have increasingly touted the concept of democracy as their guiding principle. Groups like those depicted here contest the interpretation of democracy by insisting on a meaning they adhere to. With ongoing meetings and activities, they present an alternative understanding of political practice to convince others to demand changes to the way the government is run. Meanwhile, the discourse of democracy that Mexican government officials continually use in activities and speeches contrasts starkly with the way actual decisions are taken regarding public matters. This follows a global trend of abuses of the term, or "brand" (Maeckelbergh 2009: 140). Guadalajara's political system may well be considered a case of illiberal democracy, which entails the use of state democratic institutions for private purposes (Zakaria 1997). Widespread corruption motivates those in power to ensure their ongoing access to public finances and information, which in turn means a monopoly of power by a small elite (González Llaca 2005; Lomnitz 1996). All the while, the long, difficult process of democratization unfolds like a drama in which actors and staging demonstrate various potential developments without a clear, forthright formula to pave the way (Whitehead 2002). These assessments do not intend to denigrate Mexico's political system, but rather to provide a context for understanding the uses of the concept of "democracy" for those involved in P39. Having identified "public dialogue" as the key concept behind its efforts and advanced it in meetings and interviews, P39 offered an appealing concept at a time of social unrest. But in limiting itself to providing simply a concept with related ideas and reflections, did it foster a potential "branding" of dialogue?

Although P39 did not use the word dialogue in any of its campaigns, its meaning and implications were evident in its actions and those of its splinter webs. As a central part of the network structure of what activists themselves called "the movement," it had two main purposes: (1) as described at various meetings, it was a less hierarchical, more horizontal strategy to ensure a reinvention of democracy within the movement itself (Maeckelbergh 2009); and (2) it was the key to avoiding co-optation or easy demobilization of the group's leadership. In power struggles in Mexico, co-optation has been a common strategy whereby one group, usually the power holder, convinces the leader or leaders of a critical faction to join it or lead its group on a different path. Although this is doubtless a common political strategy in many places and contexts, in Mexico it has resulted in a deep mistrust of leaders in general. Suspicion of political co-optation, coercion, and persecution in Mexico is a legacy of colonial times, reinforced by the authoritarian regime that followed the Mexican Revolution. Groups critical of those in power thus tend to rely on "loose connections," as Martin's ethnography of popular movements in Mexico suggests (Martin 2005).

Dialogue was therefore considered an essential ingredient of the concept of democracy promoted by P39, in which public dialogue would improve the process of handling disagreement. The splinter webs issued various, constant calls for public dialogue on different issues. During the campaigns for vote annulment, for example, activists asked people on the street whether their so-called representatives heeded their opinions and demands or aired them in government debates. The urban improvement network, for its part, published a newspaper ad criticizing the toll road in Guadalajara and demanding a public dialogue before any decision was taken. All these uses portray the concept of dialogue as conducive to the improvement of democratic procedures. Other uses of the term by individual organizations, however, proved contradictory. One P39 member group, staging a camping protest against a bridge it saw as unnecessary and likely to increase pollution and traffic, demanded more investment in public transport and cycle paths instead of construction of more infrastructure for cars. One of this campaign's slogans, "bridges for dialogue," appeared without clarification of what this meant. The bridge was built, and there was no dialogue with government officials on the group's aims and ultimate ideals for better public transport. In this sense, misuse of the concept may have produced contradictory ideas, causing a backlash against an organization.

Use of the concept of dialogue therefore resembles use of the notion of democracy. As with the latter, government officials use the former to legitimize their decisions on public spending or projects. Public servants commonly call for dialogue when conflicts arise, but when addressing objections by citizens' groups, the dialogues are simulated. "I think that most of our government officials first take decisions and then bring them out for a supposed public dialogue ... all they want therefore is applause, not dialogue," Holger told me in an interview, reflecting on his experience with public officeholders. "We want to participate in dialogues in order to take decisions with the government; it should be part of the governing process," he added. Many other activists involved in P39 and other networks in Guadalajara seem to share this opinion. Citizens' groups therefore claim the moral high ground of truly representing the diversity of interests in society at large. The thorny issue of representation is not in the scope of this chapter, but it is one of the conceptual problems behind what is known as organized civil society. The point is easily criticized from outside. Government officials often dismiss currents of opposition by questioning the merit of denunciations by small organizations in a city of millions.

Independent critical groups are also vulnerable to spiral into believing that regardless of any opposing views, theirs are the correct ones because "those in power" dismiss them. This susceptibility extends to the appropriation of concepts as open as "dialogue" and "democracy." By assuming that activists' interpretation of a concept's meaning is the correct one, such groups would be following a path similar to that of the government officials they criticize. The main issue here—what I term "knowledge as dogma"—is, I believe, relatively common in Mexico. In a society where patron-client relations are still common and new political scenarios often reproduce old formulas that reinforce hierarchical arrangements, people find it easier to follow a few self-proclaimed leaders than to agree on ways to negotiate a path for all.

Constant misuse of terms in Mexican public life caused it to be termed "a country of lies" (Sefchovich 2008). Through a detailed discourse analysis of public data from various Mexican government offices, Sefchovich reveals systematic use of lies as official strategy. In this situation, individuals or associations made little to no effort to inquire further about dubious official data sets or disclosures or prove them wrong. One of the organizations involved in P39 suffered greatly from this state of affairs when it denounced dangerously high levels of pollution in a suburban town, only to be dismissed by various government offices aided by supposed experts who denied the veracity of any proof presented by the organization's supporters. Different universities and their own experts got involved, trying to mediate and offer an unbiased assessment, but in vain. This points to a weak sense of what is credible. In such a context, how can dialogue exist?

Analysis of the observed network also has implications for the view of the national-level situation. Debates and diagnoses at P39 meetings often referred to a longing for a renewed sense of polity. The idea of fostering dialogues to achieve it therefore fulfills the common aspiration of grassroots participation in a dialogic process. New media, with their multiplication of channels, have renewed a sort of public sphere in which numerous arguments are displayed and debated with unprecedented scale and range.

An increasing critical mass of better-educated individuals is more vociferously demanding changes to state structures. The critical voice of P39 demanded change in government officials' handling of dissent in their projects and plans. In doing so, it reified the figure of the state. This is not a case, therefore, of society fighting against the state (Clastres 1977) or keeping it at bay (Shah 2007), but more an effort to orient the state to the demands of its critical population (Maeckelbergh 2009). In this context, a research project like mine can provide insights into how groups like P39 and its splinter networks reinvent themselves in terms of discourse and action.

Perhaps, though, explanations of more complex nuances of performance and meaning are what need improving. As Eder (2009) pointed out, it is relevant to differentiate civil society groups' vision, practice, and staging. The actual messages that activists use in their campaigns and performances shape each of these three processes differently. In doing so, they affect the public sphere that tries to achieve the changes sought in public decision-making. They are attempting to open various routes to imagining the potential future of a community. But as in any other good deed, is righteous discourse enough? Does identifying a dialogue reproduce government demobilization strategies by generating a concept-brand bandwagon?

In a complicated sociopolitical process like the one portrayed, where a long history of power abuses intertwines with grassroots resistance, public anthropology offers mixed results. When subject to activists' agenda and demands, researchers risk producing a superficial analysis of the situation. But an analysis that is too far from the group observed risks irrelevance. The potential contribution of our discipline lies in its thorough analyses of cultural inheritances and ongoing processes. The experience portrayed in this chapter taught me that our discipline's most effective public use is to clarify that analysis can be provided in two stages: a preliminary probe for the group to reflect on, and a further in-depth interpretation that considers the subsequent process of immersion and public engagement during the research project. The first stage could help shape the second by clarifying certain issues and relations. The second may offer a thick description through exhaustive scrutiny of the implications of the situations observed. Explaining this two-tier process may help researchers both face inquisitive members of observed groups and organize ideas for further analysis. Anthropological scrutiny need not conform to the agendas of studied groups, but it should not ignore them either. To prove the public relevance of our endeavor, we must be able not only to provide analysis down the line, but also to give something back when it is useful.

Raúl Acosta completed his doctoral degree in Social Anthropology at the University of Oxford with a thesis on the internal politics of advocacy networks in the Brazilian Amazon and in the Mediterranean. He is currently Research Associate at the Zukunftskolleg, and teaching fellow at the Department of History and Sociology at the University of Constance. He has worked as a lecturer in ITESO University, in Guadalajara, Mexico; and a researcher at the University of Deusto, in Bilbao, Spain. His main interests are in political anthropology, specifically activism, advocacy, liberation theology, urban governance, the political, and the social construction of what is public.

References

Acosta, Raúl. 2007. "Managing Dissent: Advocacy Networks in the Brazilian Amazon and the Mediterranean." Ph.D. diss. University of Oxford.

———. 2012. "Calidad Del Diálogo Público Según Una Red De Organizaciones Ciudadanas En Jalisco." In *El Diálogo Como Objeto De Estudio: Aproximaciones a Un Proceso Cotidiano Y Su Calidad,* ed. Raúl Acosta, 359–378. Guadalajara: ITESO.

Bakhtin, Mikhail Mikhailovich. 1981. *The Dialogic Imagination: Four Essays,* ed. Michael Holquist. Austin: University of Texas Press.

Butler, Udi Mandel. 2009. "Notes on a Dialogical Anthropology." *Anthropology in Action* 16, no. 3: 20–31.

Clastres, Pierre. 1977. *Society against the State.* Oxford: Blackwell.

Clifford, James. 1983. "On Ethnographic Authority." *Representations* 2: 118–146.

Dwyer, Kevin. 1977. "On the Dialogic of Field Work." *Dialectical Anthropology* 2, no. 1: 143–151.

———. 1979. "The Dialogic of Ethnology." *Dialectical Anthropology* 4, no. 3: 205–224.

Eder, Klaus. 2009. "The Making of a European Civil Society: 'Imagined,' 'Practised' and 'Staged.'" *Policy & Society* 28, no. 1: 23–33.

Eriksen, Thomas H. 2006. *Engaging Anthropology: The Case for a Public Presence.* Oxford: Berg.

González Llaca, Edmundo. 2005. *Corrupción: Patología Colectiva.* Mexico: Instituto Nacional de Administración Pública.

Gurdin, Julie E. 1994. "The Dialogic and the Semiotic: Bakhtin, Volosinov, Peirce, and Sociolinguistics." *Arizona Anthropologist* 11: 57–59.

Handler, Richard. 1985. "On Dialogue and Destructive Analysis: Problems in Narrating Nationalism and Ethnicity." *Journal of Anthropological Research* 41, no. 2: 171–182.

Hendry, Joy. 2007. "Building Bridges, Common Ground, and the Role of the Anthropologist." *Journal of the Royal Anthropological Institute* 13, no. 3: 585–601.

Hermans, Hubert J.M. 2001. "The Dialogical Self: Toward a Theory of Personal and Cultural Positioning." *Culture & Psychology* 7, no. 3: 243–281.

Lomnitz, Claudio. 1996. "Ritual, Rumor Y Corrupción En La Formación Del Espacio Nacional En México." *Revista Mexicana de Sociología* 59, no. 2: 21–51.

Maeckelbergh, Marianne. 2009. *The Will of the Many: How the Alterglobalisation Movement Is Changing the Face of Democracy.* London: Pluto Press.

Martin, JoAnn. 2005. *Tepoztlán and the Transformation of the Mexican State: The Politics of Loose Connections.* Tucson: University of Arizona Press.

Morgan, Bronwen. 2004. "Water: Frontier Markets and Cosmopolitan Activism." *Soundings: A Journal of Politics and Culture* 27: 10–24.

Mosse, David. 2006. "Anti-Social Anthropoogy? Objectivity, Objection, and the Ethnography of Public Policy and Professional Communities." *Journal of the Royal Anthropological Institute* 12, no. 4: 935–956.

Sefchovich, Sara. 2008. *País De Mentiras: La Distancia Entre El Discurso Y La Realidad En La Cultura Mexicana.* México: Océano.

Shah, Alpa. 2007. "'Keeping the State Away': Democracy, Politics, and the State in India's Jharkhand." *Journal of the Royal Anthropological Institute* 13, no. 1: 129–145.

Shotter, John. 1999. "Life inside the Dialogically Structured Mind: Bakhtin's and Volosinov's Account of Mind as Out in the World between Us." In *The Plural Self: Multiplicity in Everyday Life,* ed. John Rowan and Mick Cooper. London: Sage.

Surrallés, Alexandre. 2003. "Face to Face: Meaning, Feeling and Perception in Amazonian Welcoming Ceremonies." *Journal of the Royal Anthropological Institute* 9, no. 4: 775–791.

Tedlock, Dennis. 1979. "The Analogical Tradition and the Emergence of a Dialogical Anthropology." *Journal of Anthropological Research* 35, no. 4: 387–400.

———. 1987. "Questions Concerning Dialogical Anthropology." *Journal of Anthropological Research* 43, no. 4: 325–337.

Van Meijl, Toon. 2006. "Multiple Identifications and the Dialogical Self: Urban Maori Youngsters and the Cultural Renaissance." *Journal of the Royal Anthropological Institute* 12, no. 4: 917–933.

Weigand, Edda, ed. 2008. *Dialogue and Rhetoric.* Amsterdam: John Benjamins.

Werbner, Richard. 2004. *Reasonable Radicals and Citizenship in Botswana: The Public Anthropology of Kalanga Elites.* Bloomington: Indiana University Press.

Whitehead, Laurence. 2002. *Democratization: Theory and Experience.* Oxford: Oxford University Press.

Zakaria, F. 1997. "The Rise of Illiberal Democracy." *Foreign Affairs* 76, no. 6: 22.

Chapter 10

WHAT EVERYBODY SHOULD KNOW ABOUT NATURE-CULTURE

Anthropology in the Public Sphere and "The Two Cultures"

———— ⬯⬯⬯ ————

Thomas Hylland Eriksen

In more than two decades as a teacher of anthropology at the university level, preceded by ten years as a student and junior researcher, I have yet to come across an anthropology student who has never considered the possibilities of using knowledge to make the world a slightly better place to live. Indeed, the wish to understand the world in order to change it, to paraphrase Marx, may be a major source of motivation for many beginning students.

Then the weeks, months, and years go by. Coursework, reading, exams, fieldwork training, more reading, perhaps burgeoning academic ambitions, and increased knowledge of the pleasures and challenges of academic life gradually transform the initial idealism into competitive professionalism. Some end up ensconced in the stimulating cocoon of academic life, where new knowledge is produced, theories confronted, methods refined—and new cohorts of students taught. However, as the contributions to this book suggest, the academic cocoon can come to resemble a closed circuit, and many highly professional, skilled academic researchers verge on forgetting why they started to do anthropology in the first place.

A public anthropology that makes a difference in the human condition need not be activist in character, or advocate certain policies, or embed itself in a social movement. These options are certainly interesting, but they also present their own dilemmas, amply documented in several of this book's chapters. Indeed, knowledge and ideas may themselves contribute to changing the world through shifts in perspective and participation in the collective endeavor of expanding our horizons sufficiently to see the human world as a whole. This requires serious reflection on *what* we are saying to *whom*, and *how* we are saying it. Alas, in recent years academic anthropologists have mostly forgone this opportunity to concentrate instead on problems internal to the discipline, academically defined. Meantime, vigorous, skillful popularization has given neoliberal, xenophobic, and reductionist views of humanity currency as "real science." Anthropologists, who ought to be the foremost scientific interpreters of the human condition in all its diversity and unity, have been busy doing other things.

Anthropological perspectives on minorities, human nature, morality, multiculturalism, and development, to mention just a handful of topics, could in fact make a difference: we have the power to make the world slightly wiser and more humane. This chapter's story line concerns controversies about human nature. While speaking of hugely successful popularizers outside of anthropology, I envision a public anthropology that might have been just as successful, given the appropriate toolbox and a collective memory mindful of why anthropology mattered in the first place.

Preamble: A Nasty Piece of Bad Publicity

In the spring of 2010, Norwegian state television, by far the most viewed channel in the country, broadcast a series of six programs on popular science. The series, called *Hjernevask* (Brainwash), spawned an unprecedented flurry of lively and generally heated debates—about nature and nurture, biology and social science, gender and intelligence—that reached far beyond the usual audience for this kind of topic. From tabloid newspapers to prime-time televised debates and lunchtime conversations in university common rooms, the programs, the journalists' approaches, the statements scientists made in interviews, and the resulting shifts in symbolic power in the Norwegian public sphere (whether temporary or long-term it is too early to tell) were scrutinized and debated countrywide, via every conceivable media channel, for almost a year. Never before had the principles of science and epistemological issues been discussed with such fervor and engagement in the popular media.

Surprising? Yes and no. It is worth noting that the presenter of the show, a man in his forties named Harald Eia, is one of the country's most popular TV comedians. Also, the series was based on a simple, intuitively understandable contrast—nature versus nurture—and had a distinctly confrontational style. Typically, social scientists would be asked, apparently innocently, whether they believed, say, gender characteristics to be inherited or socially constructed. They might answer, oblivious of the context into which their statements would be placed, that social constructedness is essential, and they would sometimes dismiss biological or evolutionary accounts as ideological, dated, or simply wrong. In the next segment, Mr. Eia would typically talk to an American evolutionary psychologist (Steven Pinker appeared regularly) who explained why, as a matter of fact, scientific research pointed to the conclusion that nature trumps nurture, and that a Darwinian approach to human life is the only road to true insight. Truth, the shows told the viewer, is superior to political correctness, and truth is to be found in a positivist interpretation of Darwinism. As the Dean of the Faculty of Theology, Professor Trygve Wyller drily remarked later (personal communication, 2011), the main problem with this kind of popular science is it gives the impression that nothing exists that cannot be measured.

One or two of the programs had been aired and controversy was raging across the country when I ran into my vice dean for research on my way to the office. As we waited for the elevator, she said in an unequivocal tone of voice that well, it could not be denied that this kind of show was bad news for us social scientists. The programs' none-too-subtle meta-message was that by failing to incorporate evolutionary theory properly into their work, humanities scholars and social scientists had lost their way. Accordingly, they tended to produce uninformed guesswork and ideologically motivated texts with flimsy foundations in scientific method, based on debatable interpretations of empirical facts. Large segments of the public sphere received these conclusions with perceptible glee: the learned professors were finally exposed as dilettantes without specialist knowledge worth heeding, pompously parading in the emperor's new clothes. In a public sphere where anti-intellectualism is endemic, this discovery was a major selling point for the show. It told the public that there were simple answers to complex questions—in other words, there was no reason to labor over the long catalogue of arcane thinkers from Adorno to Zizek; Darwin and his present-day prophets had all the answers, and they were all simple and straightforward. Darwinism was a "universal acid" (Dennett 1995) that melted away all the ultimately futile and unnecessary complexity, replacing it with a handful of lucid questions that could be answered by way of simple quantitative methods.

The journalists of the program were no newcomers to academia. Harald Eia's researcher and co-writer of the series, Ole-Martin Ihle, holds an MA in cultural studies from New York University and took anthropology courses at my department. Eia himself holds a higher degree in sociology from the early 1990s, when he wrote a dissertation inspired by Bourdieu's *Distinction* about the transformations of taste in the Norwegian upper class. Whereas art had a generation ago been discussed in a qualified way based on aesthetic theory, paintings were now exclusively evaluated as investment objects (Eia 1992). In the preamble to the *Brainwash* series, Eia claimed to feel cheated by his alma mater, where for years his instructors had taught him the view that biological explanations had no place in research on society and culture. He said he had believed this throughout his studies and for some time afterward before discovering neo-Darwinism and evolutionary psychology, which appeared to unlock all the doors that sociology's oblique and fuzzy perspectives had kept closed.

Eia's intermittent comedy shows since the late 1990s have always revealed his grounding in sociology. His jokes and skits tend to interrogate the categories of everyday life, place persons slightly out of context, or make reflexive meta-comments on the genre of the comedy show itself. Labeled "intelligent humor," his work is visibly inspired by Erving Goffman's classic depictions of "role play." Interviews on his popular science program continued to rely on methods learned from Goffman (1959) and other interactionists (e.g., Garfinkel 1984), exaggerating his role as a naïve, sympathetic interviewer to get the criminologists and gender researchers to relax and confess to him that, for example, they had never actually sat and read biology, considering it irrelevant to their own work. The programs led to the conclusion that the kind of knowledge obtained through IQ testing is more valuable than a truckload of Bourdieu (as Mr. Eia himself once baldly put it).

Thus our vice dean saw the *Brainwash* programs as bad news for humanities and social science people, though eventually she wisely added, "in the short run." Lampooning of the *Brainwash* kind can in fact serve as a call to arms or a reminder that social scientists cannot take their intellectual authority for granted in a public sphere increasingly dominated by scholars with a background in evolutionary theory. We could not but conclude that a PR strategy was overdue.

The *Brainwash* programs applied a meta-frame of evolutionary discourse to perspectives from social science, giving the impression that standard social science was unscientific and incorrect. However, the questioned social scientists and humanities scholars also demonstrated a near total lack of interest in evolutionary theory. Some of them, probably unwisely, expressed not just ignorance of natural science but total uninterest in it.

Against a backdrop of mutual hostility or indifference between natural and social scientists, and acknowledging that the *Brainwash* series is but one symptom of the latter's loss of symbolic capital in the last two decades, one might ask what went wrong in the first place. Dialogue, interdisciplinarity, and mutual curiosity had thrived from Tylor and Morgan's days until World War II. Without going into the historical circumstances of the ensuing segregation, I shall argue that a closer relationship with evolutionary biologists, this time based on respect and ideals of complementarity rather than one-upmanship and suspicion, is key to a better public understanding of social science.

The Meaning of Research

In *Open the Social Sciences*, Immanuel Wallerstein and his interdisciplinary team of collaborators (Wallerstein et al. 1996) showed how the present-day social sciences were shaped by particular historical circumstances requiring certain forms of knowledge and a division of labor that appeared reasonable then, but perhaps not now. The professionalization of economics, political science, sociology, and social anthropology in the late nineteenth and early twentieth centuries created disciplinary boundaries; eventually a broad range of institutions, from annual conferences to scientific journals, developed to represent and guard particular disciplines' borders. The book, originally a report commissioned by the Gulbenkian Commission, called for radical rethinking of the boundaries defining disciplines in relation to questions at hand. Careful consideration of twentieth-century intellectual and social developments, they argued, may well lead to the conclusion that the established academic boundaries are in fact obsolete and counterproductive.

Over the last decade or so, I have engaged in two major interdisciplinary endeavors. The research program Cultural Complexity in the New Norway (2004–2010, www.culcom.uio.no), funded by the University of Oslo, brought together scholars and advanced students from a dozen academic disciplines. Once the group was consolidated, it became clear that shared topical interests in cultural change and complexity by far overshadowed differences in methodology and, somewhat, the theoretical references defining individual disciplines' boundaries. For example, musicologists working with hybrid styles and folk music soon found common interests with linguists studying changes in everyday spoken language on the ethnically complex East Side of Oslo. Disagreements tended to be fruitful and generate new insights. In our recurring discussions about normative and purely analytical approaches, for instance, the disciplines—theology, history, philosophy, social anthropology, and so on—might give different, but also similar answers.

The second endeavor, perhaps both less and more complex than the cultural complexity program, consists of long-term but low-level collaboration with a biologist at my home university, Prof. Dag O. Hessen. In the late 1990s, we co-wrote a book about selfishness (Eriksen and Hessen 1999), and we recently finished another joint book on competition in nature and culture (Hessen and Eriksen 2012). Working conceptually and empirically with a biologist has taught me that searching for common denominators may often expand rather than restrict the scope of enquiry. In studying selfishness, we spent considerable time exploring the implications of the congruence between the reciprocity principle as developed by Mauss, Polanyi, and others, and theories on mutual aid and collaboration in nature. Similarly, we discussed how the controversy around group selection in biology could shed light on political structures in tribal societies and vice versa. And our recent joint work, based loosely and often metaphorically on evolutionary theory's "Red Queen" principle, which posits a need to evolve in order to "stay in the same place" (Ridley 1994), has compared technological change, academic one-upmanship, and teeth whitening to the peacock's tail, the Irish giant deer, and mating "strategies" among freshwater fish. Avoiding reduction of one to the other, we tried to establish how far parallels and analogies between fields hold up before either merging or taking separate paths. Simply, we tried to ask fundamental intellectual questions without raising questions about academic turfs and boundaries on the way. I commend this method to others, although they should bear in mind that the outcome is highly uncertain and has no obvious merit-building academic outlet. The book on competition, like the one on selfishness, has been published as a trade book for the general reader.

Universities have always been irrelevant, but today they must find new ways to do so. At best, they operate by the formula "the more irrelevant, the more relevant." As Fredrik Barth once said, "The difference between basic research and applied research is that basic research is so much more applicable" (Barth, personal communication). On the other hand, applied research that is good may be used to solve a given set of problems. For example, a government that pays a research group to conduct an overview of fish consumption in different groups in the population may, following due delivery of answers (e.g., northern people eat more fish than southern people, women more than men, those older than forty more than the young), task a responsible agency with developing campaigns to change the behavior of groups that eat less fish.

On the other hand, a basic research project might ask about the role of fish in culture more generally and offer tentative answers about masculinity (fish is feminine), notions about grossness (fish are slimy and stink), health (fish is not fattening), or virility (fish is an aphrodisiac). From there, it might develop an argument concerning fish's place in cultural history, notions about food in general, or theories of classification (fish, meat, plant food, religious taboos and warnings, etc.) and social differentiation (posh people eat raw fish; the working class wants it battered and fried). These hypothetical examples illustrate the possibilities of basic research.

A background in basic research is needed to carry out a good applied research project. Admittedly, most university students will go on to jobs with no research component, but it is equally true that their studies should give them knowledge they can draw on, for pleasure and utility, for the rest of their lives. In this regard, the above formula remains valid: The more experience-distant and arcane the knowledge, the more fields there are where it can be transformed into something experience-near and relevant. One needs abstract concepts to understand the concrete. This is why Plato does not come with a use-by date.

Many anthropology students have trouble understanding why they need to learn about topics they are never going to work on. Someone who wants to become, say, a Latin Americanist might not read more than the absolute minimum about Polynesian kinship. A scholar whose passion lies in understanding gender differences cross-culturally does not waste time delving into the cultural grammar of Swedish municipal politics. But given time, the best of these students grasp how reading about Melanesian garden magic can help them understand popular religiosity in Sicily, how studies of clan feuds in southern Sudan in the 1930s may shed light on the Balkan civil wars of the 1990s, and why it is relevant to know why New Guineans do not classify the cassowary as a bird, even if one's real interest is West European understandings of the whale.

A properly educated person knows something about what unites and what separates people, and after some empirical exploration is often able to discern similarities in pattern and content, as well as fundamental cultural differences. A properly educated person also knows that simple answers to complex questions are rarely satisfactory. Able to draw on diverse sources and aware that several kinds of knowledge exist, this person sees any issue from several perspectives, approaching problems from many angles before drawing conclusions. Only a barbarian can believe that a single kind of theory or a single kind of scientific method can generate all the answers one wants or needs. Education, in the full sense of the word (as in the German *Bildung*), should strengthen and shape the ability to think several thoughts simultaneously without mixing them up. This presupposes, as Gregory Bateson might have put it, that one simultaneously has something to think *with* and something to think *about*.

On Duckrabbits and Jigsaws

Tendencies toward academic withdrawal and disciplinary boundary maintenance are a major problem militating against the above view of education. Public debates, notably about the nature/nurture complex, continuously reveal such territorial demarcations and unintentional demonstrations of mutual ignorance. Ideally, introductory courses at the undergraduate level would include a mandatory component demonstrating some of the virtues of interdisciplinarity. Just as schoolchildren in many countries are now taught to respect people whose cultural background differs from their own, university students should, in the spirit of multicultural coexistence, learn about the unique contributions of various disciplines and professions.

Were this idea realized in a responsible and suitably thorough way, much unnecessarily spent energy would be saved for other tasks. For example, evolutionary scientists would be hard put to dismiss poststructuralist theories of gender as pretentious rubbish, whereas poststructuralists could no longer claim that everything evolution teaches about gender is speculative and ideologically biased. Instead, they all might cultivate the capability to see production of knowledge in the university as a jigsaw puzzle of cosmic dimensions and astonishing difficulty, where one's own piece snaps into place with a tiny click—or a wallop, if need be—and everybody agrees that essential pieces will still (and might always) be missing when the picture appears properly.

Many of us presumably hope that between the corner pieces of philosophy, theory of science, and mathematics, a considerable part of the edge hangs loosely together thanks to logic, methodology, and belief in human reason. Meanwhile, the vast internal space is only patchily filled in. A few years ago, my children and I gave up on assembling a several-thousand-piece puzzle depicting Michelangelo's *The Creation of Adam* long before we finished the Sistine Chapel's cracked ceiling in the background. However, and hearteningly, we quickly succeeded in constructing the entire edge and the detail where God's finger nearly touches Adam's. Similarly, those interdisciplinary moments that expose one to a worldview other than the customary one can generate new forms of knowledge and make the world more exciting than it would otherwise have been.

All university students should be required to learn not only how different methods and different questions lead to different answers, but also that those answers are not necessarily incompatible or competing, but rather like pieces in a jigsaw puzzle. (That some answers are simply wrong is another issue.) One of contemporary academia's most urgent needs, highlighted crudely and insensitively in the *Brainwash* programs, was precisely formulated as early as 1959 in C.P. Snow's famous essay "The Two Cultures" (Snow 1993 [1959], which is probably more often cited than actually read). Though especially outraged at humanities scholars' prevalent lack of interest in the natural sciences, Snow admitted that the ignorance and indifference went both ways.

Sometimes, different perspectives on the same phenomenon are like the duckrabbit, an odd creature sketched by Wittgenstein in *Philosophical Investigations* (Wittgenstein 1983 [1958]) that can look like a duck and like a rabbit, but not simultaneously. If Wittgenstein is right, different perspectives on the world may be incommensurable. There is no synthesizing gaze on the drawing that encompasses both the duck and the rabbit at once, to give a total experience of the complexity of the drawing. One must accept alternating between the duck and the rabbit as two distinctive perspectives on the world.

What one ends up seeing, however, depends on what one is looking for. Whereas some see the internal incompatibility of the duckrabbit, others may discover complementarity or promised future syntheses. Moreover, a result of incompatibility sometimes means the question is wrongly asked. In our co-written book on selfishness, Hessen and I initially asked naively whether human beings are intrinsically selfish or altruistic—a classic theme in social theory and research. As the argument proceeded, with examples taken from nature, politics, and everyday life in contexts ranging from the avian world (group selection) to rush traffic (the zipper principle

Figure 10.1. The duckrabbit

when two lanes merge), and from the history of social philosophy (including a reassessment of the lamentably misunderstood Adam Smith) and neo-Darwinian games theory, it slowly became clear that the original question was wrongly phrased: human beings cannot be either selfish or altruistic, for altruism is present in even the apparently most selfish acts, while the most self-sacrificing activity contains an element of self-interest. Human beings resemble duckrabbits in this respect.

Ships Passing in the Night: Perspectives on Kinship

In the recurring and ongoing debates about nature and nurture that have been a cornerstone of scientific controversy at least since Darwin's time, the discussants clearly often talk past one another, almost like Wittgensteinian ships passing in the night. They do so at least partly because they do not know each other's disciplines from the inside. Humanities scholars, natural scientists, and social scientists alike often behave as though, upon receiving a hammer as a gift, they set out to wander the world, hitting everything in sight in hopes that the whole planet will reveal itself to consist of nails.

The nature of kinship is a classic source of frustration. A typical perspective in sociocultural anthropology would accept that kinship is universal but emphasize the relevance of its cross-cultural variation (see, e.g., Holy 1996). These very variations and local expressions of kinship are what anthropologists typically explore. In the North Atlantic, for instance, cognatic kinship is most common. Among Jews, descent is reckoned through the maternal line, whereas Arabs are patrilineal and prioritize agnatic links. Anthropologists have studied connections between kinship systems, practice, and social organization worldwide. Patrilineal kinship systems in Arab societies entail strong loyalties among brothers and agnatic cousins (i.e., those with a common grandfather) and imply societies where conflicts tend to follow lineage or clan lines. In India, patrilineal kinship entails, among many other things, access to interest-free loans as well as a moral obligation to support brothers' and cousins' children economically. Cognatic kinship among hunter-gatherers in southern Africa, meanwhile, implies a flexible social organization that expands and contracts depending on the current food supply.

Kinship may be based chiefly or exclusively on one or another form of descent, but this is not always the case. In some places—for example, on several Polynesian islands—adoption is widespread, and in some situations persons can, through shared residence or other commonalities, *become* relatives without marriage or blood ties. Some anthropologists have therefore proposed the concept of relatedness as an alternative to kinship, given that in practice, people's strongest moral commitments often are not to the people with whom they have the closest biological relationship. From a biological perspective, kinship is mostly about reproduction and "inclusive fitness" — that is, the furthering of genetic material, which takes biological relatedness into account. If my siblings and cousins share enough genetic material with me to make my supporting them rational, then it is in my interest to secure their reproduction. From this angle, the world's many extant kinship systems represent various solutions to the challenges of reproducing the genetic material of individuals directly and indirectly, that is, through inclusive fitness, helping close kin to reproduce.

Confronted with such a perspective, anthropologists tend to respond that this model does not explain variation, and that the extent to which studied forms of kinship actually promote solidarity between close biological kin varies considerably. That said, the biologists may reply, similarities between kinship systems that clearly emerged independently of each other, frequently on different continents, are strikingly numerous. Even in societies where classificatory kinship is the norm (i.e., the same term applies to every member of the same general unit, be it clan, gender, or generation), people appear to recognize their biological brothers, cousins, and so on. Exceptions may be interesting, according to this argument, but they remain marginal phenomena.

Supporting the evolutionary perspective is the fact that most of the world's peoples have similar notions about blood relatedness and its relevance for socially constructed kinship. Conflicts between households and descent groups are widespread and often expressed through fraught relationships with mothers-in-law, bitter conflicts over inheritance, and complicated negotiations surrounding major family gatherings and rituals. A man is not his wife's family's relative; they are his affines and he is theirs. Social and cultural anthropologists may rightly respond that they are interested in variation as well as actual practices (which often deviate from the given culture's principles and norms), and that this difference in emphasis significantly helps explain the controversies surrounding kinship. Thus some researchers circle the planet, as it were, in a helicopter, taking fisheye photos of huge landscapes, whereas others crawl on all fours, studying every grain of sand in a tiny territory.

A Question of Scale

In 1967, Benoit Mandelbrot, later known for his fractal theory, wrote the article "How Long Is the Coast of Britain?" His general point was simply that the answer depended on the scale of the map. On a map drawn on a

1:50,000 scale, the coast is longer than on one with a 1:100,000 scale, and as Mandelbrot shows, the coastline grows indefinitely when the scale decreases toward zero. Ultimately, one must measure not just every grain of sand, but inlets and irregularities at the subatomic scale.

Differences involving kinship and many other areas where biologists and anthropologists appear to disagree may often be accounted for, and the duckrabbit superseded, by distinguishing between different levels of scale. Many anthropologists still insist that biology is irrelevant to kinship, but I believe they speak against their better knowledge. Biologists and Darwinian social scientists, meanwhile, tend to overlook variation, which can be highly statistically significant, for the sake of the simplicity and parsimony of their explanatory models.

Obviously knowledgeable people offer such different answers to identical questions for at least four reasons. First and perhaps most importantly, they operate on different scales: some find local particularities; others, universals. Phrased differently: answers to the question "What is language?" would range from a generalizing statement to the question "What are the characteristics of language X?" Credible evolutionary accounts explain the omnipresence of language in human society, but Bengalis speak Bengali and not Mandarin because of specific historical and cultural reasons.

Secondly, the scales by which the two types of researchers operate vary not just spatially but also temporally. In a sense, evolutionary biologists watch the hour hand, while historians and archaeologists follow the minute hand and social scientists are mostly concerned with the second hand. An evolutionary approach to kinship might raise the question within the context of human evolution, a temporal horizon whose span ranges from 200,000 years to two million years or more. An anthropological approach would normally study and extrapolate from the situation here and now, whereas historians may explore why and how the kinship systems of, say, Eastern Europe have changed since medieval times.

Thirdly, natural scientists raise the question "What is a human being, seen in objective terms?" Scholars in the humanities and social sciences, for their part, might ask, "What does it mean to be a human being?" To understand the lifeworlds of others, one must use the method of cultural relativism, which, put simply, involves trying to learn to see the world as they see it—not to become one of them, but to become capable of explaining the kind of socially constructed world the X live in to colleagues, students, and others. It is fascinating to explore the Dayaks' ideas about life after death, the Maasai's view of the relationship between money and cattle, or debate among the Ainu in northern Japan on climate change's effects on their environment. Still, these questions do not in themselves generate answers about objective characteristics of humanity.

276 | Thomas Hylland Eriksen

Fourthly, natural scientists typically seek testable hypotheses and are prepared to isolate variables that can be tested so as to establish reliable knowledge about at least some segments of reality. Anthropologists, by contrast, use qualitative and interpretive methods to account for as large a part of reality as possible. The outcome is a richer empirical narrative with a downside of less accurate answers or knowledge whose validity is more locally restricted. The media researcher Marshall McLuhan (1968) —simplifying somewhat, but perceptive as always—once contrasted two "games" typical of scientific enquiry. One seeks unambiguous, precise, parsimonious knowledge, while the other strives for complexity and rich-ness. Science probably "plays" more games than these two, and many intermediate forms exist, but the contrast is illuminating. The belief in a single true method and a single true answer may be credible within some areas of scientific research, but in view of complex phenomena like kin-ship, ethnicity, gender, and class, it is absolutely imperative to furnish oneself with a toolbox containing more than hammers.

A Multidimensional Perspective

The educated person understands the need for a multidimensional view of knowledge without thereby relinquishing faith in reason and criticism. Clifford Geertz was such a person. Arguably the most influential cultural anthropologist in the later twentieth century, Geertz often argued against what he saw as positivist simplification in theorizing on complex cul-tural facts. Many Darwinian social scientists, from the anthropologist-psychologist couple Tooby and Cosmides (1992) to the linguist Pinker (2002), have used Geertz as a *Prügelknabe*, a symbol of all that is wrong in the interpretive social sciences: a typical representative of the deplorable view that humans are "tabulae rasa" without moorings in evolutionary history or their own biological nature. Regarding this background, it is worth discussing Geertz's careful development of his view on the rela-tionship between evolution and culture in two important essays from the early 1960s.

In the first, "The Impact of the Concept of Culture on the Concept of Man," Geertz departed from standard evolutionist accounts by proclaim-ing that "[t]o take the giant step away from the uniformitarian view of hu-man nature is, so far as the study of man is concerned, to leave the Garden [of Eden]" (Geertz 1973a [1964]: 36). He went on to describe, and dismiss, what he called the "stratigraphic" conception of relations between bio-logical, psychological, social, and cultural factors (37). This view presents the human condition as characterized by hierarchical stratification, that is, watertight boundaries between kinds of factors. This is not so, according to Geertz: humans are cultural all the way through. Moreover, universals are empty containers that create an illusion of similarity where in fact there is dramatic variation.

Human evolution, Geertz continued, is characterized by ongoing mutual feedback between culture and biological properties. Humans have a desperate and chronic need for "external control mechanisms" (Geertz 1973a [1964]: 44) embedded in culture. Our lack of fixity means that there is no natural way of being human. This view, which was later elaborated by scholars like Durham (1991) and Richerson and Boyd (2005), is fully compatible with a Darwinist account. Commenting on universals, Geertz (1973a [1964]: 40) considered religion as a candidate but noted the extraordinary difference between "the obsessive ritualism and unbuttoned polytheism of the Hindus and ... the uncompromising monotheism and austere legalism of Sunni Islam." Like Alfred Kroeber before him, Geertz sees alphabetic lists of "universal human traits" as establishing fake universals, mentioning cultural anthropologists from Wissler to Murdock and Kluckhohn as exemplifications (Brown 1991 might be added today).

In the essay titled "The Growth of Culture and the Evolution of the Mind" (Geertz 1973b [1964]), Geertz developed a perspective on the evolution of mind. Beginning with the familiar contrast between freedom and determinism, he approvingly quoted the philosopher Gilbert Ryle's observation that positing the two as opposites is ridiculous, since a golfer can perfectly well be subject to the laws of ballistics, obey the rules of golf, *and* play with elegance (57). Even Steven Pinker could have said that (and in fact, E.O. Wilson once did). Geertz then elaborated on the view of human evolution presented in the previous essay: culture began, embryonically, millions of years ago among proto-humans whose brains were a third the size of ours. Mutual reinforcement, as culture contributed to the growth of the cortex (presumably by changing the circumstances of natural selection) and vice versa, rendered us flexible and generally endowed. "Though it is apparently true enough that the invention of the airplane led to no visible bodily changes, no alterations of (innate) mental capacity, this was not necessarily the case for the pebble tool or the crude chopper, in whose wake seem to have come not only more erect stature, reduced dentition, and a more thumb-dominated hand, but the expansion of the human brain to its present size" (67). Finally: "In fact, this type of reciprocally creative relationship between somatic and extrasomatic phenomena seems to have been of crucial significance during the whole of the primate advance" (68), and "[t]he human brain is thoroughly dependent upon cultural resources for its very operation; and those resources are, consequently, not adjuncts to, but constituents of, mental activity" (76).

In other words, being cultural is the only way to be human, but one cannot be cultural without a body—tendons, neurons, skin, veins, a genome. Having established this insight—that human nature and human culture do not contradict each other but rather create a seamless whole—one faces two sets of choices. First, should nature-culture be seen primarily through the lens of nature or that of culture? Those choosing the first alternative search for common denominators in human behavior and organization, and may proceed far in their work without actually talking to any of the people under study. Those who pick the latter alternative must then decide whether to study Culture with a capital C—that is, what humans have in common—or cultures with a lowercase c, delving into a historical period, specific social environment, or "my tribe"?

I have always advised students to do as much as they can for as long as possible. No matter which specialization they end up choosing or what they decide to leave aside, they have a moral obligation to be aware of the alternatives and know something about the kinds of insights they might have generated.

Turf Wars and Symbolic Power

There is no intrinsic reason for evolutionary theory and sociocultural anthropology to necessarily maintain a competitive relationship over definitional power and intellectual turf. Complementarity could be as close at hand as competition, just as an ecological account of the great theater of evolution is as credible as the selfish-gene account. Besides, a world in the shape of a jigsaw puzzle is more challenging and interesting than one resembling a duckrabbit. Yet breaking down barriers between competing perspectives on humanity may be more difficult than it sounds, and the relationship between sociocultural anthropology and evolutionary science remains tense and knotty in most quarters, as I will illustrate by way of an example and some personal reflections.

A few years ago, I took part in a radio debate with an internationally recognized evolutionary biologist. The topic was an article he had co-authored that tried to demonstrate that evolutionary theory and the concept of inclusive fitness can easily explain the widespread evolutionary phenomenon of gift exchange. He and his co-author argued, briefly, that in Western society, gifts exchanged between close biological kin tend to cost more than gifts exchanged between others, such as friends. During our conversation, I conceded that evolutionary theory may say something important about gift exchange but objected that one would err by assuming that other explanations concerning individual decisions and features of the sociocultural environment can be discarded. I argued that *reasons* may sometimes be *causes*—that the causes of certain actions may actually be the subjective reasons the actors claim motivated them. To find out why people do what they do, one may ask them, and their answers may be both honest and correct. This is not always the case, but the possibility should be considered.

Leaving the radio studio, we kept talking until we reached the parking lot, and I repeated my stance that social and cultural phenomena are in fact so complex that several analytical approaches are needed to fully understand them. The biologist nodded, but added that in a sense, every scientific article can be understood as polemic promoting one particular point of view at the expense of nuance and alternative possibilities. At this, I was slightly taken aback. Should science not endeavor to describe and explain the world in as much detail and as comprehensively as possible, if necessary admitting doubt and uncertainty to avoid conclusions that the data do not support? Apparently not.

Time and again, it happens. Fervent Darwinians, convinced that the theory of evolution can explain everything human, use the currently predominant interpretation of evolutionary theory (natural selection + sexual selection + genetics) as their main analytical tool in analyzing a cultural phenomenon like kinship, religion, art, or music. The result is sometimes curious, typically interesting, usually enlightening, never boring, often irritating, and always incomplete. Academic scholars in, say, religious studies, art history, or musicology who express little interest in these analyses are seen as intellectually stagnant, reactionary, and irrelevant in the wrong way.

This is partly correct. Intellectuals who work with interpretive, semiotic, historical, and other non-evolutionist methods have nothing to lose by taking other approaches seriously, and the gains can be considerable. However, the advice should go in both directions. Those who write about human culture and society from a Darwinian point of view should learn about alternative methods and explanatory models before passing judgment on them.

Authors of Darwinian books on culture and society often begin with a few friendly nods left and right, stating with admirable restraint that, for example, evolutionary theory can only explain 10 percent (Wilson 1975) of culture, or that it is essential to study the interrelationship between biology and culture (Pinker 2002). They then go on, nearly without an exception, to pen texts that ultimately attribute practically everything to evolution. Pinker's bestselling *The Blank Slate* holds not a single example of an empirical circumstance presenting non-Darwinist explanations as the most convincing. Such books obviously testify more to their authors' self-confidence than to their broad and deep knowledge of the social sciences.

Those of us who have not yet seen the light and been converted arouse increasing, perceptible impatience. Rejoinders addressed to doubters of evolutionary theory's relevance in all aspects of social and cultural life often insinuate limited scientific understanding. Unbelievers in the omnipotence of Darwinian evolutionary theory are often lumped with creationists or believers in "intelligent design," that is, people who insist that a God is behind the amazing patterns of nature. It may embarrass an academic scholar to be associated with religious literalists who want to establish equivalence between evolutionary theory and religious myths of origin in the educational system, but the fact is, intelligent design cannot be disproved. The notion of an omnipotent God may be true or false, but it cannot be tested empirically. Because religious concepts and stories therefore do not form part of science, it makes sense for schools to teach religious worldviews in classes that deal with cultural diversity or religion (depending on country), but not in science classes.

Conflating the views of different kinds of skeptics leads to confusion between an ontological position (a worldview, a faith) and epistemological positions (which concern research methods and the kind of knowledge that is ascertainable). One need not hold that *The Origin of Species* and the book of Genesis are alternative, epistemologically equivalent narratives of the origin and evolution of life to be critical of the view that Darwinist explanation tells the whole story about such phenomena as visual art or war.

Many Darwinists painstakingly distance themselves from ideological abuse of the theory of evolution in social Darwinism, eugenics, or even sometimes the Holocaust (it is debatable whether the fervently anti-English Hitler was influenced by Darwin at all, though he would have heard of Darwin's major German evangelist Haeckel). Such criticism implies that Darwinism, when *not* being misused in ideological contexts, is true and good. However, it is hard to completely disentangle science and politics from one another. Although initially an enthusiastic admirer of Darwin's evolutionism, Marx would later write to Engels (Marx 1974 [1862]) that Darwin was himself visibly influenced by the liberal thinking of his time when he wrote of something resembling capitalist competition in nature, and many contemporary interpreters of Darwinism, from Edward O. Wilson (1984) to Matt Ridley (1997), have tried to draw normative conclusions from the theory of evolution. Wilson speaks, for example, about *biophilia* (love of all that lives), which he reckons may be an inherited trait among humans. Ridley proposes that a minimal state and free-market enterprise give people autonomy and a sense of responsibility, creating conditions for healthy social relationships based on reciprocity. Others have drawn very different conclusions. According to Kenan Malik (1999), for example,

Ridley somehow transforms *homo sapiens* into *homo thatcherus* in his book's final chapter. Thought is rarely devoid of normative judgments.

Some have argued that humans (especially men) are genetically conditioned to be warlike (although in fact, there is more peace than war in the world), but the left-leaning Darwinist Marek Kohn (1999) has called for social policy that targets inequalities, since egalitarian societies appear to enjoy better health and lower conflict levels than more hierarchical ones.

The mere fact that Darwinism has inspired both eugenics and social Darwinism shows the scope of its interpretive possibilities. Eugenics proposes strict state control over human reproduction, aimed at preventing degenerate and inferior individuals from reproducing. Social Darwinism proposes the exact opposite: free, unregulated competition.

Many humanities scholars and social scientists are dismayed by the lack of breadth in many natural scientists' education. This response is understandable but inadequate. Evolutionary theory has a lot to teach us all, but allowing it to run the show by itself would be irresponsible at best.

Food and Symbolic Kinship

Lately, some evolutionary scholars have championed "stone-age food," meaning the food humans are assumed to be biologically adapted to: the popular "low-carb" diet rich in meat and fish, berries, mushrooms, nuts, leaves, and wild tubers. Our bodies have only just left the cave, they argue, and we have not had time to adapt to Coca-Cola, white bread, and microwave pizzas.

A few remarks on this view are apropos. First, the agricultural revolution led to a steep increase in population density, making the first towns possible. Without agriculture, there would have been no towns; without towns, no literacy; without literacy, no intellectual class; without an intellectual class, no theory about stone-age diets. (To Socrates' "Know thyself!" I am tempted to add: Know the historical conditions of your own existence!) Second, as there are nearly seven billion of us now, it is hard to see how a general change to stone-age food would make it easier to survive as a human being. Third, people in the part of the world that is saturated with red meat, additives, dairy products, starches, and sweet drinks are longer-lived and healthier than any previous human population. In short, the transition from a stone-age to an agriculture-based diet cannot be seen as a continuous descent into degeneration. (Moreover, grilled meat, presumably a staple of the stone-age diet, appears to contain large amounts of carcinogens.) That said, I must add that although evolutionary theory may seem superfluous to the message that we eat too much sugar and saturated fat in this part of the world, food and evolution can make for exciting reading. An evolutionary perspective on diet is enlightening, but as usual, it is undesirable to confound one piece with the entire puzzle.

Another example indicating the limitations of a purely biological perspective on the human condition, pertains to group belonging, more specifically loyalty to large, abstract communities in which no one can personally know everyone else, such as nations, ethnic groups, and religions. One simple (but fairly common) interpretation of evolutionary theory holds that such communities are a form of kinship that ultimately serves the purpose of preserving and passing on a gene pool in which one owns stock. In other words, cheering for people who are genetically similar to oneself is somehow natural, so ethnic solidarity and racism may therefore be inevitable.

This perspective is empirically important and certainly has considerable commonsense appeal, but solidarity and the formation of abstract groups follow other patterns as well. In India, religion and caste are essential criteria for group formation. Genetically, a Brahmin from North India has more in common with low-caste Muslims from North India than with South Indian Brahmins, but may yet feel stronger solidarity with the latter. In recent decades, the assumed danger of a zealous, intolerant Muslim solidarity that threatens the West has aroused considerable anxiety. Such a religious loyalty may be abstract and full of moral obligations, but it has only a loose, metaphorical connection to biological kinship. A Bosnian may be just as Muslim as an Indonesian, and the two may meet in Mecca or elsewhere, but genetically, a Bosnian is closer to an Irishman than to an Indonesian.

An imam I met in Mauritius in 1986 gave clear expression to the flexibility in human social orientation that Darwinian scholars so often underestimate. When Muslims came to Mauritius from India in the nineteenth century, they spoke Hindi, Urdu, and Bhojpuri. Since the national census of 1972, however, a majority of them have reported Arabic as their *langue ancestrale*. I confronted the friendly imam with this contradiction, and he calmly answered that "yes, biologically, we descend from Indians, that is beyond doubt. But you must remember that we Muslims are deeply religious people, and since Arabic is the language of the Holy Qu'ran, our spiritual descent can be traced back to Arabic speakers." His eloquently phrased response left me tongue-tied. After all, on what criteria could I base a claim that biological descent is more "real" than spiritual descent?

Despite these caveats, evolutionary theory can be helpful indeed in understanding group formation. Even the most abstract communities imaginable depend on metaphors of place (territoriality) and kinship (biological proximity). But because of humans' capacity for abstract thought and inclination to metaphor, the clear tendency to protect one's genetic relatives receives highly varied concrete expression. If genetic proximity were all that counted, nobody would need to fear militant Islamism in Europe or aggressive Pentecostal prosetylizing in India, since both would be impossible.

Similar lines of reasoning may be fruitful in other areas, too. For this reason, competition over symbolic power between scholars from different disciplines is a quite unhelpful, counterproductive tendency. No one should have trouble admitting to not holding a monopoly of interesting knowledge. Certain differences between research traditions might in themselves make interdisciplinary collaboration a dynamic, exciting, unpredictable endeavor.

Darwin's significance for the natural sciences is undoubted. Before Darwin, biology was what Thomas Kuhn (1962) would have described as a "pre-paradigmatic science." The naturalists of earlier generations had merely collected, classified, and speculated, but evolutionary theory—especially after "the new synthesis" with genetics in the 1930s—led biology to develop a powerful theoretical tool capable of identifying and explaining connections and causal chains. Yet this does not mean Darwinism is a "universal acid" rendering all other theories of life, including human life, superfluous. At the same time, I must stress that a toolbox without evolutionary models is just as poor as a toolbox that holds only these same models. Studying the brick foundation does not preclude an interest in the decorative objects on the mantelpiece, but even perfect knowledge about the masonry in the cellar cannot predict wallpaper choice or kitchen fittings.

This we must accept. An educated person, anthropologist or not, cannot afford to relinquish the scientist's most essential qualities: intellectual curiosity and epistemological humility. Armed with appropriate openness and determination alongside the right combination of confidence and humility, anthropology can fulfill its promise of using knowledge to make the world a slightly wiser, slightly more humane place.

Thomas Hylland Eriksen (Ph.D. anthropology, Oslo 1991) is Professor of Social Anthropology at the University of Oslo and Principal Investigator of the ERC Advanced Grant project "Overheating: An Anthropological History of the Early 21st Century" (2012–2017). His research has largely concerned cultural dynamics and social identities in complex societies, and his books in this field include *Ethnicity and Nationalism: Anthropological Perspectives* (2010/1993) and *Common Denominators: Ethnicity and the Politics of Compromise in Mauritius* (1998). He has also published books on globalization, e.g. *Globalization: The Key Concepts* (2014/2007); basic textbooks in anthropology—*Small Places, Large Issues* (2015/1995) and *What is Anthropology?* (2004); and a book about public anthropology, *Engaging Anthropology* (2006). His latest book in English is *Fredrik Barth: An Intellectual Biography* (2015). Eriksen is currently carrying out research on the social and cultural dimensions of coal and gas in Australia.

References

Brown, Donald. 1991. *Human Universals.* New York: McGraw-Hill.
Dennett, Daniel. 1995. *Darwin's Dangerous Idea.* New York: Simon & Schuster.
Durham, William. 1991. *Coevolution: Genes, Culture and Human Diversity.* Stanford, CA: Stanford University Press.
Eia, Harald. 1992. *Lidende ledere og kompetente kalkulatører: Næringslivsfolks symbolske kamper* [Suffering executives and competent calculators: The symbolic struggles of business people]. MA thesis, University of Oslo.
Eriksen, Thomas Hylland, and Dag O. Hessen. 1999. *Egoisme* [Selfishness]. Oslo: Aschehoug.
Garfinkel, Harold. 1984 [1967]. *Studies in Ethnomethodology.* Malden, MA: Blackwell.
Geertz, Clifford. 1973a [1964]. "The Impact of the Concept of Culture on the Concept of Man." In Geertz, *The Interpretation of Cultures.* New York: Basic Books.
———. 1973b [1964]. The Growth of Culture and the Evolution of the Mind. In Geertz, *The Interpretation of Cultures.* New York: Basic Books.
Goffman, Erving. 1959. *The Presentation of Self In Everyday Life.* New York: Anchor Books.
Hessen, Dag O., and Thomas Hylland Eriksen. 2012. *På stedet løp: Om konkurranse i natur og kultur* [The treadmill paradox: On competition in nature and culture]. Oslo: Aschehoug.
Holy, Ladislav. 1996. *Anthropological Perspectives on Kinship.* London: Pluto.
Kohn, Marek. 1999. *As We Know It: Coming to Terms with an Evolved Mind.* London: Granta.
Kuhn, Thomas. 1962. *The Structure of Scientific Revolutions.* Chicago: University of Chicago Press.
Malik, Kenan. 1999. *Man, Beast, and Zombie: What Science Can and Cannot Tell Us About Human Nature.* London: Palgrave.
Mandelbrot, Benoit. 1967. "How Long Is the Coast of Britain? Statistical Self-Similarity and Fractional Dimension." *Science*, N.S., 156: 636–638.
Marx, Karl. 1974 [1862]. "Letter to Engels 18 June 1862." *Marx–Engels Werke* 30: 249. Berlin: Dietz.
McLuhan, Marshall. 1968. *War and Peace in the Global Village.* New York: Bantam Books.
Pinker, Steven. 2002. *The Blank Slate: The Modern Denial of Human Nature.* London: Penguin.
Richerson, Peter J., and Robert Boyd. 2005. *Not by Genes Alone: How Culture Transformed Human Evolution.* Chicago: University of Chicago Press.
Ridley, Matt. 1994. *The Red Queen: Sex and the Evolution of Human Nature.* London: Penguin.
———. 1997. *The Origins of Virtue: Human Instincts and the Evolution of Cooperation.* London: Viking.
Snow, C.P. 1993 [1959]. *The Two Cultures.* Cambridge: Cambridge University Press.
Tooby, John, and Leda Cosmides. 1992. "The Psychological Foundations of Culture." In *The Adapted Mind: Evolutionary Psychology and the Generation of Culture*, ed. Jerome Barkow, Leda Cosmides, and John Tooby. Oxford: Oxford University Press.

Wallerstein, Immanuel, Calestous Juma, Evelyn Fox Keller, Jurgen Kocka, Domenique Lecourt, V. Y. Mudkimbe, Kinhide Miushakoji, Ilya Prigogine, Peter J. Taylor and Michel-Rolph Trouillot. 1996. *Open the Social Sciences: Report of the Gulbenkian Commission on the Restructuring of the Social Sciences.* Stanford: Stanford University Press.

Wilson, Edward O. 1975. *Sociobiology: The New Synthesis.* Cambridge, MA: Harvard University Press.

———. 1984. *Biophilia.* Cambridge, MA: Harvard University Press.

Wittgenstein, Ludwig. 1983 [1958]. *Philosophical Investigations.* Trans. G.E.M. Anscombe. Oxford: Blackwell.

Chapter 11

REIMAGINING THE FRAGMENTED CITY/CITIZEN
Young People and Public Action in Rio de Janeiro

———— ∞∞∞ ————

Udi Mandel Butler

The questions *who* are the publics in a public anthropology and *what* such an endeavor aspires to are crucial in recent disciplinary debates striving for a more relevant, engaged anthropology. Does the "public" refer to the sector of the population interested in newspapers, books, and other media outlets where anthropologists could have a voice? Or should the public, in a public anthropology, be understood in a broader sense as promoting the use of anthropological knowledge outside the academy in domains that affect people's day-to-day lives in the spheres of policy, law, health, community development, and so on? If we accept the latter definition, do we risk conflating the technical application of knowledge with the aspiration to link certain values to the use of anthropological knowledge?

Recent writings, specifically by Beck (2009), Borofsky (2000), Eriksen (2006), and Burawoy (2005), have sought to clarify what a "public anthropology" (or sociology, in Burawoy's case) might refer to. A common factor identified in these writings is a conception that the *what* that such public engagement works *for* is a fairer, more just and equitable world. This conception may involve, as Sam Beck proposed, the idea that "local groups and communities should be able to control their own well-being and quality of life" (Beck 2009: 1). It may also be involved in what Michael Burawoy referred to as the defense of civil society and the social (Burawoy 2005).[1] This conception of public anthropology, though perhaps more narrowly defined, is also more clearly articulated and purposeful. Burawoy

Notes for this chapter begin on page 309.

clearly illustrated the distinctions and relationships between "applied" and "public," and between the "professional" and "critical" branches of the social sciences, in his presidential address to the American Sociological Association (Burawoy 2005). Though his proposal referred specifically to a public sociology, several of Burawoy's key points also seem applicable to anthropology.

Burawoy convincingly argues that sociology comprises four branches or tendencies, each with its own logic, methods, goals, and shortcomings: the *professional mainstream,* which dominates the discipline and is responsible for articulating conceptual and methodological approaches and promoting various research programs; the *critical wing,* which examines the foundations of professional sociology research programs and methods, acting as sociology's conscience; the *policy branch* involved in providing "solutions to problems that are presented to us, or to legitimate solutions that have already been reached" where the "client" that defines the goal is the state, nongovernmental, or corporate sector; and finally the *public branch,* which as the conscience of "policy sociology" engages with the public in pursuit of the broad vision of an inclusive, just world outlined above.

Burawoy further clarifies this public sociology by distinguishing between a traditional public sociology and an organic public sociology. Representatives of the former might include key figures such as Franz Boas, Margaret Mead, Ruth Benedict, Bronislaw Malinowski, and others who, having carved out a public presence with their written work, remain both popular and relevant, addressing contemporary issues of their times (see Eriksen 2006). As for an organic public sociology, Burawoy refers to this engagement as one where "the sociologist works in close connection with a visible, thick, active, local and often counter-public. The bulk of public sociology is indeed of an organic kind—sociologists working with a labor movement, neighborhood associations, communities of faith, immigrant rights groups, human rights organizations. Between the organic public sociologist and a public is a dialogue, a process of mutual education" (Burawoy 2005: 264).

In this chapter I draw on these discussions and understandings of a public anthropology to address what role images and the domain of the visual could have in them. It is noteworthy that debates about the contours, definitions, and examples of a public anthropology have focused primarily on text. Key authors in these debates, such as Borofsky and Erikson, have contributed meaningfully to advocacy for a more public presence of anthropologists through the medium of the written word, especially through more accessible styles of writing and a more vocal presence in print journalism (Borofsky 2000; Eriksen 2006).

Situated within the intellectual tradition of the academy, and beyond that a philosophical heritage that privileges the word, one may wonder whether debates for a public anthropology might have overlooked the image, which has lately enjoyed a resurgence in academic interest.² In this chapter I engage with the field of visual anthropology to further explore how the dimension of the visual and audio-visual could contribute to the project of a public anthropology more aligned with the conceptions of Beck and Burawoy outlined above. Doing so, I argue here, means focusing on different media—film, video, photography, the Internet, or exhibitions—through which the "public" might be engaged, not just as audiences but also as dialogic partners. It also means taking the visual seriously as an important site of domination and resistance in struggles for recognition and dignity, the building of community, and the flourishing of the imagination.

This chapter is based on research carried out in Rio de Janeiro between 2005 and 2009 that sought to understand how young people perceived and practiced what we termed *public action* in the context of a socially and economically divided city. I worked with a small team of researchers, and especially with Marcelo Princeswal, from a Brazilian action/research NGO, the International Center for Research and Policy on Childhood (CIESPI), based at Rio de Janeiro's Pontífica Universidade Católica (PUC). Our research explored significant spaces and practices of public action and the kinds of groups, organizations, networks, or movements that young people (mostly aged sixteen to twenty-nine) participate in (e.g. faith groups, development projects, community organizations, social movements). The term public action has been preferred over, say, civil society to emphasize the dynamic and often agonistic nature of public struggles for recognition, respect, resources, or justice.³

We did not, at the outset, intend to focus on the domain of the image or visual production. However, a set of struggles and organizations seemed deeply implicated in this domain, which I will call the *imaginary*. This imaginary consisted of several prejudiced representations, visual and otherwise, of inhabitants of favelas or shantytown communities, sometimes connected to racial stereotypes. These circulated in the dominant media and were seen, by many of our interviewees, as widespread among the population of Rio de Janeiro. Terms like *visual culture* describe the embeddedness of visual representations within broader systems of meaning and in mediating social relationships. *Visual discourse* has been used to describe particular genres and stereotypical forms of representation that come to reflect dominant ideologies or ways of understanding people and aspects of the world. For authors like Poole, the term visual culture fails to address the power inequality often present in the production, circulation, and consumption of images; instead, the concept of *visual economies* is suggested to describe these processes (Poole in Pinney 2003: 8). As the term implies, these processes are deeply intermeshed with political and economic inequalities and with the resources available to produce images. The visual domain I am describing encompasses these understandings of visual culture, discourse, and economy, but it also differs in that it tries to emphasize how images are experienced by subjects and affect their emotions, identities, and imaginations. The notion of the imaginary acknowledges that images have an important role in shaping subjectivities, while also celebrating people's capacity to reimagine, a quality inherent to the human condition.[4]

This chapter then, will address how the image has become a site for struggle in places like Rio de Janeiro and at the same time how sectors of the public have mobilized to try to reconfigure or reimagine the city, counteracting the fragmenting logic of this "imaginary of marginality." The chapter will also discuss certain social and cultural conditions that have provided spaces for reconnection—or as I term it here, reimagination of the city/citizen—in an attempt to reconfigure the city's visual economy. Given that Rio de Janeiro's visual economy proved an important site of struggle for young people, it follows that making the visual itself an important site of collaboration and intervention would be a sensible (and sensitive) means of engagement during fieldwork. The chapter will then provide an overview of a project I coordinated with a group of young activist photographers in Rio de Janeiro and conclude with a discussion of the possible role of images in public anthropology.

The Fragmented City

The exchange below took place among a group of five young people who were part of a pilot radio project in the city that trains participants to become producers of news and current affairs programs for their peers. The exchange is emblematic of a common response given by many young people involved in numerous initiatives we came to know in our research on youth participation in different forms of public action in Rio de Janeiro (in particular NGOs, cultural groups, and community organizations). Regarding the effects on their lives of their participation in a range of initiatives around issues of citizenship, the following discussion ensued:

– Before I was reluctant to say I live in the Complexo da Maré [a large urban shanty]. The person jolts, the person retreats, it is horrible, you have to own up, I always own up, you know, about the place where you live and

290 | Udi Mandel Butler

it doesn't matter, the place doesn't make you up, it is you who makes up
the place.
– My critical gaze shifted.
– Yes, our vision of society amplified, and we cannot deny our roots, I think
that is it. Many people who live in the community are ashamed of saying
that they live in a community, that they live in a favela.
– They feel shame.
– Afterward I started having this other perspective; I gave more emphasis to
the fact of the place where I live, to my origins, to the fact of being black
too.

This conversation highlights a set of key issues this chapter addresses.
First, the feeling of "shame," of being stigmatized by particular social
representations associated with the place where several young people we
talked to lived, that is, in Rio's shantytowns or favelas. Indeed, reluctance
to admit to living in a favela in Rio is common, part of an internalized
prejudice or shame addressed above. At the same time the conversation
points to how such feelings of shame are overcome through a "critical
gaze," a reappraisal of the social, political, and historical context young
people find themselves in. I describe this process as a micro-revolution of
identification where the individual feels a renewed connection with her/
his own community, race, or ethnicity—or in other cases we found in our
research, sexual orientation and even class. The effects of this are variously described as concerning a sense of self-respect and pride in being
part of a constituency with a particular history and culture, as well as
renewed feelings of recognition of oneself and oneself by others that also
connect with sentiments of dignity.

I say "micro-revolution" following philosopher, psychotherapist, and
political activist Felix Guattari, who spoke of the many levels on which
political (and therefore potentially revolutionary) change can occur
(Guattari 1996; Guattari and Rolnik 2005). Guattari provokes us to think
differently about such changes, guiding our gaze not only to the "great
revolutions" due to more traditional forms of political organization and
mobilization, but also to other places where the political is found, such as
the local level (communities, neighborhoods, schools), the interpersonal
level (how we relate with each other, our family, strangers, those who are
different), and the level of subjectivity (how we feel and react, what we
dream or identify with) where we are constituted and constitute ourselves
as subjects. Referring to micropolitics, that is, to the crossing over between
these domains, for Guattari the crucial question becomes how we reproduce (or defy) dominant forms of subjectification. Subjectification, in this
sense, has to do with how we come to be defined and to understand and

act upon ourselves through particular discourses (Foucault 1982; Hacking 2003). Most important for the present discussion is that both subjectification and reimagination operate in a visual domain.

Imaginary Struggles

Cities like Rio de Janeiro, marked as they are by deep social divisions, pose particular challenges for collective action in the public sphere and for the practice of and struggle for citizenship. Rio's residents have at times referred to this social relationship between differing socioeconomic groups as *Cidade Partida,* the divided city (Ventura 2002). This term points to the relation between the *favela x asfalto,* the shantytown and the asphalt, or the semi-legal domains and the regular spaces of the city, coming to represent—in the imaginary of scholars, politicians, the media, and other inhabitants—the lack of integration in the urban environment. The term divided city, according to Fernando Fernandes, refers to a division that separates the "formal" city, with its juridically legitimized streets and properties and range of public services, from the "informal" city, a place "without urban planning, of informal occupation of land and clearly lacking in a range of services and urban provisions" (Fernandes 2004).

Favelas are the squatter settlements that have occupied disused land in the city at least since the early twentieth century. The distinct geography of Rio, a city growing around the steep and forested hills close to the coast, has meant that older and more established favelas have grown upward into spaces where it was hard to build. With a third generation arising, favela residents make up 18.7 percent of the city's population of almost six million, up from 7 percent half a century ago.

The visual economy surrounding the favelas, consisting of the production, circulation, and consumption of images of and from them to the rest of the city and the country, has been around since their emergence more than a hundred years ago. Nowadays, the most visible aspect of the way spaces are represented in this domain of the visual, at least in the dominant media, is violence. These representations emerged alongside the rise of drug trafficking gangs that have grown in strength and operate from a number of favela communities over the last two decades (Zaluar 1994). High fatality rates have resulted from drug factions' fights between themselves for control of territory and also from police operations in these spaces. The consequences of the political economy of the drug trade in Rio, in terms of the deaths, suffering, and culture of fear, corruption, and intimidation it generates, are devastating, especially for favela inhabitants. The state's recent attempts, using the police and the military, to occupy these communities and cast out the drug gangs have mainly been positively received across different societal sectors. It remains to be seen whether more sensitive and progressive forms of policing will replace these gangs, and where the suppressed forces of the drug trade will manifest next. An undeniable effect of the drug trade and these actions taken against it has been the proliferation of images of favelas as spaces of violence, marginality, and lack, contributing to what I call the *imaginary of marginality.*

Since the middle of the nineteen nineties, several media and cinema theorists have taken up Benedict Anderson's work in an attempt to understand the role of media like television and cinema in imagining communities. *Imagined Communities* (Anderson 1983) showed how nationalism emerges as a historical phenomenon whereby large groups of people come to envisage themselves as part of a community with shared attributes and a common identity. These communities—he referred in particular to Creole communities in the Americas—acquired social consciousness as part of a larger group in parallel with processes of self-organization around the institutions of a state. For Anderson, a key catalyst in this phenomenon is the presence of what he called "print-capitalism," that is, a wide availability of printed books published in the vernacular by a newly established print industry producing literature, pamphlets, newspapers and so on.[5] For Anderson, then—as Walsh points out in an article on cinema and nationalism—imagining refers not to a psychological faculty but to a development in "social epistemology" in which historical actors generate unintended consequences such as a collective sense of identity (see Walsh 1996).

Similarly, film and media theorists have undertaken to trace the role of different media in the shaping of such social epistemologies. Their significant contributions have traced a series of "national imaginaries" in national film and television productions, analyzing tropes, tendencies, and historical shifts, as well as depictions of minority groups like immigrant communities or black and indigenous people (Araújo 2000; Ginsburg 2003; Shohat and Stam 2002; Walsh 1996).

In the context of Brazil, the chief agent of this imagining since the nineteen sixties has been the media empire of Rede Globo, one of the five largest television networks in the world. Not just a key player in terrestrial, cable, and satellite television, Globo also incorporates newspaper, magazine, and book publication, radio stations, and charitable institutions. It is by far the most watched terrestrial TV channel in Brazil, with more than 50 percent audience share, and its world-famous soap operas are a staple of the nation's viewing diet. Rede Globo, then, is the most powerful force in Brazil's visual economy. The story of Globo's rise to national dominance is interesting in itself, involving a close relationship to Brazil's military regime (1964–1985) and then continued alliance with the political and economic elite in the era of Brazilian democratization. Globo even declined to cover the huge anti-dictatorship protests that took place right up to the moment of political transition (see Mader 1993).

The extremely popular daily dose of entertainment and advertising that Globo feeds the nation, however, reflects the lifestyles and consumption habits of the country's white upper-middle-class urban residents, often from wealthier districts of Rio de Janeiro. The Globo network, and to an extent other Brazilian broadcasters too, are very much aware of television's power to shape public opinion and create a sense of national identity.[6] The corporation's slogan, constantly spoken on air—*"Rede Globo, a gente se ve por aqui"* (Globo Network—we see each other through here)—is a succinct encapsulation of what Anderson spoke of in *Imagined Communities*. Globo's almost five decades dominating the airwaves have profoundly impacted Brazil's imaginary, reinforcing social attitudes and forming opinions. But what happens to those who do not recognize themselves on Globo's screen? The passage below is from a text written by Gabriela as part of a collaborative book our research team developed with seven activists who had spent years engaged in public-sphere initiatives (CIESPI 2007; see also Butler 2009; Butler and Princeswal 2010).

> I like living in the favela but I would like people who live there to have the opportunity to chose, to be able to walk around freely without people getting frightened in hearing the magic word "favela." It is there on the top of the hill-shanty that you live a harsh reality. The hard and sweet reality that you do not read about in the newspapers. Drug trafficking exists and the violence that appears on the news is not a lie. However we know that the news is manipulated to increase ratings. All this violence is perpetuated by the same people who denounce it on TV, because most people who use drugs are from the social classes A and B.[7] The drug dealer has never left the hill-shanty and the weapons never stop arriving in ever increasing numbers. No one goes up the hill-shanty to document the fashion parades, Forró, Capoeira, Folia de reis, that is, all the cultural life of our people which is very beautiful and intense.

Like Gabriela, many people interviewed in our research, especially young people and coordinators of assorted organizations working with media and communication, expressed a feeling of *misrecognition*. In their perspective, media descriptions of the favelas, and consequently of their inhabitants, were often prejudiced. The favela was commonly described in terms of its lacks—of urban resources (e.g., sanitation, roads, adequate housing), the law, education and culture, productive power, or even morality. For Jailson de Souza e Santos, a Brazilian academic who grew up in a shantytown and founded an important favela-based NGO, Observatório das Favelas, the problem with the perpetuation of such prejudiced perceptions—apart from the discrimination that favela inhabitants face in many aspects of their day-to-day life—is the relativizing of citizenship, whereby citizenship becomes relative to skin color, level of education, income, and/or space inhabited in the city (Souza e Santos 2004).

This description sheds light on an event that took place during my fieldwork in Rio in 2005. A news item on Globo's prime-time Sunday weekly magazine program *Fantástico* showed Rio's Special Operations Forces on a routine patrol of a favela. Special Operations Forces are responsible for tackling the city's drug gangs and are considered some of the best-trained police officers. Involved in constant shoot-outs, they have developed a series of procedures for policing favelas, the latest of which is to safely enter these communities in armored personnel carriers. The nickname for such a vehicle is *Caveirão*, the Big Skull, in light of the skull and bones that is the battalion's coat of arms. Though they protect the police from shots fired by drug gangs, *favela* residents greatly fear these armored vehicles. Like tanks, they drive at high speeds into some of the most densely populated places in the city. *Fantástico* showed what such an operation is like from inside an armored car, much in the way embedded journalists covered the Iraq War. The news piece employed a videogame aesthetic: at night, the camera looks through the window of a car patrolling the streets, looking for action. When people are seen, they quickly scatter, frightened. The expected confrontation between police and gangs fails to occur in this particular episode, but the police nevertheless oblige Globo's voyeuristic expectations by subjecting some local residents to weapon searches.

Such police incursions are not atypical but have become part of the state's security policy to combat the drug gangs' favela-based operations. Here, though, I want to emphasize how the media commonly represent such operations. *Fantástico*'s report did not seek locals' opinions; nor did it address the impact of such a favela "invasion," as local residents often describe police operations. Instead it portrayed the favela as a dangerous space that must be entered with extreme caution, quickly, armed. Locals are regarded with mistrust, for all are potential criminals. These representations are part of a broader imaginary of marginality, a set of images and narrative tropes that embody a stigmatizing view of favelas,[8] not just as hotbeds of crime, violence, danger, and vice, but also as separate settlements that are a drain on the city, defiling panoramic views and occupying prime real estate.[9]

I present the example of the *Caveirão* to show how different forms of alternative media are resisting this imaginary. These different spaces, or sites of re-representation of the favela, in turn illuminate the current configuration of the field of public action in which youth participate. The patrol site of the armored car in the Globo piece happened to be next to the Observatório das Favelas, mentioned above. This community NGO is responsible for several different projects focused on research, policy development, and capacity building in large, complex favela communities. This organization, and others like it that operate in different favelas on varying scales and with different degrees of success, see their role as involving the formation of technically competent, politically aware groups inside low-income communities. A key element in many such initiatives is "critical communication": registering, producing, and diffusing everyday experiences and practices present in these communities.

Since the nineteen nineties, Rio de Janeiro has seen a marked increase in the number of NGOs focused on youth living in the city's favelas. Many of the initiatives that work with young people do so through cultural forms such as music, dance, and theater. Regarded as means of engaging people in a process of cultural and community revitalization, these forms also stimulate critical reflection on the sociopolitical situation youth and the country find themselves in. More recently, several projects and organizations have worked to similar ends using media like cinema, news production, and photography. Such approaches are directly descended from the Popular Education movement, which motivated many campaigns and projects across the Latin American Left in the 1960s and 1970s. These projects centered on areas like adult literacy, popular and union movements, and education movements in favelas, urban peripheries, and politically engaged church communities, particularly those linked to Liberation Theology. The broader political movement articulated through Liberation Theology sought to integrate historically marginalized populations into society through a Christian and Marxist political framework and imaginary.

The guiding principles of Popular Education, whose foremost advocate was Brazilian teacher, philosopher, and activist Paulo Freire, promote a struggle for education as an emancipatory force, a practice of freedom, and a precondition for democratic life (Freire 1976; 1984; 1987; 1993 [1970]). As such, Popular Education is a politico-pedagogical process opposing colonial or colonizing education and attempting to reverse the negative effects that many decades of such education have had on the popular classes (Graciani 1999).

Freire's pedagogical approach focused on the idea of dialogue and departure from the student's cultural context. By reflecting on personal experience, social relations, culture, and history, he held, individuals can develop the ability to perceive the social, political, and economic contradictions surrounding them and consequently take action against the oppressive elements of this reality, both individually and collectively (Freire

1976; 1984; 1987; 1993 [1970]). Crucially relevant here is how numerous initiatives in the public sphere, like the community organizations described above or less formalized associations centered on cultural forms like hip-hop, have acted as spaces of reimagining self and society.[10] As privileged sites for critical reflection and the re-creation of self and community, these spaces of encounter have catalyzed the micro-revolutions discussed at the start of the chapter, producing new representations that have begun to circulate through the city's imaginary.

A pioneering project of the Observatório das Favelas is the Escola Popular de Comunicação Crítica (Popular School of Critical Communication), which was launched in 2005 with a class of forty-two students. This project is a one-year vocational course in different media (print, Internet, video, photography, radio), designed to train young people from Rio's favelas and peripheries to become critical communicators able to engage with and challenge the fragmenting imaginary. The school's goal is to establish local production facilities in the students' communities of origin and equip them with the skills to enter the media market. The school also hopes to replicate its course elsewhere in Rio and has also attracted interest in its methodology from elsewhere in Brazil.[11]

The *Caveirão* was very topical when I first met people from the school. They were discussing how their reports could reflect the community's experiences facing such invasions. Some of their pieces circulated in the alternative media sphere, particularly via community news websites. The stories described the *Caveirão's* reckless entry into the favela and the Special Operations Forces' actions, which traumatized the local population—as did their language. Blared through the armored car's loudspeakers as the forces entered the favela, it was reported to be at times quite abusive and intimidating, calling, for instance: "We have come to take your souls!" (Amnesty International 2006). This community journalism has also covered occasional deaths at the hands of police during such incursions, something Amnesty International has also investigated and written about recently (Amnesty International 2006).

Significantly, considering the theme of this chapter, another Observatório project works specifically with "popular photographers": young people from favelas and urban peripheries who then go on to develop their own projects, such as photographing day-to-day life in these communities.[12]

A Public Visual Anthropology Intervention

As addressed elsewhere (Butler 2009; Butler and Priceswal 2010), our research in Rio de Janeiro also involved collaborative approaches to research and dissemination that sought to engage with audiences beyond academia. One such project was the co-creation of a book with seven young activists who were deeply engaged in the city's public sphere in diverse ways. This co-created text illustrated the trajectories of their engagement and what it has meant for them (CIESPI 2007). For instance, two of the authors, sisters Diana and Diane, described their involvement in a range of community and educational projects in the area where they live, and increasingly in committees and associations working for the rights of black women citywide. Eron detailed his political trajectory from activism in school unions to work in a youth worker union and a series of regional rights forums. Quênia wrote of her political awakening and her identifying as an Afro-Brazilian through her encounter with hip-hop culture.

In a subsequent stage of the research, we encountered various issues pertaining to the *imaginary struggle* addressed here and in response devised an experiment involving the medium of photography instead of writing (for the challenges of such collaborative writing projects, see Butler 2009). In this participatory photographic project I worked with five young photographers from Rio de Janeiro's favela communities to capture the spaces and forms of public action that involved young people. Two of the young photographers are quite accomplished: Gabriela Torres has long been involved in community education initiatives, and Manuelle Rosa wrote in the above co-created publication about her trajectory from serving in local church and community organizations to working in community media. The other three photographers on the team—Vânia Bento, Francisco Valdean, and Davi Marcos—were veterans of photography projects in low-income communities and had considerable experience of photography and involvement in community organizations. Davi and Francisco both went through Observatório das Favelas' Popular School of Critical Communication.

This photographic collaboration aimed to understand the diversity of spaces and practices of young people's engagement in public action in Rio de Janeiro from the perspective of young people themselves, using the medium of photography. We also wanted to communicate this understanding through a mobile exhibition presented to different audiences across the city: young people from different social backgrounds; practitioners working in community organizations and NGOs; local and international researchers; and the general public, too.

The project began in September 2008, when the five photographers and I held a series of meetings to discuss the concept of "participation in public action" and the kinds of activities and spaces that might be important to photograph. The group brought examples of their work, made plans of the photographs to be taken, and began to think about where and how to hold the final exhibition in Rio. From December to May 2009, we collectively selected photographs for display and made plans for the traveling exhibition. Around 150 people attended the opening event of the first exhibition, held at a media NGO in the city center. The photographers introduced their work and spoke of their experiences of taking photographs, being engaged in social issues, and growing up in favela communities. This discussion elicited lively responses from those present, a mixture of students, young people, professionals from the nongovernmental sector, and educators across the social spectrum. Whereas the audience overall was very supportive of the photographers and their chosen trajectories of engagement with community activism, photojournalism, and art photography, one or two prejudiced voices considered such media as the preserve of higher social classes. Their argument, which I have heard before at similar events involving favela residents' use of audio-visual technologies, was that people from these communities should instead concentrate their efforts on more manual occupations. Though some members of Brazilian society still hold such views, they have become less acceptable, especially since the recent surge of audio-visual productions from these communities.

The exhibition then proceeded to the grounds of Brazil's distinguished PUC University, which was hosting the Latin America Studies Association annual conference. An important reason the exhibition was shown here, at one of the city's most elite universities, was that many of its students remained unaware of the living conditions, struggles, and cultural richness of people their own age living in communities neighboring their own homes (see Figure 11.1). After PUC, the exhibition material was handed back to the photographers, who themselves subsequently organized ex-

Figure 11.1. "PUC University exhibition." Photo by Udi Mandel Butler.

hibitions in different venues, including Rio de Janeiro State University (where one of them studied) and schools and cultural venues in different favelas where three of the photographers live (see Figure 11.2). At these sites, the exhibition was accompanied by film screenings and discussions with young people and local residents.

The process of making and disseminating these images across diverse spaces in the city was exciting and challenging; most significantly, it allowed me and others to submerse ourselves in, and emerge with a clearer sense of, the *imaginaries* that many of my young acquaintances inhabited. The encounters the project entailed—between the photographers, their work, and others across the city—in turn created creative, inspiring opportunities for exchanges that forged new relationships. For instance, a "comment book" in which visitors jotted their reflections on the exhibition was filled with enthusiastic responses from people across the city's social spectrum. Studying the images themselves also increased my own understanding of the diversity of the places and actions that the photographers associated with public action, which also appear significant for many young people.

These images, including the examples displayed here, also show that occupation and transformation of public spaces and attitudes go beyond traditional understandings of the political. For instance, a photograph taken by Davi (Figure 11.3) recognizably represents political action in

Figure 11.2. "Sobrado Cultural exhibition, Maré favela." Photo by Francisco Valdean.

Figure 11.3. "Mourning in Maré." Photo by Davi Marcos.

public space but also offers an image counter to that described through the perspective of Rede Globo and the Caveirão, of *favela* residents protesting police killings of young people in their communities. Another Davi photograph (Figure 11.4) represents a form of mass occupation of public

Figure 11.4. "Gay Parade." Photo by Davi Marcos.

Figure 11.5. "*Se Benze que dá*, Maré samba school." Photo by Vânia Bento.

space, this one more carnivalesque: the city's Gay Parade, which annually attracts more than a million participants and promotes awareness about rights and discrimination in the domain of sexuality. The theme of the carnivalesque is also clear in Vânia's photograph (Figure 11.5) of a local youth samba school in the favela where she lives. In Rio de Janeiro, samba schools' long history as sites of popular expression of the art and experiences of the favelas constitutes an important lens through which to view these places, for the rest of the country and beyond.

Our group's photographs also revealed surprising—and for me previously unseen—manifestations of public action, such as Davi's shot of an-archo-punks, whose performances in the city's public squares mix music, politics, and the occupation of public space (see Figure 11.6). An approach to public space that fuses art and the political is also evident in Manuelle's photograph of a theater troupe that also uses public space to stage shows that often address political themes (see Figure 11.7).

Another important site of public action, especially for young people from favelas, involves access to university education. Multiple community organizations, often run by university students from these areas, have emerged to help young people from favelas and peripheries study to pass the university entrance exams. Francisco's photograph (Figure 11.8) of one such group of students hiking to the top of one of the large hills surrounding the urban landscape captures the sense of achievement such initiatives involve for those taking part. Gabriela's photograph of a

Figure 11.6. "Anarcho punks." Photo by Davi Marcos.

Figure 11.7. *Tá na rua* theatre troupe." Photo by Manuelle Rosa.

Figure 11.8. "Community University Entrance Exam group." Photo by Francisco Valdean.

folkloric celebration in a favela evokes the central role that young people still play in rural traditions transposed into an urban environment, as well as these activities' importance in building local communities and simultaneous invisibility to the rest of the city (see Figure 11.9). Whereas Gabriela's photograph shows the continuity of the rural in the urban, Francisco's picture of hip-hop culture (Figure 11.10) shows this new urban culture's significance to both creation of new forms of artistic expression and education and political association (see note 9).

As a form of public visual anthropology, this project allowed mutual learning and

Figure 11.9. "Folia de Reis." Photo by Gabriela Torres.

Figure 11.10. "Hip Hop." Photo by Francisco Valdean.

the quality of surprise to emerge within the group and beyond as images and ideas were produced and experiences shared in a way not restricted to a mere exchange of words. At the same time, dissemination of images showing young people across social groups engaged in action in the city's public sphere facilitated wider circulation, beyond what such images, and the ideas they hold, might have had in a solely textual form.[13]

The Role of Public Anthropology in Imaginary Struggles

The theme of media and citizenship, also called "visual inclusion," has gained importance in Brazil's public sphere since the late nineteen nineties. Though much more recent than community radio's penetration of favela communities, alternative media production centers and dissemination networks are now intensifying their activities, especially by appropriating new forms of technology such as digital video and the Internet. Interesting in this respect is that such movements have been taking place not only "from below," through civil society initiatives such as those presented here, but also through government programs. During his tenure, Brazil's Minister of Culture Gilberto Gil, also a popular musician, implemented a national project intended to motivate local cultural production in marginalized communities by disseminating their productions across

Brazil via digital technologies and the Internet. To date, more than 650 "points of culture" have been established countrywide in favelas, indigenous communities, *quilombos* (historic runaway slave communities), and other marginalized settlements (Butler and Simões 2010; Pontos de Cultura 2011). The innovation in this initiative is its emphasis on horizontal exchanges across the different communities under the slogan of "digital inclusion" (Pontos de Cultura 2011).

Local groups' appropriation of film, video, and photography to represent themselves in different contexts has had huge significance in the sphere of visual inclusion across the world. The rise of indigenous media production since the late 1980s—particularly among Australian Aborigine communities (Batty 1995; Ginsburg 1991; Michaels 1991), the Kayapo in the Amazon (Turner 1990; 1992a), Maoris in New Zealand, and First Nations people in Canada (Dowmunt 1995; Fox 1995), though examples abound— points to the importance of visual modes of representation within broader struggles for autonomy and cultural expression. Production and dissemination technologies, in particular video and satellite broadcasting, were appropriated when members of these communities perceived their culture and language as threatened by the increasing prevalence of the dominant national media, especially with the introduction of national satellite coverage (Ginsburg 1991; 1995; 2003) or else by more immediate hazards to culture and territory (Turner 1990; 1992a).

Ginsburg wrote of such communities' use of audio-visual and broadcast technologies as a powerful means of "self-production" that in many cases has had culturally revitalizing effects (Ginsburg 1991; 1994; 2002). These initiatives, some of them under way for many decades, have often directly involved anthropologists. Some of them have encouraged and promoted uptake of these tools by working with local groups, whereas others have been active writing of these ventures and analyzing them. Clearly, this project of a public anthropology involves anthropologists collaborating with historically marginalized communities to exercise the right and opportunity to produce and disseminate the audio-visual representations that they feel best represent their lifeworlds. Meanwhile, a public visual anthropology ought also to acknowledge the countless local initiatives, undertaken without the help or representation of academics, which remain outside the widely circulated history of a visual anthropology.[14]

Sarah Pink addressed the neglect of visual anthropology in the history of applied anthropology in a special edited volume of *Visual Anthropology Review* (2004). Her article there features a revealing historical overview of applied visual anthropology, citing early examples such as the photography of John Collier in the Vicos project, Eric Michaels's work training his aboriginal informants in video production, or Terrence Turner's similar training among the Kayapo (Pink 2004: 4). In Brazil, the work of the NGO Video in the Villages, founded by French anthropologist Vincent Carelli, has also meaningfully helped many indigenous Amazonian communities represent themselves through video and disseminate their productions across the country and beyond (Carelli 2009).

Another important contribution to an applied visual anthropology consists in anthropologists' work with television producers to create programs that reach a larger audience than monographs do. Figures like Paul Henley, Terence Turner, Andre Singer, David Turton, and the many anthropologists involved in the Granada Television series *Disappearing World* (comprising sixty-three hour-long episodes aired in the United Kingdom from 1969 to 1993) are key to the project of extending anthropology's reach to a more general public.[15] The academic community commonly cites this series as one of the most successful attempts to bring anthropology, with all its complexity and contemporary concerns, to a wider audience in and outside the United Kingdom. Reaching a U.K. audience some thirteen million strong with some episodes' premier broadcasts, the series showed that the public, counter to the opinion of television producers, could indeed engage with anthropological ideas and come to know other cultures as complex entities striving to cope with the challenges of the contemporary world (Loizos 1980; Turner 1992a; Turton 1992). In the United States Margaret Mead and more recently David Maybury-Lewis have figured prominently in opening up anthropology to larger audiences through television.[16]

Applied visual anthropology interventions have also concerned health settings. Key here is the work of Richard Chalfen, who for decades has been developing what he calls video intervention/prevention assessment—a way of working with patients to facilitate communication of their day-to-day experience of their condition to clinicians (Chalfen and Rich 2004). Also, Pink (2004) has mentioned her own work using visual anthropology tools and methods in consumer research as a further example of an applied visual anthropology approach.

Pink's article strove to define what applied visual anthropology might be, and her approach—much like the present essay's—covered a range of contexts in which anthropologists have been working, such as those mentioned above. Such a definition, Pink argued, should also encompass the "anthropology of visual systems" advocated by Morphy and Banks (1997: 5). In doing so, as this chapter attempts to show, such an applied (or in my case, public) visual anthropology concerns more than the use of particular tools and methods of academic visual anthropology (e.g., photography, film, drawings, or other kinds of imagery used in visual research): it also involves engagement with visual domains and its effects on the lives of individuals and communities (Pink 2004; Pinney and Peterson 2003). My discussion of the imaginary of marginality, and of the strategies and processes of reimagination found in various public action sites in Rio de Janeiro, has aimed to sketch this engagement with the role of images in the public domain.

Pink's definition of applied visual anthropology involves diverse applications of a set of conceptual, analytical, and representational tools in the private, public, and NGO sectors, including "social intervention projects, medical anthropology, consumer ethnography, and design anthropology, among others" (Pink 2004: 5). Here, the "applied" and the "public" part ways. As a form of social intervention, Pink explained, applied visual anthropology "usually takes the form of problem solving that involves collaboration with informants and brings about social change. ... This characteristic sets it apart from academic visual anthropology that may also be collaborative but is exploratory rather than problem solving" (Pink 2004: 5). But defining visual applied anthropology as a form of "social intervention" and "problem solving" does not answer the question posed in the chapter's first paragraph: *for whom* and *for what* such intervention is pursued. An applied visual anthropology thus risks becoming another set of methodological and analytical procedures through which problems, however defined, are tackled to serve a given group. In this sense of problem solving, the answer to the question *for what* is more immediate, depending on whose problem is being solved, be it the clinician who treats asthma patients or the multinational corporation that wants to learn more about customers' use of its products.

The project of a public visual anthropology, however, seems rather different. In my understanding, it entails a vision, however hazy, of a fairer, more inclusive and equitable world as the *what* that our engagement is *for*. As discussed early on in the chapter, Burawoy's notions of public and organic public sociology are relevant here (Burawoy 2005). A public visual anthropology could be defined as being concerned with the values of fairness, justice, and equality. Such an anthropology would work with people or communities to redress imbalances in the visual economies in which their present and their past are embedded, while also collaborating or assisting in the production and circulation of representations that nurture the values of fairness, justice, and equality. Anthropologists working in this vein as organic public anthropologists include figures such as Turner (1990), Michaels (1991), Chalfen in his work with young asthma patients (Chalfen and Rich 2004), Flores with the Maya Q'eqchi' (2004), and Carelli with different indigenous groups in the Amazon, to name but a few.[17]

Our research project in Rio de Janeiro did not initially aim to study media representations of the favela or focus on media productions that involved young people in these spaces. Nevertheless, we ultimately found these to be significant themes relating to youth participation in the public sphere. The sense of stigma and the feeling of misrecognition of representations of favelas in the dominant media, along with the actual prejudice and discriminations these are held to have encouraged, were common grievances among the young people we talked to. Participating in the different initiatives we came across—NGOs, cultural groups, hip-hop collectives—clearly sharpened their critical perspectives, as described in this chapter's opening. Although our interlocutors' perceptions and experiences did not necessarily reflect majority opinion in the city's favelas, they appear to be meaningful among those more engaged in the public sphere.

In this particular domain of the imaginary struggles of Rio de Janeiro's public sphere, then, public anthropology's role has been to engage with groups that are striving to reimagine the city and the idea of citizenship in a more inclusive way. The new images produced in this process of mutual learning have added to the new imaginary created by countless organizations and individuals looking to a fairer world.

Acknowledgments

The research this chapter is based on was part of the ESRC's (Economic and Social Research Council, U.K.) Non-Governmental and Public Action Programme. The research project "Parallel Lives, Different Worlds: Citizenship and Public Action" in Rio de Janeiro took place between 2005 and 2009. This research was conducted with Marcelo Princeswal, with whom I have published elsewhere (Butler and Princeswal 2010). I am also very grateful to Sam Beck, Kelly Teamey, and Carlos Flores, who provided many insightful comments on an earlier draft, as well as to Michael Butler and Nina Simões, who encouraged me to tell more about the photographs shown here.

Udi Mandel Butler's research has been mainly with children and young people living in a context of urban poverty in Rio de Janeiro, in particular those living on the street and in the favelas. His recent work has engaged with young people's perceptions of and engagement in public action in Brazil (NGOs, social movements, cultural groups, community organizations). On this theme, he has also conducted collaborative projects, through writing and photography, with young activists living in Rio's favelas, in association with the International Center for Research and Policy on Childhood (CIESPI) in Rio de Janeiro where he is a Research Fellow. Udi was a lecturer in Visual Anthropology at the Institute of Social and Cultural Anthropology, Oxford University, where he is now a research associate.

Notes

1. Burawoy defines civil society as a product of nineteenth-century Western capitalism, which produced associations, movements, and publics outside the state and the economy. These included political parties, trade unions, schools, communities of faith, print media, and various voluntary organizations. For Burawoy, sociology as a discipline flourishes when civil society flourishes but disappears when it disappears, as in Stalin's Soviet Union, Hitler's Germany, and Pinochet's Chile (Burawoy 2004: 288).
2. Several works in anthropology and beyond have engaged with the question of the visual ways of knowing in contrast with the privileging of text. Some important writings in the vast literature on these debates include Grimshaw (2001), Hastrup (1992), MacDougall (1997), and Morphy and Banks (1997).
3. The term public action as used in this chapter stems from discussions in the Non-Governmental and Public Action Research Programme, in particular through the work of Jude Howell, the program's director. These discussions set aside the notion of civil society, arguing that this term did not sufficiently convey the agonistic character of the range of actions evident in the public sphere. For more information on this program, including the range of projects within it, see its website at http://www2.lse.ac.uk/inter nationalDevelopment/research/NGPA/.
4. Some important examples of this appeared in Pinney and Peterson (2003). In a chapter on Australian Aborigines' encounter with archived photographs of their ancestors (both for anthropometry measurements and as reconstructions of "primitive" peoples), for instance, Aird describes how the descendants of those depicted managed to "look through" the image and enter into a relationship with their relatives, thus reappropriating the image for themselves (Aird 2003).
5. Other forms of widely circulated representations Anderson mentions include atlases and maps, which also contribute to a sense of national community (Anderson 1983).
6. The extent of this media influence may even be reflected in the country's declining birthrates, which some demographers have partly attributed to the *telenovelas* like those aired on Globo, which have spread through the country faster than education and show modern upper-middle-class urban families with few children and desirable lifestyles.
7. The phrase "classes A and B" refers to a sectoral classification of the population most often used in business circles and marketing and often concerns profession and training rather than purchasing power, though in this context it may well indicate upper- and middle-class individuals.
8. For an important analysis and critique of how the notion of "marginality" applied to favela communities in Rio de Janeiro in the 1970s, see Janice Perlman's *The Myth of Marginality* (1979 [1976]).
9. It is worth noting that alongside images of violence and crime, Brazil's media commonly depict favelas as incessantly growing and destroying the surrounding flora. Disingenuously aligning themselves with environmental discourses, the creators of such representations fail to take into account the greater toll taken on the city's ecology by large new condominiums, shopping centers, and private mansions.
10. Hip-hop culture is often regarded as including four elements: rap (a musical form of singing and rhyming), break dancing, graffiti, and the DJ. Hip-hop may be too diverse to be called a movement, as it encompasses various tendencies, from the more progressive to those that eulogize crime factions, to religious hip-hop, right-wing hip-hop, homophobe hip-hop, etc. Yet despite this diversity, the Brazilian case tends strongly toward mobilization for social justice and citizenship and against racism, discrimination,

and inequality. Our research observed hip-hop's proximity to feminist, landless, Black, and other social movements.

11. As some Brazilian commentators have pointed out, recognition of the dominant media's power to spread values, representations, and attitudes spurs the rise of counter-hegemonic practices in the public sphere among those who struggle for social justice and citizenship (Coutinho and Paiva 2007).

12. Photographers from this project have carried out photo assignments such as "Sport in the Favela" and "The Favela Sees the Favela," which emphasize the depiction of everyday life in these spaces on the premise that through such re-presentation, images that more faithfully depict the experiences of favela residents will come to circulate in the national imaginary. In this, they appear to have succeeded. Their photographic exhibitions have been installed in sundry places, including Brazil's parliament in Brasilia, where members of the project met with President Lula to present him with samples of their work (Valdean 2008). More recently, Francisco Valden's successful blog has shown his latest photographic work as well as his analysis and commentary regarding current issues in the city and favelas (see http://www.ocotidiano.com.br). Highlighting the non-homogenous nature of institutions such as Globo itself, the photography project Imagens do Povo was recently awarded the corporation's social project award, Makes a Difference, and its images appeared in the Sunday newspaper magazines.

13. My goal in comparing images to text is not to favor one over the other; clearly text is central to any discursive activity and our discipline would collapse without it. Yet at the same time, a rich tradition in visual anthropology argues for the importance of attentiveness to what images do in society and how we, as researchers, can deploy them to convey particular experiences and kinds of knowledge that may be hard, if not impossible, to express through the medium of words alone.

14. Carlos Flores (personal communication 10th October 2012) forcefully made this point by tracing a number of initiatives that are seldom written about in this realm of the audio-visual, especially in Latin America, and consequently remain outside the commonly held history of the field of visual anthropology.

15. Though the *Disappearing World* series is often hailed as a successful collaboration between anthropology and television, several articles have also drawn attention to the challenges such a venture poses (e.g., Loizos 1980; Turner 1992b; Turton 1992).

16. Maybury-Lewis's *Millenium: Tribal Wisdom and the Modern World* (1992) is one large-scale effort by an anthropologist to reach a wider audience in the United States.

17. Anthropologists are also doing very interesting work in different archives and museums, e.g., helping indigenous source communities reestablish links with collected photographs or objects that somehow concern them. For more examples of this kind of work see Pinney and Peterson (2003); regarding photographs specifically, as well as novel museum practices, see Brown and Peers (2003).

References

Aird, Michael. 2003. "Growing Up with Aborigines." In *Photography's Other Histories*, ed. Christopher Pinney and Nicolas Peterson. Durham, NC: Duke University Press.

Amnesty International. 2006. "'We Have Come to Take Your Souls': The Caveirão and Policing in Rio de Janeiro." Amnesty International Report (March).

Anderson, Benedict. 1983. *Imagined Communities*. New York: Verso.

Araújo, Joel Zito. 2000. *A negação do Brasil: identidade racial e estereótipos sobre o negro na história da telenovela brasileira*. São Paulo: SENAC.

Batty, Philip. 1995. "Singing the Electric: Aboriginal Television in Australia." In *Channels of Resistance: Global Television and Local Empowerment*, ed. Tony Dowmunt. London: British Film Institute.

Beck, Sam. 2009. "Introduction: Public Anthropology." *Anthropology in Action* 16, no. 2: 1–13.

Borofsky, Robert. 2000. "Public Anthropology: Where To? What Next?" *Anthropology News* 41, no. 5: 9–10.

Brown, Alison, and Laura Peers, eds. 2003. *Museums and Source Communities: A Routledge Reader*. London: Routledge.

Burawoy, Michael. 2004 "American Sociological Association Presidential Address: For Public Sociology." *American Sociological Review* 70, no.1: 4–28.

Butler, Udi Mandel. 2009. "Notes on a Dialogical Anthropology." *Anthropology in Action* 16, no. 3: 20–31.

Butler, Udi Mandel, and Marcelo Princeswal. 2010. "Cultures of Participation, Young People and Public Action in Brazil." *Community Development Journal* 45, no. 3: 335–345.

Butler, Udi Mandel, and Nina Simões. 2010. "Culture Hot-Spots: An Anthropological 'Do-In'?" http://www.lab.org.uk/index.php/cultures/263-culture-points.

Carelli, Vincent. 2009. "Presentation." http://www.videonasaldeias.org.br/2009/vna.php?p=1&.

Chalfen, Richard, and Michael Rich. 2004. "Applying Visual Research: Patients Teaching Physicians Through Visual Illness Narratives." *Visual Anthropology Review* 20, no. 1: 17–30.

CIESPI. 2007. *Nós: A Revolução de Cada Dia*. CIESPI/PUC: Rio de Janeiro.

Coutinho, Eduardo, and Raquel Paiva. 2007. "Escola Popular de Comunicação Crítica: uma experiência contra-hegemônica na periferia do Rio de Janeiro." Journal of the Associação Nacional de Programas de Pós-Graduação em Comunicação. Available at: http://www.compos.org.br/seer/index.php/e-compos/article/viewFile/142/143.

Dowmunt, Tony, ed. 1995. *Channels of Resistance: Global Television and Local Empowerment*. London: British Film Institute.

Eriksen, Thomas Hylland. 2006. *Engaging Anthropology: The Case for a Public Presence*. Oxford: Berg.

Fernandes, Fernando. 2004. "Cidade partida: Partida?" http://www.observatoriodefavelas.org.br.

Flores, Carlos. 2004. "Indigenous Video, Development and Shared Anthropology: A Collaborative Experience with Maya Q'eqchi' Filmmakers in Postwar Guatemala." *Visual Anthropology Review* 20, no. 1: 31–44.

Foucault, Michel. 1982. "The Subject and Power." In *Michel Foucault: Beyond Structuralism and Hermeneutics*, ed. Hubert Dreyfus and Paul Rabinow. New York: Harvester Wheatsheaf.

Fox, Derek Tini. 1995. "Honouring the Treaty: Indigenous Televisionin Aotearoa." In *Channels of Resistance: Global Television and Local Empowerment*, ed. Tony Dowmunt. London: British Film Institute.

Freire, Paulo. 1976. *Ação Cultural Para Liberdade*. Rio de Janeiro: Editora Paz e Terra.

———. 1984. *O Papel do Educador*. São Paulo: Documentos FEBEM.

———. 1987. *Paulo Freire e educadores de rua: Uma abordagem crítica*. Projeto Alternativas de Atendimento aos meninos de rua. Rio de Janeiro: UNICEF/SAS/FUNABEM.

———. 1993 [1970]. *Pedagogy of the Oppressed*. London: Penguin Press.

Ginsburg, Faye. 1991. "Indigenous Media: Faustian Contract or Global Village?" *Cultural Anthropology* 6, no. 1: 92–112.

———. 1994. "Culture/Media: A (Mild) Polemic." *Anthropology Today* 10, no. 2: 5–15.

————. 1995. "Production Values: Indigenous Media and the Rhetorics of Self-determination." In *Rhetorics of Self-Making*, ed. Debbora Battaglia. Berkeley: University of California Press.

————. 2002. "Mediating Culture: Indigenous Media, Ethnographic Film, and Production of Identity." In *The Anthropology of Media: A Reader*, ed. Kelly Askew and Richard Wilk. Oxford: Blackwell.

————. 2003. "Shooting Back: From Ethnographic Film to Indigenous Production/Ethnography of Media." In *A Companion to Film Theory*, ed. Toby Miller and Robert Stam. Oxford: Blackwell.

Graciani, Maria Stela. 1999. *Pedagogia Social de Rua*. São Paulo: Cortez Editora.

Granada Television. 1969–1993. *Disappearing World*.

Grimshaw, Anna. 2001. *The Ethnographer's Eye: Ways of Seeing in Modern Anthropology*. Cambridge: Cambridge University Press.

Guattari, Felix. 1996. *Soft Subversions*. New York: Semiotext.

Guattari, Felix, and Suely Rolnik. 2005. *Micropolítica: Cartografias do desejo*. Petrópolis, Brazil: Vozes.

Hacking, Ian. 2003. "Between Michel Foucault and Erving Goffman: Making Up People." Lecture held at London School of Economics. Unpublished.

Hastrup, Kirsten. 1992. "Anthropological Visions: Some Notes on Visual and Textual Authority." In *Film as Ethnography*, ed. Peter Ian Crawford and David Turton. Manchester: Manchester University Press.

Loizos, Peter. 1980. "Granada Television's Disappearing World Series: An Appraisal." *American Anthropologist* 82: 573–594.

MacDougall, David. 1997. "The Visual in Anthropology." In *Rethinking Visual Anthropology*, ed. Marcus Banks and Howard Morphy. New Haven, CT: Yale University Press.

Mader, Roberto. 1993. "Globo Village: Television in Brazil." In *Channels of Resistance: Global Television and Local Empowerment*, ed. Tony Dowmunt. London: British Film Institute.

Maybury-Lewis, David. 1992. *Millenium: Tribal Wisdom and the Modern World*.

Michaels, Eric. 1991. "Aboriginal Content: Who's Got It—Who Needs It?" *Visual Anthropology* 4, no. 3–4: 277–300.

Morphy, Howard, and Marcus Banks. 1997. "Introduction: Rethinking Visual Anthropology." In *Rethinking Visual Anthropology*, ed. Marcus Banks and Howard Morphy. New Haven, CT: Yale University Press

Perlman, Janice. 1979 [1976]. *The Myth of Marginality: Urban Poverty and Politics in Rio de Janeiro*. Berkeley: University of California Press.

Pink, Sarah. 2004. "Applied Visual Anthropology Social Intervention, Visual Methodologies and Anthropology Theory." *Visual Anthropology Review* 20, no.1: 3–16.

Pinney, Christopher. 2003. "Introduction: 'How the Other Half …'" In *Photography's Other Histories*, ed. Christopher Pinney and Nicolas Peterson. Durham, NC: Duke University Press.

Pinney, Christopher, and Nicolas Peterson, eds. 2003. *Photography's Other Histories*. Durham, NC: Duke University Press.

Pontos de Cultura. 2011. Overview of 'Pontos de Cultura' in project website. http://www.cultura.gov.br/culturaviva/ponto-de-cultura/.

Shohat, Ella, and Robert Stam. 2002. "The Imperial Imaginary." In *The Anthropology of Media: A Reader*, ed. Kelly Askew and Richard Wilk. Oxford: Blackwell.

Souza e Santos, Jailson de. 2004. "Meios de comunicação e espaços populares." www.observatoriodefavelas.org.br.

Turner, Terence. 1990. "Visual Media, Cultural Politics and Anthropological Practice: Some Implications of Recent Uses of Film and Video among the Kayapo of Brazil." *CVA Review* (Commission on Visual Anthropology, Montreal) (Spring): 8–13.

————. 1992a. "Defiant Images: The Kayapo Appropriation of Video." *Anthropology Today* 8, no. 6: 5–16.

————. 1992b. "The Kayapo on Television: An Anthropological Viewing." *Visual Anthropology Review* 8, no. 1: 107–112.

Turton, David. 1992. "Anthropological Knowledge & The Culture of Broadcasting." *Visual Anthropology Review* 8, no. 1: 113–117.

Valdean, Francisco. 2008. "Encontro com o Lula." www.observatoriodefavelas.org.br.

Ventura, Zuenir. 2002 [1994]. *Cidade Partida*. São Paulo: Compania das Letras.

Walsh, Michael. 1996. "National Cinema, National Imaginary." *Film History* 8, no. 1: 5–17.

Zaluar, Alba. 1994. *Condomino do Diabo*. Rio de Janeiro: Editora Revan.

Chapter 12

URBAN TRANSITIONS
Graffiti Transformations

———— ⌒⌒ ————

Sam Beck

This chapter focuses on a particular public art form called *graffiti*. The idea of the "public" used here is a claim public artists make to assert their right over space as a resource for creating their art. By reclaiming "the commons"—described by Donald Nonini (2008: 1) as "those assemblages and ensembles of resources that human beings hold in common or in trust to use on behalf of themselves, other living human beings, and past and future generations of human beings, and which are essential to their biological, cultural, and social reproduction"—graffitists are reclaiming a public good defined by the representations that appear as part of the built and social environment. For Elizabeth Blackmar (2006: 51), "Common property is an individual's right not to be excluded from the uses or benefits of resources ... common property is usually distinguished from 'open access' or unappropriated resources that are beyond a prescribed political jurisdiction." Public art is thus both a political and a symbolic statement. Graffitists claim identity with their creation, but not ownership. Moreover, graffiti becomes part of the streetscape and as such makes a territorial claim.

In this chapter, I explore the nature of modern graffiti art in relation to the larger context in which it appeared and developed. I assert that graffiti should not be understood in terms of objectification—as markings on a space in public view—but as a process through which identity is claimed and the forces that produce it are revealed. According to Setha Low (1999: 112), "both the production and the construction of space are contested for economic and ideological reasons; understanding them can help us see how local conflicts over space can be used to uncover and illuminate larger issues." After all, graffiti is more than an aesthetic form: it is also about capturing, using, and making a claim over space.

In most urban low-income neighborhoods, graffiti is a ubiquitous element of the built environment. In many neighborhoods, though, murals accompany graffiti. Both these communicative art forms vary thematically. Graffiti is mostly the work of amateurs who use spray paint, wide felt-tip pens, and so on to write their names, usually in black, or paint multicolor images of various sorts. They often perceive graffiti as an act of rebellion and carry it out in places that Marc Auge (1995) refers to as "non-places": lonely stretches of roadway where factories, warehouses, or abandoned buildings whose external walls, shuttered storefronts, and billboards are canvases for graffiti artists. These are "non-places" because

Figure 12.1. Mural located in Northside, Williamsburg. Photo taken on 15 March 2014, Sam Beck.

they tend not to be locations for sociability, but spaces that one passes by—though they may also be in full public view, like the subway cars once covered by graffiti.

Murals, by contrast, tend to be institutionalized as commissioned art, often oriented to social change and social justice, or commemoration of historical events. In making murals, professional artists work with community members, particularly children (Groundswell 2014). Urban community mural art began appearing on buildings' exteriors in the 1960s as part of a movement of popular political activism. By 1970, public art in Chicago was also public education. Image themes reflected the suffering of the inner-city poor living with urban decline, racial tensions, absentee landlords, and illicit drugs, but they also expressed pride. In Philadelphia, muralists involved community members in designing and creating the art. School-sponsored mural projects often represent community solidarity and may be part of community service projects to beautify an urban landscape, recount history, or express particular values and ideals. Other kinds of murals are nonpolitical and decorative in nature or advertise a

Figure 12.2. Congresswoman Nydia Velazquez in front of an El Puente Academy for Peace and Justice and Latino Arts and Culture Center mural designed and painted by El Puente high school students and their teachers. Photo taken on 30 July 2011, Sam Beck.

product or service. From an ownership standpoint, muralists' work is transactional: private or government ownership determines a mural's making based on a financial arrangement. A mural, therefore, is produced as a commodity.

The graffiti-mural binary is clear to both types of practitioners—even graffitists who do murals and muralists who do graffiti—as something that evolved over time in the world of public art. For the general public, though, the difference between graffiti and mural "art" is muddled. This chapter asks whether murals are "crowding out" graffiti in neighborhoods experiencing gentrification. Graffiti, an illegal activity, is associated with inner cities and low-income neighborhoods, whereas both government and the private sector sponsor murals. Both kinds of street art are ubiquitous in all urban areas of the United States and abroad and likewise appear throughout different parts of New York City. For example, graffiti tends to be found in Latino neighborhoods, while hipster/yuppie-oriented retail districts feature murals and painted street advertisements. One can also see murals near schools and on school buildings and playground walls painted by inner-city children under the direction of professional artists or teachers. These forms mingle in the areas where loft buildings that used to house manufacturers or function as warehouses are being converted into luxury housing.

Public Art, Gentrification, and Displacement

Gentrification and displacement cause demographic, sociocultural, and economic changes and spark movements of resistance that I have studied in prior research (Beck 1992) in Providence, Rhode Island. Gentrification normally targets areas of "creative destruction" and underdevelopment ripe for "surplus absorption." Capital gravitates to areas where profits can be generated. David Harvey (2012: 16) observed that "this nearly always has a class dimension, since it is usually the poor, the underprivileged, and those marginalized from political power that suffer first and foremost from this process." Poverty in the United States is typically found in ethnic and working-class communities, often dilapidated urban neighborhoods ripe for capital reinvestment, gentrification and displacement. Gentrification thus displaces underserved long-term residents of housing regarded as low-order land use, in a process of urban restructuring "in favor of higher-order land use," as Harvey (2012: 19) put it.

The historic preservation movement, urban renewal, and Brown University's influence in "neighborhood planning," a policy that African-descendent residents referred to as "nigger removal," fueled gentrification in Providence. My current research attempts to understand non–historic preservation gentrification dynamics in North Brooklyn, New York, including Williamsburg, an area with a highly vulnerable population of working-class Latinos that is experiencing considerable gentrification and displacement pressures. North Brooklyn's complex demographic fabric departs from the norm in studies of gentrification and displacement (Smith 1996; Smith and Williams 1986). Latinos, Poles, Italians, Hasidic Orthodox Jews, university students, luxury housing dwellers, historic preservationists, and others are all shaping the social and political process of determining the future of a hotly contested, valuable landscape with easy access to Manhattan.

Much of the gentrification narrative has focused on hipster and yuppie newcomers to urban areas, whom the media portray as "turning around the neighborhood." Hipsters originated in a 1990s youth movement associated with alternative, non-mainstream, or avant-garde lifeways and cultural styles, and with the hangers-on who follow them and their activities in the worlds of art, fashion, film, dance, and music. Yuppies (also buppies) are young urban professionals who have carved out a particular

Figure 12.3. Mural of COST who partnered with REV in roller graffiti on N 6th and Bedford Avenue, Northside, Williamsburg. Photo taken on 5 September 2013, Sam Beck.

middle-class lifestyle and consumption pattern. The media have claimed that the hipster movement first emerged in Williamsburg and has expanded all over the world.

While participating in and seeking to understand this social and political matrix that could be simplified with a narrative of gentrification and displacement narrative, I was struck by the many graphics visible on the exteriors of retail stores and loft buildings in this area of Brooklyn. Public art, whether defined as graffiti or as mural, is intersected by multiple aesthetics, political and sociocultural narratives, and discourses. Raquel Rivera (2003) described the similar richness and complexity of rap, which cuts across ethno-cultural and class diversity. Ivor Miller (2002) captured the complexity of the artistic, ethno-cultural, and political views embedded in the popular use of the term graffiti. Although certain sectors of society appreciate graffiti, governmental authorities stigmatize it as illegal and transgressive, and it is usually identified as an act of aggression and vandalism. Mural art, on the other hand, is appreciated as legalized public art that provides aesthetic relief to its urban setting, and the art-appreciating public seems to understand it more easily. Both graffiti and murals have authors, but a mural is owned because someone commissioned the

Figure 12.4. Mural commissioned and donated to the Reconnect Café, Tomkins and Vernon Avenues, Bedford Stuyvesant. Photo taken on 13 June 2013, Sam Beck.

Figure 12.5. Decorative mural on private apartment building on N 4th and Metropolitan Avenue, Williamsburg. Photo taken on 14 March 2014, Sam Beck.

art or gave permission to have it produced; it is executed on private property or property owned by the state.

Perhaps this is the crux of the matter. Graffiti has an anarchic quality: it appears and disappears; exemplifies rapid transformations in style, aesthetic sensibilities, and political messages; and most often is not sponsored by anyone. Graffiti, like murals, is very much part of a particular social domain. In the words of the muralist and labor activist Mike Alewitz, "When we make art in the studio, we assert our humanity. When we make art in public, we assert our existence as social beings" (Buhle and Alewitz 2002: 3–4). Chantal Mouffe (2007), though not addressing graffiti in particular, came close to what most graffiti writers seek to accomplish; for her, art is an "agonistic" intervention in public space. Public art interrupts, transgresses, and confuses, but it also compels interaction.

Art is not the only intervention in public space placed on exterior walls of the urban built environment. Large-scale images that advertise products and services are ubiquitous in New York City and other metropolitan environments. The earlier hand-painted advertising images that covered the sides of buildings have been almost entirely replaced by graphics created electronically on plastic tarp-like products stretched over the enormous expanse of a building's side to advertise various products. Mouffe (2007: 1) asked: "Can artistic practices still play a critical role in a society where the differences between art and advertising have become blurred and where artists and cultural workers have become a necessary part of capitalist production?" I believe the answer is yes, when artists as cultural workers create to empower, represent, or serve the most vulnerable in society, whether through murals or graffiti. In this sense, the two art forms may complement each other in the public sphere, but compete for space when complementariness eludes them despite their aesthetic value.

At the turn of the twenty-first century in Williamsburg, Brooklyn, mural art and graffiti, rather than competing and pushing one another out, coexist in a changing urban landscape. However, the dynamics of public spaces and public art in Brooklyn cannot be understood without going back to the roots of urban graffiti in the New York City neighborhoods of the South Bronx and Spanish Harlem, which since the 1960s have witnessed profound socioeconomic transitions similar to those currently affecting Williamsburg, though in different ways and at different paces of capital investment. The Bronx is by far the slowest to experience the kind of gentrification now under way in Williamsburg. In Spanish Harlem and Harlem, the pace of gentrification is somewhat more rapid, but still slower than in Williamsburg. When comparing urban transitions across these diverse communities, we need to keep in mind Walter Benjamin's (1968 [1936]: 222) notion that the "manner in which human sense perception is organized, the medium in which it is accomplished, is determined not only by nature but by historical circumstances as well." This means that the political and economic forces behind the changes that have made gentrification possible in the Bronx, Spanish Harlem, and Williamsburg are also molding a different sensory landscape, and with it a changing public art media tableau in which sponsored murals are appearing where graffiti once prevailed.

The Roots of Urban Graffiti in New York City

The case of Puerto Rican migration and settlement is instructive for contextualizing graffiti as a form of public art that can represent a cultural group's various transitions over decades. Just before and immediately after World War II, a massive population shift took place as African Americans left the South to escape Jim Crow culture and Puerto Ricans migrated from their island homeland to seek economic opportunities in New York City. Most newcomers sought a better life, but many had been forced to emigrate by displacements at home. Displaced by a postwar island economy dominated by corporations, rural Puerto Rican peasants flocked to urban centers and the United States. Between 1940 and 1970, about 533,000 Puerto Ricans emigrated from their homeland to the United States. Tens of thousands of them went to New York City, where "the Puerto Rican community became synonymous with the Latino community" (Haslip-Viera and Baver 1996: 12). However, in the two decades after World War II there arose a set of circumstances that reshaped Puerto Rican lives in ways that could never have been anticipated.

In the late 1940s, the U.S. government collaborated with Puerto Rican politicians to develop "Operation Bootstrap," a set of policies aimed at increasing investment in industries with high labor demand, encouraging Puerto Ricans to leave agrarian areas for the industrial mainland. The mass movement of agricultural workers seeking work in U.S. cities in the wake of agriculture's industrialization and corporatization had already crested. Although Puerto Ricans often suffered the indignities visited on immigrants from foreign lands, they were still entitled to the privileges enjoyed by any U.S. citizen. In these postwar years, these migrants, especially those who were poorly educated, expected that unionized manufacturing work would provide them and their families with a respectable standard of life. This image was shattered by reality.

By the 1950s manufacturing was disappearing from New York City's landscape. What remained, notably garment manufacturing, attracted Puerto Rican newcomers, though this industry was also moving to areas of cheaper labor in the United States and overseas. The Puerto Rican women who managed to find work in garment manufacturing earned very low wages in the sweatshops that remained. They joined and worked with the International Ladies' Garment Workers' Union (ILGWU), where union officials favored white ethnics. Puerto Rican workers became progressively disenchanted with the union's failure to adequately represent them in contract negotiations and joined with African American workers to march against discrimination, specifically their subordination "in the occupational ladder of the industry and in the leadership structure of the union" (Ortiz 1989: 118). Puerto Rican workers also occupied other niches in the low-wage service sector, such as the restaurant business and building custodial services. A small number found their way into the public sector and lower echelons of the private sector.

From a cultural ecological point of view, an empty niche invited new migrants—and especially immigrants—to occupy it. According to Jesse Sanchez (1996: 272), at this point the Puerto Ricans helped "salvage the city's manufacturing sector with their cheap labor." From an economic perspective, Puerto Ricans were a people who could fill low-wage service jobs and reside in increasingly available low-income housing at a time of "white flight." The transition from "white," often mostly working-class Jewish and Italian, neighborhoods to Puerto Rican and African American neighborhoods enabled a poorer, less-skilled group of people—Latinos and African-descendent folk—to settle in the housing made available by mass departures in a kind of "de-gentrification" and displacement.

Meanwhile, under the GI Bill, returning military servicemen could participate in the upward mobility of postwar society by accessing higher education and low-interest loans to purchase homes and build up equity. Occupational and social mobility translated into spatial mobility. Newly built housing, in suburbs connected to New York City by newly constructed highways, was meant to support the transition from a wartime to a peacetime economy. However, these benefits accrued to whites almost exclusively, helping generate urban white flight to the suburbs.

The massive influx of Puerto Ricans and others from the Caribbean and Latin America, together with the movement of earlier immigrant groups and their descendants from the city to the suburbs, permitted the growth and expansion of neighborhoods associated with Latino settlement after 1945. "El Barrio," or Spanish Harlem, expanded eastward from Park Avenue to the East River between 1948 and 1955. During the same period, a large new concentration of mostly Puerto Ricans emerged in the South Bronx and settled in Sunset Park and Williamsburg too. South Bronx Puerto Ricans were often related to those from El Barrio and Williamsburg, but each group developed its own sense of identity.

Jewish out-migration occurred at this time as well. Puerto Ricans continued to replace earlier, mostly Jewish residents on the Lower East Side, and they also stabilized themselves in new concentrations on Manhattan's West Side and Upper West Side. The Puerto Rican neighborhoods in Brooklyn and Queens also grew in these years. The Puerto Rican enclave in the Navy Yard district of Brooklyn expanded northward and eastward into parts of Williamsburg, Greenpoint, Bushwick, and Red Hook. At the same time, the South Brooklyn enclave around Columbia Street expanded southward to include parts of Park Slope and Sunset Park. In the early years of their migration to New York City, Puerto Ricans tended to live under crowded conditions in the worst of the available housing and generally ended up at the bottom of the economy, in terms of occupational category and income. These conditions inspired mainstream artists' romantic, though not necessarily complimentary, depictions of Puerto Rican lives in theater, film, and music, from Leonard Bernstein and Steven Sondheim's *West Side Story* (1957) to Paul Simon and Derek Walcott's *The Capeman* (1998). Now closed since the 1990s, the Teatro Puerto Rico in the South Bronx had its heyday in the 1940s and 1950s as the Latino equivalent of Harlem's Apollo Theatre, where such musicians as Tito Puente, Machito, Charlie and Eddie Palmieri, Willie Colon, and others played to broad audiences.

Puerto Ricans struggled to gain access to public housing in the 1970s, a period of significant housing decline due to New York City's fiscal crisis and policy of planned shrinkage of urban areas populated by people with the least power and greatest vulnerability. Despite organized efforts to reform the New York City Housing Authority, little changed to enable Puerto Ricans to gain access to public housing in larger numbers. Sanchez (1996: 269) discovered that Puerto Ricans were not involved in the struggle for public housing because they lacked access to an "independent institution that provides routine opportunities for congregating, sharing joys and hopes, and assisting often in the mobilization of values, resources, and people," such as the black church, a reliable source of leadership and site of social movement formation in the African American community. Ana Maria Díaz-Stevens (1994: 167) saw the dearth of viable organizing structures—notably, the local Catholic parishes' failure to effectively address their needs—as a key factor deterring Puerto Ricans from accessing public housing and other entitlements. However, some faith-based efforts, for example those of charismatic priests in Williamsburg, did provide infrastructure for gaining access to entitlements.

Despite their situation, Puerto Ricans did find housing, in both the public housing that was available to them and, more so, in rentals that enabled them to establish vibrant communities in "Puerto Rican" neighborhoods. Since the 1950s, and increasingly in recent decades, urban renewal drove thousands of Puerto Ricans, as well as members of African-descendent groups, from their neighborhoods, devastating strong, cohesive social relationships identified with the notion of community. Whites' demographic shift from cities to suburbs received much attention, as did the ethno-racial transition that cities experienced as working-class whites moved to the newly built suburbs and lower-income people of color came to predominate in urban areas referred to as "inner cities," "ghettos," and "slums." The various transitional conditions experienced by newcomers to New York City in the postwar years gave birth to a new form of public art known as graffiti.

Starting in the late 1960s, "getting up" became a rite of passage for many New York City youths as Puerto Ricans and African Americans settled in New York City neighborhoods. They "bombed" trains because their objective was to gain recognition for abundant visibility; hence, the synonyms for "getting up" included "getting around," goin' all-city," and "getting the name out." The graffiti work itself was referred to as "writing." Painting subway cars took courage and preparation. Spray cans had to be "racked up" in sufficient quantity and color variety to do the job. Athleticism, stamina, and focus were needed to hold to the prepared design, sketched out ahead of time in "piece books." A multiethnic crew worked as a team, standing up for hours, always on the lookout for the law.

In the 1970s, graffiti artists competed to put as many tags as they could on surfaces, thus preventing others from doing the same. Writing over someone else's graffiti was strictly prohibited by an unwritten social contract and could lead to violence. Recognition was the principle motivation for tagging. Those who study the ubiquity of tags on subway trains say that by tagging trains, graffiti artists gained recognition all over the city, and indeed they did. Experimentation produced more colorful designs of greater complexity, though the evolution of styles remains difficult to pinpoint because they emerged somewhat simultaneously. Works with bubble-style characters, polka dots, and crosshatches were prevalent. The single tags initially borne by subway train exteriors were replaced by "top-to-bottom" creations that literally covered train cars. The 1970s saw an explosion of graffiti in New York City. By 1973–1974, further features had been introduced; for instance, cartoon characters were included in more traditional work. It is easy to romanticize graffiti when reflecting on the successful, appreciated images that got documented by graffiti aficionados. Unfortunately, much graffiti is unsuccessful and unsightly: instead of beautifying space, it clutters and cheapens it. Photographs of subway cars' marred interiors attest to the destructive power of exuberant youth practicing their tags. Such tags abound on walls and retail store shutters.

Demetrius Taki is most often celebrated as the founder of graffiti in New York City. However, the most successful graffitists, who managed to transform street art into commercial art success, are arguably Jean-Michel Basquiat (Bischofberger 1999; Emmerling 2003; Fab 5 Freddy 2011: 96–99) and Keith Haring (Deitch 2011: 100–104). A particularly notable development by the 1970s was that sophisticated graffiti street art producers were no longer only "angry" ghetto youths but cut across class, ethno-racial, and occasionally even gender lines. Some of them grew into legitimized "artists" in their own right, Basquiat and Haring being prime examples.

The rise of graffiti in New York City in the 1970s coincided with a period of economic collapse as the world oil crisis in 1973 led into a "fiscal crisis" in 1975. Government resources contracted, leaving low-income neighborhoods to their own devices. New York City had to slash its budget, limiting among other things the resources available to fight graffiti. At this point, graffiti art exploded all over the city. Entire subway trains "bombed" by graffiti images rolled through tunnels underground to reappear at subway platforms or on elevated tracks in the boroughs, rumbling across the skyline from one neighborhood to the next. Subway graffitists enshrined narratives of bravery in tales of their nocturnal adventures "getting up." It did take courage to scale walls, climb barbed-wire fences, and elude security guards and police officers. Nowadays city budget cuts are on the rise again—and so, unsurprisingly, is street graffiti (Nagourney 2011).

In an introduction to Jamel Shabazz's *A Time Before Crack,* Claude Grunitzky (2005: 12) pointed out that 1985 was a watershed year in the inner city: "[P]eople were different before that year. The slang was different, the attitudes were different, the music was different, and social interactions were different." He attributed this dramatic change to the introduction of crack, which was cheap and highly addictive. The former Transit Police Officer Shabazz (2005: 135) noted that whereas the New York Police Department made no arrests for crack offenses in 1985, 19,000 such arrests were made in 1988. The drug trade penetrated youth culture and "transformed the social fabric of the city" (Grunitzky 2005: 12). Sale and use of drugs was ubiquitous in the inner city, and although only a fraction of people engaged in the trade and use of illicit drugs, entire neighborhoods were stigmatized, with youth in particular bearing the brunt of this characterization (to this day). This endangered graffitists who entered train yards or climbed over fences or roofs to ply their art. They had always had to overcome significant physical barriers to get to the prospective graffiti site, but now law enforcement agents circulated in the area to thwart them. This was not only a matter of getting caught "getting up," as apprehension might also involve being chased by police or guards. Youths caught trying to escape might end up with a beating never to be forgotten.

Susan Hoeltzel credited Stefan Eins with the founding of Fashion Moda, an alternative space in the Bronx that shaped the art of the 1980s. Hoeltzel (1996) identified this space as a "laboratory where untrained artists and those with art school backgrounds exchanged ideas, performed, exhibited and made art—while the neighborhood joined in." Soon the legitimate art world recognized what was happening. Hugo Martinez started the Razor Gallery, and United Graffiti Artists formed to represent graffiti artists in mainstream galleries, commoditizing what had been considered "public art" produced without a price in mind. Hardened graffiti artists declared that those who turned their street art into products to be sold had disqualified themselves as graffiti "artists" because disassociation from the marketplace was the hallmark of graffiti. Franke, a German graffitist at the July 2008 opening of Alphabeta—a Brooklyn store offering graffiti enthusiasts outdoor space for mural painting and merchandise like t-shirts, spray-painted hats, and of course aerosol cans in a wide range of colors—

Figure 12.6. Keith Haring mural in the Woodhull Medical and Mental Health Center entrance hall. Photo taken on 18 September 2010, Sam Beck.

was quoted as saying: "The real graffiti artists are in dictatorships, where writing on a wall is a courageous act. What I do is child's play. But a real graffiti artist risks a lot to make people think" (NPR 2008). Real graffiti is still characterized as an act of transgression, be it subversive, rebellious, or dissident.

The hip-hop movement brought about a synergistic merger between graffiti art and performing arts such as rapping, DJing, and break dancing. A new wave of European receptivity to American-born art forms and artists led the Italian collector and art dealer Claudio Bruni to stage an exhibition of Lee Quinones and Fab 5 Freddy in Rome. Keith Haring built his reputation in Europe before he was recognized in the United States.

"Wild style," featuring intricate compositions of letters and color that only a trained eye could differentiate, was prevalent by the 1980s. Graffiti-influenced, trained artists like Haring and Basquiat ascended the ranks of the art world. But whereas rap—even gangster rap—and break dancing reached a mass market and became respected acceptable art forms, graffiti did not match their range or marketability, perhaps because of the difference between performance art and painting as an art form. Rap in particular reached a public audience even when it transgressed, defied, or offended. Break dancing and rap found a global audience and corporate media money; graffiti fared less well.

Yet in just twenty years, graffiti made its way from neighborhoods, subways, and train yards to the halls of art galleries and museums. New York City, as one of the prime centers of the fashion world, had given birth to a creative style unquestionably tied to urban youth culture. Rapidly assimilated by art school–trained practitioners, this style evolved into high-priced commodities. Some urban youth, recognized for their raw talent, also rose in the ranks of art producers by commoditizing their graffiti.

Master Graffitists: TATS CRU and James De La Vega

My earlier fieldwork was with TATS CRU (2014) and James De La Vega, variously identified as "graffiti," "public," "spray can," or "street" artists. I also participated in the art world, subjecting myself to the vicissitudes of making art for art's sake and producing art for sale in the marketplace. I experienced modest success but also failure. Though not directly participating in public art, I developed a sense of its world in the two years I spent with De La Vega, who worked the streets of various parts of Manhattan (Goldberg 2009). During my fieldwork, a literature on public art emerged and grew, much of it in the form of book-length photographic collections accompanied by text and transcriptions of interviews with graffiti writers. Photographers like Cooper and Chalfant (1984), Miller (20012, Sutherland (2004), the Murrays (2006), and Naar (2007) created such volumes. Others

Figure 12.7. James De La Vega, Become Your Dream. Photo taken on 18 September 2010, Sam Beck.

are field-researched analyses by sociologists like Castelman (1982), Snyder (2009), and Austin (2001).

One summer evening, James De La Vega invited me to join him as he drove a mutual friend home from Spanish Harlem, where James lived and had his studio and store, to the Bronx, where our friend lived. On the way back, James eyed a prominent wall facing a highway and opposite a well-frequented McDonald's restaurant. Passing the wall, we discussed its striking suitability for one of his images, *Become Your Dream,* whereupon he suddenly turned back, stopped, and popped open the trunk of his car. Pulling out a gallon can of white paint and his favorite brush, both of which had seen previous use, he quickly painted a huge fish jumping into the air toward a glass it could not have fit in, had it actually reached it. He was partway through painting his name at the bottom of the fresh image when a police cruiser pulled up and two officers stepped out, asking us what we were doing there and whether we had permission to paint on the wall. James said no (Goldberg 2009). They briskly confiscated his equipment, turned him, restrained him with plastic handcuffs, pushed his head down, and edged him into the back seat of the patrol car. Over the next few days, his mother, a mutual friend, and I looked for James, who was being transferred from one local cell to another.

Figure 12.8. James De La Vega, Homage to Singer Celia Cruz. Photo taken on 16 October 2011, Sam Beck.

After receiving a degree in fine arts from Cornell University, De La Vega returned to his native Spanish Harlem "to give back," as he put it. The various art forms he developed in giving back gave him notoriety in New York City and abroad. He painted on traditional canvas and painted murals on public walls all over the neighborhood. To De La Vega, these works of art were not graffiti; nor did he consider them "murals," although that was what they looked like to me. While some of the work was commissioned, other work was done surreptitiously, graffiti-style, with a few quick strokes of paint. De La Vega also used chalk and masking tape on New York City sidewalks and streets to do his art and considered this kind of work as much performance art as anything else. This artwork was defined by its impermanence and by what he identified as "interruptions." While carrying out his art, whether on walls or on the sidewalk, he was always interrupted by people asking questions about what he was doing, usually also complimenting him or making suggestions about what else he could do. He meant his completed work to interrupt people's everyday lives, helping them stop their doing and thinking to just interact with their surroundings. Moreover, he invited people in suits on their way to work or returning home to "live out their passion," or at least consider the meaning of his *Become Your Dream* image. He saw them as having lost sight of their "dream" and settled for less. When he was arrested, it was as a graffitist who had vandalized private property.

Figure 12.9. James De La Vega, Homage to Picasso. Photo taken on 16 October 2011, Sam Beck.

Figure 12.10. James De La Vega, Homage to Picasso. Photo taken on 16 October 2011, Sam Beck.

Graffiti in particular but murals too "hold an element of power that is personal, social, symbolic and political" (James De La Vega, personal communication). Making them is not only about defacing private or governmental property—the struggle is also about who controls public discourse in public and private spaces in city neighborhoods, who rules the streets, and who defines deviance in those spaces. Graffiti is an accepted art form only when taken from the street, displayed in galleries and museums, and thereby sanctioned by the marketplace. The artists' collective, TATS CRU has been a party to court cases involving free speech and copyright issues. It challenged the City of New York for painting over its "Stop Snitching" mural painting on the side of an East Harlem bodega. It initiated a lawsuit against Fiat because a commercial featuring Jennifer Lopez used an image of its Hunt's Point wall art as background without permission, attribution, or compensation. Similarly, Peter Rosenstein and Isabel Bau Madden's (2006) book *Tattooed Walls* was taken out of circulation because it included one hundred photographs used without permission from graffiti artists.

From time to time, I visit the Point Community Development Corporation in Hunts Point in the South Bronx (www.thepoint.org). Established to lay the foundation for community sustainability in the arts, this community-based organization operates out of a former mint that the Point rehabbed for its own purposes. A small building next to the main build-

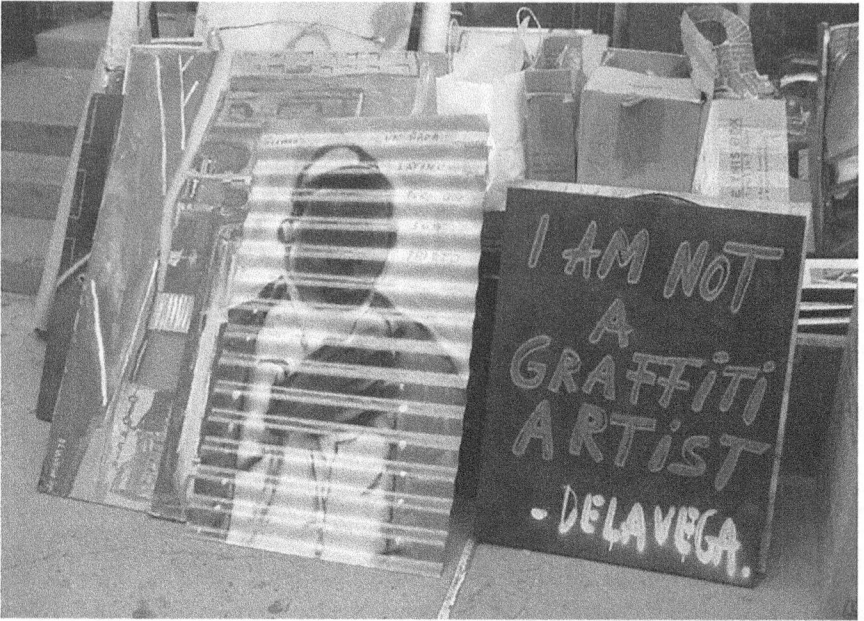

Figure 12.11. James De La Vega, East Village store closing, photo taken on 16 October 2011, Sam Beck

ing holds the offices and studio space of TATS CRU (Top Artist Talents), founded by a group of young Puerto Rican (Bio, Nicer, and BG183) graffitists. These young men spray-painted subway cars with graffiti designs in the 1980s, but now they produce commercial art for such companies as Coca-Cola, M&M's, Reebok, and Firestone, for hip-hop CD covers, and so on. They identify themselves as "aerosol muralists" (Marcano 1995) and continually evolve their art form using computer-aided design. Their works may be regarded as both landmarks dotting the South Bronx and expressions of their identity with the South Bronx. In line with Snyder's (2009: 63) observation that "today's writers have a more intimate relationship with the entire city. In the 1970s and 1980s graffiti was location specific and was mainly written on trains," today TATS CRU's art can be seen in different parts of New York City. Since TATS CRU's turn to commercial art, its members have known that other graffitists see them as "sellouts" because they no longer involve themselves in the surreptitious, illegal form of graffiti. However, they identify themselves as artists and consider their art form as a creative, aesthetic advancement that takes spray-can art to another level (see Beighley 2014). A recent book on New York City community murals included them as an example of community mural artists with an anti-war message (Braun-Reinitz and Weissman 2009: 179–180).

Figure 12.12. TATS CRU, Nicer, Bio, and BG183 at their art show opening at gallery Toy Tokyo, Blood Sweat and Tears, in the East Village. Photo taken on 28 February 2014, Sam Beck.

Key to understanding these artists is their art's connection to their Puerto Rican identity and their sense that part of their work is to gain recognition for their community. Much like African Americans, upon arriving in New York City Puerto Ricans were quickly racialized and vilified as a minority population degrading the neighborhoods where they settled. Even now they are only beginning to be recognized for their contributions to New York City and the United States. Large numbers of Puerto Ricans fought in the Korean War in the segregated 65th Army Infantry Regiment, and in the Vietnam War. At the start of the neoliberal era in the 1970s, Puerto Rican families stabilized neighborhoods at a time when New York City was withdrawing basic resources. Even more important, Puerto Ricans

Figure 12.13. BG 183 in front of his recent work at TATS CRU opening show at gallery Toy Tokyo, Blood Sweat and Tears, in the East Village. Photo taken 28 February 2014, Sam Beck.

strengthened their communities, creating binding ties, supporting each other in the hardest of times, and raising their children as best they could, enabling for many the social mobility most Americans sought when they first arrived.

Public Art in New York City: Transgression or Commodity?

What happens on New York City streets often passes us by as so much peripheral noise, at worst an annoyance, at best a momentary distraction or interruption. A closer look uncovers a controversy implicating urban political, economic, and law enforcement powers that is all the more intense for public artists because it centers on the very meaning of their art. How it is defined, and who defines it? Is art produced based on the producer's aesthetic value alone, or is art a commodity bought and sold in the marketplace, reflecting the appreciation of consumers who are willing to purchase goods created for sale? The tension between graffiti, murals, and images for outdoor advertisements is very much part of the urban aesthetic. Government or the private sector sponsors some public art, while other public art is idiosyncratic, personal, and transgressive. Mural art, in contrast to graffiti art, is more often a tool for educating the public, although some graffiti artists seek to educate as well.

Whether at ground level, above the ground, or underground, New York City's public face is "eye candy." Virtually any space, even the body, bodily adornments, or articles of clothing, is canvas for various forms of planned or spontaneous graphic art, be it oriented to public consumption or not. These ubiquitous art forms may represent marketing of goods and services, or simply be consumer objects themselves. The point is that whenever our gaze apprehends a graphic piece, two impressions must be held simultaneously: one of the particular isolated graphic itself, and the other of the larger context—the environment—in which it is situated. More often than not, only local people in the neighborhood know the location of graffiti street art, and graffiti blends into their daily activities. Strangers who come upon a graffiti-strewn urbanscape for the first time can feel interrupted by the artwork, or even antagonized or disturbed. Some fear neighborhoods where graffiti is found. For others, graffiti in urban settings is a destination for touristic voyeurism.

Like other public art, graffiti is situated in a changing city environment whose landscapes, ranging from postindustrial to gentrified, both signify and reflect a dynamic urban ecology. Transgressive graffiti especially is in constant transformation as its material form and function interact with its physical and social environment. In some instances graffiti is touched up, refreshed, and sustained over time, but much graffiti gets worn down by the elements or obscured by added graffiti, stray markings and tags, and replacement graffiti. Often building owners just paint right over the images, or the building is torn down. Graffiti, like any other material form present in the urban infrastructure, decay and disappear.

Figure 12.14. Bodega wall at Myrtle and Willoughby Avenues, Bedford Stuyvesant. Photo taken on 25 September 2011, Sam Beck.

The Chicago-based muralist John Pitman Weber (2003) claimed that much of the community public mural art from the 1960s, 1970s, and even the 1980s has disappeared, and that the work of those decades' social activists has similarly almost vanished. Buildings on which this art appeared were demolished, the paintings disintegrated as a result of weather conditions, some were painted over, and others have faded, slowly losing visibility (Weber 2003). According to Janet Braun-Reinitz and Jane Weissman (2009), much of New York City's public art fortunately has remained. Yet as someone living in this city for decades, I have noticed the disappearance of many prominent murals. Much of De La Vega's public work in Spanish Harlem is gone. Weber (2003), who is interested in keeping public art visible, turned to producing murals in mosaic and cement relief instead of paint, too easily destroyed. American urban change appears to be the ultimate arbiter of what disappears and what remains, as large tracts of land are transformed, neighborhoods change, and new property owners appreciate other aesthetics (Vergara 1999). Ironically, the Philadelphia Anti-Graffiti Network, which campaigned against tagging, also generated the Mural Arts Program, which supported the painting of two thousand murals in the city between the 1980s and the early 2000s (Golden et al. 2002) to thwart the writing of graffiti.

According to Weber (2003: 6), "Despite the relative impermanence of paint exposed to sun, despite North American winters and acidic urban atmospheres, the ultimate danger is that a mural outlasts the community consensus that it originally reflected and helped shape." Whoever occupies a given space will define the expression of its particular public aesthetic. Gentrification redefines space and the urban aesthetic, yet this aesthetic sense moves through developmental stages that reflect the developmental stages of gentrification itself. Certain public art is perceived as disposable or unappreciated, but other public art may be encouraged, sponsored, or tolerated due to its message or marketability. For example, a new mural painted on a restaurant wall advertises a café, marketing and "branding" the enterprise, conceptually, to various publics: hipsters, yuppies, and luxury housing dwellers.

Graffiti has been a bone of contention among New Yorkers ever since the late 1960s. The 1960s and 1970s could be described as a peak of youth culture, which flourished in the rebellions against America's war in Vietnam and the struggle for civil rights as young people spilled out into the streets to protest and demonstrate. In the mid 1970s, when New York City experienced something close to financial collapse, government withdrew services from inner-city areas as minorities settled in formerly white ethnic neighborhoods depopulated by so-called white flight. In this era of "creative destruction," land values plummeted, and housing in working-class neighborhoods decayed. It was then that the modern forms of graffiti and community murals were invented. Graffiti, as an urban public aesthetic, paralleled government- and private sector–funded public mural art.

Graffiti started as part of a marginal, urban social youth movement that came to be politicized as a war of ethnicity, race, class, and gender in a space of urban decay defined as the inner city. There, settlements of working poor were considered "marginal," now that the generations of mostly working-class white ethnic residents who once considered them "home" had abandoned them for suburban living. One difference between graffitists and muralists is that graffitists tend to have few expectations of permanence, and to seek respect and status rather than remuneration. In the context of poverty, life changes are severe. Being poor can breed a certain impermanence. Moving constantly in search of low-cost housing, transferring children from school to school, and other forced transitioning are normal forms of existence in poor communities. Youth seeking status in these conditions must gain respect to stand out and "stand up," and graffiti is one vehicle for doing this. They initially acquired notoriety by writing names or initials on walls, known as "signaturing," or "tagging" and then moved on to whole subway-car paintings. Sponsored mural art, commoditized graphic advertisements, and graffiti developed simultaneously, influencing each other and sometimes even "speaking to each other."

The impermanence of graffiti, especially whole subway-car art, generated the impetus to record the images through photography. A substantial body of art made by graffiti artists was reproduced in photographic and academic books before being cleansed or otherwise disappearing. Alongside this publishing trend, industries arose around the policing of graffiti spaces (part of former Mayor Rudolph Giuliani's "quality of life" initiative) as well as around the supply of graffiti materials and retailing of graffiti-influenced goods. Since 2004, the New York City Police Department has gone all out to deter "graffiti vandalism crimes." According to its website, "the New York Police Department has created a centralized intelligence graffiti database to identify known graffiti vandals with their tags" (New York Police Department 2014).

In 2006, New York City Mayor Michael Bloomberg and City Councilman Peter Vallone Jr. sought to ban and make illegal the possession of spray paint and broad-tipped markers by youth aged eighteen to twenty. Marc Ecko, a former graffiti artist and serial entrepreneur who uses graffiti images in his design work, spearheaded a lawsuit against the City of New York for violating first amendment rights of free speech. The judge sided with Ecko, supporting freedom of expression ("Bomb the City" 2006). Graffiti law enforcement is a multibillion-dollar effort across the country. Various products for cleaning graffiti off subway cars, private and public buildings, and billboards have entered the economy (Graffiti Hurts 2014). Meanwhile, graffiti art supplies like aerosol paint and nozzles, markers, stencil materials, and so on are now available online (33third 2014).

Photographic publications on graffiti provide documentation of artwork. These books are commodities in their own right but also, importantly, serve to circulate design and color ideas. Observers of graffiti associate its impermanence with the temporariness that characterizes ghetto life. Others see graffitists as members of households in New York City neighborhoods but also perceive them as unrepresentative of the American mainstream, as intruding into "real" America. Some see the transient nature of graffiti art as its most important quality (Camilo José Vergara, personal communication). Transgressive graffitists believe that no one should own their art. REVS of Brooklyn, for example, showed no interest in anything commercial except for "getting up." He innovated by pasting sheets of paper high on walls with his printed REVS signature. COST, who often joined him did similar art and continues to this day. (See *Gothamist* 2013.)

Figure 12.15. COST in lower Manhattan. Photo taken on 3 September 2013, Sam Beck.

Photography, however, accords a sense of permanence and legitimacy, even ownership. Transgressive public artists moving between illegal graffiti and commoditized art understood the need for photographers and videographers to create their histories, even when their original art no longer existed outside of photos, film, and videos such as Banksy's (2010) Oscar-nominated documentary film *Exit Through the Gift Shop,* or the film *Wild Style* (Aheam 1983). MacPhee (2004) affirmed that stencil artists photograph their own work, and members of TATS CRU do so as well (personal communication). Digitized graffiti graphics circulate in cyberspace. Stencil graffitists circulate their designs, the simplicity of their materials allowing their work to be reproduced all over the world. Amateur photographers' postings on various websites make innovations almost instantly available worldwide.

As graffiti gained legitimacy in the art world, the style became an incentive for young people to enter the creative world of art and design. Children and youth commonly sketch their versions of graffiti in notebooks. At a time when art no longer has a place in school, youths' desire—or perhaps even their innate need—to be creative finds its outlet elsewhere.

Placement of Graffiti in New York City's Public Spaces

American-rooted art forms, especially performance art forms, tend to arise on the social margins. Tap dancing, jazz, the blues, and rock and roll are all syncretic art forms connected intimately to African roots, which remained part of the syncretism that traveled from the Caribbean islands to New York City. Claims that these contemporary urban aesthetics concern a particular ethnic or ethno-national identity remain farfetched. Much like hip-hop, modern graffiti is a product of American urbanism and the Americanization of diverse people's aesthetic sense. There is no one meaning, no one origin. Graffiti is a fantastic combination and recombination of diverse influences that continue to evolve. If anywhere, its roots are found among the urban youth living in America's low-income working-class neighborhoods.

In an appreciative sense, graffiti popularly implies the painted decoration of the urban built environment. In disapproving speech it refers to the defacing of private and public property, an act of illegal vandalism. Between the 1960s and 1980s, street youth associations usually portrayed as "gangs" of various types entered the scene. In New York City, only a few "gangs" devoted themselves at least partly to graffiti writing to mark turf. Yet the media and police portrayed graffiti crews—groups of graffitists who collaborated to paint together—as "gang members." Graffiti was also linked to hip-hop culture. Some participants characterized b-boying and or break dancing, which emerged at about the same time (Rahn 2002: 2; Rivera 2003: 12), as a means of expressing the frustrations in their lives through dance. Joseph Rivera's account of his lived experiences as a member of the New York City Transit Police Department lends much-needed insight into how the city's authority structure viewed graffiti and graffiti artists (2008). A youth culture complex emerged and has continued to evolve over time, expanding and diffusing from U.S. urban centers into the suburbs and internationally. Every urban aesthetic style, from rap to breaking to graffiti, can now be found in virtually every part of the world. The authorities similarly characterized graffitists as rebellious and transgressive, rather than creative and innovative. In this manner, the establishment attacked urban youth culture by reducing it to its worst elements instead of praising its creativity and innovation. In some ways this is unsurprising because "urban culture" is not only associated with poverty but with youth of color, who are persistently characterized as threatening, violent, and crime-prone.

Not all graffitists are the same. Some regard graffiti as a political act of social activism; others see it as a highly individualistic, even anarchistic form of self-expression competing with corporate advertising at a time of job scarcity and the explosion of the culture of the American consumer society. As the paintings became larger and more complex, graffiti turned into a team effort by groups of individuals creating their tableaus in "crews." In his book *Graffito,* Michael Walsh (1996: 11) asserted, "Most media coverage lumps graffiti crews and urban gangs as if they were the same thing. Whereas gangs use graffiti solely for the purpose of marking their territories and sending messages to rival gangs [*sic*]. Gang-related graffiti represents only about twenty percent of U.S. graffiti." Walsh points out that graffiti results from various motivations. Some graffitists are simply angry; feeling alienated, they express their sense of estrangement through their work. Likening graffiti to a sacred, healing shamanic ritual, Walsh (1996: 1) also joins most other graffiti commentators to assert its political power as an act, possibly a revolutionary one, that challenges the art gallery system and art market, and thus the "utilitarian values of capitalist social order." Analyzing generational differences, Walsh maintains that teenage graffitists view their practice as fun and exhilarating, providing a set of euphoric, transgressive experiences; older graffitists, meanwhile, see theirs as a way of life. Some see themselves as "tricksters" who create their own language and produce their own calligraphy; according to Walsh (1996: 12), "They want you to see it but don't want you to understand it."

Graffiti has been used to mark territory in marginalized neighborhoods patrolled by paramilitary police forces and ruled by the ubiquitous "gangs." In Los Angeles and Philadelphia, for example, graffiti could delineate one gang's neighborhood from others. This was less the case in New York City, where "gangs" took on a different configuration and graffiti among gangs was highly organized and practiced in crews. Jay "J.SON" Edlin began his career as a middle-class white graffiti artist in 1973. By the early 1980s, when crack and angel dust spilled into the graffiti world, Edlin understood that graffiti territoriality meant that certain crews controlled specific [train] yards and lay-ups. "To venture into hostile turf was akin to suicide" (2010: v).

An important form of graffiti is the memorial to fallen youth, often associated with a drug culture in which sales territories were openly contested through violence and vendettas were common among competing individuals and their "posses" or crews. Cooper and Sciorra (1994: 7) documented "memorial wall art" on the sides of buildings in New York City's Latino and African American neighborhoods, positing that: "The ongoing violence in the public sphere contributes to an overwhelming despair and necessitates a communal response to help neighborhood residents overcome their bereavement collectively. Memorial walls are reminders of, if not indictments against, civil society's inability or unwillingness to address the systemic poverty and the pervasive racism that promote the rampant flow of drugs and guns into inner-city communities."

Families and communities also employ graffitists to help in their grieving process by commemorating individuals who died under other circumstances. Some of these memorials are painted on walls by permission of the buildings' owners; others are created without consent. In a video interview posted by Rosenblum (2011), graffitist Alfredo Oyague Jr. discusses such memorials in the Bronx's Mott Haven. Family members hired graffiti crews to throw up images of murder victims in scenes associated with their short lives and the dates of their deaths. Portraits spray-painted on neighborhood walls also commonly bore farewell messages and statements of remembrance. Commissions of this sort were ubiquitous in the 1980s and 1990s; TATS CRU is still commissioned to paint such memorials. Vestiges of earlier memorials remain visible in many neighborhoods, as they are left untouched even when the paint fades or peels away. Memorials are well respected and rarely purposely damaged or defaced, as this is understood as a prohibited act of disrespect that could incur punitive retaliation.

In the 1980s, a new style emerged on the urban scene: stencil graffiti, which used cutouts as a way to rapidly create images. The notorious Banksy

Figure 12.16. Old memorial on the corner of Marcy and Tompkins Avenues, Bedford Stuyvesant. Photo taken on 18 March 2014, Sam Beck.

Figure 12.17. Retouched old memorial, Havemeyer Avenue and South 2nd, Southside, Williamsburg. Photo taken on 8 February 2014, Sam Beck.

is purported to have been one of this style's originators and developers. In his own words:

> I started off painting graffiti in the classic New York style [in the late 1980s during the Bristol, England, spray-can movement] you use when you listen to too much hip-hop as a kid … but I was never very good at it. As soon as I cut my first stencil, I could feel the power there. The ruthlessness and efficiency of it is perfect. I also like the political edge. All graffiti is low-level dissent but stencils have an extra history. They've been used to start revolutions and to stop wars. They look political just through the style. … Painting the streets means becoming an actual part of the city. It's not a spectator sport. (Manco 2002: 76–79)

Josh MacPhee (2004: 9) declared that stencils "opened up a world of public expression to me, and I want to share that with everyone that's felt like they had no control over their environment." In the built environment, stencil images are an alternative to corporate street advertising and government signage. Stencils are meant to interrupt. Their meanings, if they actually have them, are ambiguous—unless they are political, whereupon they are most likely harsh and "in your face." Much like tagging, stenciling is about "getting up" as much and as often as possible, gaining visibility everywhere. Shepard Fairey's images, including OBEY and Andre the Giant, are ubiquitous the world over. Like Banksy and MacPhee, Fairey is an example of a street artist turning transgressive work into commodities. Similarly, REVS and COST gained fame not only for their work's wide distribution, but also because they innovated by using rollers to write their huge tags, often at the top of buildings, 6 feet high and 15 or more feet across. They also photocopied their names on sheets of A4 paper and pasted them by the thousands all over New York.

New York City, like cities everywhere, ramped up its campaign against graffiti vandalism, spending millions of dollars. The MTA prioritized graffiti eradication on subways, a policy that created hardships for graffiti artists, who could be accosted, beaten, fined, and jailed by graffiti eradication officers. Deterred by these punitive measures, many graffitists abandoned their efforts. Others made it a game of hide-and-seek in which they "counted coup" (i.e., demonstrated bravery in combat against efforts to obliterate their images), later recounting stories of tagging and escape that bolstered their prestige and status.

This was a time when hardware stores locked spray paint in glass and metal storage cabinets, not just in observance of restrictions on its sale, but also to stop the pilfering of this product. Stealing spray paint, another trend in youth culture, became an actual part of graffiti production and the narratives associated with this art form. The Clean Train Movement, an effort to rapidly remove graffiti from subways, had two outcomes: graffiti artists increasingly moved to the streets, covering available walls; and youths started to deface subway train glass by etching images, usually letters, into windows and door glass in a process known as "Scratchiti" or "Scribing."

Amid the cocaine and crack epidemic that spawned violence and wide-scale death in marginalized communities of color in the 1980s, the most renowned graffitists moved from the streets to the galleries. Jean-Michel Basquiat (Cortez et al. 2007) and Keith Haring (Kolossa 2004) each had art school training, but they first made their reputations in the streets. As they gained recognition in the gallery world, they moved to commoditized aesthetics and developed identities as professional artists. Their young careers ended abruptly with Basquiat's heroin overdose and Haring's death due to AIDS.

Later, though, the significance of graffiti art became established in museums and galleries. The Brooklyn Museum of Art, in line with its mission to bring in a Brooklyn-based audience mounted a hip-hop show that included graffiti art. In 2006, in association with the publication of *Graffiti Women: Street Art from Five Continents* (Ganz 2006), the museum mounted an exhibit and sponsored a panel discussion with Lady Pink, Toofly, Swoon, and Lady K Fever ("Exhibitions" 2006). The Tate Gallery in London organized a graffiti show in 2008, and the Grand Palais in Paris assembled one in 2009.

Meanwhile, the market for graffiti art lives on in its street art form, despite its criminalization through graffiti enforcement codes. In 1995, New York City Mayor Giuliani founded the Anti-Graffiti Task Force, which many cities subsequently emulated to combat graffiti vandalism. The sale of aerosol spray-paint to anyone under eighteen was criminalized. Spray-can art interrupts public spaces and serves many purposes in the urban landscape. Some see it as a way to enhance and beautify empty, monotonous urban walls, providing an avant-garde mood tamed by color and form. Contrariwise, some identify it as marking a neighborhood space perceived as dangerous, violent, abandoned, wild, or uncontrolled. To relieve talented graffitists of the onus of doing illegal public art, some private property owners and government-sponsored programs commissioned graffiti art on their buildings. Clearly, graffiti continues to generate contradictory and confusing responses from the general public and the private and government sectors.

The Legacy of Graffiti in New York City's Public Art World

No matter how it is viewed, graffiti in its modern urban appearance in New York City is a tourist attraction and has become, whether the authorities like it or not, part of the appreciated urban aesthetic. At the Graffiti Hall of Fame, located at 106th Street and Park Avenue in East Harlem's El Barrio, graffiti artists have displayed their talent since 1980 (Rivera 2003). Virtual tours of graffiti landmarks are available online. A *Soundwalk* (2014) CD of Hunts Point in the Bronx takes people to landmark graffiti created by TATS CRU, about whom Mark Kotlinski (2006) produced a DVD Video interviews with TATS CRU are available on YouTube ("TATS CRU" 2014). I used to take students on excursions to South Bronx neighborhoods that included graffiti tours and visits with TATS CRU at their office and studio, where graffiti artist Nicer would speak to us. We also visited James De La Vega, at first in El Barrio in East Harlem and later in the East Village, after he moved downtown.

Both Nicer and James spoke about their respective histories and what *their* form of public art meant to them. TATS CRU saw the real estate boom, gentrification and displacement, and the nation's economic decline as having little impact on their work in the Bronx. TATS CRU continues to have a stable relationship with the Point, the community arts development organization in Hunts Point that provides TATS CRU with its workspace in exchange for new images that the group paints annually on the building's exterior wall. However, James De La Vega told a different story in which the same economic factors had dramatically shifted his professional development. Gentrification in East Harlem had displaced him. When Hope Community, Inc., the community development organization with which he had bartered a monthly artwork for his work space, asked him to move to a less desirable space, he decided to move to the East Village. Though already heavily gentrified, this area was home to the kind of population that bought the commodities he produced. After five years, he eventually closed what he called his "museum" shop and studio space on St. Mark's Place in the East Village, deciding not to renew his lease, as the rent was too high. Like other transitions in the past, he decided, this was less the end of something than a new beginning, a potential reinvention. His art strongly reflects this change. It is as much about the disappearance of what he produces as it is about its existence: chalk is washed away by rain, wall paintings are painted over, his shop and studio space are here today, gone tomorrow and now available at the "De La Vega online store."

Some urban spaces are imbued with history, like the East Village wall made famous by Keith Haring in 1982, and more recently by Shepard Fairey. Until recently it held Barry McGee's and Josh Lazcano's commissioned *Ultimate Graffiti Writer's Roll Call*, a painting that included the names of the most well-known taggers. Whether transgressive or not, graffiti art, as street art, public art, or mural art, continues to evolve and is here to stay. At a time when people are rejecting corporate power, whose commoditized images intrude on an urban visual environment they cannot avoid, and occupying parks and public squares, artists engage the public to provide an alternative. In MacPhee's words, "There is no question that corporations are fighting to control every square inch of our visual landscape. It has become increasingly difficult for individuals and groups outside of institutions and corporations to get their ideas, beliefs, and aesthetics into the public eye" (2004: 141).

Returning to North Brooklyn, the site of my current fieldwork, where graffiti and other public art within the genre have taken hold, the ubiquitous graffiti and murals have covered the skyline of old former factories, newly converted loft apartments, retail shops, cafés, and restaurants. Young people, artists of various sorts, and their hangers-on are currently gentrifying Williamsburg's North Side and areas not occupied by Latinos, Hasidic Jews, or luxury housing developments. Initially, high Manhattan rents had pushed hipsters into Williamsburg, which boasted affordable rents and subway lines intersecting the community. Rezoning the waterfront from manufacturing to residential enabled luxury housing developers to build the towers that now overlook the East River, bringing the area a substantially more affluent population and the amenities they desire and causing a wave of further property development all along and near the subway lines, again pushing hipsters out into neighborhoods with more affordable rents, like Bedford-Stuyvesant and Bushwick, current hotspots for artists where murals and graffiti abound.

In hipster-based "urban transformations," graffiti and murals accompany the revitalization of public spaces. In North Brooklyn, spray-can artists, stencil artists, and sticker artists appear next to more conventional artists, covering whatever wall space is available. They do not compete but rather produce a complementarity of aesthetic innovation to accompany the energies of young people creating an alternative space within the neoliberal economy in which virtually everything is commodified. Graffitists express themselves by struggling against commodification, occupying public space and its visual environment, and defining its aesthetic. They block out corporate influence and imagery, impart an aura of resistance, inject a healthy dose of democratization, and in the process reclaim the commons.

Sam Beck is Senior Lecturer and Director of the Urban Semester Program at Cornell University. His interests have focused primarily on inter-group relationships expressed as ethnicity, race, and class under a variety of conditions, processes, landscapes and modes of production. He teaches a fifteen-credit academic program in which students learn ethnographic methods as tools for learning from experience. He guides students' experiences in their internships and community service/participation in critical reflection seminars. He is actively engaged in the North Brooklyn community, receiving from Churches United for Fair Housing (CUFFH) the Daisy Lopez Outstanding Leader of the Year Award. Cornell University recognized him with two Merrill Presidential Scholar Outstanding Educator Awards (2011, 2012) and the Kendall S. Carpenter Memorial Advising Award.

References

Aheam, Charlie. 1983. *Wild Style*. http://wildstylethemovie.com.
Auge, Marc. 1995. *Non-Places: Introduction to an Anthropology of Supermodernity*. London: Verso.
Austin, Joe. 2001. *Taking the Train: How Graffiti Art Became an Urban Crisis in New York*. New York: Columbia University Press.

Banksy. 2010. *Exit Through The Gift Shop.* http://www.banksyfilm.com.

Beighley, Jacqueline Santillan. 2014. *Legendary Tats Cru: The Guys Who Brought Color to the Bronx.* Online video and article posted 12 April 2013, updated 7 January 2014. http://fusion.net/culture/story/tats-cru-mural-kings-bronx-18454.

Benjamin, Walter. 1968 [1936]. "The Work of Art in the Age of Mechanical Reproduction." In *Illuminations.* New York: Harcourt Brace Jovanovich.

Bernstein, Leonard, Steven Sondheim, and Arthur Laurents. 1957. *West Side Story.* New York: Columbia Records.

Bischofberger, Bruno, curator. 1999. *Basquiat.* Catalogue of Basquiat exhibit produced by the Gallleria d'Arte Moderna of the Civico Museo Revoltella in Trieste, Italy. Milan: Edizioni Charta.

Blackmar, Elizabeth. 2006. "Appropriating 'the Commons': The Tragedy of Property Rights Discourse." In *The Politics of Public Space,* ed. Setha Low and Neil Smith. New York: Routledge.

Braun-Reinitz, Janet, and Jane Weissman. 2009. *On the Wall: Four Decades of Community Murals in New York City.* Jackson: University Press of Mississippi.

Beck, Sam. 1992. *Manny Almeida's Ringside Lounge: The Cape Verdean Struggle for Their Neighborhood.* Providence, RI: Gávea-Brown.

"Bomb the City." 2006. *NYpress.com,* 10 May. http://nypress.com/bomb-the-city/.

Buhle, Paul, and Mike Alewitz. 2002. *Insurgent Images: The Agitprop Murals of Mike Alewitz.* New York: Monthly Review Press.

Castelman, Craig. 1982. *Getting Up: Subway Graffiti in New York.* Cambridge, MA: MIT Press.

Cooper, Martha, and Henry Chalfant. 1984. *Subway Art.* New York: Thames & Hudson.

Cooper, Martha, and Joseph Sciorra. 1994. *R.I.P: Memorial Wall Art.* New York: Thames & Hudson.

Cortez, Diego, Glen O'Brian, Gerard Basquiat, and Franklin Sirmans. 2007. *Jean-Michel Basquiat: 1981, the Studio of the Street.* New York: Charta/Deitch Projects.

Deitch, Jeffrey. 2011. "Keith Haring." In *Art in the Streets,* ed. Jeffrey Deitch. New York: Skira Rizzoli; Los Angeles: Museum of Contemporary Arts.

Díaz-Stevens, Ana María. 1994. "Aspects of the Puerto Rican Religious Experience: A Sociohistorical Overview." In *Latinos in New York: Communities in Transition,* ed. Gabriel Haslip-Viera and Sherrie L. Baver. Notre Dame, IN: University of Notre Dame Press.

Edlin, Jay. 2010. *Graffiti 365.* New York: Abrams.

Emmerling, Leonard. 2003. *Basquiat.* Cologne: Taschen.

"Exhibitions: Graffiti." 2006. Brooklyn Museum. http://www.brooklynmuseum.org/exhibitions/graffiti/.

Fab 5 Freddy. 2011. "Samo/Jean-Michel Basquiat." In *Art in the Streets,* ed. Jeffrey Deitch. New York: Skira Rizzoli; Los Angeles: Museum of Contemporary Arts.

Ganz, Nicholas. 2006. *Graffiti Women: Street Art from Five Continents.* New York: Abrams.

Goldberg, Rachel. 2009. *Discovering New York Artist De La Vega.* North Miami, FL: Rachel Goldberg.

Golden, Jane, Robin Rice, and Monica Yant Kinney. 2002. *Philadelphia Murals and the Stories They Tell.* Philadelphia: Temple University Press.

Gothamist. 2013. "Photos: Elusive Graffiti Artist REVS Has Been Tagging NYC Recently." http://gothamist.com/2013/11/10/photos_elusive_graffiti_artist_revs.php#photo-1.

Graffiti Hurts. 2014. http://www.graffitihurts.org.

Groundswell: Art-Community-Change. 2014. http://www.groundswellmural.org.

Grunitzky, Claude. 2005. "Introduction." In Jamel Shabazz, *A Time Before Crack.* New York: powerHouse Books.

Harvey, David. 2012. *Rebel Cities: From the Right to the City to the Urban Revolution.* London: Verso.

Haslip-Viera, Gabriel, and Sherrie L Baver. 1996. "Introduction." In *Latinos in New York: Communities in Transition,* ed. Gabriel Haslip-Viera and Sherrie L. Baver. Notre Dame, IN: University of Notre Dame Press.

Hoeltzel, Susan. 1996. Introduction. *Fashion Moda.* http://www.lehman.cuny.edu/vpadvance/artgallery/gallery/talkback/fashionmoda.html.

Kolossa, Alexandra. 2004. *Keith Haring: 1958–1990; A Life for Art.* Cologne: Taschen.

Kotlinski, Mark. 2006. *TATS CRU: The Mural Kings.* New York: Anthem NYC.

Low, Setha M. 1999. "Spatializing Culture: The Social Production and Social Construction of Public Space in Costa Rica." In *Theorizing the City: The New Urban Anthropology Reader,* ed. Setha M. Low. New Brunswick, NJ: Rutgers University Press.

MacPhee, Josh. 2004. *Stencil Pirates.* Brooklyn, NY: Soft Skull Press.

Manco, Tristan. 2002. *Stencil Graffiti.* London: Thames and Hudson.

Marcano, Tony. 1995. "NEW YORKERS & CO.; TATS Cru Wins Coca-Cola Account." *The New York Times,* 16 April. http://www.nytimes.com/1995/04/16/nyregion/new-yorkers-co-tats-cru-wins-coca-cola-account.html.

Miller, Ivor L. 2012. *Aerosol Kingdom: Subway Painters of New York City.* Jackson: University Press of Mississippi.

Mouffe, Chantal. 2007. "Artistic Activism and Agonistic Spaces." *Art & Research: Journal of Ideas, Contexts, Methods* 1, no. 2: 1–5.

Murray, James T., and Karen L. Murray. 2006. *Burning Windows: Graffiti NYC.* Berkeley, CA: Gingko Press.

Naar, Jon. 2007. *The Birth of Graffiti.* New York: Prestel Press.

Nagourney, Adam. 2011. "Cities Report Surge in Graffiti." *The New York Times,* 18 July. http://www.nytimes.com/2011/07/19/us/19graffiti.html?_r=0.

New York Police Department. 2014. "Crime Prevention: Anti-Graffiti Initiatives." http://www.nyc.gov/html/nypd/html/crime_prevention/anti_graffiti_initiatives.shtml.

Nonini, Donald M. 2008. "Introduction: The Global Idea of 'The Commons.'" In *The Global Idea of "The Commons,"* ed. Donald M. Nonini. New York: Berghahn Books.

NPR. 2008. "Brooklyn Store Celebrates The Art Of Graffiti." *All Things Considered,* 14 July. http://www.npr.org/templates/story/story.php?storyId=92521444.

Ortiz, Altagracia. 1989. "Puerto Rican Workers in the Garment Industry of New York City, 1920–1960." In *Labor Divided: Race and Ethnicity in United States Labor Struggles, 1835–1960,* ed. Robert Asher and Charles Stephenson. Albany: State University of New York Press.

Rahn, Janice. 2002. *Painting without Permission: Hip-Hop Graffiti Subculture.* Westport, CT: Bergin & Garvey.

Rivera, Joseph. 2008. *Vandal Squad: Inside the New York City Transit Police Department, 1984–2004.* Brooklyn, NY: powerHouse Books.

Rivera, Raquel Z. 2003. *New York Ricans From the Hip Hop Zone.* New York: Palgrave.

Rosenblum, Daniel. 2011. "Mott Haven Walls Keep Memories Alive." *Mott Haven Herald,* 4 June. http://www.motthavenherald.com/2011/06/04/mott-haven-walls-keep-memories-alive-3/.

Rosenstein, Peter, and Isabel Bau Madden. 2006. *Tattooed Walls.* Jackson: University Press of Mississippi.

Sanchez, Jesse M. 1996. "Education and Community: Puerto Ricans and Other Latinos in the Schools and Universities." In *Latinos in New York: Communities in Transition,* ed. Gabriel Haslip-Viera and Sherrie L. Baver. Notre Dame, IN: University of Notre Dame Press.

Shabazz, Jamel. 2005. *A Time Before Crack.* New York: powerHouse Books.

Simon, Paul, and Derek Walcott. 1998. *The Capeman.* New York: Universal Music Classical. https://itunes.apple.com/us/album/capeman-original-broadway/id160812504.

Smith, Neil. 1996. *The New Urban Frontier: Gentrification and the Revanchist City.* London: Routledge.

Smith, Neil, and Peter Williams, eds. 1986. *Gentrification of the City.* Boston: Allen & Unwin.

Snyder, Gregory J. 2009. *Graffiti Lives: Beyond the Tag in New York's Urban Underground.* New York: NYU Press.

Soundwalk. 2014. "The Bronx: Hunts Point—Graffiti Walk." http://www.soundwalk.com/#/TOURS/bronxgraffiti/.

Sutherland, Peter. 2004. Autograf New York City's Graffiti Writers. New York: powerhouse Books

TATS CRU. 2014. *TATS CRU: The Mural Kings.* http://www.themuralkings.com/home.php.

"TATS CRU: The Mural Kings—Graffiti." 2014. *YouTube.com.* http://www.youtube.com/watch?v=IFVua4Y79ow.

33third: the art alternative. 2014. http://33third.com/default.aspx?ibp-adgroup=adwords&ibp-keyword=33third&ibp-matchtype=b&gclid=CPjlqqDKirwCFUVyQgodxS8AWQ.

Vergara, J. Camilo. 1999. *American Ruins.* New York: Monticelli Press.

Walsh, Michael. 1996. *Graffito.* Berkeley: North Atlantic Books.

Weber, John Pitman. 2003. "Politics and Practice of Community Public Art: Whose Murals Get Saved?" *The Getty Conservation Institute.* http://www.getty.edu/conservation/publications_resources/pdf_publications/pdf/weber.pdf.

Chapter 13

RECREATING COMMUNITY
New Housing for Amui Djor Residents

———— ∞∞∞ ————

Tony Asare, Erika Mamley Osae, and Deborah Pellow

Slums shock, because they appear unruly and squalid to outsiders, who often interpret residents as dirty and morally degraded. Slums develop when urban populations grow faster than cities' capacity to support them, resulting in non-enforcement of basic land and building regulations. The barely adequate shelter and deteriorated environments of these areas are home to the most visible concentrations of poor people. Yet not all slum areas are socially disorganized or overrun by criminals. Many are increasingly socially cohesive places offering opportunities for security of tenure, local economic development, and income improvement. Moreover, not all people who live in slum areas are poor. Many are active in the informal economy, working, for example, in various home-based enterprises or as domestics, security guards, and hairdressers.

Thus, slums result not only from urban poverty but also from failed policies, poor governance, inappropriate legal and regulatory frameworks, dysfunctional land markets, unresponsive financial systems, and not least a lack of political will. Over the years, social reformers and town planners have joined forces to "better" the circumstances of slum area residents. Meanwhile, many communities have been displaced by renewal. Whereas planners and other outsiders see the demolition of such areas as desirable, their dwellers often resent the denigration of their community (Marris 1979) and, when it happens, their resettlement (Fried 1963; Marris 1961). All told, many different approaches and methods are needed to tackle slum problems in developing countries.

Notes for this chapter begin on page 373.

This chapter documents a new kind of project, an apartment complex, for improving living conditions. Known in UN-Habitat parlance as a Slum Upgrading Facility (SUF), it was carried out in Amui Djor, a low-income housing area outside Tema, Ghana's major port (eighteen miles east of the capital Accra), in response to the Millennium Development Goal 7, Target 11 (UN-Habitat 2005). Launched in 2005, the SUF was "designed to mobilize domestic capital for urban upgrading activities by facilitating links among local actors, and help prepare local projects for potential investment by international donors and financial institutions, and, potentially, investors in the global capital markets—with the specific intent of leveraging further, domestic capital for slum upgrading" ("Slum Upgrading Facility" 2005). SUF specialists on international and domestic financial institutions and financing models coordinate financing institutions with UN-Habitat while seeking ways "to mobilize domestic savings and capital for affordable housing" ("Slum Upgrading Facility" 2005).

Below we will outline the project and how it began; why Tony Asare, the architect, signed up for the job; what responsibilities Erika Osae had as project manager; the roles of community members; and Deborah Pellow's sense that the innovations introduced to help solve the housing shortage through appropriate design and accessible financing would pique anthropologists' interest. Numerous conflicts can arise when a community partners with an NGO as well as donors and management teams, especially when nonresident participants fail to appreciate residents' cultural issues. At Amui Djor, experts and community members worked hard to iron out issues and largely succeeded.

What was achieved? How much has the process benefited community members? Project manager Erika Osae has mused about eligibility for the project, which targeted the poor. How is a person deemed "poor?" Is it only poor people who live in deteriorated environments? Working in a long-established migrant community in Accra, Pellow (2008) found that some residents chose to remain in such surroundings despite having a solid income and in some cases even owning property elsewhere. To qualify for the Amui Djor project, people had to identify themselves as slum dwellers and join the housing association, even if they owned a shop or had other sources of income. According to Osae, this indicates that the reason some people live in these areas is not poverty but accommodation constraints and other factors. Irrespective of their economic status, project participants made sure to benefit from their community identity. In considering these and other questions, we take anthropology out of the academy to confront critical public concerns and, as anthropological pioneer Sandy Davis put it, "work with citizens in promoting fundamental change" (Davis and Mathews 1979: 5).

Slums, Culture, Attachment

Years ago, British town planner Peter Marris observed that the word slum is like the word dirt: "evocative, disapproving, and indefinable except in the context of our expectations of what should be" (Marris 1979: 419). "What should be" is, of course, in the eye of the beholder. Policy makers and the middle class condemn housing as a slum when it does not fit their society's requirements or conform to their values or perceptions of urban form. This also makes the term problematic to those looking in. Marris goes on: "If, then, we are to discuss slums, we need to remind ourselves, at the outset, that we are not talking about overcrowding, lack of amenity, poverty or want as such; but about the relationship of such conditions to a context of meaning that changes with your point of view" (420).

Do people who live and work in Amui Djor consider it dirty? Do they regard it as an eyesore? And do those who bought into the new apartment building funded by the project feel rescued? Conditions in Amui Djor, a local hub of small-scale commerce and family networks, were surely no worse or more anomalous than those in central Lagos in the 1950s (Marris 1961), an area that was "cleared" of a large, inadequately housed population of poor people. The clearance scheme for central Lagos relocated its residents to a suburb five miles away, disrupting their family networks, robbing them of their livelihoods, and housing them in British-style bungalows unsuited to their traditional understanding of proper spatial layout. Inversely, the Amui Djor intervention strove to maintain the community with a design that acknowledged customary social and spatial needs and enabled the return of those who, having bought into the project, were being temporarily re-housed.

The Amui Djor design is sympathetic to the courtyard prototype and what it represents. Ubiquitous throughout Africa, the courtyard house boasts climatic and functional efficiencies that account for a long history globally as well (Oliver 1987). It was present in Mesopotamia in the seventh millennium in the Chaldean city of Ur in 2000 B.C., and in Kahun, Egypt, five thousand years ago (Oliver 1987; Schwerdtfeger 1982). Variations on its ancient plan range as far east as India in cities developed under Moghul influence, to the Mediterranean in Greece and Rome, to Hispanic Latin America (Oliver 1987; Rapoport 1969) and China (Boyd 1962; Knapp 1989).

The common Ghanaian version of the courtyard house is the compound house with its enclosed yard. Northern Ghanaian compounds feature round dwellings that are conjoined (Prussin 1969). However, geometrized buildings and courtyards prevail (Prussin 1986) in southern Ghana among the forest-belt Asante (Rutter 1971), Accra's indigenous Ga (Field 1940), and Muslims or those influenced by Islam. "The original architectural norm in Accra was a round house made of swish and topped by a conical roof" (Parker 2000: 25), but by the 1850s, most houses in Accra were rectangular. At that time, Accra's elite were building multistory stone residences that also reproduced the courtyard style (Parker 2000: 25).

The compound style is culturally significant. Social composition and physical form are mutually constituted, rooted in social and cultural values, and expressed in people's daily routines and exchanges. The compound is both public and private space. In Islamic societies, the courtyard is used only by the family (Ozkan 2006). The Muslim Hausa in northern Nigeria delineate compound space in such a way that no unrelated male can even glimpse the resident women. Courtyards with only a single entrance ensure the privacy of the inside rooms. The type of compound created by four buildings joined in a square around a courtyard and having just one entrance, common among the Asante, ensures not only privacy but also security and easy defense (Denyer 1978: 164).

The compound house satisfies basic family needs: sleeping accommodations for each family member; a place to cook; food storage; pens for chickens, goats, and sheep; and a place to eat and socialize (Denyer 1978: 21). It is everywhere congenial to economic activity and social organization (King 1984). In all compounds, demarcated spaces are often multifunctional.

In Africa, such housing is a suitable environment for the development of community living, testifying to the definite place of the individual within the group (Kulturmann 1963). In the typical southern Ghanaian house, the individual rooms are on average 12 feet by 12 feet and open onto an internal courtyard where daily interaction among residents occurs. The courtyard is the living area of the house, the location of arbitrations, cooking, children's play, storytelling, and family celebrations and funerals (Faculty of Architecture 1978: 458). This is also true in Ghanaian cities like Accra and Tema and their adjacent areas. The communal lifestyle, of course, is directly tied to the extended family, which in turn is facilitated spatially by the "family house." But no matter the residents' genealogical relationship to one another, rooms are used primarily for sleeping—in part due to crowding, in part due to the heat (Pellow 1991) and the courtyard space, in effect an outdoor room, takes primacy. It has been documented as "the spatial arena in which social interaction and inter-household co-operation are typically nurtured" (Korboe 1992: 1160).

In much of urban West Africa, the communal family lifestyle and spatial compound organization have enabled the survival of many poor who as family may live there rent-free. This family house-form is also easily adapted to accommodate tenants. In this situation of unrelatedness, the compound yard becomes a space that is conceptually zoned, from the private bedroom to semipublic shared facilities (e.g., a shower room) to the public perimeter, for those who do not live there or have clear right of access. Tenants (who carry a mental blueprint of the kin-based compound) must structure their behavior to mesh with the unrelated social setting (Pellow 1991). The zoning of regions creates a spatial hierarchy to control interaction and to allocate roles to spaces. As a territorial structure, the compound is a framework for social organization (Kuper 1972).

Compound dwellers are fundamentally attached to this shared space for various reasons. Most notable is the courtyard tradition, which highlights what it is that people do with the space and makes their attachment so pronounced, even if they are unaware of it (Pellow 1991). The yard is a staging place for behavior, and as a place, it contributes to the development of a sense of self as the individual learns roles and behaviors, and bonds with the group (Laufer et al. 1976). It is here that activities come together. Bourdieu (1984: 18) understood this attachment to the compound and the idea of the compound as habitus, "a system of schemes of perception and thought," of dispositions, skills, and habits. The habitus appears to incorporate an individual's past experience in the social world, but it is a socially structured phenomenon "derived from a common set of material conditions of existence to regulate the practice of a set of individuals in common response to those conditions" (Garnham and Williams 1980: 213). Social life consists in the interaction of structures, daily practices, experiences, and dispositions of individuals and groups. The most basic link between social structure (roles and relationships) and action (what people in these roles and relationships perform), including practices between individuals, is that of habitus. Thus habitus is a group circumstance. Sahlins referred to its system of generative schemes as "the cultural consciousness" or "a cosmic principle of order" (1983). Sahlins was writing of heroic history, but the principle seems to hold also for the quotidian practices of commoners, which are a site of enactment and reproduction of much of daily life. Knowing the compound to be the prototypical space, the architect based his design at Amui Djor on this form as best fitting and enabling people's practices.

The Site

The population of Ghana in 2010 was 24.3 million, up from 22.9 million in 2000 ("Population: Total in Ghana" 2011). Urban residents numbered 11,270,812 or 49 percent in 2000, and 12,561,790 or 51.5 percent in 2010 ("Ghana: Urban Population" 2011). Ever since Kwame Nkrumah became

Ghana's first president in 1957, successive governments have sought funding for affordable housing schemes. For example, Nkrumah created the State Housing Corporation and Tema Development Corporation (TDC), which operate in all of the regions and the newly developing Tema industrial area, respectively; during the Second Republic Prime Minister K.A. Busia created the Ministry of Housing and the Social Security Fund to help build low-cost housing; and the J.J. Rawlings regime promoted the SSNIT (Social Security and National Insurance Trust) housing scheme. None were particularly successful.

"The whole provision of shelter is to target the economically viable poor and below—starting with someone who sells groundnuts by the roadside or the basic trader, a carpenter" (Tony Asare, 24 June 2010). Today Ghana's housing deficit is in excess of one million units, needed largely in the growing urban areas. Many urban dwellers live in substandard housing in areas that outsiders characterize as slums, believing them to have low levels of solidarity or organization, their residents bootlegging water and electricity connections.

Amui Djor is one such area. A large unplanned settlement outside Ghana's port city of Tema, Amui Djor covers 37.31 acres and has an estimated resident population of 6,138 (Standard Surveys & Construction Services 2008). Amui Djor falls under stool (chieftaincy) lands but is vested in the state and managed by the TDC. Anybody who needs land goes to the stool, which is represented by the Traditional Authority, in this case the Tema Traditional Council (TTC) and the TDC. The TTC collaborates with the TDC to process land titles, which ultimately are granted by the national Land Title Registry.

Amui Djor is also part of the Tema Municipal Assembly (TMA), which occupies 565 square kilometers and has a population of 620,000 (Ghana Statistical Service 2000). This well-planned city is the country's main port and industrial hub (Figure 13.1). The TMA area is divided into six subunits, referred to as zones; Amui Djor is a part of the Ashaiman zone, itself characterized as a slum.

In the late 1950s, Ashaiman grew as construction of the new port and town of Tema created a demand for labor. According to Patrick Wakely (Osae 2007:12), construction jobs became fewer in the 1960s but were replaced by industrial work at the port and in factories. Ashaiman provided an affordable alternative to the high-cost housing in the formal communities of Tema. Its slum areas provide most of the municipality's urban poor with cheap accommodations and continue to supply the harbor and industrial areas with cheap labor.

The relationship between the TMA and its subdistrict structures (zonal councils), especially in poor urban areas, was generally one of conflict,

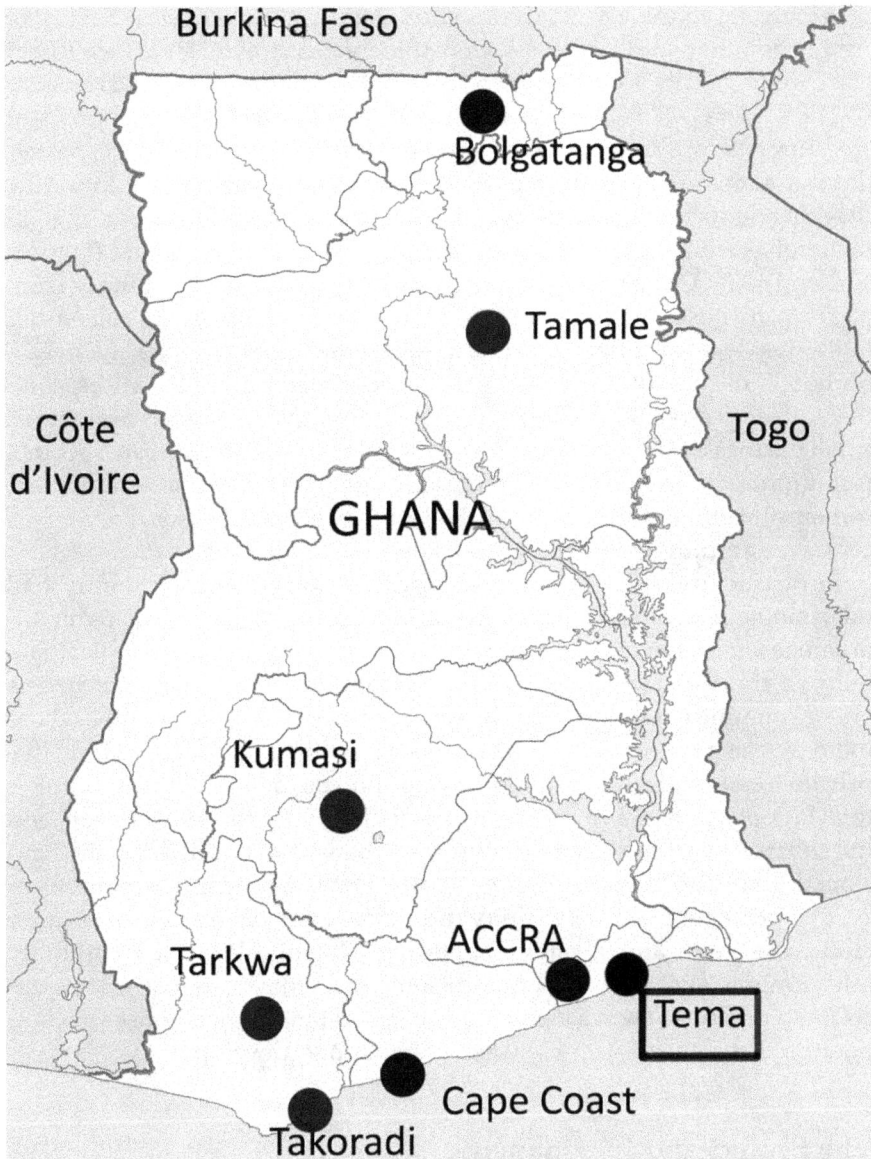

Figure 13.1. Tema, Ghana. Map modified from an original by NordNordWest.

mistrust, misunderstanding, and uneasy interdependence. However, this arrangement changed in 2008 with the elevation of Tema to metropolitan status and Ashaiman to municipal status. The new municipality has since assumed control of its area and worked to upgrade its slums and reinvent the community.

According to the Project Completion Report of the Physical Survey of Amui Djor (Standard Surveys & Construction Services 2008), 25 acres held 604 dwelling units, as well as two schools, two mosques, and a church.

The settlers—all squatters—built their own houses as semi-permanent structures because the permits they held, called Temporary Certificates, did not allow erection of permanent structures. About 99 percent of the dwelling units were built of wooden materials, but a few were of solid materials such as sandcrete with corrugated aluminum roofing (Figures 13.2 and 13.3). Close to four hundred wood or metal kiosks built for commercial purposes were also used as residences. Four-story mixed-use buildings, located in an area of low residential density along the neighborhood's major road, served largely work-related purposes: offices, commerce, service-related activities. The community contained numerous small businesses, including provisions stores (for non-refrigerated foods), restaurants, tailors' shops, and mechanics' garages. Most occupants were self-employed, meaning they worked in the informal sector; only 8 percent were employees or salaried workers.

Infrastructural development was sadly lacking. The community had not a single refuse bin, so residents used a nearby wetland area as an unorganized garbage dump, a practice that threatened the ecological stability of the area (Standard Surveys & Construction Services 2008). The only community latrine was in the southern part of the community, where there was also a refuse dump. The physical survey crew counted only five private toilets and twenty-seven private shower rooms. The community's total lack of drains was a problem, especially during the rainy season, and the southern part of the community had the worst of it because the land sloped gently to the south (Standard Surveys & Construction Services 2008). Fortunately the community did manage to acquire power lines for electrical service, and a water main though the middle of the community ran from one end to the other, with some residents developing commercial water points. Few residents, however, had taps in their houses or compounds. Thus, the project site was severely underdeveloped.

The Project and Its Financing

Housing is a basic need, but it is sadly lacking in many low income developing countries. Those with high rates of urbanization in relation to economic growth are affected by considerable poverty, unplanned settlements and slums, crowding, and an absence of basic infrastructure and services. The 2002 International Conference on Financing for Development recognized the need to mobilize domestic financial resources, both generally

Figures 13.2 and 13.3. Amui Djor squatters' structures. Photo by Deborah Pellow.

and with regard to housing. The international community responded by adopting Target 11 under Millennium Development Goal 7, an effort to significantly improve the lives of at least 100 million slum dwellers by the year 2020 (Tweneboa 2011).

For UN-Habitat, to better housing in low-income areas and promote affordable housing finance, it is crucial to devise mechanisms and systems enabling sufficient financial resources from the public and private sectors. In 2003 the Governing Council requested UN-Habitat to work with banks, private sector and other relevant partners to field test approaches through pilot projects to mobilize resources to increase the supply of affordable credit for slum upgrading and other pro-poor human settlements (UN-Habitat 2003).

Under the Human Settlements Financing Division of UN-Habitat—and with funding from SIDA (Swedish International Development Cooperation Agency), DFID (Department for International Development, UK), and the Cities Alliance—in 2005 UN-Habitat established the SUF as a "technical advisory facility to assist national Government, local government and community organizations in the development of their own slum upgrading, low cost housing, and urban development projects so they can attract funding primarily from domestic capital markets using seed capital grants where necessary and bringing in existing guarantee and credit enhancement facilities, the whole process being packaged in such a way that the projects can be regarded as financially sustainable" (UN-Habitat 2005). SUF coordinates initiatives to raise seed capital for slum upgrading, support affordable housing for low-income households, and improve urban infrastructure in developing cities worldwide. One of its central objectives is to mobilize domestic capital for these activities by bringing together the relevant local actors from central and local government, civil society, and the private sector, while also taking into account the initiatives' financial, technical, and political elements (UN-Habitat 2005). SUF liaises between financing institutions and UN-Habitat's normative and technical cooperation activities.[1]

SUF had an initial fund of 11.8 million dollars, provided by the governments of the United Kingdom and Sweden. After identifying potential operations in ten cities in Africa and Asia, it set up field projects in Tanzania, Indonesia, and Sri Lanka, in addition to Ghana (UN 2005). SUF Team Leader Michael Mutter stated: "Ghana satisfies many of the criteria we are looking for in assessing the financial viability of slum upgrading projects. These include a well-established local government recognized by the central government, a vibrant private capital market base, and functioning community organizations" (UN-Habitat 2005).

The Amui Djor pilot project was undertaken as a model slum-clear-ance project. Entitled Development of Mixed-Use Low-Income Demon-stration Housing Scheme, it was undertaken through the Tema/Ashaiman Municipal Slum Upgrading Fund (TAMSUF). The Tema and Ashaiman Metropolitan Assemblies, along with SUF (UN-Habitat) and other poten-tial investors, combined and helped fund TAMSUF, which guaranteed a loan from the Commercial Bank. TAMSUF's initial funding consisted of a UN-Habitat grant of $400,000 for capital enhancement; a further UN-HABITAT grant of $100,000 was also provided for administration and development (Tweneboa 2011).

Once work began, construction took about seven months (see Figure 13.5). First, the Ashaiman Municipal Authority asked people to leave the site. Some two weeks were needed to clear the site for the commission-ing ceremony." TAMSUF facilitated the clearing; and it was funded by an NGO devoted to slum upgrades, the People's Dialogue on Human Settle-ments. Squatters on the land where the building was to go up were tempo-rarily re-housed in a building the People's Dialogue put up in partnership with the project (Figure 13.4). Built next to the site, this wooden structure equipped with lights and toilet facilities accommodated all the squatters

Figure 13.4. Temporary housing. Photo by Deborah Pellow.

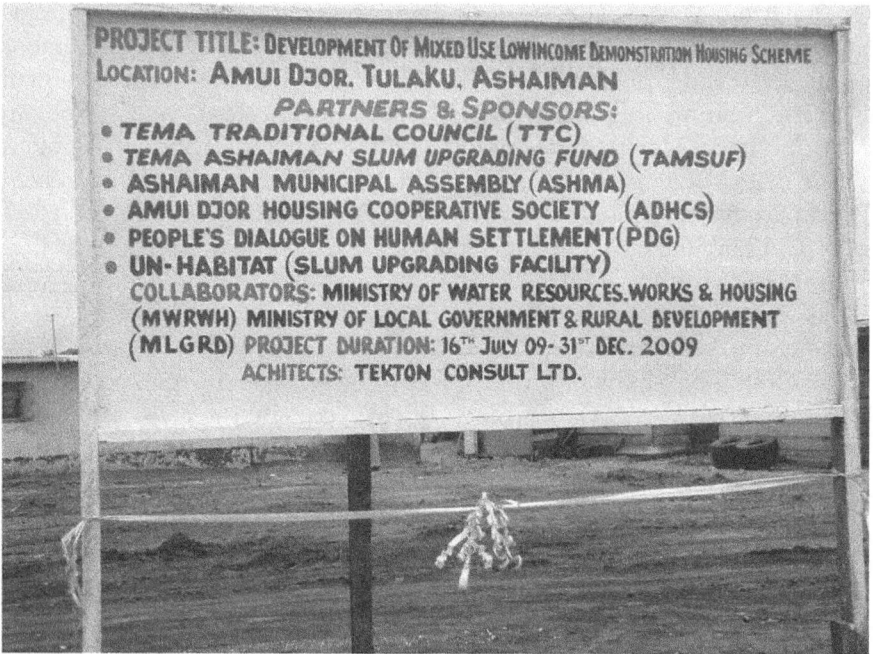

Figure 13.5. On-site signboard for Amui Djor. Photo by Erika Mamley Osae.

and all but three of their enterprises. Once the mixed-use residential-commercial facility was finished, people were served notice to vacate, but people still occupied it. Thus the temporary structure defeated its purpose by becoming a permanent abode.

The new low-income demonstration housing units were to provide good, affordable accommodation to community residents who could obtain long-term mortgages from a commercial bank. As mentioned above, prospective residents of the new dwelling units were members of the Amui Djor Housing Cooperative Society, an active community association and itself a member of the Ghana Federation of Urban Poor, an organization that receives support from the People's Dialogue.

Prior to the signing of the contract by all of the stakeholders, a stakeholder consultative meeting was held to formally inform the Amui Djor Community Development Committee (ACDC) about the project and agree on the modes of their involvement in the implementation process. This meeting set out the responsibilities of all stakeholders, including the ACDC, which was assigned the tasks of helping the surveying agency find the boundaries of the site to be surveyed, and arranging the permits the survey teams required to access all areas on the surveyed site.

The SUF and People's Dialogue leadership were also represented at this meeting.

Tony Asare, the architect, was very clear about the purpose of this project: "This is not a business venture—it is a social venture. There will be a point when it pays for itself" (personal communication, 25 June 2010). The whole concept was not based on the benefit principle alone but on residents' and shop owners' ability to pay, as the project's replication hinged on recoupment of the funds sunk into the pilot.

Construction costs (adjusted) came to Ghc 420,072; post-construction expenses brought the adjusted total to Ghc 429,672. Subsidies from the government of Ghana and the People's Dialogue, as well as land contributed, brought costs down to Ghc 365,958. These costs were to be recovered by a loan from the Amal Bank (Ghc 144,000), the "sale" (i.e., paid use) of toilets (Ghc 67,500), deposits on residential units (Ghc 90,000), and shop rentals (Ghc 128,172). Actual construction costs were Ghc 10,801 for a bedroom-and-living room unit and Ghc 21,603 for a self-contained two-bedroom unit. Income from public bathing and toilet facilities and stores on the ground floor reduced those costs to Ghc 6,577 and 13,157, respectively. Community members paid a deposit of Ghc 1,000 plus another 1,500 they received from the People's Dialogue. The balance was bank-financed for ten years, guaranteed by TAMSUF. This left residents with a monthly payment of Ghc 75.

The Design and Its Designer

How did the project in Ashaiman start? Architect Tony Asare had a relevant specialty: "I am a fan of design economics—it deals with how you can create a more cost-effective building in a standard area. If you have a 50 sq meter area, which design would make the [project] cheaper?" In 2005, a few friends who were interested in social housing approached Asare, hoping to co-opt him into a new project. One of them, the housing consultant Dr. Ohene-Sarfo, was working with UN-Habitat Ghana as the country coordinator for the SUF. "He contacted me and said he knew People's Dialogue, an NGO, was organizing slum dwellers and wanted to do some sort of slum clearance project. It was pro bono work." Ohene-Sarfo, who knew Asare from a project they had worked on in the town of Elmina, approached him upon hearing about the Amui Djor plan. "He asked if I was interested. I said, 'as the people would benefit from it'" (Asare, personal communication, 12 November 2011). Asare and Ohene-Sarfo both saw the project's potential as a case study of use in developing a model for slum upgrading. "In our quest to come up with the design, we felt that poor people in such communities get 'visitor fatigue' [from] so much intrusion in their lives and very little results" (Asare, personal communication, 25 June 2010).

Asare and others involved in the design and development of the site asked a chief to allocate land in Ashaiman for the pilot. The total land area of the project was 37.31 acres. Before Asare started the design process, UN-Habitat through Emerging Markets Group (EMG), a consortium contracted to implement the SUF project, did a very detailed evaluation report—the settlement and everything within. "So you see the vocations, you see their way of life, you see the age structure, you see from even the various interactions they have, their hopes and aspirations. You could actually feel that you needed to improve the densification" (Asare, personal communication, 24 June 2010).

The Metropolitan Assembly wanted every unit to have its own bedroom, and data collected by the People's Dialogue revealed that the design had to improve on the ratios currently existing in slum circumstances. The objective was very simple: the chief "wanted us to design 1-bedroom units that cost $5000 and 2-br to cost $10,000. Anytime you work on those areas, you shrink [them]" because the space created for $5,000 would be almost nothing. "We [the managers and technical people] came up with a brief we would cross-subsidize so we would be able to bring down the cost of the unit" (Asare, personal communication, 10 November 2011). The idea of a mixed development, with vendors, showers, and toilets on the ground floor to serve the community, was seen as a way to subsidize the housing on the two upper levels, since demand for the shops and toilets was high.

The ground floor of the Amui Djor project is nonresidential, except for one 2-bedroom unit adjacent to the communal bathrooms. Fifteen commercial shops face the road. The core is a courtyard with access to a twelve-seat public toilet and bathing facility at its back. The second and third floors each contain sixteen dwelling units: fourteen 1-bedroom units with sitting room; two 2-bedroom with sitting room, kitchen, and bathroom/toilet. The two self-contained bedroom apartments are for families that can afford not to share their space with the rest, though the staircase and corridors are used by all. Each residential floor has separate male and female communal toilet and bathing facilities, and each 1-bedroom apartment has its own kitchen in the courtyard.

Such a mission carried special value for Asare:

> In our part of the world, there are more poor people than rich people, and if you are an architect you should be able to serve both the very rich and the economically vulnerable. I tried to research what is minimal to give a person housing. Estimate on basic personal needs—a place to have a bed, to

be able to have a place for a few belongings, small living area with sectional sofa, a place to cook, spaces that are expansive and that should be shared like kitchen and bathroom. Endeavor to have people share. It is easier to share bathrooms and toilets. Kitchen is harder because it becomes a point of conflict. (Personal Communication, 10 November 2011)

The kitchens are grouped together back-to-back, seven facing northwest, seven southeast, bisecting the open courtyard space across from the apartments on the same level. The women keep their wooden mortars and pestles for pounding yam and cassava in their respective kitchens upstairs and carry them down to pound the foodstuffs in the courtyard on the ground floor, an inconvenient but necessary practice in a storied building.

Asare's design (Figure 13.6) testifies to the importance of the compound structure, replicating the situation in mixed-tenant housing in other urban areas such as Accra: everyone shares the semipublic space of the compound yard—hanging out, playing board games, and such—and facilities like the water tap and shower room. In the many urban compounds that lack toilets, residents use nearby communal toilets kept up by the municipality. But each dwelling unit claims the space just in front of its

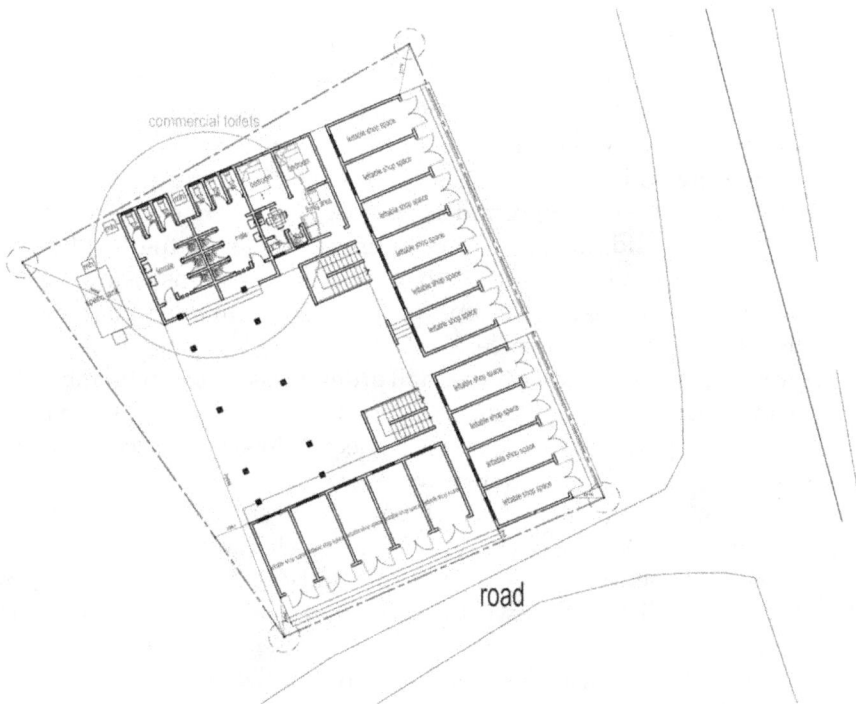

Figure 13.6. The site plan and ground-floor layout. Plan by Tekton Consult, Accra.

respective door as its own. It is here that each woman cooks her meals and feeds her children, separate from other women but within sight of them. She often has a cupboard by the door for storing cooking utensils. As is visible in Figure 13.2, even the local so-called temporary structures share a compound yard. Maintaining this organizing principle in the built form acknowledges its organic significance in peoples' lives.

The building occupies a corner plot. Asare's design splits the building in two to create a breezeway. He came up with three different designs and organized several charettes to take stakeholders through the design process until all their concerns were incorporated and explanations issued as to why some could not be accepted. This paved the way for the finalization of the design, which all the stakeholders involved approved as land preparation arrangements kicked in. The design process took about two months; the construction, initially slated to take six months, was completed in seven. The project was then handed over to the Amui Djor Cooperative Housing Society.

Managing the Construction

In January of 2008, when the SUF Ghana project was in its implementation stage, EMG hired Erika Osae as its SUF country coordinator. She got involved quite simply because it was a job: "I changed jobs and wanted something a bit flexible—couldn't take on a job with lots of travel. A friend approached me and I applied" (Osae, personal communication, 12 November 2011). Osae's background is in geography and resource development, and she did an MA in development studies at the Institute of Social Studies in The Hague, the Netherlands. Now she was testing a UN-Habitat model in a "demonstration project" that combined community savings with commercial finance.

Osae explained that her job "was a tall order: I was to help with the business plan, solicit funds from the banks, loan agreements from the banks, government agencies that oversee the project (Ministry of Local Government and Ministry of Water Resources, Works and Housing)." (personal communication, 12 November 2011). She was basically micromanaging negotiation of the loan and land arrangements. Her key role was to coordinate the implementation of the Ghana Country Project Implementation Plan (CPIP) in collaboration with the SUF international pilot team (PT) and local project partners.[2]

When the contract with EMG expired in April 2009, Osae was hired directly by UN-Habitat in Nairobi as the Ghana SUF country advisor for a term ending in August 2010. In this position, she liaised with all stakeholders—the community, NGO partner and affiliate members, Amui Dzor Housing Cooperative Society, Habitat Program Manager's Office and Local Finance Facility Board, and TAMSUF. TAMSUF's board consisted of the Ghana Real Estate Developers Association, TTC (the traditional custodians of the land), Ashaiman Municipal Assembly, People's Dialogue on Human Settlements, Ghana Institute of Architects, Ghana Federation for the Urban Poor, Ashaiman Housing Cooperative, Ghana Institute of Engineers, Ghana Association of Bankers, TDC (in whom government land ownership is vested), and Ministries of Local Government and Rural Development, and Water Resources Works and Housing.

The diversity of the stakeholders and their interests complicated Osae's work. For example, eleven squatter families occupied the earmarked land, and some of them held Temporary Certificates permitting them to be there. To vacate the site, most squatters demanded some form of compensation and some form of assurance that they could continue with their businesses, which included tractor repair, welding, and photography. Osae's mediation between the squatters and the People's Dialogue, which was mobilizing them, led some squatters eventually to join the Amui Djor Housing Cooperative Society, whereupon they had priority to benefit from the new project, provided they were able to pay.

Another condition of creating the mixed-use facility was conclusion of a land agreement with the TTC (the traditional owners of the land) and the TDC. TTC's nonobservance of the urgency of the timetable made this process particularly frustrating. TTC insisted on certain concessions, for example, a percentage of the facilities given to the TTC to rent out to its indigenes as a way of maintaining local Ga culture. This then had to be negotiated with the board. It was more than two years before construction could commence.

In the meantime, meetings about the new structure's design were also held with the target beneficiaries: members of the Ghana Federation for the Urban Poor, Ashaiman Amui Djor branch members, the Amui Djor Housing Cooperative Society, and the Structure Owners Association. Discussions covered the types of materials to be used and the costs involved. Selected group representatives were taken round to see construction sites and available technologies. Always, the production team aimed to keep costs low. The beneficiaries were impressed by the various technologies; however, some also considered the building materials incongruent with their environment, especially the steel frame which used plaster boards for the facial plastering. Community members understood the lower cost of these new technologies, but most still believed a proper building is made of brick and mortar. Osae and her crew found this quite frustrating, as their main concerns were cost, durability, and aesthetics.

Figure 13.7. Clearing for the project. Photo by Deborah Pellow.

With the District Assembly's help the squatters or occupants on the land were cleared without much difficulty and moved into transit quarters close to the site. Also, the construction company agreed to hire local residents as laborers as long as they met quality standards and bought building supplies from local shop. Both were important players in the supply chain of materials and construction of the facility.

As the project's manager and country advisor, Osae supervised the activities of the architect and his team, the contractor, and the community with its NGO partner. This presented more challenges, as individuals' vested interests had to be negotiated for the good of the whole. Decisions were never unilateral but always taken in consultation with board members via telephone, e-mail, or emergency meeting. The transparency of the process made some uncomfortable, but it worked to prevent complications or confusion. The entire construction phase, which took nine months, was done on schedule without compromising building quality.

The building was ready in August 2010. The experts were very pleased:

At the culmination of a recent three day Conference for Housing Excellence the UN-HABITAT sponsored Slum Upgrading Facility project in Ashaiman—an Accra low income housing area—was judged the best social innovative housing project for the urban poor and low income people.

Figure 13.8. Internal view. Photo by Deborah Pellow.

Figure 13.9. The finished building. Photo by Deborah Pellow.

The panel of judges consisted of housing Experts from U.K based organization the Chartered Institute for Housing, and ConsultASH, a professional social housing body based in the U.K.

The Amui Djor project also took a further award on the same night which went to the architectural firm Tekton Consultants which designed the building for the best designed architectural concept for a mixed use development in social housing for the urban poor. (UN-Habitat 2011)

The cooperative members appear to concur. The building is completely inhabited, and the ground-floor businesses (including a barber, grocery store, and office of child welfare) are open.

Conclusion

Anthropologists speak of a "sea change" reorienting our discipline's practice and focus toward collaborating with communities to tackle social problems, influencing social policy to benefit the larger society, and "bringing knowledge to publics outside of the academy" (Checker et al. 2010; Lamphere 2004: 431; see also Rob Borofsky and Naomi Schneider's California Series in Public Anthropology). The idea is to enrich our collective understandings of people around the globe while helping to transform many people's lives.

In the case at hand, we addressed the pressing issue of inadequate housing, illustrating how members of a poor community became participants in a housing project that radically changed their living circumstances. At Amui Djor, the architect and the agency overseeing the project brought the community in throughout the planning and execution of the structure. The architect, a Ghanaian, understood the cultural imperatives underlying a successful outcome—an advantage that does not necessarily pertain when a planner is foreign or insensitive to cultural needs. At Amui Djor, the collective team supported the architect and cared about getting the community something tangible in the form of a building. They buttressed Asare's sensitivity to the sorts of issues Marris (1979) wrote of in his discussion of poor environments. In the absence of such support or local knowledge, an engaged anthropology can make a difference.

Being poor does not mean that people are dirty or disorganized. Indeed, in Amui Djor, it was an infrastructure of social organization that enabled the local community to be brought into the effort of revitalization. They joined an organization, participated in meetings, worked as laborers, and then occupied the new building. And the new building is significant. As a storied building, its silhouette differs from what the locals may be used to. Yet its imprint echoes the traditional space because it incorporates a prototypical element—the compound yard, a space that acts as a transitional zone where people can easily meet and be together without consequence. As in any compound, traditional activities such as food preparation can be carried out in the yard. But each family also has its respective kitchen, which prevents the conflicts that can arise in situations of sharing. The structure is also significant in that it represents what one Ghanaian architect referred to as "incremental housing": [T]he commercial interest ... should be considered part of the housing; assuming that you don't have a wife, you don't need a kitchen. Once you recognize those who cook, the caterers as part of the house—when you create the bedrooms, you create the kitchen unit also, for that is where you eat. And since you can't afford a bathroom, you also create a public bathroom. So you have your unit—you somehow manage to take your bath. When you have a little bit of money you add some bathroom. There's no order" (OK Agyemang, personal communication, 24 June 2010).

The Amui Djor project is fully occupied. The base prices are $7,000 for a 1-bedroom unit and $10,000 for the larger 2-bedroom flat, which also has an en suite kitchen and bathroom. A sign of its success is the way owners have claimed their space. Many have upgraded their apartments, tiling the floors, buying new front doors, and changing the louvered windows for sliding glass encased in aluminum. Each respective kitchens is outfitted according to its owner's taste—some installed tile backsplashes; others hung cabinets. Although the bathrooms are shared, each apartment has its own shower, which may have been tiled. The architect and developers now know of a shortcoming: space in the apartments is too tight. A possible fix for this would be to make the rooms a bit larger but put in less finishing—which is not an issue, given that so many have upgraded their apartments anyway.

Time will tell how successful Amui Djor is. For now, the experts are pleased. They succeeded in getting the people and the project together, and persuading agencies, banks, and governments that this project matters. They oversaw and cajoled cooperation between the UN and local NGOs, outside governments, and the government of Ghana; financial organizations' acquiescence to using a different metric in guaranteeing loans; and the requirement that potential residents pay their share, both monetarily and through involvement in planning. Moreover, the SUF plan points to the possibility of replication elsewhere—in Ghana, Africa, the developing world.

The project withstood challenges (Tweneboa 2011), such as the issue of affordability for UN-Habitat. Despite subsidies, it is not certain that community members will be able to make their monthly payments. But one important lesson was that slum upgrading and urban renewal are possible when commercial banks can be persuaded that such projects can and should be financed at affordable interest rates. This persuasion is well worth the effort, if it helps to adequately house the millions globally who are in need.

Tony Asare is an ardent social housing enthusiast and loves to write on urban planning issues. He graduated from Kwame Nkrumah University of Science and Technology with a Post Graduate Diploma in Architecture in 1997. He has worked as an architect for more than seventeen years, handling both design and supervision of various projects. He became an Associate of the Ghana Institute of Architects in 1999. His interest in urbanism was sharpened by training in Urban Planning and Infrastructural Management at the Human Settlement Management Institute in New Delhi. He won an award from ConsultASH in 2011 for his work in Ashaiman on Slum Upgrading and first prize of a competition organized by the Home Finance Company and the G.I.A on affordable housing designs.

Erika Mamley Osae is a Development Practitioner and Managing Partner in TUAL with sixteen years experience in development practice both in local and international sectors engagement with civil society actors, local actors, and the private sector. She has extensive experience in training and capacity building, project and program implementation, project and program design, gender development and organizational systems development, and change management processes.

Deborah Pellow is Professor of Anthropology in the Maxwell School, Syracuse University. Her research program is grounded in the roles and relationships enacted by individuals in the urban arena and plural society, under conditions of social change. Most of her work has involved the conception, use, and social reproduction of identity and access to power. Her primary approach deals with the interrelationship of social and physical space. She did a long-term project on socio-spatial arrangements in a migrant community in Accra, Ghana, which resulted in the book *Landlords and Lodgers* (Chicago 2008). Her latest research focuses on members of the new Dagomba (northern Ghana) elite, who live and work as professionals in the capital Accra while remaining attached to and involved in home-town affairs.

Notes

1. SUF works with international donor facilities such as the Private Infrastructure Development Group; international financial institutions including the World Bank Group, International Bank for Reconstruction and Development, International Finance Corporation, Asian Development Bank; and others, e.g., United Cities and Local Governments, Slum and Shack Dwellers International, and the UN-Habitat Governing Council.
2. The full list of Osae's tasks:
   - Identify capacity-building requirements of the project partners.
   - Assist in provision of capacity-building services to the project partners through sourcing of local available information, recruitment and coordination of local technical advisors, and provision of training.
   - Coordinate support to SUF initiatives in negotiating appropriate commercial loan agreements with local financial institutions.
   - Ensure all the local SUF initiatives are provided with appropriate technical assistance inputs including engineering, architecture, and legal support made available by means of the SUF PT.
   - Oversee the work of the Tema and Sekondi-Takoradi SUF project advisors.
   - Monitor, document, and report on the progress of the projects.
   - Build links, partnerships, and communications with SUF local partners and, where appropriate, liaise with urban-sector stakeholders on project-related activities.
   - Represent SUF and EMG at conferences and workshops.
   - Ensure effective exchange of inputs and information between SUF PT, their consultants, and project partners.
   - Maintain regular contact and communication with the SUF PT Ghana Team Leader.
   - Coordinate production of project documentation for use in disseminating SUF progress in Ghana.
   - Participate in local and international workshops and forums appropriate for the dissemination of SUF project experience and achievements.
   - Assist in drafting an Annual Implementation Plan, progress reports, and other project documents.
   - Assist in drafting Terms of Reference for consultants and other technical assistance providers.
   - Provide monthly/quarterly reports to the SUF PT Ghana Team leader.
   - Prepare regular budget information and report on SUF program expenditure in Ghana.
   - Make all necessary arrangements for visits by the SUF PT and UN-HABITAT officials.

References

Bourdieu, Pierre. 1984. *Outline of a Theory of Practice.* Cambridge: Cambridge University Press.

Boyd, Andrew. 1962. *Chinese Architecture and Town Planning: 1500 B.C.–A.D. 1911.* Chicago: University of Chicago Press.

Checker, Melissa, David Vine, and Alaka Wali. 2010. "A Sea Change in Anthropology?" *Public Anthropology Reviews* 112, no. 1: 5–6.

Davis, Shelton H., and Robert O. Mathews. 1979. "Public Interest Anthropology: Beyond the Bureaucratic Ethos." *Practicing Anthropology* 1, no. 3: 5, 25–26.

Denyer, Susan. 1978. *African Traditional Architecture*. New York: Africana.

Faculty of Architecture. 1978. "Traditional Forms of Architecture in Ghana." *International Social Science Journal* 30: 449–476.

Field, M.J. 1940. *Social Organisation of the Ga People*. London: Crown Agents.

Fried, Marc. 1963. "Grieving for a Lost Home." In *The Urban Condition*, ed. Leonard J. Duhl. New York: Basic Books.

Garnham, Nicholas, and Raymond Williams. 1980. "Pierre Bourdieu and the Sociology of Culture." *Media, Culture and Society* 2: 209–223.

Ghana Statistical Service. 2000. "Ghana—Population and Housing Census 2000." http://www.statsghana.gov.gh/nada/index.php/catalog/3.

"Ghana: Urban Population." 2011. *Index Mundi*. http://www.indexmundi.com/facts/ghana/urban-population.

King, Anthony. 1984. *The Bungalow: The Production of a Global Culture*. London: Routledge and Kegan Paul.

Osae, Erika Mamley . 2007. "Operationalizing the Subsidiarity Principle in Ghana's Local Government for the Urban Poor: The Case of the Tema Municipality." Accra: Charles F. Kettering Foundation.

Knapp, Ronald G. 1989. *China's Vernacular Architecture: House Form and Culture*. Honolulu: University of Hawaii Press.

Korboe, David. 1992. "Family-houses in Ghanaian Cities: To Be or Not to Be?" *Urban Studies* 29, no. 7: 1159–1172.

Kulturmann, Udo. 1963. *New Architecture in Africa*. New York: Universe Books.

Kuper, Hilda. 1972. "The Language of Sites in the Politics of Space." *American Anthropologist* 74: 411–425.

Lamphere, Louise. 2004. "The Convergence of Applied, Practicing and Public Anthropology in the 21st Century." *Human Organization* 63, no. 4: 431–443.

Laufer, Robert S., Harold M. Proshansky, and Maxine Wolfe. 1976. "Some Analytic Dimensions of Privacy." In *Environmental Psychology: People and their Physical Settings*, ed. Harold M. Proshansky, William H. Ittelson, and Leanne G. Rivlin, 2nd ed. New York: Holt, Rinehart & Winston.

Marris, Peter. 1961. *Family and Social Change in an African City: A Study of Rehousing in Lagos*. London: Routledge and Kegan Paul.

———. 1979. "The Meaning of Slums and Patterns of Change." *International Journal of Urban and Regional Research* 3: 419–441.

Oliver, Paul. 1987. *Dwellings: The House Across the World*. Austin: University of Texas Press.

Ozkan, Suha. 2006. "Foreword: Courtyard; A Typology that Symbolizes a Culture." In *Courtyard Housing: Past, Present and Future*, ed. Brian Edwards, Magda Sibley, Mohamed Hakmi, and Peter Land. New York: Taylor and Francis.

Parker, John. 2000. *Making the Town: Ga State and Society in Early Colonial Accra*. Portsmouth, NH: Heinemann.

Pellow, Deborah. 1991. "Spaces that Teach: Attachment to the African Compound." In *Place Attachment*, ed. Irwin Altman and Setha Low. New York: Plenum Press.

———. 2008. *Landlords and Lodgers: Socio-Spatial Organization in an Accra Community*. Chicago: University of Chicago Press.

"Population: Total in Ghana." 2011. *Trading Economics*. http://www.tradingeconomics.com/ghana/population-total-wb-data.html.

Prussin, Labelle. 1969. *Architecture in Northern Ghana: A Study of Forms and Functions*. Berkeley: University of California Press.

————. 1986. *Hatumere: Islamic Design in West Africa.* Berkeley: University of California Press.

Rapoport, Amos. 1969. *House Form and Culture.* Englewood Cliffs, NJ: Prentice-Hall.

Rutter, Andrew. 1971. "Ashanti Vernacular Architecture." In *Shelter in Africa,* ed. P. Oliver, 153–71. London: Barrie & Jenkins Ltd.

Sahlins, Marshall. 1983. "Other Times, Other Customs: The Anthropology of History." *American Anthropologist* 85, no. 3: 517–544.

Schwerdtfeger, Friedrich Wilhelm. 1982. *Traditional Housing in African Cities: A Comparative Study of Houses in Zaria, Ibadan, and Marrakech.* New York: John Wiley & Sons.

Standard Surveys & Construction Services. 2008. "Physical Surveys of Amui Djor Settlement and Associated Works in Ashaiman." Accra.

Tweneboa, Alexander. 2011. "TAMSUF's Role in Providing Affordable Housing in Ghana." African Union for Housing Finance Conference Johannesburg, South Africa, 7–9 September.

UN-Habitat. 2003. "Governing Council of the United Nations Human Settlements Programme HSP/GC/19/1/Add.1. 27 January." http://ww2.unhabitat.org/governingbodies/documents/english/K0360262E.pdf.

————. 2005. "Ghana Slums Lined Up For Investment." http://ww2.unhabitat.org/ghana_invest.asp.

————. 2011. "UN-Habitat Project in Ghana Awarded for Positive Impact." http://mirror.unhabitat.org/content.asp?cid=10671&catid=7&typeid=6&AllContent=1.

INDEX